THE IMPOSSIBLE PRESIDENCY

THE IMPOSSIBLE PRESIDENCY

THE RISE AND FALL OF AMERICA'S HIGHEST OFFICE

JEREMI SURI

BASIC BOOKS
New York

Basic Books
Hachette Book Group
1290 Avenue of the Americas, New York, NY 10104
http://www.basicbooks.com/
@BasicBooks

Printed in the United States of America

Published by Basic Books, an imprint of Perseus Books, LLC,
a subsidiary of Hachette Book Group, Inc.

The Hachette Speakers Bureau provides a wide range of authors for speaking events. To find out
more, go to www.hachettespeakersbureau.com or call (866) 376-6591.

The publisher is not responsible for websites (or their content) that are not owned by the
publisher.

Library of Congress Cataloging-in-Publication Data has been applied for.

ISBN: 978–0–465–05173–1 (HC)
ISBN: 978–0–465–09390–8 (EB)
First Edition
LSC-C
10 9 8 7 6 5 4 3 2 1

To Alison, Natalie, and Zachary—
current and future leaders.

CONTENTS

Alone

The presidency is the most powerful office in the world, but it is set up to fail. And the power is the problem. Beginning as a small and uncertain position within a large and sprawling democracy, the presidency has grown over two centuries into a towering central command for global decisions about war, economy, and justice. The president can bomb more places, spend more money, and influence more people than any other figure in history. His reach is almost boundless.

Reach does not promote desired results. Each major president has changed the world, but none has changed it as he liked. Often just the opposite, especially in recent times. Today, power elicits demands, at home and abroad, that exceed capabilities. Power also inspires resistance, from jealous friends as much as determined adversaries. Power pulls the president into mounting commitments, exaggerated promises, and widening distractions—"mission creep," in its many infectious forms.

Despite their dominance, modern presidents have rarely achieved what they wanted because they have consistently overcommitted, overpromised, and overreached. They have run in too many directions at once. They have tried to achieve success too fast. They have departed from their priorities. And they have become too preoccupied with managing crises that inevitably appear, rather than leading the country in desired directions.

Extraordinary power has pushed even the most ambitious presidents to become largely reactive—racing to put out the latest fire, rather than focusing on the most important goals. The crises caused by small and distant actors have frequently defined modern presidents. The time and resources spent on crises have diminished resolve and attention to matters with much greater significance for the nation as a whole. Presidents frequently lose control of their agendas because they are too busy deploying their power flagrantly, rather than targeting it selectively.

Unmatched capabilities and ambitions encourage undisciplined decision-making, followed by stubborn efforts to make good on poor choices. These are the "sunk costs" that hang over the heads of powerful leaders determined to make sure nothing sinks, except their own presidencies. As much as they try, presidents cannot redeem the past nor control the present. Their most effective use of power is investing in a limited set of national economic, social, and military priorities. Priorities matter most for successful leaders, but presidents forget them in the ever-denser fog of White House decision-making.

THOMAS JEFFERSON ANTICIPATED THESE CIRCUMSTANCES TWO centuries ago. Although he valued virtue and strength in leaders, Jefferson recognized that these qualities were potential sources of despotism as much as democracy. The virtuous and the strong often try to do too much, and they adopt tyrannical practices in pursuit of purposes that at first seem worthy, but often become corrupted. Machiavelli's prince, who promotes the public good through ruthless policies, was a warning against centralized power run amok.[1]

Like other founders steeped in the history of empires, Jefferson wanted to insure that the United States remained a republic with restrained, modest, and cautious leaders. He envisioned a president who embodied wisdom above all, a philosopher more than a warrior or a businessman. For Jefferson, the essential qualities of leadership came from the intellect of the man who occupied the office.

The US Constitution divided power to prevent presidential tyranny, but it did not, of course, guarantee the necessary intellect, prudence, or personal restraint of the people in charge. Fragmented authority could be just as misguided as centralized authority, and it could franchise its despotism in multiplying offices and agencies. A powerful democracy ultimately relied upon the wisdom and self-denial of its leaders, not constitutional barriers, according to Jefferson. Democratic leaders had to remain introspective and ascetic as their country grew more dynamic and prosperous.

Writing on the eve of the country's first burst of expansion, Jefferson warned that the nation's leaders may one day "shake a rod over the heads of all, which may make the stoutest of them tremble." Restrained use of power and disciplined focus on the national interest were the only antidotes to excess, despotism, and decline. "I hope our wisdom will grow with our power," Jefferson wrote, "and teach us that the less we use our power the greater it will be."[2]

Jefferson's heirs did not heed his words. Over two centuries the United States strayed from its values more than any elected president could correct, despite repeated public hopes for a savior. Leaders pursued goals—of wealth, influence, and security—that undermined the democracy they aimed to preserve. By the mid-twentieth century the growth of American power made frequent misuse unavoidable, and effective leadership nearly unattainable.[3]

The widening gap between power and values produced President Donald Trump, elected to promote raw power above all. He is the final fall of the founders' presidency—the antithesis of what they expected for the office. This book is not about Trump's election, but one of its aims is to help us understand the deep historical forces that made it possible. Although President Trump was not inevitable, the rise and fall of America's highest office has a historical logic that explains the current moment, and how we might move forward.

THE DESCENT JEFFERSON FEARED DID NOT HAPPEN OVERNIGHT. THE first century-and-a-half of American presidents led a very different nation. They had fewer temptations and clearer priorities. They were pioneering executives who invented the modern presidency to nurture a stronger, wealthier, and more democratic society. Their ambitions were big, but focused on a small number of issues: union, opportunity, growth, and security. They were idealistic in their aspirations, and realistic in their pursuit of compromise and balance—rather than total victory and dominance, both of which were inconceivable in their world. They made the presidency more powerful, even as they affirmed its limitations.

The most influential early American presidents were wise, strategic, and wary of excess. These qualities contributed to the slow and steady rise of the American presidency as a powerful institution. It affected more lives with each generation, and it drove the expansion of American wealth and influence, decade after decade. The first six chapters of this book recount that history, through the lives of five transformational leaders. None of their successors have surpassed them in their enduring contributions to American prosperity.[4]

George Washington invented the role of democratic executive. Part king, part elected representative, he was neither and both at the same time. He used his very limited presidential powers to lay the foundations for a national economy, territorial defense, and a common "American" identity among citizens still defined primarily by their states of residence. He was the father figure for a young republic.

A child of the violent American frontier, Andrew Jackson brought the presidency to the people, promising to protect their local needs against the elites in New York, Philadelphia, Boston, and other cities who dominated many of the founding national institutions—including Congress, the Supreme Court, and the Bank of the United States. Jackson's populism increased the influence of the president as a fighter (and an Indian killer) who opened opportunities for "ordinary" citizens, but did not interfere in their daily lives. Jackson was the first Democrat—responsive to the least powerful white citizens, and a defender of their rights within the Union.

Abraham Lincoln was the first Republican. Also born on the frontier, he transformed the Union from a political arrangement among rival regions into a sacred whole defended by a powerful national executive. With little oversight from Congress or the courts, Lincoln used wartime powers to abridge civil liberties, raise the largest army in the world, and free the slaves in the South. He widened the Northern industrial economy across the continent, and he crafted the language to justify its triumph over alternatives. Although he expanded the powers of the president to reconstruct the nation, subsequent events showed that those powers would be limited to wartime, at least for another generation. After the surrender of the Confederacy and Lincoln's assassination, the Union was stronger but still governed by local institutions, especially in the South.

Theodore Roosevelt returned to Lincoln's legacy four decades later. He converted the presidency into a wellspring of progressive reforms at home and aggressive military strength abroad. He personally involved himself, as no president had before, in breaking up monopolies, preserving the wilderness, building a world-class navy, and negotiating peace between foreign powers. He made the president a model of the "strenuous life" that he extolled. Citizens felt Theodore Roosevelt's presence, sometimes more than they wanted. His bullying, however, had its limits. He was a whirlwind of energy, often overextended, but his presidency remained focused on a coherent set of policy reforms. Although he was a know-it-all, his knowledge applied to a still small set of national issues.

Theodore's cousin, Franklin, fused Lincoln's wartime presidency with his namesake's progressivism. He made the president into *the* national reformer to heal a country suffering through the Great Depression, and he mobilized the nation's enormous resource base to defeat enemies who threatened to enslave much of the world. Lasting an unprecedented twelve years, Roosevelt's presidency created a permanent, and often dominant, executive presence in all corners of society—on farms and factory floors, in schools and national parks, and on radio and other media. Roosevelt was father figure and economic manager and war commander. He was the culmination of one hundred and fifty years of growth in the reach of the presidency, the personal role of the president, and the public expectations surrounding the office and the man in it. Roosevelt's New Deal seeded a sprawling welfare state with global influence. The country never looked back.

Franklin Roosevelt broke the mold. He tore down many of the last limits on executive power as he took over the economy and many parts of the world. He placed the president in charge of countless agencies, programs, and projects in communities across the country. And he spoke directly to citizens through the radio, motivating them to act on his behalf. Roosevelt created a modern presidency that organized a complex society behind his vision. He did more than any other leader in American history.

Roosevelt was the only president to master the responsibilities of the office, responsibilities that he, to a large extent, invented. His successors possessed even greater institutional capabilities, but they experienced deeper disappointments in the exercise of that power. The slow rise of the presidency triggered a rapid decline, and ultimate fall, after 1945. Since the Second World War, presidents have failed, repeatedly, as the office became bloated, undisciplined, and self-defeating. Whether out of necessity or personal ambition, presidents from George Washington to Franklin Roosevelt expanded the powers of the executive, unwittingly creating a presidency too big for its own good.

The second part of this book recounts the struggles of more recent presidents, who have been overwhelmed by abundant capabilities, diffuse interests, and ever-increasing demands. Presidents John F. Kennedy, Lyndon Johnson, and Ronald Reagan responded to a wide variety of national and international pressures, and they fell tragically into a pattern of excess, isolation, and decline—just as Jefferson predicted. Bill Clinton and Barack Obama sought to escape this pattern, but the demands of the presidency pulled them into ever more diffuse responsibilities, with even less satisfying results.

Abandoning wisdom for crisis management, the postwar presidents threw their power at problems, rather than thinking about the best uses (and non-uses) of their capabilities for important national needs. The pressure to act at ever greater speed diminished the opportunities for these leaders to think about why, how, and where they acted. The twenty-four-hour news cycle left no quiet time for the introspection Jefferson thought necessary for all democratic leaders.

As a consequence, strategy became a lost art in the White House. Instead of thinking deeply, late twentieth-century presidents proclaimed their virtue, opened their wallets, and flexed their muscles. This approach to the office required less time for rushed leaders. It came most easily for figures with enormous power at their disposal. And it played to the prejudices of their staffs and citizens. Yet as these presidents learned through hard experience, undisciplined power is self-defeating.[5]

No recent American president has been prepared for the overwhelming power of the office, and the responsibilities and challenges that define it. The leader of the wealthiest and most powerful country in the world is much more than a CEO, a general, or a party leader. The American president is closer to a mythological figure, expected to rise above normal human limitations and manage a constant barrage of local and international problems. The pace is breathless, even on the quietest days, and the stakes are enormous, even for the smallest decisions. Nearly every waking hour is monumental for the president of the United States. Mere mortals do not live (or survive) in these circumstances.

Despite the crushing intensity, the president is expected to be ever-ready for crises yet strategically minded; deeply connected to ordinary citizens but independent of special interests; a manager of democratic institutions and a fearless commander of lethal force. Although no human being can do all the things expected of the president, each individual elected to this mighty office must claim that he can. Like the power of the Greek gods, the promise of the presidency always exceeds what is possible.

Every modern president has struggled with this gap between promise and possibility. Some came to rely on a growing group of advisors, others sought to centralize authority with a small set of loyalists. Most have done a little of both, relying on their own energy, insight, and instinct to determine which issues require attention at a given moment. It is a grueling and lonely experience. Self-doubt creeps into the minds of even the most confident presidents.

The more powerful the leader, the more isolated he becomes from anything like a normal life. Power induces fealty in friends and self-interested advocacy in acquaintances. Franklin Roosevelt described this experience: "Someday you may well be sitting here where I am now as president of the United States. And when you are, you'll be looking at that door over there and knowing that practically everybody who walks through it wants something out of you. You'll learn what a lonely job this is."[6]

THE MODERN PRESIDENT IS CONSTANTLY BEATEN DOWN BY demands, large and small. His work is never done. He is alone in his struggle to fight off those who want a piece of him. Every hour brings another demand, another obligation, another crisis.

Few leaders are impeached or assassinated; most die from a thousand cuts. The cuts come from those closest to them—the people who walk through the president's door each day. They have problems that demand attention and solutions that merit action. They want to get things done and the president is the most powerful agent for helping them to achieve their goals. Abraham Lincoln, Franklin Roosevelt, and Lyndon Johnson (among other presidents) struggled with this dynamic. Despite war and expansive government policies, they faced a continuous stream of requests for *more*—more programs for the needy, more assistance for the productive, more weapons for the warriors, and more support for the peacemakers. Expansive government activities also created multiplying conflicts between different bureaus and their chiefs—conflicts that the president, reluctantly, had to mediate.

Reading over the daily calendars of presidents, it is startling how much time they spend fending off small demands and mediating petty conflicts. Lincoln, Roosevelt, and Johnson were not unique. Their days were filled with solving other people's problems. Lincoln had to contend with the incompetence and infighting of men overseeing the acquisition of supplies for the Union Army. Roosevelt assembled a New Deal empire with powerful issue advocates and monumental egos. Most famously, Johnson's White House telephones kept the chief executive in constant touch with advisors, congressmen, and governors—even when he was in the bathroom—so that he could solve their problems and procure the favors he wanted in return. Listening to Johnson on the phone, one hears more hectoring, pleading, and horse-trading than one might expect, given the aura of the office.

ONE OF PRESIDENT JOHNSON'S TENSE CONVERSATIONS WITH Alabama Governor George Wallace reveals how modern executive leadership really works. Although the president had promoted an ambitious civil rights agenda from the moment he assumed office, he felt embattled in his encounters with impatient advocates, including the Reverend Dr. Martin Luther King, Jr., and recalcitrant opponents, especially Wallace. Johnson needed to navigate between the extremes, trying to address everyone's concerns.

On 18 March 1965, the president had to protect marchers in Selma, Alabama, who had been brutally beaten by state troopers for demanding voting rights, and he had to restore order in a Southern state that had already descended into street violence—much of it encouraged by its segregationist governor. Johnson wanted Wallace to allow a peaceful civil rights march and limit white violence. He had to help Wallace as he also helped Wallace's adversaries.

JOHNSON: I am always standing by, and you can always call me anytime you want to.

WALLACE: These people are pouring in from all over the country. . . . All I want to say quite frankly is that they've been stirring up by a lot of things, and of course, I know you don't want anything to happen that looks like a revolution, but if these people keep pouring in here and conducting themselves in the manner they are, it's going to take everybody in the country to stop something.

JOHNSON: When you talk about a revolution, that really upsets us all, and we don't want, I know you don't, and I know I don't, and we just got to work together as best we can to see we discharge our duties, and I am willing to do it, if this is what you want.

WALLACE: What about the next day after the march is over?

JOHNSON: I guess no one can really prophesize...I sure don't know, I wish I knew...I might issue a statement later today saying, I ask people not to go into the state, and we're going to jointly try to protect the march...If you call up your guard, I'll put the best people we've got to work right with them...I think I just ought to say that I am asking people in the country not to let this thing get out of hand. And we don't need any more marching down there.[7]

Lyndon Johnson relished his power to manipulate people, but he was hardly unique in his need to do so. The presidency has always been a shell game where the man on top moves the pieces around the table to fend off challengers, appease advocates, and keep his supporters on the team. There are always too many problems without obvious solutions for the president to lead as decisively as one might expect. Uncertainty and complexity undermine every president's desire for simple, strong action.

IN ITS EXTREMES OF POWER AND RESPONSIBILITY, THE US presidency is the most talked about and least understood office in the world. Presidents are elected to accomplish big things, but they spend most of their time focusing on problems that do not serve, and frequently contradict, their larger agendas. Presidents command the most powerful military in the world, but they repeatedly confront the frustrating limits of what they can achieve by force. Presidents are revered around the globe, but they have trouble translating their celebrity into tangible influence. Most of all, presidents are elected by the people, but they spend most of their time in office cut off from any unscripted contact with ordinary citizens. Presidential power is awesome and pathetic at the same time.

The president has too many people to please and too many issues to address. The scholar Richard Neustadt made this point more than fifty years ago when he observed that leaders—even those with the popularity of Franklin Roosevelt and John F. Kennedy—are forced to "bargain" for their power with numerous stakeholders, and they are often bargaining from weakness. President Barack Obama must have felt this acutely during budget disputes with a defiant Republican Congress. President Ronald Reagan had a similar experience when he failed to convince a Democratic Congress to adopt his promised spending cuts.[8]

As George Washington recognized, the president is institutionally constrained by Congress, the Supreme Court, the states, and various partisan factions. The president cannot raise money or make laws without the approval of these institutions. He cannot appoint the diplomats, generals, judges, and cabinet advisors that he wants without their consent. The president cannot even enter foreign negotiations without the intervention of other parts of the US government. Confronted by popular dissent from his treaty with Great Britain (the "Jay Treaty") and the efforts to undermine his policies by a popular French visitor ("Citizen" Edmond-Charles Genêt), Washington was only the first president to lament the domestic "encroachments" on his ability to lead as the public expected. Every one of his successors has voiced the same frustration as the encroachments only became more frequent and intense with each passing decade.

In addition to the institutional limitations on power, presidents confront ever-greater difficulties in managing their time. Washington often felt overextended by his daily responsibilities, and that problem has multiplied exponentially across two centuries. Due to the breadth of his responsibilities and the ever-faster movement of international developments, the contemporary presidency is in perpetual "crisis" mode, constantly running to catch up with events. On any given day, a president will have to respond to a mass shooting in an American city, the failure of a major financial firm, an attack on American forces abroad, a credible terrorist warning, and Russian and Chinese bullying of neighbors, as well as ceremonial duties with a visiting foreign leader and a recent national championship sports team.

The pace of the presidency is punishing, and the president himself becomes necessarily defensive. Instead of storing up their energy to make winning shots, presidents find themselves hitting frequent soft returns to keep the ball in play and avoid unforced errors. President Obama admitted as much, revealing the pressure to respond without risk to numerous challenges and the anxiety about doing too much of anything. [9]

President Obama was hardly alone. Even President Ronald Reagan, who tried to focus his attention on a few big issues, found himself pulled into budget disputes, hostage crises, and an international AIDS epidemic that defined much of his time in office. The imperial appearance of the modern president is belied by the fragmented experience of the global policy-maker.

With a country as large and complex as the United States, and international responsibilities that extend to every region of the globe, it is impossible for the leader of the free world to master the overwhelming number of conflicts that reach him for comment and reaction. If he makes sense of some of them, thanks to his advisors, it is difficult for him to understand their connections to one another, and the consequences of American action in one area for other regions. Every day—

almost every hour—presidents are asked to make decisions that will affect millions of lives in distant places they barely comprehend, with severely constrained information, and profound uncertainty about consequences.

Presidents also know that their every move will be carefully scrutinized and savagely criticized by friends and foes alike. This was true for the partisan press of Washington's time, and it has become pervasive with the twenty-four-hour news cycle, the Internet, social media, and contemporary "news-entertainment," where manufacturing political scandals is part of the regular reporting diet. Presidents know they will only face greater condemnation if they reveal the hesitation and real limits that surround everything they do. They overcompensate by exaggerating their confidence, their commitment, and the promised consequences of their actions.

Even though recent presidents have sent American soldiers abroad with uncertainty about the threat the nation faced and the military's prospect for success, they have still promised to "eliminate tyranny as we know it" and build democracies on short deadlines. Similarly, even though they recognized how little direct control they had over the economy, the environment, education, and health, presidents repeatedly predicted big achievements in each of these areas. Rising expectations of presidential power encourage unrealistic promises, followed by popular disappointment and perceptions of executive "weakness."

The problem is that policies are oversold and then underperform. Presidential rhetoric creates commitments that undermine effectiveness. This was true for both George W. Bush's Global War on Terror and Barack Obama's Affordable Care Act, which became prisoners to caricatured definitions of "success," despite some real but largely ignored accomplishments.[10]

OUR POOR UNDERSTANDING OF THE PRESIDENCY HAS PREVENTED us from addressing the structural impediments to effectiveness in office. In the speeches citizens hear and the advertisements they watch, candidates talk about the outcomes they want to achieve—from robust economic growth to impregnable national security—without any serious discussion about *how* the presidency can make those outcomes a reality. Few reporters ask about implementation. Most candidates do not really know how they will generate the promised results.

We elect presidents based on aspirations—ours and theirs—not on effectiveness, since we cannot know how they will perform in office, even if they have had long careers in politics. Once in office, newly elected presidents are overwhelmed by the constraints on their power, and they fall into the same reactive and fragmented pattern of their predecessors. The pattern tightens with every successive administration because the demands and constraints increase along with the unpreparedness of the candidates. The power that looks so impressive outside the presidency becomes imprisoning and debilitating for those who hold it—just as Thomas Jefferson predicted.

These circumstances, not the personal failings of leaders, explain why it has been at least fifty years (since Lyndon Johnson) that a new president had a successful first year in office. After Johnson, nearly every president has seen his agenda stymied and his popularity decline—despite all the misleading talk of presidential "honeymoons." In reality, new presidents begin a quick and often irreversible slide into mediocrity from the moment of inauguration, when the onrush begins. We can expect the same for future presidencies.[11]

THE PRESIDENTS MOST WORTHY OF STUDY ARE THOSE WHO recognized their impossible predicament and found a way to maximize the benefits for American society—conscious that they could never do enough, that they would probably create as many problems as they solved, and that they would be alone in their struggles, despite all the advisors around them.

Strategy starts small: finding the quiet and focus to accomplish a few important things. That is the only true wisdom for modern leadership. Better to win the key battles, rather than pursue dominance in all places.

Identifying the key battles is hard without the benefit of hindsight. That is why a historical approach is so valuable, because it allows us to learn from our predecessors. The temptation for powerful actors, especially recent American presidents, has been to hedge by pursuing dominance everywhere. That expansive approach has characterized our foreign policy since at least the late 1950s, and it has not served the United States or the world well.[12]

American power has underperformed because it has been overused, spread too thin by hard-working leaders who are afraid to prioritize and prefer insurance policies—at home and abroad—to selective risks. That might be an effective electoral tactic, appeasing numerous groups, but it is a proven recipe for a reactive presidency, rather than real leadership. Too often leaders use power to manage crises, not to move beyond them. Constant crisis management is counterproductive, draining resources without producing real advances. Crisis management squeezes out creativity and innovation because there is just "no time"—the recurring lament of powerful, overburdened, underperforming leaders.

The most successful presidents recognized their condition, honestly assessed the constraints they faced, and defined realistic priorities. They spent less time considering how much power they had; they preserved their maximum attention for determining *where* and *when* to use it. They also prepared for partial accomplishments and unforeseen outcomes. Even the most powerful must make difficult trade-offs and expect the unexpected.

This history of the presidency is, therefore, a study of cleverness and aggression, and the tension between the two in leaders who grew more powerful and burdened from George Washington's day to our own. The transformational presidents struggled with the many dimensions of their power. In their best moments, they found the wisdom to deploy their power strategically and to learn from failure as they focused on a few priorities. In their worst moments, talented and hard-working men succumbed to the hubris of power and the cowardly incoherence of doing a little of everything for everyone. The arc of history has bent toward the latter behaviors.

The presidency is impossible because there is no obvious pathway to success, but many clear roads to doom. Presidents improve when they learn about the enduring struggles of leadership and think deeply about their own world in that light.

The best leaders see and feel how their world emerged, locate themselves accurately in it, and imagine new possibilities. They help their country travel forward by looking back and learning from past experiences—not formulas, false analogies, or inherited truisms. They use the past to discipline their power, define their priorities, and pursue well-considered goals. They also use the past to define what they are not.[13]

Even the most capable modern presidents are doomed to fail. Limiting the failure and achieving some good along the way—that is the best we can expect. Disciplining the office to focus power on the issues that matter most to the nation as a whole—that is the key lesson from the slow historical rise of the presidency, before its recent precipitous fall. We cannot go back, but we can gain wisdom and modesty from the past, especially in an age when both are so lacking in our chosen leaders.

PART I

Rise

CHAPTER 1

Origins

In the summer of 1787 a small group of rebellious farmers and merchants, living on the edge of the British Empire, came together to
"form a more perfect union" by writing a new constitution. The fifty-five
men who met in Philadelphia were not united and they were far from
perfect. They did not believe "all men are created equal," despite the
words of their earlier Declaration of Independence. The writers of the
Constitution were slaveholders and businessmen who benefited from
slavery at a time when leaders in other parts of the world were abolish-
ing that inhuman practice.[1]

With the exception of Benjamin Franklin, the men who came to
Philadelphia were not respected figures beyond their local communities.
These wealthy former colonists spent a hot, uncomfortable summer in
conversation in Independence Hall, the home of the Pennsylvania State
House. Frontiersmen with powdered wigs, they were provincial upstarts
with boundless ambitions and audacious ideas. They were young and
immodest. They believed that they could design a good government
that would improve on what had come before. They put their fortunes
on the line because they had a lot to gain if they succeeded in creating
a society that was more free and secure for men like themselves.

James Madison, the Constitution's leading scribe, captured the seri-
ousness of the men in Philadelphia and their poor preparation. They did
not have a model or a clear picture of what they wanted. They made it
up as they went along, trying to plunder useful ideas from the history

they had read, inconsistently. They were in uncharted territory, exploring a new political frontier.

These circumstances made the Constitutional Convention an exciting and uncertain endeavor. Madison was deeply concerned, even as he and his colleagues signed the final document on 17 September 1787, just before the Philadelphia summer gave way to a stormy fall of debates around the country. "It is a melancholy reflection," Madison wrote, "that liberty should be equally exposed to danger whether the Government have too much or too little power, and that the line which divides the extremes should be so inaccurately defined by experience."[2] Madison recognized that good government is about navigating between extremes. It is never pure and never simple. It requires a complex mix—a little bit of one philosophy, a little bit of another; limited power for one set of interests and limited power for another. Mixture does not mean incoherence or lack of direction. Good government has a purpose, a strategy, and ideals. It is free, but not chaotic; ordered, but not repressive. Good government is ever-evolving, and it is "inaccurately defined," in Madison's words, because it has no recipe.

The big question of the late eighteenth century was how to design good government, striking a balance between the extremes of royal tyranny and what Thomas Hobbes called the "war of all against all." Citizens across Europe and the "New World" had experienced some of both. The "age of revolution" was an era of enduring creativity in pursuit of the golden mean—a "well-balanced republic" in the language of the time.[3]

The debates in Europe and the New World focused on three political ingredients: institutions, rights, and leaders. The institutions of the state (including the parliament, the military, and the courts) protected public safety, economy, and basic justice. The state operated through law, and it used money and guns as its primary tools. The rights of the individual insured freedom and humane treatment ("life, liberty, and property," in John Locke's famous formulation.) Individual rights were codified in law, recognized in common practice, and derived from "nature," many claimed. Rights affirmed the independence of individuals, and placed limits on the authority of the state and other actors. According to this line of thought, the institutions of the state and the rights of the individual were mutually dependent, but also in permanent tension.

They were co-signers and adversaries in what some called a "social contract," or in the American case, a "constitution."[4]

Before 1787, constitutions almost always included a king, in part because it would be too heretical (and life-threatening) to discount the royal figures who dominated most societies at the time. In countries like England the king did not always directly control the institutions of government, but he was the supreme authority. A constitution was a negotiation designed to affirm and limit power simultaneously between the people, the state, and the king. In the emerging modern world, "good government" was an unequal bargain between citizens, officials, and a "sovereign."

There was a deeper historical reason to include kings, or some other leading figure, in new government designs. Thinkers on both sides of the Atlantic Ocean were avid readers of Greek mythology and Roman history. They believed, following this tradition, that healthy societies needed an Odysseus or a Cincinnatus to unite the people, fight off foreign foes, and model an ordinary life of virtue and selflessness. Society had rarely, if ever, functioned well with institutions and rights alone. Governments needed leaders who acted as a glue and an inspiration. Leaders turned design into practice, dealing with the crises and contingencies of everyday life. To make government without a leader would be like traveling by horse and carriage without a driver. You could have a worthy vehicle of conveyance (the carriage), and strong movers (the horses), but they would ride a wild, directionless, and ultimately suicidal path without a driver.

State leaders, mostly kings at the time, were the drivers who steered the institutions of the state and directed the people to favorable destinations. Kings did not "manage" or "administer" like current heads of organizations. In the best of circumstances, which were rare, they set the course and kept all the parts of government together, helping them to coordinate better when necessary, especially in moments of crisis. Kings protected the state and the people, and they were responsible for stability, safety, and prosperity. The king embodied what diplomats called the "*raison d'état*"—rights and institutions merged as the "reason of state."[5]

THE ADVOCATES OF GOOD GOVERNMENT WHO ASSEMBLED IN Philadelphia had a rather different understanding of leadership. They feared abuses of power, as they also recognized the need for powerful leaders. They sought to restrain and empower a strong national leader at the same time.

For the founders, the national leader had to be energetic and heroic, but he also had to be humble and respectful of citizens. An effective leader could not, in Alexander Hamilton's words, show "unqualified complaisance to every sudden breeze of passion, or to every transient impulse which the people may receive from the arts of men, who flatter their prejudices to betray their interests." *Raison d'état* for Hamilton required leaders "to be the guardians of those interests, to withstand the temporary delusion."[6]

Humility and restraint, however, meant the energetic leader could only go so far. He had to remain firmly attached to the people, to their rights, their beliefs, and their passions. A good leader could not dictate to his citizens or he would become an oppressor. Hamilton was very clear on this point. Although a powerful head of state did not simply mirror public whims, he led by staying close to the people and embodying their deepest beliefs. That is why Hamilton and the other founders wanted the citizens, not the states, to elect the president. "The ingredients which constitute safety in the republican sense are," Hamilton explained, "a due dependence on the people" and "a due responsibility." The citizens empowered the leader, but they also kept him grounded.[7]

The mix of heroic power and humble restraints was difficult to maintain. The experience of overweening monarchies in Europe, especially in pre-revolutionary France, gave evidence to the dangers of leaders drunk on privilege, distant from the needs of the people. Selfishness, corruption, and incompetence in a hereditary system contributed to the problem. Samuel Adams captured the common disdain for those who inherited great wealth and power: "The cottager may beget a wise son; the noble, a fool. The one is capable of great improvement; the other, not." Thomas Jefferson agreed, calling for government to dismantle the "aristocracy of wealth," replacing it with "an opening for the aristocracy of virtue and talent."[8]

Many kings could not manage the delicate balance between heroism and humility, even if they tried. The immediate availability of power in the form of the treasury and the army, and the tendency for monarchs to attract power-hungry advisors, encouraged an overuse of crown authority. This was a pattern of creeping despotism that, according to eighteenth-century political thinkers, brought degeneracy and decline in Rome, in France, and in the "Oriental" societies that many Europeans studied. The majesty of the royal court that attracted awe in prior centuries inspired derision and demands for far-reaching reform from the pens of Voltaire, Locke, Hume, Rousseau, Jefferson, and Adams. The rationality of the Enlightenment and the free enterprise of capitalism raised serious questions about the legitimacy of hereditary authority, and its service to the cause of good government.[9]

LEGISLATIVE AUTHORITY DID NOT LOOK MUCH BETTER. THE experience of expanding parliamentary power, especially evident in the ability of the British parliament to tax the American colonies arbitrarily, convinced early Americans that a representative assembly could threaten liberty perhaps as much as a king. A parliament spoke for the interests of its members and the people they represented—often a small fraction of the total population, most of whom were ineligible to vote. The unrepresented were ignored and sometimes exploited by an empowered legislature. That is precisely how many British residents of North America felt in the years before the American Revolution. A strong parliament replaced the arbitrariness of a single king with the domination of a select few who sought, in the eyes of the American revolutionaries, to exploit the colonies. Late eighteenth-century legislatures often looked as despotic as the royal dictators they tamed.[10]

Madison made this precise point at the Constitutional Convention: "Experience had proved a tendency in our governments to throw all power into the Legislative vortex. The Executives of the States are in general little more than Cyphers; the legislatures omnipotent. If no effectual check be devised for restraining the instability and encroachments of the latter, a revolution of some kind or other would be inevitable." Madison argued that good government needed an "executive" who was much more than a "cypher" to stand between chaos and aggressive representative assemblies.[11]

The American founders hoped to restrain what they viewed as legislative "tyranny." This had been the context for Thomas Jefferson's adaptation of Locke's triad of individual rights ("life, liberty, and property") in the Declaration of Independence. Jefferson eloquently argued that the rights of "life, liberty, and the pursuit of happiness" limited the excesses of legislative bodies, as well as royal figures. Monarchies and elected assemblies were equally threatening to liberty, according to this view. Good government needed an executive and a representative legislature, but they had to be restrained by deeper protections for citizens. Without these protections, Americans felt they had suffered a dual tyranny from the British Parliament that taxed the colonists and the British crown that sent soldiers to enforce its rule.[12]

THE YEARS UNDER THE ARTICLES OF CONFEDERATION, 1781 TO 1789, showed another side of political dysfunction—the dysfunction of legislative division. The disagreements between the states and their ability to block legislation made it impossible for the Continental Congress to govern the newly independent country. Ratified during the war against Britain, on 1 March 1781, the Articles required nine of thirteen states to approve all legislation, treaties, acts of war, and activities related to "managing the general affairs of the United States." Each state had only one vote, so a combination of small states (New Hampshire, Rhode Island, Connecticut, New Jersey, and Delaware) could easily hinder the efforts of large, populous states (especially Pennsylvania, New York, Massachusetts, and Virginia). In return, the small states were too few to pass legislation opposed by the large states. It was nearly impossible to craft laws for a new government in these circumstances.

The "United States" of the Articles of Confederation was a collection of self-governing states largely surrounded by threatening imperial forces. With the British fortified in Canada and Spanish forces in Mexico, the future independence of the disunited American states was in immediate peril. Security required more unity.[13]

Divisions between the states became routinized as representatives frequently failed to show up in the Continental Congress. More often than not, the legislative body lacked the necessary quorum of nine states to decide on legislation. Without a quorum, the attending members could not vote. This was a particular problem at the end of the war with Britain, when the Congress could not even muster enough members to ratify the peace treaty that ended hostilities. American and British delegates signed the document in Paris on 3 September 1783, but the Congress only ratified it with great difficulty on 14 January 1784, jeopardizing the future of the new country during this period of delay. Under the Articles of Confederation there was no mechanism for preventing a few absent state representatives from damaging the welfare of the entire United States.[14]

There was no national figure who could assume emergency powers, as European monarchs often did, when their legislatures did not perform their duties. The "president" created by the Articles of Confederation simply presided over the Congress, and he served for no more than one year. He was neither a leader nor an administrator, but a figurehead for a divided and frequently absent collection of state delegates. The president was a creature of Congress, and he was as ineffectual as Congress was in building a truly unified country. Neither Congress nor the president could articulate a larger national interest or enforce agreements.

Without an effective leader or legislature, the rivalries between states deepened, a common consequence of the withdrawal of a foreign power from a territory. The separate interests of thirteen states defied the hopes of revolutionaries for a broad consensus formed organically through a common legislature.

The Articles of Confederation encouraged fragmentation and weakness. A strong, dynamic society—free from British rule—required central leadership that could unify competing interest groups without simultaneously denying their freedom. The new country needed a powerful leader who was not a king, but also not a creature of the Continental Congress. Americans looked to history and the wider world for models, but none existed. They had to invent a new concept of leadership.

THE FOUNDERS TURNED PRIMARILY TO THREE THINKERS FROM the British Isles: John Locke, David Hume, and Edmund Burke. Writing in the shadow of the parliament-led revolution that brought a new king, William III, to the English throne in 1689, Locke substituted the word "executive" for royal. He advocated separation of "legislative and executive power" in a more consensual government, rooted in representation of the people. The legislature would give voice to the needs of citizens and it would hold leaders accountable; the executive would act on the laws passed by the legislature and bring the different parts of society together for common purpose and defense.

Locke's executive was a monarch, but his rule was justified less by divine right, and more by the governing functions he served in a society based on the public good. Locke's king had a right to rule justified by the duties he performed as leader of his people. Locke described executive authority, "not as an arbitrary power depending on his good pleasure, but with this trust always to have it exercised only for the public weal, as the occurrences of times and change of affairs might require."[15]

The king had to protect and unify his countrymen, and he had to support their prosperity. The king was essential in this role, according to Locke, and forfeited his right to rule when he did not serve these duties. The king-as-executive was to be powerful, just, and effective as a national leader; he had contractual obligations to his people in return for their obedience. In his most radical passage, Locke explained that the people had a right to revolt against their executive when he violated his country's trust: "I say, using force upon the people without authority, and contrary to the trust put in him that does so, is a state of war with the people. . . . In all states and conditions, the true remedy of force without authority, is to oppose force to it."[16]

Although other British political thinkers did not share Locke's sanction of revolt against an unjust king, they echoed his analysis of the monarch's public duties. Hume and Burke defined the king as a civil "executive," rather than a divine ruler. Fifty years after Locke formulated his ideas, Hume wrote: "The principal weight of the crown lies in the executive power," which he defined as enforcing laws, defending the country, and protecting the welfare of the citizens. Hume described necessary tensions over the control of government between the king-as-executive and the parliament-as-legislature. These tensions, he reasoned, were necessary to find the "proper medium between extremes" for good governance.[17]

Edmund Burke offered the most sustained discussion of executive power in early modern Europe. Burke criticized the French Revolution's emphasis on unlimited popular rule. Without any check on the people's power, the revolutionaries descended into extremes of violence and destruction, as the country lurched from one new policy to another. Speed and force were enemies of deliberation and stability. The dictatorship of the revolutionary legislature (the National Assembly) prevented real debate and consensus-building, in what Burke described as an increasingly barbaric war of the ideologically pure against all critics—at home and abroad.

Burke's description of the French Revolution was partisan, but it accurately captured the problems of chaotic government without an effective executive to protect order. The overthrow of the monarchy had, according to Burke, left France without the leadership it needed to hold antagonistic factions together, assess different policies, and control the most extreme popular appetites. Burke made an impassioned case for why a powerful executive—royal or not—was essential for a well-ordered society: "It is a trust indeed that has much depending upon its faithful and diligent performance, both in the person presiding in it and in all its subordinates. . . . It ought to be environed with dignity, authority, and consideration, and it ought to lead to glory. The office of execution is an office of exertion. It is not from impotence we are to expect the tasks of power."[18]

Burke was not defending the king's right to rule, but the function of an executive in maintaining a peaceful and civil society. His executive was a unifier in a time of revolutionary disunity, and an enforcer of reason in a time of popular emotions and violence. Burke's executive had a political, intellectual, and symbolic gravity that controlled what the writer viewed as the destructive qualities of mass human behavior (what some came to call "the mob") on display in France and other revolutionary settings. The judicious executive, for Burke, tamed the unruly crowd. Burke believed that a republic needed a powerful figure to lead the people in their assertion of freedom, rather than the other way around.

The "executive," absent from countless treatises on leadership in prior centuries, became the conceptual hinge for discussions of good government after 1700—inspired by Locke, Hume, and Burke. These men provided a canon for thinking about political leadership in an age when traditional kings were under assault, and talented men (especially in North America) looked to build a new society. The British thinkers created a secular basis for executive authority in new republics as they discredited incompetent monarchs, royal tyrants, and the aggressive parliaments that often replaced a hated king. The authors imagined a new kind of ruler.[19]

The executive of Locke, Hume, and Burke became a fulcrum for discussions of democracy. The concept of the "executive" quickly rose as a keyword for defining what the British political philosophers sought: a pathway between royal tyranny and popular anarchy—both of which were exhibited in France before, during, and after that country's disorienting revolution. Leading American thinkers believed they had suffered under each of these burdens from the initial discipline of the British Empire and the subsequent fragmentation of the Articles of Confederation. By the late eighteenth century it became clear to observers on both sides of the Atlantic that good government required effective institutions and enlightened leadership to locate Hume's "proper medium between extremes." There was no obvious blueprint; Locke, Hume, and Burke attempted to invent good government, with the executive playing a crucial role.

The executive would lead by reason and talent, he would unify different groups, and he would encourage collective work for the common good—especially in national defense. The executive would not tyrannize, however, because he would be bound by laws made by the people, and he would be judged by the fulfillment of his duties to the people as a whole. The executive would steer the ship of state, as he remained accountable to everyone on board.

THE WORD "EXECUTIVE" RARELY APPEARED IN POLITICAL WRITINGS before the eighteenth century. After 1750 it became a much more common part of the literate vernacular. It appeared most often as an adjective in European writings—"executive power" and "executive government" replaced "royal power" and "royal government" in the most widely read treatises. As these new writings crossed the Atlantic and entered American politics, the word "executive" became a more forceful and certain noun—the "state executive" for governors and very soon after the "national executive" for the presidency created in the US Constitution. Madison, Hamilton, and others began to write about "executives" in general when they referred to government leaders and defended the Constitution, especially in the Federalist Papers. By the end of the eighteenth century "executive" was a staple word among those elites who read books, bought newspapers, and wrote constitutions.

The word was so popular that it soon seeped into discussions of religious, business, and even family leadership. Locke's executive power of 1689 became the American presidential executive of 1787, and soon the corporate executive of the post-Civil War world. This was a new word for a new leader of large institutions, accountable to many people for his actions.[20]

The growing use of the word does not indicate consensus on its meaning, but it does show that the terms of debate had changed. Observers of politics thought about leadership in more active terms, involving a newly defined ability to execute the functions of government in a way that would simultaneously bring people together, promote their freedoms, and protect them against evildoers at home and abroad. The executive was, by definition, deeply embedded in the contractual obligations, bargains, and negotiations of the time. He was secular, even if he was still a religious figurehead. The executive worked with diverse groups of people and various institutions of authority, including legislatures and courts. Most important, the executive was accountable to the people, even as he rode above the fray to articulate and defend broader national interests.

It is obvious, but also worth emphasizing, that the executive written about more commonly in the eighteenth century, and after, was male and singular. Only men, it was assumed, possessed the strength and decisiveness expected of the executive, not to mention the knowledge, adaptability, and trustworthiness. The singularity of the executive was necessary to insure a unitary voice and avoid the very divisions evidenced in congresses, parliaments, and society at large. The executive would give focus to society by being a strong, persuasive, trusted, and revered public voice. He would lead by doing big things, by speaking eloquent words, and by presiding over numerous groups. He would go far beyond the possibilities of a traditional aristocrat, a collection of ordinary citizens, or any woman in the eyes of male writers at the time.

THE ARTICLES OF CONFEDERATION HAD REFLECTED THINKING about political leadership in the eighteenth century that ignored the relatively new—sometimes radical—writings about executive power. The American revolutionaries initially reacted against any figure who looked or acted like a king. They followed Locke on the importance of a dynamic, representative legislature, but they neglected the Locke who advocated a central leader to bring the divergent groups together.

The anti-royal assumptions of the first American government motivated a counterproductive rejection of executive power as a whole. A supreme Continental Congress, dominated by the separate states, seemed the safest bet against a return to British-style tyranny. Later generations, opposed to strong presidents (from Andrew Jackson and Abraham Lincoln to Lyndon Johnson and Donald Trump) would make the same argument.

Of course, the rejection of one perceived tyranny created a different set of challenges. As early American citizens lived with the divisions of their post-revolutionary government, the new writings about executive power became more persuasive. The strained conditions of national government without an effective executive made one appear more necessary than ever before. Absent a strong national leader, Americans struggled with unity, order, and common purpose.

THE DRAFTING OF THE US CONSTITUTION IN 1787 MARKED A major re-thinking of good government and the role of national leadership within it. The Constitution, as a whole, was an experiment in designing an anti-royal government that recreated some of the centralizing qualities associated with royalism. The founders of what became the second American republic imagined executive power for a large territory, with many diverse states that jealously guarded their independence. The challenge of the Constitution was to create executive authority that was powerful enough to hold the country together, but not so powerful that it crushed local representation.

The twin experiences of revolution against empire and disunity after independence convinced a group of influential American thinkers that the United States had to invent a democratic executive who could rise above faction and region as a distinguished citizen, and not a king. Locke, Hume, and Burke pointed the way forward, but a set of creative American thinkers had to put somewhat vague philosophical ideas into practice. Inventing a new executive meant inventing a new kind of politics.

That was the guiding motivation for the fifty-five men who met at Independence Hall. They were veterans of the American Revolution who had risked their lives and fortunes to break with Britain, and they now feared the consequences of a chaotic postwar world. They were stubborn defenders of local liberty who believed an effective national government was necessary to protect against liberty becoming a license for disunity among citizens and an invitation to foreign threats. The men who assembled in Philadelphia were also in dialogue with the leading writers in Europe—many of whom, like Burke, sympathized with the American Revolution. Freed from empire and monarchy, and blessed with rich resources, the United States offered a promising land to imagine a "more perfect union."

Defining stronger executive power immediately became central to discussions about the new national government. James Madison's Virginia Plan, presented to the convention on the fourth day, proposed "that a National Executive be instituted" with "general authority to Execute the National laws" and that he "enjoy the Executive rights vested in Congress by the Confederation." Separating executive powers, Madison explained, would give them fuller force in the daily management of government affairs. A separate executive would also have the ability to speak for the entire country, rather than just the legislature, as in parliamentary systems.[21]

Madison's initial proposal for the executive drew on the logic of the leading writers at the time, and it adapted their ideas to the unique challenges of American society. Madison's fellow Virginian, Edmund Randolph, enumerated the details of the plan, emphasizing, above all, the fundamental reasons for creating an effective national executive who could lead the government at home and abroad. Madison's notes on the Convention record that Randolph pointed to "the prospect of anarchy from the laxity of government everywhere," including the following principal defects:

> 1. The Articles of Confederation "produced no security against foreign invasion; Congress not being permitted to prevent a war nor to support it by their own authority."
>
> 2. "The federal government could not check the quarrels between states, nor a rebellion in any, not having constitutional power nor means to interpose."
>
> 3. "There were many advantages, which the United States might acquire, which were not attainable under the Articles of Confederation—such as a productive impost [tariffs], counteraction of the commercial regulations of other nations, [and] pushing [promotion] of commerce."
>
> 4. "The federal government could not defend itself against the encroachments from the states."[22]

Madison and Randolph's colleagues generally accepted these propositions. Within a week, they decided to support the creation of a national executive, separate from the Congress, with clearly prescribed duties for implementing and defending national laws, and the ability to offer a contingent veto (subject to overturn by a legislative super-majority) on acts of Congress. The national executive also acquired the "Power to Grant Reprieves and Pardons for Offenses against the United States, except in Cases of Impeachment."[23]

The executive's power to veto and to pardon—two traditional royal prerogatives excluded from the Articles of Confederation—animated debates in Philadelphia over the subsequent weeks. A consensus emerged that the greatest threat to an effective executive came from both the states and the Congress. For a president to lead he had to exercise independent authority over government resources and institutions, free from daily interference by the states and Congress, but with continued accountability to them. Frequent election through a system run by the states and dependent on financial appropriations from Congress would protect accountability. So would the threat of impeachment, if the president broke the law.[24]

The men at Independence Hall agreed that the president needed the previously royal powers of veto and pardon to assert his influence and combat efforts by the Congress to dictate his actions. The executive would not only "check" the legislature; he would have the right to assert an agenda of his own within constitutional limits. This was the point of creating a separate executive—to give the country a steady and effective leader who merited trust. The president had to push back against Congress and the states, just as he relied upon them for his resources and legitimacy.

The Constitution gave the president numerous independent powers: commander-in-chief over the military, chief diplomat and treaty negotiator for the nation, chief enforcer of national laws, and defender of the people as a whole. Especially when Congress was out of session or unable to reach agreement, the president would insure the continuity of political order and the strength of the republic. Congress would meet intermittently to pass budgets and make laws, but the president would keep the country running in line with the national laws and the national interest. This was the core of what Americans defined, then and now, as "executive power"—the capability to navigate unexpected challenges at all times. "The Constitution created," what one observer calls "a presidency that, officially, would never sleep." In the late twentieth century that became the literal truth.[25]

For the framers, however, the role was less time-intensive and more conceptual than literal. The president would take an oath to defend the Constitution, remain bound to the Congress and the states, and embody the nation as a whole. He would oversee government affairs and act as the representative of the entire people and territory. Gouverneur

Morris, a key contributor to the drafting of the Constitution, explained that the president would be the "general Guardian of the National interests." A later commentator defined this executive role as "a generalist focused on the big picture."[26]

Morris's colleagues differed on what "Guardian of the National Interests" meant in practice. Some, including Madison, wanted to see a more dynamic Congress helping to manage domestic affairs and international negotiations. Hamilton, by contrast, hoped for a more powerful president who could set an economic and foreign policy course for the country, and then gain consent from Congress after the fact. Most of the founders came down somewhere in between, and the debate in Philadelphia went back and forth on presidential powers with continued uncertainty about what the executive would actually do. The founders did not have a model. No other nation had created such a governmental position.[27]

The one expectation that the framers could all agree upon was that the national executive should be an individual who stands above others, by merit and distinction, to inspire better citizenship. The president would be impartial, fair, forward-looking, and unifying. He would bring diverse citizens together around his commitment to the nation and his model of virtuous behavior. The founders imagined the president "as an executive who would rise like a patriot king above party, free from the habits of intrigue and corruption that the lessons of history ascribed to both Stuart kings and Georgian ministers." This was the wisdom of Locke, Hume, and Burke about the need for a statesmanlike executive in a democratic republic.[28]

For the men meeting in Philadelphia, the obvious choice for the nation's first president was General George Washington. He had led American forces against the British and then returned peacefully to his Virginia farm. Called upon to help revise the Articles of Confederation, Washington served as "president" of the Constitutional Convention, moderating debates during the summer of 1787, speaking only on very rare occasions. Washington was indeed a proven patriot, leader of people, and impartial mediator between different groups. He had the gravity to unify different parts of American society, he commanded authority, and he respected democracy. Even if the framers could not agree on the precise parameters for the new executive, their overwhelming consensus on who the first president should be meant that they could tolerate continued vagueness. Washington would mold the office to his image; more than the words of the Constitution, he would define the expectations of the American president.

Even if he took on a certain regal air, as though he were above ordinary politics, Washington clearly affirmed the anti-monarchical definition of the new executive. He had no heirs, and began his presidency with the clear presumption that he would serve his country for a time, subject himself to reelection, and eventually resign from office, as he had in the past. Washington would not pass on his office as a property to relatives. As he wrote in a draft of his first inaugural address: "I have no child for whom I could wish to make a provision—no family to build in greatness upon my Country's ruins." Washington was the perfect executive for the framers: a proven national leader with ultimately limited personal ambitions. Although he was more widely respected than the Constitution when he became president in 1789, he endowed the document, and its creation of a national executive, with legitimacy that would long outlive his service.[29]

Washington promised to create not a dynasty, but an enduring institution that would unify and protect the new nation. He was a trusted wise man and a vessel for a group of anxious framers who, despite their learned arguments, could not foresee exactly how the presidency would develop. So they relied on an uneasy balance between principles of leadership and representation. The contradiction between a president with royal powers and a government founded on a rejection of monarchy, as well as the conflict between a powerful legislature and an assertive president, were not resolved in the Constitution—or thereafter. These are the enduring tensions of American governance, played out at national, state, and local levels. In his time, Washington, as a near-universally trusted executive figure, created a bridge between differences that, more than the text of the Constitution itself, brought the president to life as a national leader.

The key line in the Constitution simply says: "The executive Power shall be vested in a President of the United States of America." The meaning of this clause was clearest in what it did not say: the position

was not royal, legislative, or judicial. The Constitution required leadership on behalf of the nation and its laws, but what it meant beyond that
would be up to Washington to define.

THE PRESIDENCY WAS THE MOST ORIGINAL INNOVATION OF
America's founding moment. The enduring strength of the office comes
from its original lack of definition. It is an ever-changing role. The
president is commander-in-chief, head of state, and chief executive for
the US government; he is simultaneously an ordinary citizen subject to
the same laws as everyone else, an elected official who serves at the
discretion of the voters, and a public servant who depends on Congress
for money, legislation, and war-making. The founders made the president into a powerful but severely limited leader: part monarch, part
prime minister; part warrior, part administrator. The presidency is big
and small at the same time. The mix of purposes was the genius of the
US Constitution, and also its severest shortcoming. Although the
founders envisioned the United States becoming a large and powerful
country, they wanted it to remain anchored in the freedoms and virtues
associated with small agrarian societies. Madison expounded the advantages of size and diversity in his famous claim that a vast union
would be less susceptible to domination by one faction or another than
a small republic: "Extend the sphere, and you take in a greater variety
of parties and interests; you make it less probable that a majority of the
whole will have a common motive to invade the rights of other citizens; or if such a common motive exists, it will be more difficult for all
who feel it to discover their own strength, and to act in unison with
each other."[30]

But the advantages of pluralism, in Madison's terms, were supposed
to encourage the virtues of a free citizenry filled with diverse voices, not
just an uneasy mix of competing views. Inspired by the "classical republican traditions" of Greece and Rome, Madison and his counterparts
expected free citizens to avoid financial dependence on others, to live
comfortably but not extravagantly, to prize the public good, and to show
their worthiness of respect in their service to community. For all the
talk of national institutions and individual rights, the framers conceived

of successful democratic politics in terms of virtuous participation in an extended family of citizens.

John Adams, hardly a naïve optimist, told his wife that the success of the American Revolution required the nurturing of more virtue, not less, in the former colonists. "There is," he wrote, "in the human breast, a social Affection which extends to our whole Species." Adams, Madison, Jefferson, and their contemporaries believed that the absence of European-style feudalism in the United States and the replacement of colonial rule by a well-run democratic government would make Americans benevolent in their dealings with one another.[31]

"In most European countries," one early American speaker explained, "the dependence of peasants on the rich, produces on the one side, callousness and pride, and on the other, depressing and humiliating debasement." In North America, where there were no feudal lords, "the dependence of our citizens is only on each other for the supply of mutual wants," and this "produced mutual confidence and good-will."[32]

Slaves, American Indians, women, and propertyless workers were excluded from this image of independence and free sociability. They were not seen as sufficiently virtuous for the democratic participation that Madison's pluralism promised. If the vast territory of the United States extended the circle of American citizenship, the requirements of virtue and independence kept the circle tightly closed. Race, sex, and class were biological markers of virtue, or its absence, for even the most democratic thinkers of the era. That continued exclusivity made Madison's pluralism appealing to men who feared the ignorance of the "masses" and the immorality of an open society. Virtue protected high standards for those—including Madison, Jefferson, and Adams—who wanted democratic government to embody superior principles, not just the aggregated interests of countless citizens.

Federalism promised this uneasy balance between competing claims on authority by building a machinery of national government separated from the local controls exercised by states, counties, and towns. The president would head the national government, but also stay strictly within boundaries that limited what that government and its leader could do.

The precise boundaries for presidential power have been uncertain from the start. Washington's presidency mapped the initial lines, based on loose constitutional guidelines. Subsequent eras would reinterpret and redesign what Washington drew. Washington's presidency was the beginning of a modern presidency that would remain tied to his experiences, but grow well beyond his imaginings—and his fears.

CHAPTER 2

First Executive

The first chief executive of the first constitutional democracy, President George Washington gave the first "State of the Union" address to Congress on 8 January 1790. He had been in office for a little more than eight months, and it was the first time he officially visited the nation's legislators in joint session at New York City's Federal Hall. Washington and his counterparts were aware that this moment would set many precedents for relations between the president and Congress, and the exercise of power within the US government as a whole.

How would Washington address Congress? As a king instructing his ministers on policy? That was clearly unacceptable in a republic. As a supplicant requesting assistance from the legislature? That would diminish the executive power of the presidency, showing him to be a creature of Congress—a position the founders rejected when they empowered a president rather than a prime minister. The Constitution created a presidency that was separate from and equal to Congress, with required reporting to the legislature "from time to time." The president's reporting to Congress included the expectation that he would "recommend to their Consideration such Measures as he shall judge necessary and expedient." The Constitution said nothing more about precise timing, frequency, content, or form for executive statements. Washington had to make it up.

As with almost everything he did during his first months in office, Washington's address to Congress had enormous impact on the evolution of executive leadership in the United States and abroad. The president wished to cultivate some deference from Congress as *the* representative of the American people and *the* defender of their national interests. Although a man of few words, Washington was accustomed to commanding. He wanted to set a limited, but focused, policy agenda for the new government and push members of Congress to support it. That is how he interpreted the constitutional expectation: "Measures as he shall judge necessary and expedient."

Washington intended to lead on the big national issues, leaving the details of most programs to Congress and the states. The president did not want to pronounce on local topics like farming and family, and he sought to empower state and county governments, rather than asserting federal primacy—which had not been established on issues other than war in early America. Washington reserved his time and attention for only the most important shared issues bearing on the future of the young nation. He avoided divisive issues like slavery, where presidential action would only ignite conflict. He kept the presidency small, by design.

Washington wanted to demonstrate the modesty of his office and its dependence on congressional support. His leadership would gain democratic legitimacy from the affirmative consent of the nation's legislature. To be an executive, for Washington, meant to stand apart but remain deeply connected to representatives of local interests. He did not see the president and Congress as partners or competitors. Rather, they were parallel parts of a government, exercising different kinds of authority, with overlapping responsibilities to the national interest. For this reason, Washington was forceful about what he perceived as the needed direction of the country, but self-consciously restrained when it came to the specifics of any new laws, which would of course be the prerogative of Congress. The president would articulate a national goal for the laws and enforce them; the Congress and the states would determine the content of the laws and how to pay for them.

Washington used his words and actions at the first State of the Union ceremony to demonstrate this parallel and mutually dependent relationship. The chief justice of the Supreme Court and the secretaries of treasury and war accompanied the president as part of the entourage that he led, but they traveled to visit Congress, not vice versa. Members of the legislature greeted the president as an extraordinary official and they granted him a unique audience. The listeners, however, had no obligation to do anything that he said or follow any of his recommendations. The president had a dignified pulpit, but he commanded no rights of enforcement or obligation in Congress. He was a visitor and they were his hosts.

Members of Congress stood respectfully when he entered their chamber, they listened politely while he spoke, but when he finished he bowed to them and quickly departed, with little consequence. The event symbolized Washington's exalted status and the limits of his power at the same time. It gave him unique voice in speaking for the country and its needs as a whole, and it reminded all observers that his power was more in the vision than in the doing.

It was up to Congress to take his agenda and turn it into programs and laws. Congress was not obligated to act on the president's words, but if persuaded, it could convert executive strategy into day-to-day tactics. Washington's State of the Union was the first example of executive direction-setting for a complex and democratic American government. In subsequent decades this executive role would grow even more important. It would have few figures who understood its potential and its limits as acutely as the first president.

WASHINGTON BEGAN HIS FIRST STATE OF THE UNION by extolling the accession of North Carolina to statehood in November 1789. Rhode Island would follow six months later as the thirteenth and last of the original British colonies to ratify the Constitution. For Washington, the expansion of the country, the growth in its economic capabilities, and the increasing cooperation between the states were clear priorities. Invoking divine guidance and good fortune, he praised the new government for "the rising credit and respectability of our country, the general and increasing good will toward the government of the Union, and the concord, peace, and plenty with which we are blessed." As he saw it, the executive was responsible for promoting these values.[1]

Washington called upon Congress to give him the resources necessary for their pursuit. He began with the "common defense"—what later generations would label the president's responsibility for "national security." "To be prepared for war," the former general explained, "is one of the most effectual means of preserving peace." In early 1790 the country was not prepared for war, lacking a strong organized military, and it was not prepared for international diplomacy, lacking an effective system for sending ministers abroad.

Washington presented an agenda to build up capabilities in both areas, particularly through the preparation of ordinary citizens for participation in the common defense. The point was not to create a large standing army or navy, but to cultivate a citizen body ready for service, when necessary. Washington explained: "A free people ought not only to be armed, but disciplined: to which end a uniform and well-digested plan is requisite; and their safety and interest require that they should promote such manufactories as tend to render them independent of others for essential, particularly military, supplies."[2]

Unity and self-sufficiency were crucial to this vision. Washington called for investments in infrastructure, including the "post office and post-roads." He specifically advocated national support for trade and inventions to strengthen the nation. He also asked for national support of the arts, sciences, and education to nurture a more capable democratic citizenry.

His vision in this last area was especially prescient, anticipating the importance of public higher education more than a century later: "Knowledge is in every country the surest basis of public happiness," Washington explained. "To the security of a free constitution it contributes in various ways," including: "teaching the people themselves to know and to value their own rights; to discern and provide against invasions of them; [and] to distinguish between oppression and the necessary exercise of lawful authority." Washington argued that the president had to help the people "discriminate the spirit of liberty from that of licentiousness—cherishing the first, avoiding the last—and uniting a speedy but temperate vigilance against encroachments, with an inviolable respect to the laws." Democracy required public virtue, derived from education and experience, and the president had to be its paragon.[3]

Although Washington had no constitutional authority over education, he set a clear agenda on the matter, encouraging the government's support for new institutions of higher learning—even a "national university." He left the details of funding and institutional design to others (above all, the states), but he articulated a strong national interest in education: "Whether this desirable object will be best promoted by affording aids to seminaries of learning already established, by the institution of a national university, or by any other expedients will be well worthy of a place in the deliberations of the legislature."[4]

In short, Washington used his State of the Union, and his presidency as a whole, to define what the new country was about. He set priorities, he asserted opportunities, and he addressed challenges. Washington imagined some of the new institutions that would govern and grow American society, but he did not try to manage or control many of them. His role as an executive was to point a direction, set a strategy, and bring people together. For his first visit to a joint session of Congress, and all subsequent visits, that meant a short speech (barely more than 1,000 words) and a clear statement of goals. He wanted the president to be a figure who helped the country look forward and pursue high aspirations, moving beyond the daily ordeals of governance that were necessary, but often distracting from what really mattered most. Washington grasped what Bernard Bailyn has called the "creative imagination" of the founding moment, seeing an opportunity to create new conventions and traditions. Even though he was not a monarch, he acted with the formality and distinction necessary to make experiments in government look stable and significant. The delivery of the first State of the Union was one of many moments when Washington lent gravity to an awkward, perhaps poorly prepared, event. He achieved this result with a deliberative approach to leadership that showed deep care and consideration for controversial issues, but also a willingness to invent new practices and policies.[5]

The first president could ride above controversy and lend credibility to decisions because he showed understanding and objectivity. He was not partisan, or biased, or venal, or petty—at least not in public. He was intentionally aloof and always dignified in demeanor. Washington understood the power that came from restraint, remoteness, and an "elegant simplicity" in style. During the years of the revolution and then his presidency, he cultivated an image of humble command and complete concern for the national interest. That image made him the natural arbiter for contending positions.[6]

EXECUTIVE LEADERSHIP REQUIRES A COMBINATION OF GRAVITAS and radicalism. A leader must be reliable and experimental at the same time. Washington brilliantly combined the two—better than any president before Abraham Lincoln. His gravitas was a careful construction on his part; his radicalism came from his willingness to challenge orthodoxies as the provincial leader of a nascent nation. Washington was far from a monarch in breeding and far from London in his rule. Both characteristics contributed to his willingness to push boundaries, even as he embodied a most traditional demeanor.

The new nation's distance from Europe and the limited powers of its president stimulated creative leadership. Washington rejected monarchical precedents and avoided micromanagement of policy issues, even in military affairs. He brought a farmer's common sense and modesty to his work. These qualities appear repeatedly in his diary, especially when he recounts his various travels and meetings. Washington was obsessed with the agrarian conditions of the lands he visited, and he was acutely conscious of the local constraints on his ability to change the land and its people. He sought to understand and encourage the best qualities in the free individuals around him.[7]

Washington emphasized limited but still aspirational priorities. He avoided, wherever possible, unnecessary commitments and conflicts. He recognized that a small presidency built around the most important national needs would produce more benefits than a large, expansive ministerial machine—on the model of the contemporary monarchies across the European continent. Anticipating the writings of Alexis de Tocqueville a half century later, Washington understood that a selective and modest executive was most effective for a growing democracy. He used the new office to encourage creativity and pragmatism, while building a set of basic rules and routines for the nation.[8]

The president pursued this leadership model by surrounding himself with talented people. It helped that many of the most talented Americans of his generation were already close to him personally; later presidents, who governed a far more populous and complex nation, would not have the same luxury. Washington understood that effective leadership is built upon the performance of key figures—the conduct they model, the ideas they generate, and the actions they support in their subordinates and followers. He had famously remarked early in his military career: "It is the actions, and not the commission, that make the Officer—and...there is more expected from him than the Title."[9]

As a military leader Washington learned to identify diverse men of talent, attract them to him, and derive both technical knowledge and strategic wisdom from them. He always had a close circle of advisors whom he encouraged to think creatively about the goals he articulated, implementing bold plans his team agreed upon. He integrated his talented advisors through frequent councils, careful deliberations, and decisive action when necessary. Washington was an informed and dispassionate arbiter who commanded their total loyalty, but not their intellectual sycophancy.[10]

As president, Washington followed the same approach. His most important initial advisors were James Madison and Alexander Hamilton, both of whom were instrumental in writing and promoting the Constitution. Madison served in the US House of Representatives during Washington's two terms, but he nevertheless drafted many of the president's speeches. Hamilton had been Washington's military aide-de-camp, and he became the first secretary of the treasury.

The two young men revered Washington, but they did not perceive him as all-knowing. Quite the contrary, Washington encouraged them to see themselves as superior intellects, capable of understanding complex policy issues in more depth than the president, as well as more gifted writers. Washington instructed them to bring him their best ideas about economy, diplomacy, and society. He was firm in wanting thorough explanations, and in guarding his role as the final decision-maker. Madison and Hamilton loyally followed that stricture, even as they repeatedly pushed the thinking of the president beyond his initial assumptions.

Thomas Jefferson and John Jay joined Madison and Hamilton as frequent advisors to the president. Both Jefferson and Jay had distinguished themselves during the revolution and in subsequent years. They combined accomplishments of the pen (the Declaration of Independence and the Federalist Papers, respectively) with experience as international diplomats representing the new republic in Europe. Jefferson served as the first secretary of state and Jay as the first chief justice of the US Supreme Court. Washington relied on these men to advise him on his proposals to Congress about the methods for conducting foreign policy and adjudicating legal disputes between overlapping local, state, and national jurisdictions. Washington's ultimate determination of what he believed best served the interests of the nation depended on their expertise.

On most issues, if not all, Washington prodded his brilliant subordinates to new thinking. He solicited feedback from multiple advisors on a given topic, quietly assessed the merits of different advice, and avoided rushed judgments. Often, Washington believed, it was wise to let events take their course, keep options open, and then make a decision when a promising opportunity arose. These were deliberative tactics he cultivated as a military strategist and later applied to civilian leadership. He defined his role predominantly as a listener who relied on trusted and talented experts, and made decisions only when the stakes were high and the evidence was carefully weighed.

WASHINGTON DREW AN IMPORTANT DISTINCTION BETWEEN democratic decision-making and executive decision-making in a democracy. The former involved the necessary deliberations about laws, programs, and budgets by Congress and state legislatures. They had an obligation to insure that the daily actions of government reflected the will of the people (or the "consent of the governed" as John Locke put it), manifested by the directly elected representatives of the people.[11]

To Washington, executive decision-making within a democracy was something different. It echoed his own experiences as an accomplished military commander. For complex issues of great national importance, the leader of the government (like the leader of the army) had to deliberate in depth with a group of learned and trusted advisors. By necessity, they possessed more information, experience, and expertise on most topics than the average citizen. After carefully defining the issues where high-level knowledge and attention was most crucial, the executive had to assess thoughtful advice, often delivered in confidence, and then define a path forward for his advisors, and the nation as a whole. It was his job, after the decision, to explain what he had decided and why, encouraging support from the other necessary institutions of government (especially Congress) and the people as a whole. Executive deliberations were rigorous, confidential, and the decision of the president; executive decisions were open and carefully explained for ultimate consent by the people and their representatives.

Presidents, in Washington's model, were different from generals because they did not issue orders, except in military matters, when they acted as commander-in-chief. Washington defined presidential authority as knowledge and trust-based. He would persuade by virtue of his special access to informed deliberation and the shared faith that he acted in the national interest. He would inspire confidence from his rigorous and disinterested decision-making, and his repeated personal restraint. Most of all, he would cultivate consent from the evidence that he exercised considered judgment, based not on personal whim or prejudice, but collective analysis by some of the best minds.

Washington's executive was far from a dictator or monarch or wise man; he was more like the fatherly "guardian" of a large and talented family. His "cabinet" was a collection of energetic cousins who looked to the father figure for unifying guidance and approval. Congress was the assembly that represented all family relations. Washington chose his moments carefully, and he always used a voice that resonated with other respected individuals. He spoke *for* the family as much as he spoke *to* the family.

WASHINGTON'S FATHERLY MODE OF EXECUTIVE LEADERSHIP defined early American economic and foreign policy. During the Revolutionary War, Washington had dealt extensively with both matters. He had to raise an army, feed it, and sustain it—despite the desire of many enlistees to return to their farms. To Washington's frustration, the Continental Congress never provided sufficient resources, in part because of its inability to tax the population. Washington looked to the nation's alliance with France as a key source for depleted resources. He also encouraged the Continental Congress to take on debt for the purpose of financing his army. Washington was not a deep thinker about finance, but he understood very well the importance of building a reliable system for procuring credit, distributing resources, and managing their uses. He presciently remarked that an extended war, like the conflict with the British in the late eighteenth century, quickly became a "war of finance" where the state with the best access to key resources acquired a winning advantage.[12]

In the years after the revolution, Washington feared that the new country was not prepared for competition on the international stage. He viewed the absence of centralized powers for regulating American finance and trade as debilitating weaknesses of the Articles of Confederation, especially when competitor nations (including Great Britain) benefited from well-established institutions that managed resources at home and abroad. In Washington's eyes, the dominance of the states over currency, taxes, and trade amounted to "surrendering" the power necessary for Americans as a whole to thrive. The British might have ceded political control of their thirteen former colonies, but they still dominated the economy of North America. The independent country created under the Articles of Confederation lacked the cooperative institutions to stand on its own for very long.[13]

As president, and empowered by the new Constitution, Washington moved quickly to rectify this shortcoming. He used his executive powers to formulate a national economic plan that he pushed Congress to approve. In his first State of the Union speech Washington singled out "provision for the support of the public credit" as a national priority. He called it "a matter of high importance to the national honor and prosperity."[14]

Acting as Washington's secretary of the treasury, Alexander Hamilton took this guidance to heart when he authored the key proposals for building a national economy. Hamilton's technical knowledge and creative imagination filled the pages of his forty thousand-word *Report on Public Credit*, submitted to Congress on 14 January 1790. Hamilton began by explaining the importance of national debt: "exigencies are to be expected to occur, in the affairs of nations, in which there will be a necessity for borrowing." Pointing to the limits on "monied capital" within the United States at the time, and the importance of investments in industry, infrastructure, and defense, Hamilton argued "that to be able to borrow upon *good terms*, it is essential that the credit of a nation should be well established."[15]

Following Washington's direction, Hamilton set out the necessary steps for the United States to become an attractive magnet for foreign capital and for the investment of that capital in productive industries. First, the federal government would assume all the revolutionary war debts from the states ($25 million) and the Continental Congress ($54 million), insuring the good credit of the new government. Foreign lenders would know that the United States repaid its loans. Second, the Treasury would manage a series of national taxes (mostly on whiskey) and import duties to service existing and future debts. Third, the federal government would create a National Bank and a national currency to facilitate trade and investment, and manage the flow of finance in the marketplace.[16]

Hamilton shared Washington's admiration for how Britain's centralized state managed its economy to increase access to capital at lower cost for businesses and public (often imperial) institutions. Hamilton's proposals were an adaptation of similar measures to the United States. The new American government would leverage capital through loans and taxes to invest in national economic growth. It would stitch together a national economy, wrenching some control away from states and other local groups. The Treasury's management of debt and investment would create new loyalties to the federal government and encourage nation-wide industry.[17]

Washington's presidency made the formulation of this economic plan possible, but he could not, of course, impose it. Congress had to approve it, and for more than a month critics attacked the scheme. To Washington's chagrin, James Madison led the charge, accusing the executive of overstepping his bounds and creating too much centralized power over the economy. He accused Hamilton of trying to establish monarchical powers. Although Madison's criticisms resonated in Virginia and other parts of the South that distrusted the dominance of Northern industry, Hamilton's scheme prevailed. In return, however,

Madison extracted an agreement in July 1790 (the Residency Act) to move the national capital—then in New York City—farther south, first to Philadelphia for ten years, and then to a new city in the marshlands along the Potomac River, soon to be called Washington, D.C.

The nation now had a defined economic policy. Hamilton submitted subsequent reports to Congress on public credit and manufacturing that contributed to the creation of his proposed national bank, the US Customs Service to enforce import duties, and the US Revenue Cutter Service (later the US Coast Guard) to enforce federal regulations on trade. The president set the agenda for these increases in national economic regulation, the Treasury managed the new powers, and Congress gave the authority, the resources, and the necessary consent. This was how Washington hoped effective, but still limited, executive leadership would work on behalf of core national interests.

Economic growth was a presidential priority, and Washington mobilized talent and congressional support for more coherent central power. The executive still did not "control" the economy, but his officials (especially his secretary of the treasury) used new powers to encourage trade, investment, and sound public credit. These were national goals, executive-led, and congressionally authorized—a unique separation of powers for a uniquely democratic society.

ECONOMIC GROWTH, HOWEVER, WAS NOT ENOUGH. PROSPERITY required security, and Washington was one of many Americans who perceived multiplying foreign threats to the new country in the late eighteenth century. Although American revolutionary forces benefited from the support of French soldiers, dispatched to defeat rival British armies, Washington recognized that supporters one day would become potential adversaries the next. Like the British, the French had extensive territorial ambitions in North America, particularly in Canada. They also had a long tradition of allying with native Indian and other forces on the continent against the citizens of what became the United States.

Washington revealed his acute concern for American security and his sophisticated understanding of power politics in a November 1778 letter he sent to Henry Laurens, then president of the Continental Congress: "It is a maxim founded on the universal experience of mankind, that no nation is to be trusted farther than it is bound by its interest; and no prudent statesman or politician will venture to depart from it. In our circumstances," Washington continued, reflecting on the relative weakness of American national institutions and military forces, "we ought to be particularly cautious; for we have not yet attained sufficient vigor and maturity to recover from the shock of any false step into which we may unwarily fall."[18]

National independence did not solve the problems of insecurity; if anything, it amplified them. The British maintained their fortresses in North America with garrisoned troops, and they continued to dominate trade along the Atlantic coast. Spanish forces remained south of the United States, with control over Florida, New Orleans, Cuba, and other valuable territories. Diverse Indian groups continued to dominate the middle of the continent, and they remained a threat to American settlements in the Ohio and Tennessee Valleys, among other regions. France maintained its claims in Canada, and it acquired the vast Louisiana territory in 1800, during Napoleon Bonaparte's rule. The new American nation lived in a very tough neighborhood, surrounded by jealous, condescending, and heavily militarized imperial powers, all of whom planned to take advantage of the immature country that few Europeans expected to survive for long.

Washington's frustration with the Articles of Confederation centered on his fear that, without effective executive leadership, the country would crumble before its adversaries. He had dealt with the problems of fragmentation and infighting when he commanded American revolutionary forces. The states never provided the promised personnel or financial support. Each state looked to others to shoulder the burden, and distrust among state leaders encouraged more rivalry than unified action. Washington repeatedly had to make personal appeals to individual legislators because the Continental Congress was not an effective forum for implementing a national defense strategy.

After the war, Washington believed the problem would only deepen as the absence of immediate conflict allowed for further distraction. The states jockeyed with one another while the European powers strategized for advantage on the continent. Internal disorder and external threats brought the great revolutionary commander to a point of despair, rarely seen in a man of such controlled emotion. "How melancholy is the reflection," he wrote James Madison in November 1786, "that in so short a space, we should have made such large strides towards fulfilling the prediction of our transatlantic foes!—'leave them to themselves, and their government will soon dissolve.'"

"Thirteen Sovereignties pulling against each other, and all tugging at the federal head, will soon bring ruin on the whole," Washington predicted. He supported "a liberal, and energetic Constitution, well guarded & closely watched, to prevent incroachments." For Washington, the president had to be vigilant in defending the United States from threats that exploited internal divisions and weaknesses.[19]

Washington's words helped shape the thinking of Madison and other framers. The Constitution was a "peace pact," written in the shadow of foreign threats and domestic disorder, to secure the new nation. As president, Washington intended to use the executive office to hold the country together and mobilize, where necessary, for the common defense. He saw that as the highest executive duty, above all other presidential responsibilities, including that of battlefield commander-in-chief. His actions far from the sites of conflict would be more important. The president had to be the strategist and diplomat-in-chief for the nation's defense—roles dangerously absent from American government before 1789. Washington created a precedent for other presidents to do the same, with more far-reaching military force.[20]

LIKE OTHER EXPERIENCED GENERALS, WASHINGTON HOPED TO avoid military conflict by building a strong and secure foreign policy. He recognized that unity and strength would deter external challenges. He also understood that a relatively small and tightly controlled military establishment would neither seek nor stumble into needless wars. Although he was a professional army officer who saw the limitations of a temporary citizen militia, Washington agreed with many Americans who perceived a large standing military—modeled on France or Prussia—as a threat to civil liberties. A firm and steady foreign policy was, for Washington, the best defense. As he wrote, a large army is "a dangerous instrument to play with."[21]

Washington devoted his greatest efforts as president to the national defense. He favored a small standing army (about 5,000 men), state militias (placed under federal command when necessary), and a small but capable navy. These forces would protect the territory and its trade against interference. They would fight pirates, Indians, and domestic law-breakers—such as the Whiskey rebels in Western Pennsylvania who refused to pay taxes and threatened federal officials.

In October 1794, Washington confronted these stubborn farmers. The nation's small military and state militias, which Washington saw primarily as a police force, acted together to preserve the law. The president served as the national police chief, relying on Congress for funding and the states for troops.

That was how he assembled 13,000 soldiers who marched with him into rural Western Pennsylvania. State governments mustered the troops and the governors of Virginia, Pennsylvania, and New Jersey served on the battlefield in subordinate command to the president. Washington gave the military forces, including the governors, clear direction in defining and securing national order. He was their *political and military leader*. Under the direction of the president, citizen-soldiers served the laws and interests of the country as a whole. Washington made this clear in his instructions:

> You are to exert yourself by all possible means to preserve discipline among the troops, particularly a scrupulous regard to the rights of persons and property and a respect for the authority of the civil magistrate; taking especial care to inculcate and cause to be observed this principle, that the duties of the army are confined to the attacking and subduing of armed opponents of the laws, and to the supporting and aiding of the civil officers in the execution of their functions.[22]

The laws to be preserved were national laws for federal taxation of alcohol, part of Secretary of the Treasury Alexander Hamilton's controversial economic policy. The civil magistrates were inspectors and tax collectors employed by the Treasury, and therefore part of Washington's executive administration. In suppressing the Whiskey Rebellion during the fall of 1794, Washington effectively asserted that the president could use federal and state military capabilities to enforce national laws and preserve national order, above local objections. Congress passed the laws for taxation with the president's encouragement, and now the president was obligated to enforce the laws across the nation, through force if necessary.

Washington's use of military coercion in Western Pennsylvania set a precedent for subsequent executives, including Abraham Lincoln in the Civil War, and Presidents Dwight Eisenhower, John F. Kennedy, and Lyndon B. Johnson during the civil rights movement. They all used federal and state policing powers to enforce federal laws above the objections of state leaders. They all argued they were, like Washington, defending the national order—the highest presidential duty.

To WASHINGTON, DEFENDING THE NATIONAL ORDER ALSO MEANT avoiding commitments that would embroil the new nation in foreign wars. The appearance in April 1793 of the flamboyant French minister Edmond-Charles Genêt posed the first direct challenge to Washington's position. Genêt arrived demanding American support for Revolutionary France. He extolled the common bond between the two nations, forged in the American war against Britain, now evident in the new French government's determination to destroy English power in Europe.

Genêt was a dashing and urbane thirty-year-old who spoke English very well. He called himself "Citizen Genêt"—a citizen of liberty and world revolution. He appealed directly to American crowds for support, and he was greeted enthusiastically in Charleston, Philadelphia, and other cities. Genêt also undertook to outfit ships seized by French supporters for war against Britain. These were often small British ships captured at sea by French sympathizers and brought to the United States. Genêt helped turn these "prizes" into armed French vessels, launched from American ports.

The French minister had many American advocates, especially among supporters of Thomas Jefferson, who maintained a disdain for the British and an abiding concern about the monarchist sympathies of Alexander Hamilton, and perhaps even President Washington. This conflict played out in the partisan press. One newspaper supporting Jefferson, the *National Gazette*, scolded Washington for forgetting the ideals of the American Revolution. Another, the *Aurora*, depicted Genêt as the defender of republicanism, and his detractors as reactionaries. Americans had just fought a long war against Britain; many veterans of that struggle still saw London as the enemy, and Paris as a loyal friend.

For all his prestige, the president found himself on the defensive. The *National Gazette* condemned his "cold indifference" toward friends who "support their own liberties against a host of despots." Washington was the first of many presidents to feel intensive public pressure to support a foreign ideological ally. Many critics asked: If the United States stands for liberty, shouldn't it devote its power to that cause abroad?[23]

Washington thought not. To the contrary, he believed that the president had to restrain public passions, channeling them into policies that defended the nation's enduring interests, rather than its popular causes. He was, in this sense, a classical realist. Writing to Secretary of State Thomas Jefferson in the same month as Genêt's arrival, Washington explained: "War having actually commenced between France and Great Britain, it behooves the Government of this Country to use every means in its power to prevent the citizens thereof from embroiling us with either of those powers, by endeavouring to maintain a strict neutrality." The president ordered his chief foreign policy aide to "give the subject mature consideration, that such measures as shall be deemed most likely to effect this desirable purpose may be adopted without delay."[24]

Although he favored France, Jefferson himself, if not his followers, saw the dangers in the United States becoming a co-belligerent. He hoped to stay out of the war, but to still lend support to the revolutionary government. At the cabinet meeting that Washington called on 19 April 1793, it became clear that the president and Hamilton strongly supported strict neutrality, fearing that any direct involvement on one side would justify attacks by the other. Washington and Hamilton also recognized that the French were not, in fact, more favorable to American trading and territorial interests than the British. That was what mattered most, they argued, not ideological predispositions or the appeal of figures like Genêt.[25]

Moved by the urgency of the moment, and following what he viewed as the necessary role for the president as guardian of the national interest, Washington signed a proclamation of neutrality three days later—the first of its kind in American history. The short document, less than three hundred words, pledged that the United States "should with sincerity and good faith adopt and pursue a conduct friendly and impartial toward the belligerent powers." To enforce this posture, the president announced that the United States would not protect the property or safety of citizens who violated its neutrality. In addition, Washington ordered government officials to "cause prosecutions" in American courts for those citizens who aided one side in the war. Americans could continue to travel and trade, but they could not provide military assistance to France or Britain, or any of their allies.[26]

Genêt challenged Washington's right to make this decision on behalf of the American people. So did Jefferson and Madison. As secretary of state, Jefferson did not feel that he could criticize the president in public, but he asked Madison, then a member of the House of Representatives, to do just that. In a series of articles, published under the pen name "Helvidius," Madison condemned what he saw as Washington's usurpation of congressional authority: "The natural province of the magistrate is to execute laws, as that of the legislature is to make laws." In proclaiming neutrality, the president had prohibited the Congress from making war, Madison argued. "As the Constitution has not permitted the Executive *singly* to conclude or judge that peace ought to be made," he wrote, "it might be inferred from that circumstance alone, that it never meant to give it authority, *singly*, to judge and conclude that war ought not to be made."[27]

Madison's co-author in the Federalist Papers, Alexander Hamilton, defended the president and his authority to declare neutrality. Hamilton published a series of arguments under the apt pseudonym "Pacificus." Hamilton contended that the executive was "the *organ* of intercourse between the Nation and foreign Nations." Congress represented the states, not the country as a whole; approving treaties and declaring war were, Hamilton asserted, "exceptions" to presidential primacy in foreign policy.

For all other international issues the power of the executive was unlimited in the Constitution, and concentrated in the one person who could speak for the interests of the entire country.[28]

Hamilton devoted most of his defense to the merits of the neutrality policy for the survival of American democracy. His comments echoed Washington's emphasis on interests over ideology and a realist vision of self-interested nation-states competing for power. "Morality," according to Hamilton, is "not exactly the same between Nations as between individuals." An individual, he continued, "may on numerous occasions meritoriously indulge the emotions of generosity and benevolence; not only without an eye to, but even at the expense of his own interest. But a Nation can rarely be justified in pursuing a similar course; and when it does so ought to confine itself within much stricter bounds."[29]

Awareness of the self-interested and ungoverned nature of international relations "ought to teach us," Hamilton continued, "not to overrate *foreign friendships*—to be upon our guard against *foreign attachments*. The former will generally be found hollow and delusive; the latter will have a natural tendency to lead us aside from our own true interest, and to make us the dupes of foreign influence." Speaking for Washington, he called figures like Genêt manipulators of "our passions, under the auspices of national prejudice and partiality." They led the country to "corruption" and further division because, Hamilton reminded readers, "one foreign power can employ this resource as well as another."[30]

Hamilton's words placed meat on the bare bones of the April 1793 Neutrality Proclamation. The president was not only adopting a posture of impartiality and non-involvement in foreign wars; Washington was doing something more profound. Despite opposition in Congress and across the states, he asserted an executive right to speak for the nation's interests in its relations with foreign societies. This power did not mean the president could take the country to war, nor that he could implement treaties—two areas where the Constitution gave Congress a required role. The president was, however, claiming the position of primary strategist and manager for other international issues. He would put aside the passions and preferences that guided domestic debates and focus the nation's resources on policies that protected its long-term security.

Washington took for himself and gave to his successors the power to conduct diplomacy with little day-to-day oversight by Congress. The president became the dominant figure in American foreign policy. He set the agenda for the nation's foreign policy, he defined the national interests, and, most important, he created situations on the ground to reinforce his policies. He had the clear first-mover advantage over Congress, the states, and other parts of the US government.

In the case of Genêt, Washington asked the French to recall their minister. When a new government in Paris did so, Genêt was discredited, and he was forced to live in private (and silent) exile in the United States, fearful of returning to a revolutionary situation in France where he would probably face death. As president, Washington could isolate and ultimately muzzle a foreign advocate who challenged him. Some of his successors, including John Adams, would take this power too far through measures like the Alien and Sedition Acts of 1798 that silenced dissent and targeted foreigners. Although Washington often bridled at his critics, he did not use the presidency to repress differences of opinion. Rather, he focused on pursuing firm foreign policies, despite differences of opinion. He believed that the executive had to insure a unified and consistent international posture, even when such unity and consistency were not mirrored at home.[31]

Americans remained divided over France and Britain, with Jefferson and Madison's supporters favoring the former and Hamilton's supporters the latter. To Washington's deep regret, these divisions gave rise to the first American party system with Democratic-Republicans on one side, Federalists on the other. Nonetheless, the president's Neutrality Proclamation survived numerous challenges because most Americans, including those in Congress, trusted Washington to defend the nation's interests against foreign threats. Many citizens agreed with Washington and Hamilton's assessment of the competitive international system and the needs of the United States in this perilous environment.[32]

To survive, the country required a strong foreign policy leader who could assess threats and protect the interests of the nation. For all the ideological rhetoric of the day, many Americans were—and still are—fundamentally pragmatic in their devotion to security and prosperity above other international preferences. Although they disagreed with specific judgments made by the president, they wanted someone in the executive role to lead the rest of the government on foreign policy choices. Presidential foreign policy protected security from foreign predators, just as more pluralistic congressional and state-driven domestic policy protected democracy from potential oppressors. Unity mattered most beyond the nation's borders. Washington's leadership set the enduring precedent for the United States to jealously guard its interests abroad as it passionately pursued utopias at home.[33]

In the years after the Neutrality Proclamation, Washington reinforced his commitment to a unified foreign policy, despite the deepening partisanship at home. He sent two representatives, John Jay and Thomas Pinckney, to London and Madrid in 1794 and 1795 to negotiate treaties with foreign empires that preserved American neutrality and protected basic national interests. The Jay Treaty, signed 19 November 1794, avoided a war between the United States and Great Britain in response to British seizures of American ships trading non-military goods with France. American merchants asserted a right to trade as neutrals with all belligerents—a claim Americans would maintain through the early twentieth century. The British denied this claim because they viewed any trade with France as support for their enemy.

Washington understood that the United States did not have the power at sea to force a change of British policy. As a consequence, Jay signed an agreement with London that allowed for increased Anglo-American trade, stipulated the removal of British military fortifications northwest of the United States, and promised payment for American goods seized at sea. In return, the United States accepted British interdiction of ships bringing goods to their enemies.

The Jay Treaty met stiff resistance at home from merchants who resented the continued British restrictions on their trade with France and other British adversaries. The treaty was also a clear offense to the United States as a sovereign state: the British retained the right to control the seas around the new country and limit its trade. Other unresolved issues in the treaty included the boundary between the

United States and Canada, and unpaid pre-revolutionary British debts to Americans.

Washington put his prestige behind the treaty, as he had with the Neutrality Proclamation. It was the best deal the United States could get in the nation's attempt to avoid a disastrous war with Great Britain. In addition, the treaty improved American security by reducing the British military presence north of the border, and it increased trade with Britain and its possessions. The agreement fell short of living up to American principles, but it was a sensible deal that improved the position of the country. Washington's personal leadership made the treaty possible; its close two-thirds approval in the Senate depended on his persuasion of senators. Although the debate around Jay's diplomacy heightened partisanship at home, the treaty was a success, another instance of the president steering foreign policy toward consistent neutrality, security, and the best possible economic advantage.[34]

The Pinckney Treaty, signed between the American representative and Spanish Prime Minister Manuel de Godoy on 27 October 1795, was less controversial, although it stemmed from the same approach to foreign policy. The United States did not challenge Spanish possession of Florida or New Orleans or other lands west of the Mississippi River. In return, the United States gained the right to free navigation on the mighty river flowing north to south through the center of the continent.

This was a favorable treaty for the United States, one that created many commercial opportunities and avoided military conflict. Like the Jay Treaty, the Pinckney Treaty focused on interests, not ideology; both treaties bespoke a clear understanding of the realities of power in the international system. Washington's presidential guidance promoted this outcome at the negotiating table and in the positive Senate vote. The treaties of 1794 and 1795 extended the principles of the Neutrality Proclamation and the power of the president as the nation's diplomat-in-chief.

THE BURDENS OF EXECUTIVE LEADERSHIP WORE WASHINGTON down, as they would later presidents. Washington led a new and imperiled government, and although he faced fewer crises than his successors, the pressures on the first president were already very heavy. He had to please countless groups across the country as he contended with numerous actors abroad. He had to perform as a powerful leader when his powers were really quite constrained. He had to be authoritative but democratic, accessible but still aloof.

Washington's diary is filled with lamentations over his loss of privacy and the multiplying controversies swirling around his policies and his office. Politics in the young democracy were then—as they are now—a full contact sport, filled with personal attacks, partisan positioning, and deep disagreements over principles. The president is at the center of the democratic cacophony, and Washington was naturally the first to experience how mentally and physically exhausting that position is. He had considered retiring after one four-year term, but he was certain that he would not stay more than two terms in the eye of the political maelstrom. He sincerely wished to preserve himself and the office by setting a precedent for a new leader every eight years, at the most. One of the most enduring insights from the anti-monarchists was that no one can or should hold executive office for too long. Regularized succession is necessary for consistent and effective democratic leadership.

Washington designed his Farewell Address, initially drafted by Madison and then revised by Hamilton, as a personal testament that would further define the office he had held and the policies he had pursued. Published on 19 September 1796, Washington's words clarified the still strange (and frequently awkward) role for a powerful executive in a democratic society. Recounting his efforts to encourage economic growth and insure the independence of the nation, he argued that "a government of as much vigor as is consistent with the perfect security of liberty is indispensable." Acknowledging the regional and political differences that divided many Americans, Washington defined the presidency as a necessary office to bring the country together around vital national interests. "Liberty itself will find in such a government, with powers properly distributed and adjusted, its surest guardian."

The absence of a strong presidency, as witnessed under the Articles of Confederation, threatened the prosperity, unity, and ultimate success of the American experiment. According to Washington: "It is, indeed, little else than a name, where the government is too feeble to withstand the enterprises of faction, to confine each member of the society within the limits prescribed by the laws, and to maintain all in the secure and tranquil enjoyment of the rights of person and property."[35]

In Washington's reflections, the president had a delicate and essential role to play, protecting liberty simultaneously from foreign tyranny and domestic anarchy. External adversaries and internal factions threatened the young democracy, often exploiting one another, as Citizen Genêt's lobbying of Americans for the French cause illustrated. The president had to recognize dangers at home and abroad, and he had to help the people navigate between them, preserving their values but insuring their interests. He had to bring the divided institutions and citizens of the country together for a common economic and foreign policy agenda that preserved the foundations for freedom and democracy.

"To the efficacy and permanency of your Union," Washington wrote, "a government for the whole is indispensable." As guardian of the national interest, the president was responsible for making the parts cohere, for bringing the people together, for making sense of diverse challenges and articulating priorities. This unifying function, traditionally the work of monarchs, was the essence of the presidency for Washington. He was not "above politics," as some supporters claimed; he more accurately lifted politics to the higher purposes of union, prosperity, and liberty, as he believed the Constitution defined them. The president led the country through "disinterest," "example," and "virtue"—crucial words in his Farewell Address—and he sought to "enlighten" citizens about their common interests. In Washington's view, the president protected national priorities; he did not rule over policies, programs, or people.[36]

Washington's presidency was narrow in its scope, but wide in its influence. He largely avoided positions on issues that affected the daily lives of citizens, including local commerce, education, religion, and social relations between groups. When asked by Quakers to address the divisive topic of slavery, he famously avoided any public comment.[37]

Washington's vision of a focused executive set the standard for his successors. The Constitution and historical experience offered little guidance. The first holder of this first executive office in a new democracy wrote the script.

Beginning with presidents John Adams and Thomas Jefferson—two very different leaders—presidents prioritized union, economic growth, and foreign policy. They were agenda-setters around these issues, and they did little else. Their staffs remained small and their presence in domestic society remained severely limited, by design. As in Washington's first address to Congress on 8 January 1790, the president spoke for the Union as a whole, and its fundamental national interests, but he did not speak for specific individuals, groups, or policies within the daily course of the nation's life. The president set general parameters for the country, in line with the Constitution, but he did not manage society in any real way. He relied on Congress, the states, and other institutions to run most things. As the Constitution intended, the national democratic executive was a paragon and a guardian, not a governor, judge, legislator, or even a general. The office was small, despite its enormous importance.

CHAPTER 3

People's President

A little more than forty years after George Washington published his Farewell Address, Andrew Jackson wrote his own political testament. Jackson was the nation's first president from a post-founding generation. Although he had fought as a thirteen-year-old in the Revolutionary War and participated in the Tennessee state constitutional convention in 1795, Jackson was born a decade after Madison and Hamilton. He was more than thirty years younger than Washington.

Jackson was the first president born to non-English parents and also the first president who did not come from Virginia or Massachusetts—the cradles of the American Revolution. He was a self-taught frontier lawyer, politician, and farmer who commanded American soldiers in the War of 1812, but he was never a man of letters (like Madison, Hamilton, and Jefferson), a diplomat (like the two Adams presidents and Monroe), or a traditional military officer (like Washington). Jackson was the first outsider president. The bullet lodged in his left upper arm from an 1813 duel—one of many in his violent career—was evidence of his distance from the dignified Virginia and Massachusetts gentry.

Washington embodied a classical image of leadership with his powdered wigs and public displays of refinement and virtue. Jackson revered Washington, but rejected his image. He was not a Greek god or a Roman Cincinnatus. Jackson was harsh, volatile, and bullying. He was a common man with uncommon drive and talent, and that combination made him incredibly inspiring to thousands of other Americans who

49

knew more of Jackson's poverty and the frontier than the founders' elegance and sophistication. "If we would preserve the original simplicity of our institutions and perpetuate this grand republic," one supporter wrote, "we would choose our presidents not for the splendour of their manners, but their simplicity and plainness." Jackson's common roots gave him a claim to democratic virtue that contrasted with the sophisticated cosmopolitanism of the nation's traditional elites, which many white Americans still associated with the hated British aristocracy.[1]

Jackson became famous for fighting the British and thwarting their effort to capture New Orleans near the end of the War of 1812. He had fought to defend the settlers in the south and the west who relied on the port city at the mouth of the Mississippi River for the sustenance of their cotton plantations. He was, in fact, quite contemptuous of, and often insubordinate toward, his commanders in the US Army. That was also part of Jackson's appeal—he was, in the view of his supporters, a righteous rebel who broke the rules, when necessary, for the interests of common citizens. His violence and willfulness were marks of democratic authenticity, showing that he was uncorrupted by the personal compromises that often led politicians to depart from the country's vaunted ideals. One newspaper described Jackson as a "Hercules" who could use his toughness and common sense to clean out the self-serving figures who occupied the "Giant Augean Stable at Washington."[2]

Jackson showed fealty to the virtues of Washington's generation, the Constitution they wrote, and the union they built and preserved against countless adversaries: "Our Constitution is no longer a doubtful experiment, and at the end of nearly half a century we find that it has preserved unimpaired the liberties of the people, secured the rights of property, and that our country has improved and is flourishing beyond any former example in the history of nations." Washington and the founding generation had created a virtuous, successful, and sacred union, according to Jackson. He firmly believed it was the best hope for the protection and prosperity of white settlers.[3]

Yet the challenges confronting that union had changed with its emergence. The first president and his immediate successors combatted the twin fears of monarchy and anarchy, born of American experiences with the British Empire and the Articles of Confederation. The founding generation also confronted dangerous foreign adversaries in Paris, London, and Madrid. Washington's model of a focused and restrained executive defending broad national interests had steered the country through these difficulties to the point where, as Jackson put it, the "progress of the United States under our free and happy institutions has surpassed the most sanguine hopes of the founders of the Republic." Jackson reminded his readers: "You have no longer any cause to fear danger from abroad; your strength and power are well known throughout the civilized world, as well as the high and gallant bearing of your sons."

New dangers now stalked the land. "It is from within, among yourselves," Jackson warned, "from cupidity, from corruption, from disappointed ambition and inordinate thirst for power—that factions will be formed and liberty endangered. It is against such designs, whatever disguise the actors may assume, that you have especially to guard yourselves." Secure in its basic institutions and national defense, the United States was, according to Jackson, deeply divided between those who wielded power and those who did not; those who had access to land and money, and those who did not.[4]

Jackson re-defined the presidency as the voice and protector of the people, particularly those who did not traditionally wield power, own large tracts of land, or maintain large bank accounts. He spoke for the "planter, the farmer, the mechanic, and the laborer," modest, God-fearing, and patriotic citizens who "know that their success depends upon their own industry and economy, and that they must not expect to become suddenly rich by the fruits of their toil." These virtuous white workers were, according to Jackson, the "bone and sinew of the country—men who love liberty and desire nothing but equal rights and laws." They wanted a fair chance to live freely and improve their lives. They were honest strivers who hoped to improve the lot of their families.[5]

If Washington believed that his presidency insured the national order and freedom from tyranny, Jackson proclaimed that his presidency gave often forgotten ordinary citizens the representation and support that they deserved. Washington's presidency stood for national independence and stability; Jackson built on that foundation and fought for the expansion of opportunity among those who felt free but left behind by the prosperity of the nation's most successful, sophisticated, and gentrified citizens living in Philadelphia, Boston, New York, and a few other East Coast cities.[6]

Jackson defined his presidency by his self-proclaimed mission of defending ordinary American people, or as he put it, "the great body of the citizens of any State or States." He railed against what he perceived as the dominance of crafty financial and political elites who had hijacked the constitutional system and turned it to their particular interests. These elites were George Washington's allies, but they were now Jackson's enemies. In his analysis, they were the "moneyed powers," the banks and corporations run by big shots in crowded cities, and the defenders of "monopoly and exclusive privileges" who "besiege the halls of legislation" to make the laws sources of their enrichment.[7]

In Jackson's view, the men who succeeded the founders as America's leaders had created a conspiracy of self-interest. These elites excluded the mass of new citizens—many the descendants of poor non-English immigrants, like Jackson—from the fruits of constitutional democracy by controlling legislatures, businesses, and newspapers. They were monopolists and manipulators who commanded fancy words and printing presses for empty paper money. Jackson professed to speak common truth in response to their sophisticated lies. He exposed them, shamed them, and destroyed them. Jackson used the presidency as a massive hammer to hit back against the elites, and he hit hard. He was an experienced barroom brawler, and he made the national executive into a popular heavy who fought to protect the smaller people. He was "Hercules" on horseback with pistol and sword.

Jackson did not hold back in language or action. He was hot-headed, determined, fearless. He defended the Union of the founders, but he conspicuously abandoned their gentrified language. Speaking of one of his most distinguished, life-long opponents, Kentucky Senator Henry Clay, Jackson characteristically abandoned the political courtesy that George Washington had modeled for a national executive who was meant to stand above the fray. Jackson dived into the dirtiest political melees, and he promised to punch his way out. He wished to "remove the robes of office" that had constrained his predecessors, and, in the case of Clay, "bring the rascal to a dear account." There was little room for compromise in his attitude and his actions as president.[8]

For better and for worse, Jackson's frequently unhinged zeal contributed to his broad appeal. He was elected in 1828 with a huge popular majority, reelected in 1832 with similar support, and left the presidency in 1837 as one of the most revered men in America. He has continued to attract lavish praise from generations of struggling citizens and craven historians.[9] At the same time, his critics have grown in number; they point to his persecution of Indians and his defense of slavery, among other things. He recently lost his position on the twenty-dollar bill due, in part, to these criticisms.[10]

Jackson remains controversial because he was so different from any democratic executive before him, and from what the founders anticipated. The men who made Washington president never expected a ruffian like Jackson to succeed him. At the same time, Jackson was the great national democratic hope. He advocated a strong Union and he defended the freedoms of all white male citizens. He showed violent animosity toward many other groups—including Indians, slaves, and women—but he was still a remarkably strong advocate for poor, working-class farmers and laborers. His was a Union for the white "common men," overseen by a vigilant president.[11]

Jackson transformed the president from guardian to activist, from protector to liberator. He fused visceral patriotic nationalism with emotional populism in his wielding of presidential power. He justified his actions not on the ground that they resulted from a careful balance between institutions, as Washington claimed, but from a strong and deep connection to the "masses"—what he and his supporters called "popular sovereignty." Jackson's executive would intrude in society to help citizens and keep them united. He would act in their name, and he would use their consent to pulverize groups that stood in the way. Jackson revered the institutions and laws that Washington's generation crafted, but he frequently ignored them in the pursuit of what he viewed as the more fundamental interests of common citizens.

The executive served the people, according to Jackson, and only through broad public support could the Constitution, the Union, and the national interest find enduring security. Washington and his generation would never have agreed on the primacy of popular opinion. Jackson turned the founder's pursuit of objectivity and dispassion on its head with a more engaged, passionate, and partisan vision of national leadership. He was not a philosopher, but Jackson had a clear democratic philosophy: "the Constitution can not be maintained nor the Union preserved, in opposition to public feeling, by the mere exertion of the coercive powers confided to the General Government. The foundations must be laid in the affections of the people, in the security it gives to life, liberty, character, and property in every quarter of the country, and in the fraternal attachment which the citizens of the several States bear to one another as members of one political family, mutually contributing to promote the happiness of each other."[12]

If Washington was the revered grandfather who inspired the American political family, Jackson was the warrior father who, through forceful action, carried Washington's hopes to each and every good white citizen. Jackson was the people's president, and the people empowered him to claim presidential powers unseen in a democracy to that time. Under Jackson's leadership, the United States had a stronger executive and a more democratic polity—with more citizen participation—than ever before in its history. That was true despite the continued exclusion of a majority of the nation's residents, especially women and slaves.

Centralized power and local freedom became closely linked in Jacksonian America. Jackson advocated a strong presidency and strong state and local governments at the same time. He defined Congress and the courts as the enemies of freedom, and he viewed federal and state executives as the rightful defenders of the people. In this way, Jackson boosted executive power in general, and he challenged the basic separation of powers between the legislative, judicial, and executive branches. Despite Jackson's firm advocacy for the Union, this emphasis on executive power seeded a growing conflict between national and state leaders, which Congress and the courts would struggle unsuccessfully to mediate in the decades before the Civil War.

Executive power was the best protector of freedom for Jackson and his many supporters. Legislatures and courts, dominated by elites, could not be trusted. Only a leader connected to the people could represent their interests. Adulation for the popular strongman—who fights for the forgotten—has outlived Jackson's day, influencing future generations at least as much as the founding fathers' focus on humility, restraint, and deliberative decision-making. For all its sins, Jacksonian leadership became modern American leadership.

ANY ACCOUNT OF ANDREW JACKSON AS LEADER MUST BEGIN WITH his Indian obsession. He viewed Indians as enemies of the opportunity and security that he and other settlers sought in American society. Unlike Washington and Jefferson, who predicted that the native peoples of North America would assimilate into the United States, Jackson believed otherwise. There was not enough land to share, the Indians did not conform to settler habits, and they could not be trusted, according to Jackson. He fell into a familiar pattern for insecure outsiders—he hated the elites who condescended toward him and he also hated the other outsider groups who competed with him for resources and respectability. Elites could afford a paternalistic relationship with American Indians; poor white Americans, struggling to survive, could do no such thing.[13]

Jackson's conflicts with Indians began at an early age in South Carolina and escalated as he migrated farther west into more contested Indian country. During the War of 1812, many of the most powerful Indian tribes in the Southeast, particularly the Shawnee and Creek, allied with the British and attacked American positions. American soldiers attacked Indians as part of the war, and also out of fear that they were hindering the growth of the United States.[14]

Jackson was keen to destroy threatening Indians and avenge the American blood spilled in prior conflicts between white settlers and native tribes. Leading Tennessee volunteers into battle against Creek Indians in 1813, Jackson issued a rousing call to killing with his typical urgency, self-confidence, and battle euphoria. To fight the Indians was to claim manly possession of what was still disputed North American territory: "We are about to furnish these savages a lesson of admonition; we are about to teach them that our long forbearance has not proceeded from an insensibility to wrongs, or an inability to redress them," Jackson proclaimed. "How glorious will it be to remove the blots which have tarnished the fair character bequeathed us by the fathers of our Revolution!"[15]

Jackson's attacks on Indians did not end after the War of 1812. In 1818 Jackson led three thousand Tennessee volunteers and other white soldiers into battle again, this time against the Spanish, Indian, and free black forces resisting American expansion in Florida. Placed in command by Secretary of War John C. Calhoun—his future vice president and political enemy—Jackson seized the Spanish fort of St. Mark's and destroyed a group of Seminole Indian settlements. He captured and executed two Seminole chiefs, as well as two British citizens who were accused of supporting American enemies in the region. The summary executions, without fair trials, violated American law and risked further inflaming conflict in the region. As in the past, controversy did not deter Jackson, in this case from his mission to expel Spanish, free black, and especially Indian influences from the vital southeastern region of the United States. If anything, criticisms only encouraged him to act with greater determination.

Although Calhoun and President James Monroe regretted Jackson's extreme measures, it remains unclear whether they really intended to stop him. Some circumstantial evidence indicates that they quietly encouraged him. As Secretary of State John Quincy Adams—another future rival—astutely observed, Jackson's militancy convinced the overstretched Spanish empire to cede Florida to the United States.

In February 1819 Spanish Minister Don Luis de Onís and Adams signed what became known as the Transcontinental Treaty, which opened land east of the Mississippi River and farther northwest, along what became the Oregon coast of the Pacific Ocean, to American settlers. Jackson's followers credited the hero from Tennessee with making this outcome possible, and they were at least partially correct. Of course, the violence that forced the Spanish retreat was largely aimed not at the Spanish themselves, but at Indians.[16]

Intimidating foreign armies and killing "savages" made Jackson popular with many Americans who were drawn to his defense of white citizens' dominance over the land. He seemed to stand for the "ordinary" settler, craftsman, farmer, and factory worker who wanted more freedom. These citizens saw Indians and other foreigners as threats to their freedom, and they resented government laws that restricted settlers' access to land. Jackson's violence was a form of rebellion, an affirmation of freedom, and a seizure of control for those Americans who felt they had too little control over their lives.[17]

Jackson's defense of slavery, and his own slaveholding, also appealed to many ordinary white people—white Southerners above all. The first half of the nineteenth century witnessed rising abolitionist sentiment among Northerners, especially in respected figures like John Quincy Adams and Daniel Webster. Jackson fused support for territorial expansion with a defense of slavery—a fundamentalist position for Southern citizens who feared that the federal government would prohibit slavery in new states, and eventually use a majority in the US Senate to eliminate slavery nationwide. Jackson's violence supported white land ownership and local freedom to manage that land with the labor of slaves. Although he strongly promoted the Union against all sectional and secessionist impulses (including Calhoun's calls for "nullification" of federal laws), slaves were essential to Jackson's national vision.[18]

INDIAN-KILLING, DEFENSE OF SLAVERY, AND SUPPORT FOR THE "common man" catapulted Jackson into the presidency. Like Washington, he was a war hero, but he was not a gentleman of letters or a dispassionate father figure. He was a patriot and a nationalist who spoke for a growing segment of the population that had been underrepresented in American politics. Jackson was the first populist president, with all the brutality and prejudice that entailed.

Jackson's success in rising to the presidency, despite continued opposition from traditional elites, deepened his prejudices and those of his supporters. There seemed little reason to re-think the frontier values that had, at last, defeated the established political powers. Excluding Indians and African Americans went hand in hand with including new white Americans. The logic was simple: the United States had a bounty of resources, but a growing number of people claiming those resources, especially land. President Jackson saw his role as promoter of the white rural and working-class citizens who voted for him in overwhelming numbers and needed access to the resources around them. All contrary claimants to resources—East Coast financiers, federal government elites, foreign representatives, and especially Indians—had to be eliminated.

That was the job of the elected national executive—the true representative of the people, according to Jackson.

In his inaugural address he made it clear that his power came from the people, and that popular foundation gave the president authority to act decisively on their behalf. Rejecting assertions that the most talented and best born should make decisions for the nation, Jackson exclaimed: "The will of the people, prescribed in a constitution of their own choice, controls the service of the public functionaries, and is interested more deeply in the preservation of those qualities which ensures fidelity and honest devotion to their interests."

From his first speech as president, Jackson affirmed "state rights" and "state sovereignty" against "the tendencies to consolidation." He neglected to assign any role to Congress or the Judiciary. Jackson's exclusive focus was on executives—national and state—and their role in serving their voters, without restriction. His populism promoted executive supremacy on a scale that would have frightened most of the founders.

Jackson believed his presidency should have an unmediated connection to the American people, protecting their freedom from foreign and domestic intruders. He would not only articulate the national interest, as Washington had done; he would now act personally to rip away the impediments to freedom for his people. That was Jackson's definition of the "executive"—an elected leader with strong powers to act on behalf of popular causes, and few limitations beyond the will of the people. Mass popularity determined presidential legitimacy for Jackson, as it had not for any of his predecessors. The Constitution and other institutions and traditions were secondary considerations for Jackson, at best.[19]

From the start, Jackson acted to affirm the power of the voters and his connection to them. His first annual message to Congress, delivered on 8 December 1829, called for future election of presidents by popular national vote. This would require an amendment to the Constitution, eliminating the Electoral College and the role of the House of Representatives in determining the president. In 1824, four candidates split the vote; Jackson and his supporters remained bitter about what they perceived as the "corrupt bargain" in the House that had made John

Quincy Adams president, despite Jackson's plurality of popular and electoral votes. Finally attaining the presidency in 1828, Jackson wanted to insure that the man with the most support from citizens could thwart the maneuverings of opponents in Congress.

"To the people belongs the right of electing their Chief Magistrate," Jackson announced. "It was never designed that their choice should in any case be defeated, either by the intervention of electoral colleges or by the agency confided, under certain contingencies, to the House of Representatives. Experience proves that in proportion as agents to execute the will of the people are multiplied there is danger of their wishes being frustrated."[20]

Though he claimed to speak for the founders, on this matter Jackson diverged from them. The founders expected that many close presidential contests would be decided in the House of Representatives, and they created the system of electors (later called the "Electoral College") to limit popular control over the selection of the president. Jackson knew that, but he wanted to redefine his office as a more direct representative of the people, to eliminate the impediments to majority will in the election of the president. He also wanted to eliminate Congress's influence over the reelection of the executive, proposing that presidents serve "a single term of either 4 or 6 years," and that the law disqualify current members of the House of Representatives from seeking the presidency.[21]

This proposal created a paradox: Jackson wanted to make the election of the president more direct and majoritarian, by limiting the power of the branch of Congress that was most directly elected and majoritarian. Jackson was the first president to claim that his national majority superseded other directly elected majorities. This was a firm rejection of James Madison's argument that the legislature was the most authentic representative of the people. Jackson sought to make the president into a more powerful law-making voice than the Congress, and this ambition not only set him apart from his predecessors, but put him permanently at odds with the members of Congress who jealously guarded their constitutional powers.

For obvious reasons, the new president was unable to muster the necessary two-thirds support in the House of Representatives and the Senate for his amendment. The proposal never went to the state legislatures for the required three-fourths approval, but Jackson had made his point. Washington used the first annual presidential message to Congress to protect the careful balance of powers in the Constitution; Jackson sought to destabilize that balance, giving more power to the president by relying directly on the people.

Where he did not need an amendment, he succeeded in this endeavor. Jackson proclaimed that his role as national executive allowed him to demand a "rotation" in public offices held by appointed officials in the federal government. That included positions in the postal service, the customs service, the Treasury, the State Department, and even the Army and Navy. Jackson argued: "In a country where offices are created solely for the benefit of the people no one man has any more intrinsic right to official station than another. Offices were not established to give support to particular men at the public expense. No individual wrong is, therefore, done by removal, since neither appointment to nor continuance in office is a matter of right."[22]

Jackson turned the presidency into a human resources agency for the federal bureaucracy, replacing long-standing officials with new appointees who were not more qualified, but who were more acceptable to the national executive and his supporters. Advocates of this new system viewed it as a democratizing revolution, removing self-serving and corrupt office holders who had turned their positions into private fiefdoms. Critics, however, described Jackson's move as the creation of a "spoils system," where party loyalists and friends would get federal jobs as a reward for their electoral support. A Senate committee condemned the president for overstepping his bounds and violating propriety by trying to "convert the entire body of those in office into corrupt and supple instruments of power." That was, in fact, Jackson's aim.[23]

The senators voiced a legitimate criticism, and they were deeply offended by what felt like a presidential incursion into the basic administration of the federal government—a power to be shared with Congress, according to the conventional reading of the Constitution and established precedent. Jackson, as always, returned to his fundamental point about popular will. The people elected him president, and he needed individuals in various federal offices who would carry out his programs, on behalf of the people. If he kept the old appointees in place, they would simply resist, distort, and prohibit the president from serving the people. Jackson's argument for partisan appointments was an argument for democratic effectiveness behind a strong, popular executive.

The new appointees allowed Jackson to lead the country in his chosen directions. They gave him the tools to transform the government. In practice, it appears Jackson used his appointments for that purpose, and they were neither less qualified nor more corrupt, as a whole, than his predecessors' appointments. The real difference was that Jackson fired so many inherited employees. His spoils system was the first presidential effort to make all the offices of government match the preferences of the man on top, and it worked. It also set an enduring precedent; every president after him has used this same power. For some, it became the most important executive lever for controlling an ever-growing federal bureaucracy. To lead, Jackson understood, is to fire and hire.[34]

Jackson did not just fire holdover appointments. He slashed a number of inherited agencies that limited his power and, he claimed, denied citizens control over their lives. The Bank of the United States, housed in the most affluent part of Philadelphia, was a prime target. Jackson hated the bank and bankers in general. They were urban elites who loaned money at high rates to hard-working men, and then confiscated their property when they could not pay. They encouraged indebtedness, which Jackson believed was a source of dependence and sin.

The president believed bankers were undemocratic, since in his view they used their wealth, connections, and technical knowledge to limit the freedoms of ordinary citizens. These were, of course, common beliefs in rural and backwoods areas; they had motivated opposition to Alexander Hamilton's Economic Plan in 1790.

As president, Jackson condemned the chief banker in the nation, Nicholas Biddle. Born to a prosperous Philadelphia merchant and educated at Princeton University, Biddle was a highly regarded man of letters and finance. President Monroe appointed him one of the directors of the Bank of the United States in 1819, and then president of the Bank in

1823, at age 37. Biddle used the large reserves of the bank, including the annual revenues of the federal government, to make loans to businesses, farmers, and state banks. The Bank of the United States issued the most trusted paper currency in the country, and it largely determined the supply of money in the economy. Biddle carefully monitored a slow increase in available capital and he guarded against inflation. With twenty-five branches across the country, the Bank underwrote a decade of stable capital markets, sound currency, and continued national economic development. It was the prime source of funds for the expansion of industry.[25]

The Bank of the United States was a public corporation with private shareholders and directors. The US government held just 20 percent of the voting stock in the bank, and the president only appointed five of the twenty-five directors. The bank blended private business and financial knowledge with a broad national mandate from the federal government. As smaller state banks were quick to complain, it benefited enormously from the assets that the federal government placed under its control. It stabilized the economy, but that also meant that it produced profit and influence for a select group of people, especially Nicholas Biddle and his fellow directors. Some observers in the 1820s viewed Biddle, who was not subjected to election or any other rigorous public oversight, as the most powerful figure in the United States.

That was precisely Jackson's criticism. The president believed that public-private partnerships contributing to national development—as advocated by John Quincy Adams, Henry Clay, and other traditional elites—served established interests at the cost of ordinary citizens. Jackson distrusted paper money, he condemned unelected figures (like Biddle), and he opposed special laws for privileged institutions, especially the Bank of the United States. "It is to be regretted," Jackson wrote, "that the rich and powerful too often bend the acts of government to their selfish purposes."[26]

IF GEORGE WASHINGTON PERCEIVED THE PRESIDENT AS THE guardian of the national interest against fragmentary impulses, Jackson defined the president as the guardian of the national interest against manipulation by privileged elites. This change of emphasis transformed the nature of executive power, especially the relationship between the presidency and the other branches of government. Jackson proclaimed the independence of the president to speak for the nation as a whole. He denied the right of any branch to impose a particular interpretation of the Constitution or public needs on the executive: "The opinion of the judges has no more authority over Congress than the opinion of Congress has over the judges, and on that point the President is independent of both."[27]

Following this assertion of independence, Jackson used his executive powers as none of his predecessors had to make his preferences the law of the land. When a bill for federal support of a national road linking the Potomac and Ohio Rivers (the "Maysville Road") came to Jackson's desk in May 1830, he vetoed it. Washington and other presidents had only used the veto when they questioned the constitutionality of legislation. Jackson wielded the veto to strangle projects that, he believed, served special interests and raised the federal debt. He argued that his preferences represented the will of the American public, and he used his veto to supersede legislative majorities. Jackson rebuffed congressional opinion with greater frequency than any of the founders anticipated. He issued more vetoes in eight years than all six presidents before him had over the course of the nation's first forty years. Intent on building consensus between the branches of government, Washington vetoed only two pieces of legislation. Jackson exceeded that number in his first term alone, and he vetoed twelve bills before he left office in 1837.

Congressional opponents charged Jackson with dictatorial behavior. He was an American "Napoleon," in Henry Clay's words. John Quincy Adams accused Jackson of acting like an "overseer," not a president. The US Senate went so far as to censure Jackson in 1834, but that action only reinforced the president's determination to make himself the final arbiter of law on behalf of the people. Despite resistance, Jackson transformed the president into the most powerful policy-maker in the country—a title Washington would never have accepted. He probably would have resisted it, siding with those who feared excessive executive authority.[28]

JACKSON'S MOST SHOCKING EXERCISE OF PRESIDENTIAL POWER occurred between 1832 and 1837, when he refused to renew the Bank of the United States and forced a redirection of the nation's monetary system. His veto of the bank's charter rejected Biddle's role as the country's chief money manager. Jackson condemned that "monopoly" behavior, accusing Biddle and his supporters of generating "gratuities" and "bonuses" for themselves and "aliens" who did not serve the nation's true interests. Jackson maintained that the bank profited "out of the earnings of the American people."

The bank's powers affected the whole country and it operated as a regulator for national finances, but it did not consult the elected national executive. It was therefore, Jackson reasoned, unacceptable: "Neither upon the propriety of present action nor upon the provisions of this act was the Executive consulted. It has had no opportunity to say that it neither needs nor wants an agent clothed with such powers and favored by such exemptions." Jackson concluded: "There is nothing in its legitimate functions which makes it necessary or proper."[29]

The president did not deny that the bank supported economic stability, sound credit, and industrial growth across the country. He recognized its effectiveness in these areas. Jackson's argument was that the very effectiveness of the bank denied states and local communities the ability to control their own money, industry, and development. Through the bank, the federal government allowed and even encouraged northeastern elites to dominate the economic choices in other regions and profit from them at the cost of local residents. Through the bank, federally favored figures like Biddle gained power, and local representatives became less relevant. In this sense, monetary management was a mechanism of social and political control—and a direct affront to the Jacksonian belief in direct citizen democracy.

Jackson wanted the president to protect democracy above monetary stability, freedom above wealth. He articulated what became a fundamental argument for states' rights, and the role of the president in protecting them against an allegedly trespassing Congress. Jackson called institutions like the bank "invasions of the rights and powers of the several States." The "true strength" of democratic government, according to Jackson, required "leaving individuals and states as much as possible to themselves."[30]

As national executive, Jackson had an obligation to defend the Union, but he wished to see a union of largely independent states. A powerful president was one, in his vision, who worked against centralizing tendencies to preserve regional diversity. His Union would be economically and socially diverse, which would keep it close to ordinary citizens and far from the small and homogenous elites. Jackson's populism preserved the wild frontier from the encroaching cities, the settlers from civilization. He relied on federal and state executives, ironically, to give people voice against their legislative representatives and judges of the law.

JACKSON'S VISION OF EXECUTIVE POWER DIVERGED FROM HIS predecessors' in other ways, too, including his treatment of the Indian tribes just beyond the nation's borders. The subject of Indian removal was a centerpiece of his first State of the Union address in December 1829.

Jackson contrasted the "arts of civilization" that white settlers brought to the land with the "wandering life" and "savage habits" of the Indians. Those were common judgments among American citizens at the time. Where Jackson differed from his predecessors was in his determination to use the power of the presidency to evict the "savages," rather than try to integrate them in the United States—as advocated by many prominent Northeastern politicians of his own time, including John Quincy Adams.

The citizens of the South and the West who voted for Jackson lived near more Indians than their Northeastern counterparts. Jackson channeled the eagerness of southerners and westerners to eliminate threatening "foreigners." States like Georgia were already taking matters into their own hands, and Jackson wanted to use the presidency for guiding this removal process.[31]

Writing in the first person to emphasize his personal role in Indian Removal, Jackson recounted: "I informed the Indians inhabiting parts of Georgia and Alabama that their attempt to establish an independent government would not be countenanced by the Executive of the United States, and advised them to emigrate beyond the Mississippi or submit to the laws of those States." The president acted boldly in what would otherwise have appeared to be a domestic matter for congressional and state authorities. He acted without input from the other branches of government, merely informing them after the fact. This behavior echoed Jackson's attitude as a military leader in the past, when he had shown contempt for his commanders, and it characterized his leadership as national executive.[32]

The Supreme Court ruled—in *Worcester v. Georgia*—that the "Indian nations" were "distinct, independent political communities retaining their original natural rights," but Jackson ignored the justices. "The decision of the Supreme Court has fell still born," Jackson exclaimed, "and they find that it cannot coerce Georgia to yield to its mandate." As executive, Jackson asserted that the president had the right to determine which laws merited enforcement. He opposed the sovereign claims of Indians in land coveted by white settlers, and he used the presidency to supersede the law in violently denying those claims. This was, as Jackson's critics contended, a major rebalancing of power toward a presidency that was now planning to force thousands of people off their land, despite constitutional injunctions to the contrary.[33]

The Indian Removal Act, signed by Jackson in May 1830 after passing a deeply divided Congress, gave the president the authority to encourage what was essentially ethnic cleansing in the American South. Jackson aided Georgia and other states in coercing entire communities of Indians to re-settle in far western lands that were resource poor, inhospitable, and undesirable for white settlers at the time. The goal was clearly to seize valuable Indian land and secure white settlers against threats and rivalries.

The president was the chief advocate, enforcer, and defender of this policy. With widespread divisions across the United States about whether and how to "civilize" or "remove" Indians, Jackson turned the president from an adjudicator of Indian disputes into a perpetrator of Indian elimination. Like no other president before, Jackson used executive powers to re-shape the ethnic and cultural mix of the population within the United States.

The president collaborated with the governors of Georgia, Alabama, North Carolina, Tennessee, and Mississippi to expel more than 100,000 Indians from their lands, many of which they held under treaty with the

United States. Jackson often worked personally to coerce Indian representatives into signing new treaties that ceded their territory and created a false image of "volunteerism" for what was in reality a massive forced migration of entire tribes: Cherokee, Choctaw, Chickasaw, and Creek, among others. Some Indians, especially the Seminole in Florida, resisted, but Jackson was happy to send in the US Army. Small bands of Seminole managed to hold on in remote areas of Florida, but the tribe was devastated by American forces. For the Cherokee, Choctaws, and others, forced migration—along what came to be called "The Trail of Tears"—brought death to more than one-fifth of their population. Those who survived and settled in Oklahoma territory were confined to reservations that bred isolation, poverty, and resentment—lasting into the twenty-first century.[34]

Even the most "anti-Indian" of the American founders had never imagined that the president would have the power to force the movement of so many people, with such rapidity. Of course, Jackson acted with the support of thousands of local white residents, but the role of the federal government was crucial because it gave unity to the effort, including support from the US Army and the emerging Bureau of Indian Affairs, both of which belonged to the Department of War and reported to the president.

The growing military, economic, and organizational capabilities of American society made Indian Removal possible. Although he staked his reputation on combating the corruption of self-serving elites, Jackson brought an explicit form of favoritism to the actions of the president, accompanied by a targeted and extreme form of subjugation. Jackson's anti-elitism was an elitism of its own kind. This irony had genocidal implications. He was the people's president, and he acted to promote *his* people by all means necessary.

Jackson believed that the people's—his people's—voice was inherently virtuous and effective. "Never for a moment believe," Jackson warned, "that the great body of the citizens of any State or States can deliberately intend to do wrong. They may, under the influence of temporary excitement or misguided opinions, commit mistakes; they may be misled for a time by the suggestions of self-interest; but in a community so enlightened and patriotic as the people of the United States argument will soon make them sensible of their errors, and when convinced they will be ready to repair them."[35]

By one important measure, Jackson's claim to power from the people was accurate. He received more than 54 percent of the popular vote in two consecutive presidential elections (1828 and 1832), soundly defeating two political titans: John Quincy Adams and Henry Clay. Jackson commanded deep loyalty from tens of thousands of farmers, laborers, recent immigrants, and slaveholders. They looked to him as their hero, and he sincerely acted on their behalf. He was the most beloved president since Washington, and the affections Jackson inspired were even more personal. The first president remained intentionally aloof, as he had been in his days as a military leader. The seventh president bonded with his friends and battled with his enemies, both as general and as national executive. Washington and Jackson knew how to inspire followers, but they did it in different ways.

Jackson's personal approach motivated many more enemies than Washington ever had. He was the first president to be censured by the US Senate for trying to take his power too far. The 1834 resolution, written by Henry Clay and supported by a 26 to 20 vote, condemned Jackson's infringements on congressional authority. According to the censure document, Jackson had "assumed upon himself authority and power not conferred by the Constitution and laws, but in derogation of both." Congress did not have the evidence to impeach the president for "high crimes and misdemeanors," as required by the Constitution, but the censure resolution condemned him in the strongest possible terms.[36]

Although Jackson resented this attack upon his integrity, it made little difference. Jackson had what many critics called a "kitchen cabinet" of advisors, especially Vice President (formerly Secretary of State) Martin Van Buren, but he was his own man. Censure from senators or frequent advice for restraint from cabinet officials could not throw him off course. Jackson was tenacious, sometimes zealous, about the supremacy of presidential leadership on behalf of the people. He defined the United States as a presidential democracy, not a democracy with a presidency. The president was to the democracy what the minister was to the church congregation—he embodied, united, and pushed the community forward. He kept the flock together and close to God. Critics were heathens in need of reeducation or removal. There was little room for compromise in Jackson's vision of presidential power.

EUROPEAN MONARCHS AND PRIME MINISTERS HAD DISTINguished pedigrees. Wealth, family connections, and education were the prerequisites for leadership. Executives were expected to rise above the harshness of ordinary life, offering inspiration and enlightenment. They were imagined as Greek gods, Roman warriors, and medieval scholars—and for that reason most leaders-in-training learned Greek, Latin, and theology. They were expected to be selfless, objective, and superior.

The founders of the United States—a powder-wigged group of gentlemen farmers and cosmopolitan merchants—internalized these assumptions. Their innovation was to inscribe an elite executive position, the presidency, within a large democratic polity. They demanded that presidents serve the interests of a broad and diverse population, but they expected presidents to look and act like them. And their expectation was fulfilled. The first six presidents were learned, highly regarded Virginia gentry and Boston Brahmins.

Jackson broke the mold. His presidency was unimaginable before it happened, and he made it nearly impossible for the old gentry and Brahmins to recapture the office. Jackson brought the godly image of leadership down to earth, emphasizing a direct identification with ordinary people and a channeling of their deepest passions. He did not instruct the people from atop the mountain, but instead joined their shouts (and gunshots) in the valley. Jackson was a populist who self-consciously rejected the symbols, actions, and assumptions of elites. He rooted his presidency in the interests and expectations of ordinary citizens, rather than the refined institutions and ideas that had guided his predecessors. He made the presidency anti-elitist.

Jackson's anti-elitism greatly increased the power of the American executive. Flaunting his democratic popularity, Jackson broke through many of the inherited limitations on the presidency. He vetoed congressional legislation that contradicted his preferences, he ignored Supreme

Court decisions that he did not like, he fired government employees who were not loyal to him, he closed the Bank of the United States, and he personally pushed the ethnic cleansing of American Indians. George Washington never anticipated that the president would do any of these things, and he would have been distraught—probably disgusted—to see the mutation of the president-as-statesman into the president-as-populist.

Of course many of Jackson's contemporaries, especially in Congress, disagreed with him. The opposition to his expansive view of the presidency set up an enduring adversarial relationship between the president and the other branches of the US government. Washington sought to make the president a consensus-builder. Since Jackson, however, the president has acted as a partisan policy advocate who fights with the other branches to implement his program. Montesquieu's model for scientific balances between stately institutions, adopted by the framers of the Constitution, disintegrated in the fires of a passionate executive advocate. Jackson created the modern image of the president as domestic, as well as foreign, policy leader. He anticipated the rhetorical belligerence of later presidents, including Theodore Roosevelt, Ronald Reagan, and even Donald Trump.[37]

JACKSON'S IMMEDIATE SUCCESSORS DID NOT EXERCISE PRESIdential power with the same reach and determination as the formidable Tennessean, affectionately called "Old Hickory" by his many supporters. During the 1840s and 1850s members of Congress dominated the important national policy debates, especially surrounding slavery. Jackson's successors found themselves torn between increasingly irreconcilable sectional positions. Poor health and partisan divisions also limited many of them to one term or less in office. There are good historical reasons why Presidents Martin Van Buren, William Henry Harrison, John Tyler, and others are largely forgotten. Jackson's successors were overshadowed by his populist presidency and the backlash that it inspired, especially in Congress.

Abraham Lincoln was the first president after Jackson to win election to a second term in office. Although he revered Jackson's rival,

Senator Henry Clay, Lincoln carried forward the seventh president's interventionist vision of the national executive. He claimed that he had authority from the people to fight a civil war, abolish slavery, and impose an industrial vision of economic development on the country. Lincoln was a Republican, not a Jacksonian Democrat, and his policies rejected Jackson's defense of slavery and economic localism. Nonetheless, Jackson's populist presidency made Lincoln's war presidency possible. Rooting presidential power in the people, rather than the Constitution alone, freed the executive from many institutional restraints. It also enabled the president to advocate big social changes, rather than small-scale bargaining with Congress. George Washington led the government, Andrew Jackson led the people, and Abraham Lincoln would do both—with force of arms and words.

CHAPTER 4

Poet at War

Words become things *and powerful things too.*

John Murray Forbes,
27 December 1862[1]

In June 1862, more than a year into what Abraham Lincoln later called the "fiery trial" of the Civil War, a group of Quakers visited the president in the Executive Mansion. They called upon Lincoln to abolish slavery immediately.

Warner Mifflin, a prominent Delaware Quaker, had visited George Washington more than seventy years earlier to make the same demand. The first president and the sixteenth responded in identical ways. They listened politely and sympathetically. Neither defended slavery and each agreed that it was a threat to American democracy—more pressing to Lincoln as he struggled to force the seceding slaveholding states back into the Union.

Washington feared this exact nightmare. Both presidents, however, responded that there was little they could do. Under the Constitution, the president could not abolish slavery. The federal government had no authority to confiscate property, which is what slaves were considered. Regulating unfree labor was not a presidential power.[2]

Lincoln reminded his Quaker visitors that the causes of the Civil War centered on the expansion of slavery in new territories and the sanctity of the Union, not the legal justification of slavery in the Southern states, which Lincoln (and Washington) both accepted. Lincoln articulated his position on defending the Union, rather than pursuing abolition, in a famous letter published two months later. "I would save the Union," Lincoln proclaimed. "If there be those who would not save the Union unless they could at the same time save Slavery, I do not agree with them. If there be those who would not save the Union unless they could at the same time destroy Slavery, I do not agree with them. My paramount object in this struggle is to save the Union, and is not either to save or destroy Slavery."[3]

Lincoln's position was clear: he followed George Washington in his belief that the national executive had to protect the Union, above all, against threats at home and abroad. Lincoln echoed Washington in his observation that without the Union the states would not exist as self-governing entities. "What is a 'sovereignty' in the political sense of the term?" Lincoln asked. "Would it be far wrong to define it 'a political community without a political superior'? Tested by this, no one of our States, except Texas, ever was a sovereignty; and even Texas gave up the character on coming into the Union, by which act she acknowledged the Constitution of the United States and the laws and treaties of the United States made in pursuance of the Constitution to be for her the supreme law of the land. The States have their status in the Union, and they have no other legal status. If they break from this, they can only do so against law and by revolution. The Union, and not themselves separately, procured their independence and their liberty."[4]

The founders designed the presidency, Lincoln understood, as a guardian, charged to preserve the Union. That was the "imperative duty" he affirmed from his earliest days as a member of Congress, a public speaker, and a president. Before reaching national office, Lincoln articulated his own long-standing opposition to slavery, but once elected president he focused on his larger duty to the Union. Washington had, of course, done the same on numerous issues. The president, according to each man, had to stand above party, ideology, and prejudice to affirm the broader national interests and, in Lincoln's words, "keep the government on foot."[5]

IN HIS FEALTY TO WASHINGTON AND HIS DEVOTION TO UNION, Lincoln smuggled in the presidential activism pioneered by Andrew

Jackson. The sixteenth president's emphasis on a dynamic executive—"freeing the slaves," or not, in defense of the Union—went far beyond the limits Washington imposed on himself and the office. Lincoln's rhetoric positioned the president at the center of controversial political debates that Washington would have found uncomfortable.

Like Jackson, Lincoln claimed to "derive all his authority from the people," not the Constitution. Based on his plurality (not majority) of votes in 1861, Lincoln asserted the right of the president to move people, restrict freedoms, confiscate property, and wage war in defense of the Union. He envisioned the president as a powerful and passionate actor, not just an adjudicator between different groups and institutions. In this way, Lincoln echoed Jackson's claim that popular support justified more expansive and direct executive powers. Lincoln and Jackson both believed that the president needed to set a public agenda for the people and pursue it vigorously.[6]

Lincoln came from Jackson's world, not Washington's. Each was born poor and made his way as a self-taught lawyer, businessman, and politician. Each saw politics as bar-room conflict, law office argument, and county fair horse-trading—not detached philosophical contemplation, in Jefferson and Madison's mode. Lincoln, like Jackson, was a populist, in that he relied on his ability to appeal to ordinary people who were less talented than him, but instrumental for his success. Both men attracted followers by virtue of their personalities, their life stories, and their courage against great odds. They were men of action who defined leadership, especially the presidency, in those terms.

Their boldness helped them to climb, remarkably, from poverty to great achievements—from log cabin to the presidency. Jackson returned to the battlefield time and again, exposing himself to bullets and disease, for uncertain rewards. Lincoln built a lucrative law practice, which he exposed to controversy by his repeated, and frequently unsuccessful, forays into electoral politics. Neither Jackson nor Lincoln contemplated "retirement" to comfort and quietude, unlike Washington, who repeatedly attempted to retreat to his beloved Mount Vernon estate. Neither Jackson nor Lincoln was content to feign political reluctance, as prior presidents had in the founder's mold. Jackson and Lincoln possessed the driving ambition of men who came from very little, and the stubborn impatience with caution, retirement, and detachment that comes from those who are always looking to move up. They were instinctive climbers, and they continued to climb after they reached the nation's highest office.

Washington looked down from a secure perch; Jackson and Lincoln always looked up for more, fearing that they—and all that they cared about—would otherwise fall back to their lowly origins. They feared failure and therefore had to succeed again and again at new ambitions. Their personal ambitions became the ambitions of the nation.[7]

Insecure men of the frontier, Jackson and Lincoln were dogged, often ruthless, campaigners for themselves and what they believed in. More than anything, this quality made them *modern* American presidents. Washington condemned political parties, but Jackson and Lincoln each helped to create one and assumed leadership of that party *before* leadership of the nation. Parties mobilized ordinary people to support a candidate, provided resources for a campaign, and justified expanded uses of power. Active executive leadership gained democratic legitimacy, for Jackson and Lincoln, because presidents had parties behind them, not just personal interests. In Washington's conception, a detached president protected non-partisan democracy. For Jackson and Lincoln, an energetic president represented partisan democracy. In an expanding nineteenth-century American nation filled with deep divisions over slavery and other issues, the argument for partisan democracy and a powerful executive made the most sense. The world of the non-partisan founders, mythical from the start, was already lost.

Though today we often see them as starkly different figures, Jackson and Lincoln shared other, perhaps more troubling, characteristics. What Jackson and Lincoln wanted most was a secure national government that would continue to expand opportunities for talented white men, like themselves. They wanted dynamic economic growth with consistent law and order. They advocated protections for individual freedom and property. Above all, they desired a Union that would insure movement, unity, and security for the efforts of common white men—their core voters.

In words that Jackson would have affirmed, Lincoln explained that defense of the Union was "a struggle for maintaining in the world, that form, and substance of government, whose leading object is, to elevate the condition of men—to lift artificial weights from all shoulders—to clear the paths of laudable pursuit for all—to afford all, an unfettered start, and a fair chance, in the race of life." Partisan democracy with a strong president was the best defense of opportunity for Jackson, Lincoln, and their many supporters.[8]

Lincoln learned what this meant in practice by observing Jackson's many battles with Congress, the Supreme Court, and other parts of government. To defend the Union, Lincoln famously explained, the executive had to break a few laws to save the rest. "Are all the laws, *but one*," Lincoln asked, "to go unexecuted and the government itself go to pieces, lest that one be violated? Even in such a case, would not the official oath be broken, if the government should be overthrown, when it was believed that disregarding the single law, would tend to preserve it?" In this Jacksonian analysis, the president makes difficult trade-offs between conflicting laws and interests within the nation. He necessarily breaks some laws to protect the others. He uses all his powers to defend the Union on behalf of the people. The Union was made up of laws, but it was also above the law.[9]

Like Jackson, Lincoln defended selective presidential law-breaking particularly in times of "emergency." He returned to his predecessor's claim that the president should interpret the Constitution himself, without veto from the Supreme Court. Judicial review, in fact, was not an explicit part of the Constitution. Jackson and Lincoln did not deny the Supreme Court's prerogative to judge the constitutionality of executive actions, but they resisted the enforcement of its judgments, especially when the overwhelming needs of the Union and its people were at stake. The president, they contended, managed the relationship between the Constitution and the people. The president and the people determined the most important laws, not the unelected judges on the Supreme Court.

Accountable to the American public, the president had to be a tenacious defender of the deepest national interests that might conflict with various laws. Lincoln believed the president should avoid narrow factionalism, as Washington had advised, and actively promote the core of constitutional meaning for a new population, as Jackson had advocated.

Lincoln wanted to be a more populist Washington and a more states-man-like Jackson—an executive who spoke for ordinary people and preserved fundamental governing institutions. He would use central authority to create local opportunities, especially for white men seeking to improve themselves.

"Was it possible to lose the nation, and yet preserve the constitution?" Lincoln asked a group of skeptical visitors. "By general law life *and* limb must be protected; yet often a limb must be amputated to save a life; but a life is never wisely given to save a limb. I felt that measures, otherwise unconstitutional, might become lawful, by becoming indispensable to the preservation of the constitution, through the preservation of the nation. Right or wrong, I assumed this ground, and now avow it." The president had to preserve the life of the Union above all.[10]

Lincoln's eloquent defense of "measures, otherwise unconstitutional," echoed Jackson's defiance of established legislation and law. For Jackson, presidential prerogative included Indian Removal, destroying the Bank of the United States, and halting national infrastructure programs. For Lincoln, the necessities of his time meant denying writs of habeas corpus for some prisoners and waging an ever more brutal war against the Confederacy. Both Jackson and Lincoln turned the civilian presidency into an office of perpetual war, Lincoln out of necessity. Like fighting Indians for Jackson, the Civil War was a "people's contest" for Lincoln.[11]

Washington never spoke in these terms. His executive stood above the people and avoided people's wars. In protecting the Union, Washington saw himself as strengthening emerging constitutional adherence in the young nation. He never believed or justified the president taking "measures, otherwise unconstitutional." That would have been un-presidential behavior, in his view. For Lincoln, by contrast, the Constitution alone did not make the Union; the Union made the Constitution—without the Union it could not function.

That Lincoln drew from both Washington and Jackson was not a coincidence. Lincoln had studied both men intensively, and he revered different elements of their leadership styles. Like Washington, he sought to cultivate an image of the president as a mythological Roman prophet-warrior (a "founding father"). He was also a popular frontier-town politician, like Jackson, who wanted to use executive powers to promote the economic, political, and social changes that his voters demanded. Lincoln was elite and populist at the same time, idealistic and pragmatic.

EVEN AS LINCOLN COMBINED ELEMENTS OF WASHINGTON AND Jackson, he set new precedents and new standards that few of his successors would reach. When he entered the presidency, Lincoln was not a war hero; he had served only briefly in the Illinois militia, and he never saw combat. Lincoln was not a farmer or a large landholder either; he owned only a modest family home and some small land tracts in Springfield, Illinois, where he also rented an office. A full-time lawyer and politician, Lincoln made his case for executive leadership through argument. He was a litigator for what he believed and those who followed him. He advocated for the Union by marshaling law, tradition, logic, and common sense as he had for his clients in the hundreds of cases—more than most of his lawyer peers—he litigated before moving to Washington.

In his 1860 presidential campaign and after his election, Lincoln's clients became the American voters. The Constitution was the field of rhetorical battle—the central source of law—and the adversaries were the slaveholding Southerners who wished to use that document for their peculiar purposes. Lincoln's experience as a litigator was the background for his mobilization of words to attract supporters to his reading of the Constitution and isolate opponents with alternative interpretations. Lincoln looked to empower the national executive, and strengthen the Union, by winning the key arguments about constitutional rights.

He litigated through his speeches, his letters, his stories, his orders, and, when necessary, the force of arms. Jackson had done the same, only on a smaller scale, and with less attention to constitutional argument. Unlike Jackson, Lincoln devoted extensive effort to explaining his actions, exposing his opponents, and trying to persuade. He re-interpreted the Constitution to serve the Union cause, and he promoted his interpretation widely and forcefully. He worked harder than any of his predecessors to make his arguments stick, even in a deeply divided nation.

And he largely succeeded. We understand Lincoln today as a master of words; indeed, the Gettysburg Address and the Second Inaugural Address are the two most famous and influential political speeches in American history. What we understand less often is how Lincoln's rhetoric laid the foundation for his view of presidential power. Careful reading of his words leads one to appreciate his firmness and his subtlety—his ability to make arguments that defended a controversial position and disarmed opponents at the same time. Lincoln used language to inspire and restrain simultaneously, to build a common ground that advocates could accept and opponents had trouble refuting. His arguments, like his language, were vivid and supple, easy to understand but difficult to deny. Despite receiving barely a year of formal education, Lincoln used words to redefine presidential power as no one before or after has matched.[12]

"I remember," Lincoln explained, "how, when a mere child, I used to get irritated when any body talked to me in a way I could not understand. I don't think I ever got angry at anything else in my life. But that always disturbed my temper, and has ever since. I can remember going to my little bedroom, after hearing the neighbors talk of an evening with my father, and spending no small part of the night walking up and down, and trying to make out what was the exact meaning of some of their, to me, dark sayings. I could not sleep, though I often tried to, when I got on such a hunt after an idea, until I had caught it; and when I thought I had got it, I was not satisfied until I had repeated it over and over, until I had put it in language plain enough, as I thought, for any boy I knew to comprehend. This was a kind of passion with me, and it has stuck by me; for I am never easy now, when I am handling a thought, till I have bounded it North, and bounded it South, and bounded it East, and bounded it West."[13]

Lincoln's "hunt" after the right words gave his presidency powerful ammunition. The simple appeal of his language and the tactile clarity of his arguments allowed his audiences to digest them easily. He built his claims around sophisticated thought, but he replaced the platitudes of other politicians with precise words and evocative comparisons that moved bodies and minds, even among his opponents. In a deeply divided nation, he was able to attract a strong, diverse, and enduring following, as no president had since Jackson.

Instead of lazy abstractions, Lincoln used carefully chosen words and metaphors. Instead of clichés, he found poetic voice for his most important goals. His first inaugural address is an example of presidential poetry in defense of concrete policy aims: "We are not enemies, but friends. We must not be enemies. Though passion may have strained it must not break our bonds of affection. The mystic chords of memory, stretching from every battlefield and patriot grave to every living heart and hearthstone all over this broad land, will yet swell the chorus of the Union, when again touched, as surely they will be, by the better angels of our nature."[14]

Lincoln found this simple, clear, inspiring voice in speech after speech, and letter after letter. He appealed to popular hopes and aspirations. He used language to paint a picture—a vision—of the world he wanted to create. This was his method of executive leadership: popular inspiration and visionary aspiration, appeal to the heart and mind and then challenge for action. Lincoln's goal as president was to speak directly to the American people, as Jackson never had, and to raise them up to "the better angels" of their nature, as Washington had wished.

Lincoln expanded executive power through his language above all. His skills as a wordsmith gave him a continual edge against competitors who had more experience, but could not speak or write as well. The historian James McPherson makes this point about Confederate leader Jefferson Davis, in particular. Davis had a far better education than Lincoln, including training in classical literature, rhetoric, and logic. Davis, however, expressed himself with pedantic phrases, arcane words, and platitudinous claims. Even his supporters were rarely moved by his proclamations, and few remembered what he said. Lincoln, in contrast, was simple, direct, inspiring, and memorable. His words clarified a larger purpose for his readers; Davis simply reinforced what his readers already believed.[15]

In this way, Lincoln was different from his most influential predecessors. Washington led by the supreme dignity of the office and Jackson by the popularity of the executive. In a time when the dignity and the popularity of the national leader came under wide attack, Lincoln gave the president a strong and clear voice to cut through the ugly debates all around him and point people in a new direction. His speeches, which were widely reprinted, breathed new life into American leadership. Later presidents and other politicians would return to his words, but they rarely echoed the vividness and clarity of his expression. Lincoln helped listeners and readers, who often disagreed violently, to imagine a new shared society—a new American nation.

LINCOLN USED HIS COMMAND OF LANGUAGE TO EXPLAIN THE stakes involved in the secession crisis that began immediately after his election in November 1860. Before his inauguration the following March, seven Southern states (South Carolina, Mississippi, Florida, Alabama, Georgia, Louisiana, and Texas) voted to leave the United States and form their own country: the Confederate States of America. At least four other states were on the verge of joining them. Most residents of Northern states opposed these acts of secession, but opinions on what to do next varied widely. Fighting a bloody war to return the Confederate states to the Union was not a universally popular position, even among the staunchest opponents of slavery and secession.

From his first day in office, Lincoln had to convince his Northern voters, and especially the citizens of the border states, that he was doing everything he could short of war to save the Union. If war came, as the president thought it would, he wanted to show that it was "forced" upon the North by uncompromising Confederate belligerence. Lincoln knew that he had to be seen as defending the Union, the Constitution, and general peace against aggressive Southern behavior that attacked the American way of life.

Thus even as Southern states seceded, Lincoln's Inaugural Address offered reconciliation if they returned to the Union, absent any interference with slavery inside their borders. The president knew that Confederate leaders would not accept this offer because the spread of slavery, not its mere survival, was their goal, but he made the gesture to appear open and peace-loving: "One section of our country believes slavery is 'right' and ought to be extended, while the other believes it is 'wrong' and ought not to be extended. This is the only substantial dispute." Lincoln pledged to maintain the Union by avoiding any direct conflict between these two worldviews, offering coexistence within the same nation to both North and South. The new president counseled: "There needs to be no bloodshed or violence, and there shall be none unless it be forced upon the national authority."[16]

On 12 April 1861 the Confederate army's seizure of Fort Sumter, near Charleston, South Carolina, gave Lincoln the pretext he needed to claim that the secessionists had forced war on a peace-loving president. "They knew," Lincoln explained to Congress, "that this Government desired to keep the garrison in the Fort, not to assail them, but merely to maintain visible possession, and thus to preserve the Union from actual, and immediate dissolution." The Confederate attack was an act of aggression. Lincoln focused on the violence of that attack, not the causes of the violence. There was now, in his words, a "giant insurrection" and "this government has no choice left but to deal with it, *where it finds it.*"[17]

Lincoln now took the war to the Confederacy and appealed for support from the Northern public. This was a war of necessity in his framing, which became the standard Union narrative after April 1861: "It was with the deepest regret that the Executive found the duty of employing the war-power, in defense of the government, forced upon him. He could but perform this duty, or surrender the existence of the government." As executive, the president was fulfilling his elected obligation and calling upon Northern citizens to fulfill theirs—nothing more, nothing less. The commander-in-chief deployed unprecedented force to save the Union, not to pursue a chosen political program for slavery or any other controversial issue. Lincoln expressed a desire only "to preserve the government, that it may be administered for all, as it was administered by the men who made it."[18]

Lincoln greatly expanded presidential power in the interests of "defense." He carefully explained radical changes in military service, civil liberties, and citizenship as conservative protections of an old nation—even as the nation had changed, and was changing, beyond recognition. The long and bloody Civil War had the effect of destroying slavery and the Southern plantation system. Lincoln's prose made the president, not Congress or the states, the leader of that transformation, even as the president did not truly control all events. Lincoln's words gave shape and meaning to the conflict, and in doing that he exerted unmatched influence over the chaos of the nineteenth century's most violent war.[19]

THE LOSS OF FORT SUMTER SPURRED AN IMMEDIATE NORTHERN effort to expand the Union military. On 15 April 1861 Lincoln called for the mustering of an additional 75,000 soldiers in the US Army and their preparation for war against the Confederacy. Like Washington and Jackson before him, the president had to rely on the states and their militias for these soldiers. Secretary of War Simon Cameron apportioned the request among the states that remained in the Union, most of which enthusiastically furnished the needed men. Some states exceeded their quotas for new soldiers in the early months of the war. Lincoln was, however, entirely dependent on the state legislatures and governors for the expansion of the Union army.

Early defeats for the Union, beginning with the Battle of Bull Run on 21 July 1861, forced Lincoln to return repeatedly to the states for more troops. Enthusiasm for what many had hoped would be a short conflict quickly turned to frustration and even defeatism in parts of the North. Governors and state legislatures began to resist calls for more troops and had trouble filling federal requests even when they agreed to them. In Massachusetts and Wisconsin, two strong pro-Union states, governors criticized federal troop demands just months after their initial enthusiasm for the war.[20]

Lincoln had to find a new way of recruiting soldiers, boosting Northern morale, and discouraging foreign actors—especially the British—who might aid the Confederacy in anticipation of its victory. He realized that state legislatures and governors were too fragmented in their power. Only the national executive could lead a campaign to defeat the Confederacy.

The commander-in-chief of the military, responsible for overseeing the generals, now had to become the chief manager of the war effort. Lincoln recognized that the strength of the Union was its superior resource base—human, industrial, and agricultural—not its generalship. (The South had the clear advantage with General Robert E. Lee, particularly in the war's first years.) To win the war, the president needed to mobilize superior Union resources on a scale never before seen. This was a "people's contest," Lincoln explained, and it therefore required a centralized executive to organize the masses.[21]

In previous wars presidents had left domestic affairs to the states, as Lincoln claimed he would do at the start of the Civil War. Congress had vigorously rejected presidential efforts to recruit soldiers and sailors for past conflicts. Personal liberty, at its most basic level, meant freedom for American citizens from forced conscription by a distant federal government. The vast majority of participants in prior conflicts had been "volunteers" who did not sacrifice their freedom, or their primary loyalty to their states, when they joined a national war effort.

Lincoln changed this assumption not with a full-throated defense of a national army, but with an emphasis on the necessities of fighting the Civil War. He worked through the state legislatures and governors as long as possible, and he then slowly moved to expand the federal role in recruiting, training, and deploying forces. To the end of the conflict, regiments were defined by their state of origin. Nonetheless, officials employed by the president, not the state governors, became the key figures for determining who served, where, and when. By 1863 the president commanded military service from young males across the Union as a condition of citizenship—a power never held by Washington or Jackson. Lincoln was the first modern commander-in-chief with supreme war powers at home.

The process of assuming these powers began with federal conscription of freed blacks into the Union Army. Although many state leaders opposed giving African Americans guns, the need for additional manpower, and the desire among many white citizens to avoid service, encouraged the use of this untapped resource. Lincoln made the argument in these pragmatic terms, avoiding mention of any other purpose. He emphasized the use of African Americans as "laborers" supporting the Union Army, not full soldiers who could turn on the white population. A delegation of Western state representatives visiting with Lincoln on 4 August 1862 received this explanation: "It is the determination of the Government not to arm negroes unless some new and more pressing emergency arises."[22]

The shortage of soldiers, especially following Lincoln's request for 300,000 more recruits in July 1862, meant that the Union now faced a "pressing emergency." As soon as Lincoln spoke with the Western representatives his generals began placing black soldiers under arms. Henry Halleck, appointed general-in-chief by the president, ordered his subordinates, including General Ulysses Grant (then in western Tennessee), to "take up all active [rebel] sympathizers, and either hold them as prisoners or put them beyond our lines. Handle that class without gloves, and take their property for public use. . . . It is time that they should begin to feel the presence of the war." As everyone knew, seizing Confederate property meant seizing former slaves whom General Grant and others began to use for military purposes. Grant wrote about this to his family, admitting that while he did not have a strong personal view about the future status of freed slaves, he was "using them as teamsters, hospital attendants, company cooks, and so forth, thus saving soldiers to carry the musket." He continued, "I don't know what is to become of these poor people in the end, but it weakens the enemy to take them from them."[23]

The Militia Act, passed by Congress in July 1862, approved enlisting African Americans as soldiers in the US Army. It allowed the president to recruit "persons of African descent" for "any war service for which they may be found competent," including direct combat with the enemy—often their former slave masters. The Second Confiscation Act, also passed by Congress in July 1862, authorized the federal seizure of slaves held by Confederates. The former slaves would become free citizens of the Union, and they would be encouraged to serve with Union forces.[24]

The states did not govern the process of recruiting and organizing free black soldiers in what was rapidly becoming a multiracial Union army. The federal government managed that process, as it did for tens of thousands of recent immigrants (many of whom were not yet citizens) and other residents of the North pulled into a massive military machine. The Union army grew larger than any of its European counterparts, exceeding the imagination of the nation's founders, who distrusted large centralized militaries. The Union army looked more like a Napoleonic invasion force than the ragtag militia of the revolutionary era. By 1865 Lincoln commanded one million men from diverse backgrounds—a nation within a nation, led by presidential order. Much had changed from the small forces and local control overseen by Washington and Jackson.[25]

The Enrollment Act, passed by Congress in March 1863, allowed the gigantic Union army to recruit directly from the Northern population through the first mandatory conscription of young males (ages twenty to forty-five) in American history. The vast majority of soldiers remained "volunteers," not conscripts, but federal coercion to enlist deepened. Young men were promised better commissions if they "volunteered," rather than await mandatory enlistment at the hands of a federal commissioner. Justifying his actions as necessary for waging the war, Lincoln superseded traditional state control of American armies and created a presumption that free male citizens—white and black—would follow orders from the president to defend the Union. Lincoln centralized enormous power in the presidency. He made the president the most important local actor for determining many questions of life and death, as well as citizenship and freedom.

Lincoln nationalized the North through the military, as so many of his less democratic counterparts did in Europe. He was engaged in modern nation-building, rather than leadership of a small republic. Lincoln's new executive powers were highly coercive over lives and property, but they remained rooted in a powerful language of democracy and opportunity. That is what he meant by a "people's war." The Civil War presidency was distinctive because it constructed an industrial nation-state, on a European model, but Lincoln led through promises of unparalleled citizen participation.[26]

The Union army was the largest military in the world, and it was also the most powerful democratizing force on earth. It was the president's massive constabulary and his main lever for changing lives—North and South, free and slave. The president had to manage an apparent contradiction: making democracy by force of arms. Lincoln and all of his successors would struggle to control this contradiction on a continental, hemispheric, and eventually global scale.

FREEING THE SLAVES HELPED FUEL LINCOLN'S MILITARY MACHINE, but the war and his presidency did not begin with that aim. He entered the war committed to avoiding the slavery issue to the extent possible. He had famously commented in 1858 that the United States was a "house divided" on the question of slavery, and he hoped to "arrest the further spread of it, and place it where the public mind shall rest in the belief that it is in the course of ultimate extinction."[27]

"Ultimate extinction" did not mean immediate abolition, or anything close to it. Lincoln condemned radicals on both sides for threatening to bring the Union tumbling down through hasty and aggressive blows. Instead, Lincoln sought to preserve the divided Union by slowly reducing the national influence of slaveholders. He hoped to stop slavery's spread in new territories, but not deny current slaveholders the right to keep their human property. He wanted to compensate them, through the federal treasury, for the consensual and gradual abolition of the institution. As late as the summer of 1861, he still attempted to convince slaveholders that they did not have to live among former slaves, but could send them to a Caribbean island or an African nation—what proponents of these ideas, Lincoln among them, called "colonization"— with the assistance of the federal government.

Lincoln believed slavery was "an evil not to be extended." In the short run, it had "to be tolerated and protected"; its slow and steady extinction had to occur with the support of all parties—North and South—and the leadership of the president. Lincoln argued that this was the ultimate goal of the founders. He pointed to Washington's manumission of his slaves and his prohibition of slavery in territories settled under the Northwest Ordinance, Congress's elimination of the US slave trade after 1807, and Thomas Jefferson's encouragement that "it is still in our power to direct the process of emancipation, and deportation, peaceably, and in such slow degrees, as that the evil will wear off insensibly."

Lincoln called for compromise, which to him meant a shared antislavery vision over time: "Wrong as we think slavery is, we can yet afford to let it alone where it is, because that much is due to the necessity arising from its actual presence in the nation; but can we, while our votes will prevent it, allow it to spread into the National Territories, and to overrun us here in these Free States? If our sense of duty forbids this, then let us stand by our duty, fearlessly and effectively."[28]

Lincoln's stirring words met with stiff resistance from his Southern opponents, leading to secession. And as it became clear that the war effort would demand an ever-larger Union military under the president's command, he found himself moving faster toward the immediate abolitionist position he had resisted for so long. A bigger war necessitated bolder aims to justify the accumulating death and destruction. The people Lincoln appealed to for support—including African American soldiers—needed to know their sacrifices would bring about a necessary moral transformation. To convince his almost entirely white base of supporters, a more powerful president had to escalate his promises.

This became a common phenomenon for most presidents after Lincoln: wider aims announced to encourage support of less-than-popular wars. In a democracy, where presumptions of personal freedom are sometimes sacrificed in the face of military necessity, leaders must emphasize the "danger to freedom" and the promise of "expanded liberty" in order to mobilize the population for war. Inflated threats and promises help turn war reluctance and fatigue into popular support. Inflated threats and promises also justify deviations from constitutional limits on federal reach and assertions of direct presidential authority ("war power").[29]

Lincoln was the first president to define an extended military conflict as a "new birth of freedom." The Civil War was not about independence, trade, or territory, as in 1776, 1812, and 1846. It was, in Lincoln's inimitable formulation, a world-historical trial for the vitality of democracy: "This issue embraces more than the fate of these United States. It presents to the whole family of man, the question, whether a constitutional republic, or a democracy—a government of the people, by the same people—can, or cannot, maintain its territorial integrity, against its own domestic foes." Though none exhibited the same rhetorical skill, every American war president after Lincoln made idealistic claims about defending and expanding democracy, while asserting more direct powers at home and extended reach abroad. [30]

LINCOLN FUSED FREEDOM AND WAR, IMAGINING EXPANDED PERsonal freedom through what was the most brutal and inhumane conflict anyone had seen to that time. To make a pervasive "culture of death" worthwhile and meaningful—rather than absurd and abhorrent—Lincoln had to strive for idealism, to make it a religious mission more than a political-military dispute.[31]

This was the genius of his Gettysburg Address—the most enduring war speech in American history, written in Lincoln's own hand and delivered after a battle that resulted in nearly 50,000 Union and Confederate casualties. Speaking on 19 November 1863 at the dedication of the national cemetery on the battlefield, still strewn with maimed body parts, Lincoln declared that the Civil War was now about something much larger than the defense of the Union. To justify the mountains of dead and the masses of newly drafted men, including former slaves, the president connected the conflict to the Declaration of Independence and its promise of individual freedom.

His address opened with what became the most famous presidential lines about the founding of the United States: "Fourscore and seven years ago our fathers brought forth on this continent a new nation, conceived in liberty and dedicated to the proposition that all men are created equal."

Lincoln defined the purpose of the Civil War as a redemption of basic American equality and self-governance:

Now we are engaged in a great civil war, testing whether that nation or any nation so conceived and so dedicated can long endure. We are met on a great battlefield of that war. We have come to dedicate a portion of that field as a final resting-place for those who here gave their lives that that nation might live. It is altogether fitting and proper that we should do this.

But in a larger sense, we cannot dedicate—we cannot consecrate—we cannot hallow—this ground. The brave men, living and dead, who struggled here have consecrated it far above our poor power to add or detract. The world will little note nor long remember what we say here, but it can never forget what they did here. It is for us the living, rather, to be dedicated here to the unfinished work which they who fought here have thus far so nobly advanced. It is rather for us to be here dedicated to the great task remaining before us—

that from these honored dead we take increased devotion to that cause for which they gave the last full measure of devotion—that we here highly resolve that these dead shall not have died in vain—that this nation under God shall have a new birth of freedom—and that government of the people, by the people, for the people shall not perish from the earth.[32]

In less than 300 words, Lincoln "transformed the ugly reality" of the Gettysburg battlefield "into something rich and strange," as Garry Wills has put it. Lincoln authored "a new lean language to humanize and redeem the first modern war." He turned the terrible deaths around him into a shared obligation not just to continue fighting ("these dead shall not have died in vain") but to complete an unfinished mission ("a new birth of freedom") announced to the world at the origin of the American dream ("government of the people, by the people, for the people"). At Gettysburg, Lincoln created a biblical narrative for transforming pervasive death into national rebirth, even democratic renaissance. He made the Civil War into a collective religious awakening.[33]

Through the address, Lincoln seized control of the nation's historical narrative. He did not mention slavery, or union, or even Gettysburg itself. He did not mention the Constitution. Instead, he defined the Declaration of Independence as the wellspring of legitimate government power, and he made himself the spokesman for its values. Those who died in battle died not for the Union army alone, but for a larger historical cause. And the president was empowered to call upon the remaining citizens to carry that cause to its conclusion. The president stood at the head of an inevitable (perhaps divine) movement to expand liberty, with the citizens who served under his command asserting their right to govern themselves by force of their arms.

The honored dead at the Gettysburg commemoration were martyrs, and Lincoln was a preacher leading the flock to the promised land built on their dreams, their blood, and their memory. The president assumed the posture of a national prophet, speaking across generations. The president became leader of a social and spiritual movement, transcending what was usually expected of a political figure.

The Gettysburg Address replaced the language of "union" that Lincoln had invoked so frequently with the concept of "nation." Lincoln used the word five times at Gettysburg. His speeches and correspondence after Gettysburg relied on the same vocabulary. The United States was not a collection of separate political bodies, Lincoln claimed after 1863, but an organic whole united by a common set of ideas about freedom. The president was the articulator-in-chief for these ideas, on behalf of the people. The United States was, according to Lincoln, a diverse collection of people growing ever-closer through the executive's unifying voice. The progress of self-governance required more centralized protections of freedom, and a more forceful executive committed to democratic participation.[34]

Most major Northern newspapers printed the Gettysburg Address in its entirety. Book and pamphlet publishers immediately reprinted it, and they never stopped. Most Southern newspapers condemned the address, meaning that it framed the arguments of both sides in the Civil War.

Edward Everett, the president of Harvard University who gave an extended speech before Lincoln's short remarks, recognized the "eloquent simplicity and appropriateness" of the Gettysburg Address. "I should be glad if I could flatter myself," Everett wrote the president, "that I came as near to the central idea of the occasion, in two hours, as you did in two minutes." Indeed, Lincoln's words proved more inspiring—and enduring—than traditional political prose, party politics, or declarations of war.[35]

For all the debates about the Civil War, historians have agreed that it was a war about the fundamental meaning of America. No one painted a more compelling picture than Lincoln. Reading his words, many citizens disagreed about the shape of the nation's future, but few citizens saw it the same way as before. His words continue to hold that power today.

Lincoln articulated new possibilities that, once described, seemed so real, so close. No one since Thomas Jefferson in 1776 had done such a thing for American politics. Few presidents after Lincoln have achieved anything similar, despite repeated efforts. The power of Lincoln's words was hard to resist, and difficult to replicate. Their artistry gave them, and their author, unique authority.[36]

LINCOLN'S WORDS IN THE GETTYSBURG ADDRESS EXPLAIN HIS evolving vision for the Emancipation Proclamation, issued by the president more than ten months earlier, on 1 January 1863. The Proclamation, a military order, officially freed the slaves in the Confederate states. Thousands of long-suffering slaves had already escaped to Union lines and taken up arms against their former masters. The immediate impact of the Emancipation Proclamation was to legitimize a new national language of black freedom and anoint the president as the figure who, almost like Moses, could declare bound men free.

"I do order and declare," Lincoln wrote, "that all persons held as slaves within said designated [Confederate] States, and parts of States, are, and henceforward shall be free; and that the Executive government of the United States, including the military and naval authorities thereof, will recognize and maintain the freedom of said persons."[37]

Congress did not announce the freedom of the slaves, nor did the judiciary. The president did. He turned slave self-liberation and Union army recruitment of former slaves into national policy.[38]

The president called upon the freed slaves to become regular workers and citizens—to "labor faithfully for reasonable wages" and only resort to violence "in necessary self-defense." He also encouraged their enlistment in the Union army: "I further declare and make known, that such persons of suitable condition, will be received into the armed service of the United States to garrison forts, positions, stations, and other places, and to man vessels of all sorts in said service." Lincoln ordered these radical changes—by almost royal decree—as "an act of justice, warranted by the Constitution, upon military necessity." With his signature, the president expanded the language of freedom to include black citizens, as it never had before in the nation's history.[39]

The slaves were property at the start of the Civil War, the conflict made them contraband, and the president welcomed them as citizens of the Union. Emancipating the slaves, the American president oversaw the largest official government re-distribution of property, and the most sudden redefinition of citizenship, in the nineteenth century. No other society turned so many unfree laborers into free citizens so quickly. No other society eliminated an entire class of property with the stroke of a president's pen.

Lincoln made these decisions mostly alone; he consulted his cabinet, but did not rely on them to the same degree Washington depended on his cabinet members. Lincoln's "team of rivals" was really a team of one.[40]

"We must free the slaves," Lincoln explained, "or be ourselves subdued." Removing this institution that Lincoln hated, but had first sought to appease, was the key to his power by the middle of the Civil War. The Confederacy repudiated his national authority, his generals (especially George McClellan) challenged his command, and countless citizens questioned his right to send them to fight. Lincoln needed the cause of slave emancipation to show his power and give truth to his words.[41]

Freeing the slaves expanded Lincoln's influence. He was speaking to the men and women who were liberating themselves. He was also speaking to their increasing number of sympathizers, especially in the North, frustrated with the slowness of the war effort. The president now entered personally into the struggle as a partisan not just for Union victory, but for a new kind of society. Although Lincoln did not advocate equality between the races (few of his time did), he embraced political and economic freedom for all males, white and black. With emancipation the president became, as never before, a movement leader—an abolitionist.[42]

Lincoln had little choice. By 1863, if he had tried to leave slavery intact he would have lost all credibility as a leader. The war would have become an end in itself, rather than a spark for improving the country, as he promised. Without the moral authority derived from freeing the slaves, and the labor they provided for the Union, the president could only expect an endless civil war. Without evidence of moral and political progress, he could only anticipate growing acceptance of the Confederacy as a *fait accompli*, perhaps even a sovereign republic.[43]

Through emancipation Lincoln highlighted the backwardness of the Southern secessionists and their unworthiness for separate statehood. As he memorably explained: "With rebellion thus sugar-coated, they have been drugging the public mind of their section for more than thirty years." The Emancipation Proclamation was an antidote. Creating an unmistakable contrast between the free North and the slave South, the president could define the war as a legitimate defense of progress and justice, rather than the violent imposition of a "Northern way of life," as the Confederates claimed.[44]

Moral authority shifted decisively to the slave emancipators, rather than the slaveholders, and Lincoln exploited that comparison to recruit soldiers and win over skeptics. "We cannot escape history," he reminded readers. "The fiery trial through which we pass, will light us down, in honor or dishonor, to the latest generation." He went on: "In *giving* freedom to the *slave* we *assure* freedom to the *free*—honorable alike in what we give, and what we preserve. We shall nobly save, or meanly lose, the last best, hope of earth."[45]

As Lincoln hoped, emancipation gave the army new dynamism and Union supporters—at home and abroad—new determination. Ending slavery opened a new avenue for executive power, across regions and races. It made the president a force for change in what was a largely stalemated war. Eight months after signing the Emancipation Proclamation, following the Union victory at Gettysburg, he reported to one skeptic: "The war has certainly progressed as favorably for us, since the issue of the proclamation as before." Lincoln recounted: "Some of the commanders of our armies in the field who have given us our most important successes, believe the emancipation policy, and the use of colored troops, constitute the heaviest blow yet dealt to the rebellion; and that, at least one of those important successes, could not have been achieved when it was but for the aid of black soldiers." To add credibility to these opinions, "the commanders holding these views are some who have never had any affinity with what is called abolitionism, or with Republican party politics; but who hold them purely as military opinions."[46]

Lincoln extolled the positive effects of emancipation, arguing against detractors within the Union. "You say you will not fight to free negroes.

Some of them seem willing to fight for you; but, no matter. Fight you, then exclusively to save the Union. I issued the proclamation on purpose to aid you in saving the Union." Lincoln continued:

> I thought that in your struggle for the Union, to whatever extent the negroes should cease helping the enemy, to that extent it weakened the enemy in his resistance to you. Do you think differently? I thought that whatever negroes can be got to do as soldiers, leaves just so much less for white soldiers to do, in saving the Union. Does it appear otherwise to you? But negroes, like other people, act upon motives. Why should they do any thing for us, if we will do nothing for them? If they stake their lives for us, they must be prompted by the strongest motive—even the promise of freedom. And the promise being made, must be kept.[47]

Lincoln wrote these words to justify his aggressive use of presidential power in emancipating the slaves. His words were widely commented upon in newspapers, pamphlets, and public rallies. The Northern reaction was overwhelmingly supportive. For many citizens, the war had become a great cause, not just a battle against Southern secession. The moral and military ammunition provided by freeing the slaves relieved Northerners who feared defeat or endless stalemate. Lincoln's words were a palliative for an anxious and uncertain public.[48]

Emancipation, however, raised lingering anxieties about just what a post-slavery society would look like. The question of black rights remained uncertain, and Lincoln avoided any discussion of that topic, except repeated efforts to minimize concerns. The president used his words to envision a Civil War victory with freed slaves, but he kept his pen dry when it came to the question of race in America after the war. He knew how to fire his powerful words for a purpose, and how to mute them when necessary. The opening created by emancipation did not resolve continued limits on presidential power over race relations, and enduring conflicts over resources and rights across the nation.

THE CIRCUMSTANCES OF THE CIVIL WAR PUSHED THE PRESIDENT toward freeing the slaves and remaking parts of American society. He played a personal role in this "revolution"—expanding the influence of the executive beyond the imaginings of Washington, Jackson, and even Lincoln himself on the eve of his election. The president, not Congress, ordered the end of slavery in the South. The ordeal of the Civil War transformed the presidency at least as much as the presidency changed the war. A more muscular commander-in-chief, hardened by repeated battle, was also a more hydra-like national executive subjected to multiplying pushes and pulls in countless directions.

Lincoln admitted as much in a letter written more than a year after he signed the Emancipation Proclamation. "I attempt no compliment to my own sagacity," he explained. "I claim not to have controlled events, but confess plainly that events have controlled me. Now, at the end of three years struggle the nation's condition is not what either party, or any man devised, or expected."[49]

Lincoln authored the words to turn necessity into virtue, long overdue reform into moral revolution. His powerful language about a "new birth of freedom" helped nudge the engine of history in that direction. He guided changes that were more powerful than him or the office of the presidency. Lincoln's executive authority focused on winning a war and promoting social changes (like the end of slavery) that had begun before his order, but gained scale and scope from his nation-wide advocacy.

The president put language, law, money, and military force in the service of broad social changes. His language was crucial because it made change seem sensible, logical, and even traditional, when it was really quite radical. The simplicity and directness of Lincoln's words cut through fear and complexity. The inclusiveness of his language made readers feel that the changes he advocated were natural and connected to the deepest needs of the American people as a whole. The president promised not punishment, but improvement and redemption for all Americans—Union and Confederate; former slave, slaveholder, and abolitionist.[50]

This was the enduring genius of one of the greatest presidential speeches: Lincoln's Second Inaugural Address, delivered in front of the new Capitol dome on 4 March 1865. Like the Gettysburg Address, this speech was short (only 703 words) and aspirational. It rose above the chaos of the moment to articulate a higher purpose. It created order, inspiration, and direction from its eloquent vision. And it brought an enduring poetry to Lincoln's leadership.[51]

The war was not yet over, but Lincoln looked forward to what would come next. He explained what the war was about, why it was fought, and how it had transformed American society for everyone—including the president himself. He did not claim control over events, he did not propose a perfect solution to the remaining challenges, and he did not claim "victory," a word he avoided.

Lincoln used his carefully chosen words to fill the moment with a common mission and a strong president steering the nation through great tides of change. If there was an all-powerful figure for Lincoln, it was God. The president was his interpreter for a born-again nation emerging from a redemptive war and the collective penance of slavery. Lincoln's speech was laced with humility and self-criticism. He pointed to a new "high hope for the future" earned in common suffering by his "fellow countrymen":

> If we shall suppose that American slavery is one of those offenses which, in the providence of God, must needs come, but which, having continued through His appointed time, He now wills to remove, and that He gives to both North and South this terrible war as the woe due to those by whom the offense came, shall we discern therein any departure from those divine attributes which the believers in a living God always ascribe to Him? Fondly do we hope, fervently do we pray, that this mighty scourge of war may speedily pass away. Yet, if God wills that it continue until all the wealth piled by the bondsman's two hundred and fifty years of unrequited toil shall be sunk, and until every drop of blood drawn with the lash shall be paid by another drawn with the sword, as was said three thousand years ago, so still it must be said "the judgments of the Lord are true and righteous altogether."[52]

Slavery was an inherited evil for Lincoln, and the Civil War expunged it from American society. Lincoln claimed neither that he ended slavery nor that he determined the outcome of the war. His executive role was to understand the changes to the country, help citizens adjust to them, and bring all groups together behind a common vision. The president was a national minister for a battered and divided people, grappling for some shared salvation:

> With malice toward none, with charity for all, with firmness in the right as God gives us to see the right, let us strive on to finish the work we are in, to bind up the nation's wounds, to care for him who shall have borne the battle and for his widow and his orphan, to do all which may achieve and cherish a just and lasting peace among ourselves and with all nations.[53]

In this last valedictory paragraph, the president withdrew as a powerful commander or a determined law-giver. He made himself more of a prophet than a ruler, more of a fatherly overseer than a manager or a director. George Washington would have recognized the unifying vision of Abraham Lincoln, but Lincoln's transformative ambitions would have astounded the first president.[54]

"The war came," Lincoln wrote; the president acted to help the people find their way through to a better future. He was an active visionary and a collective redeemer, as never before. His beautiful words made him a new kind of leader for a new kind of nation, searching for the "better angels" of its originally sinful nature.[55]

LINCOLN'S ASSASSINATION, ONE MONTH AFTER HIS SECOND Inaugural Address, gives the speech a "farewell address" quality. Lincoln delivered another more informal speech on 11 April 1865, just a few days before his murder, but the Second Inaugural reflects his deepest thinking about the role of the American president. It also shows the fundamental transformation in the presidency from the troubled beginning of his time in office to his sudden and shocking death.[56]

In response to admirers of his Second Inaugural Address, Lincoln admitted that he expected it "to wear as well as—perhaps better than—any thing I have produced." But he doubted its popularity: "Men are not flattered by being shown that there has been a difference of purpose between the Almighty and them. To deny it, however, in this case, is to deny that there is a God governing the world. It is a truth which I thought needed to be told; and as whatever of humiliation there is in it, falls most directly on myself, I thought others might afford for me to tell it."[57]

The war over slavery was a war over the future of the nation. Could it survive in its still largely decentralized and regionalized form, or did it require more centralized efforts to promote freedom, opportunity, and economic growth? The new Republican Party emphasized centralization, and Lincoln as president carried that choice forward more quickly and extensively than anyone expected. Centralization was a cause and a consequence of the Civil War.

The Civil War president emerged with more authority than any of his predecessors. He commanded the largest army in the world, he directed one of the world's fastest industrializing economies toward his war aims, he created new domestic institutions and agencies to strengthen the Union, and he ended slavery. Of course, his authority in each of these areas was challenged repeatedly by the Confederacy and by Northern dissenters. The president became more powerful not because he could always achieve his aims, but because he managed to imbue his centralizing efforts with legitimacy through the force of his actions, and especially his words.

Lincoln as president was something other than a virtuous Washington-like guardian or a Jacksonian fighter for frontier communities, although he drew on both traditions. Lincoln made the president into a true national executive, articulating a transformative vision and forcing the nation's resources and policies in that direction. His Gettysburg Address and his Second Inaugural Address described an integrated nation of free men, individual opportunity, and economic growth. His words brought that vision to life as a national narrative, a widely shared dream. Union victories made that vision real; they helped to flesh out the narrative. The guns and greenbacks were the grammar for Lincoln's larger story.

As national storyteller and poet, Lincoln was telling a Truth. That was what made him a new kind of national executive. Although he still controlled a government of limited means, he had a message of extraordinary appeal. He drew power from his words, and he made the president into a visionary-in-chief, a real national strategist. That is why he took so much care in his words. That is why he kept his message so clear, so tight, so focused.

Lincoln believed the nation needed an executive who could raise the consciousness of citizens, beyond constitutional principles and popular interests. He sought to lead through persuasion, as he had during his long legal career. His skill with words allowed him to rise from a poor country boy to a revered man of influence, and he promised to help all Americans do the same.

Lincoln turned a terrible civil war into a narrative of national redemption, and he imagined the president as Truth-Teller to *freedom, opportunity, and wealth*. Those words are the closest approximation to *the* American civic religion. Lincoln made the president their most articulate defender.

His legacy encouraged expanding power for future presidents to promote American values and interests. His words inspired greater ambitions for the nation and its leaders. The mixed results of Reconstruction after the Civil War, particularly the resurgence of racial subjugation in the late nineteenth century, pointed to the disappointed expectations that accompanied rising presidential power. No president, not even Lincoln, could live up to the hopes described so beautifully in his words.

Lincoln's tall shadow hangs over all of his successors. It symbolizes possibility and tragedy. It inspires as it haunts powerful leaders struggling to measure up.

CHAPTER 5

Progressive President

I preach to you, then, my countrymen, that our country calls not for the life of ease but for the life of strenuous endeavor.

Theodore Roosevelt, 10 April 1899[1]

Theodore Roosevelt was the first president born in a big city, and although he reveled in his rugged frontier adventures, he made the national executive into a pushy, self-confident, and impatient reformer—a New Yorker. He did not have patience for tradition or even gradual change. He did not accept that post-Civil War America, bursting at its seams with new immigrants and growing industries, could conduct business as usual. Roosevelt envisioned the United States as a powerful engine, and he wanted to steer it to higher achievement at home and abroad. His executive was a driver as much as a father figure, a populist, and a poet. His ideal leader was an intellectual and an athlete, a man of thinking and doing, organizing the best of a crowded world around him.

That was what he meant by the "strenuous life," a term he invoked in 1899, when he spoke to citizens in America's other great early twentieth-century city, Chicago. "We do not admire the man of timid peace," Roosevelt announced. "Far better it is to dare mighty things, to win glorious triumphs, even though checkered by failure, than to take rank with those poor spirits who neither enjoy much nor suffer much, because they live in the gray twilight that knows not victory nor defeat." Roosevelt wanted to bring energy, wisdom, and courage to what he called "new problems"—the domestic dislocations of an industrializing economy and the international rivalries of growing empires—without getting "sunk in a scrambling commercialism."[2]

The pursuit of wealth was acceptable to Roosevelt, and he recognized that it fueled New York's rise as a cosmopolitan, dynamic city. Money, however, was not something Roosevelt admired. He took it for granted in his own life and he resented its misuses by those who possessed too much of it. Roosevelt was no leveler or socialist—he accepted inequality in all forms, and in all areas of life—but he was a utilitarian. Wealth and other advantages were justified so long as they produced greater value for society. Privilege brought public responsibility, in Roosevelt's view.

As a twenty-four-year-old member of the New York State Assembly in 1883, initially distinguished by his family name (the Roosevelts were prominent business leaders, philanthropists, and socialites) and his Harvard education, he expressed his core belief about the civic obligations of wealth. Justifying his own departure from the established gentleman's traditional avoidance of public office and the indignities that came with it, Roosevelt proclaimed: "Every man must devote a reasonable share of his time to doing his duty in the Political life of the community." The wealthy had to sacrifice for the good of society, and they had to justify their advantages: "You can no more have freedom without striving and suffering for it than you can win success as a banker or a lawyer without labor and effort, without self-denial in youth and the display of a ready and alert intelligence in middle age."[3]

Roosevelt never veered from his commitment to the burdens of civic duty. He believed that rich and poor citizens alike needed to pursue a higher calling in this world. Future salvation was not enough. Although Roosevelt was a deep believer in a Christian God, his politics were motivated by the vision of a present-day kingdom of human righteousness and achievement inherited from Greece, Rome, and an earlier British Empire. He wanted to make the United States the center of a new world "civilization," and that required the use of wealth for social improvement, not just the acquisition of more things. If the rugged wilderness would build the muscles on the body of the urban citizen, education in the arts, literature, and sciences would improve the sophistication and acuity of the American mind. A modern industrial democracy, rapidly breaking old boundaries, required the physical and mental soundness to devote its increasing power to virtue, not vice. Leaders had to model this behavior, inspire it, and, when required, enforce it.

"I suppose," Roosevelt admitted, "my critics will call that preaching, but I have got such a bully pulpit." It was an apt phrase, as Roosevelt sought to bully citizens to serve the public good. Once he became president, he did not wait for citizens to come to him or for other branches of government to act. He moved more quickly and forcefully than other politicians or prominent citizens, articulating the national purposes of wealth, the obligations of citizenship, and the needs of the country. He transformed the presidency from a distant office into a pulpit that projected the president's words into as many homes and offices as possible.

He talked about duty to the richest and the poorest citizens, and he did it personally. Roosevelt's president acted directly with the public, despite constitutional assumptions to the contrary. He had little use for the humility of Washington or the caution of Lincoln. His bully pulpit was purposely impulsive. He echoed Jackson, but with more eloquence and sophistication.[4]

Roosevelt's civilizing ambition explains his disdain for those rich citizens, especially in his own city, who put their wealth above the public good. In 1901, just two months before he unexpectedly became president, Roosevelt explained: "I do not see very much of the big-moneyed men in New York, simply because very few of them possess the traits which would make them companionable to me, or would make me feel that it was worth while dealing with them. To spend the day with them at Newport, or on one of their yachts, or even to dine with them save under exceptional circumstances, fills me with frank horror."[5]

"Money is undoubtedly one form of power," Roosevelt acknowledged. He was thankful for his own inherited fortune, but he confessed he knew only "a few men of wealth who use their wealth to full advantage." He pledged to educate his children and others to "do good work" with the resources at their disposal. Absent strong civilizing leadership,

Roosevelt feared, the "moneyed and semi-cultivated classes," along with corrupt politicians, would "bring this country down to the Chinese level." (Roosevelt was what we today might call a racialist; he saw each race as possessing distinctive attributes that differently suited each to civilization.)[6]

Virtue was neither inherited from family nor acquired through wealth, according to Roosevelt. It grew from learning and experience. The true elites—those of real talent, not just high birth station—served as role models, as educators, and as inspirational leaders. Roosevelt defined his public life, and the American presidency, around these activist functions. He was a progressive because he devoted his enormous energies to fostering virtue in a society producing so much directionless wealth. He was a progressive because he believed that the true elites could improve the world for less privileged citizens—both at home and abroad.[7]

ROOSEVELT COMBINED JACKSON'S POPULISM WITH WASHING-ton's paternalism. He was tireless in his efforts to reach the "common man" through his words, images, and actions. An English friend, Cecil Spring-Rice, observed that Roosevelt acted like a six-year-old, always seeking the attention of a large crowd. Between the beginning of his political career in 1882 and his death in 1919, Roosevelt gave more speeches and published more books and articles than almost anyone else. He was everywhere, traveling ceaselessly from one corner of the country to another by rail to speak to citizens of all backgrounds. His broad shoulders and bespectacled, mustached face were recognizable to countless Americans from constant newspaper coverage of his exploits. He was the unparalleled political celebrity of his time. A century later, his visage remains more recognizable (in drawings, photos, and even Halloween costumes) than most other presidents.[8]

Roosevelt was Jacksonian in his heroic, hypermasculine, and larger-than-life qualities. Richard Washburn Child, a keen observer of politics at the time, said that "you shake hands with Roosevelt and hear him talk—and then you go home to wring the personality out of your clothes." He was magnetic, overfilled with fascinating talk, physical bombast, and contagious energy. He moved those around him to action. He intoxicated his listeners with his sense of purpose and destiny. Roosevelt had his detractors, including Mark Twain, who was then one of the nation's most prominent cultural figures, but he had few encounters that left his audience indifferent. Like no other president before him except Jackson, Roosevelt was a visceral politician of the people. He got under the skin of the electorate; people far and wide felt his presence.[9]

Roosevelt's popularity did not diminish his elitism. He believed that the "common man" lacked the cultivation to make major decisions. Homespun wisdom was not sufficient for enlightened policy-making. Roosevelt directed popular sentiment, even as he appealed to it. During President William McKinley's first term in office, before Roosevelt became vice president, he lamented the limitations on presidential power and expressed the thought that "if this country could be ruled by a benevolent czar we would doubtless make a good many changes for the better." He recognized that was not possible, but he called upon national leaders to "get the best work we can out of the means that are available." Stronger central power, within a democratic setting, was imperative for the progress Roosevelt desired.[10]

He later described the president as a "short-term elective King" who was different from a hereditary monarch in that he served a limited term of office, depended on popular opinion, and was restricted in many respects by constitutional law. Nonetheless, Roosevelt believed that the president had to be "even greater" than a "Prime Minister" in his ability to unite the people for common purpose. The elective king would stand above party, as Washington hoped, and he would envision a new future, as Lincoln did, but he would direct the complex machinery of society as none of his predecessors had done. That was what Roosevelt called his "real philosophy of statesmanship."[11]

ROOSEVELT IDEALIZED AMBITION AND TENACITY IN WHAT HE famously called the "man in the arena…whose face is marred by dust and sweat and blood; who strives valiantly; who errs, who comes short again and again, because there is no effort without error and shortcoming; but who does actually strive to do the deeds; who knows great enthusiasms, the great devotions; who spends himself in a worthy cause; who at the best knows in the end the triumph of high achievement, and who at the worst, if he fails, at least fails while daring greatly, so that his place shall never be with those cold and timid souls who neither know victory nor defeat."[12]

One example of Roosevelt's "man in the arena" was, obviously, himself. He sought to direct the energies and resources in America's great cities to push the whole country toward a brave new world. He wanted prosperous cities with productive citizens who made great things. He wanted pristine "wild" landscapes where busy city residents, like himself, could retreat to reinvigorate their bodies and their minds. He pursued big international "adventures"—especially in Cuba and the Philippines—where Americans could expand their ambitions and showcase their talents. Overall, Roosevelt wanted the nation to "go forward" without hesitation, and he encouraged Americans to do more, achieve more, and experience more for their collective betterment.

Roosevelt was obsessive about progressive change, and he agitated for it incessantly before, during, and after his presidency. He was inspiring, but also frightened some observers. Mark Twain saw him as more of a dangerous zealot than a judicious leader. Twain labeled him "insane": "Mr. Roosevelt is the Tom Sawyer of the political world of the twentieth century; always showing off; always hunting for a chance to show off; in his frenzied imagination the Great Republic is a vast Barnum circus with him for a clown and the whole world for audience."[13]

Twain's resentment was well founded. Roosevelt was often a caricature of himself—vain, fanatical, even demagogic. As president, his popular appeal endangered a government built around checks on individual power. Roosevelt's undemocratic qualities—at least as Washington, Jackson, and Lincoln understood the limits on the presidency—were tempered by a commitment to broad social progress. He was devoted to making the lives of citizens better, not just getting himself elected.

In contrast to his predecessors, Roosevelt wrote, spoke, traveled, fought, and bullied citizens into embracing progressive change, and he never let up. Progressive politics was more than his vocation; it was his life. In this sense, he broke with the mold of the wealthy gentleman politician who temporarily enters the public arena. Roosevelt was a full-time progressive politician—a professional reform leader. He never really did anything else. All of his adventures and obsessions pointed to the same goal: reforming the country for greatness behind his personal leadership.

Unlike Washington, Jackson, and Lincoln, he relished every minute in office, and when he retired in 1909, he could not wait to try and get back. He was intoxicated with power and an exaggerated sense of his own superhuman capabilities. That was what frightened Mark Twain and other critics.

For all his fame and success, Roosevelt would have an enduring, and in some ways negative, effect on the office. He changed the presidency and the image of executive leadership by creating a model of rapid forward change—later called "transformation"—that motivated his successors for decades to come. Future presidents from Franklin Roosevelt to Ronald Reagan would try to live up to Theodore Roosevelt's model, and they would inevitably fall short. Theodore Roosevelt made the presidency into a whirlwind that neither he nor any other individual could control. He mastered most of the issues, but the range of presidential concerns began to exceed even his formidable capabilities. By expanding the scope of an energetic presidency far beyond what his predecessors imagined, he deepened the disillusion when he, and especially his successors, could not fulfill ever-greater demands. Roosevelt's ambitious "man in the arena" was set up to fail because he could never do enough, even as he did more than ever before.

ROOSEVELT WAS FASCINATED BY POWER AND ITS USES FOR NAtional greatness. He believed that a powerful country needed a powerful central government, staffed by the most talented and patriotic citizens. Without "men in the arena" the government could not reach its potential of helping the people to improve their lives and those around them. "Here in America," Roosevelt explained, "we the people have a continent on which to work out our destiny, and our faith is great that our men and women are fit to face the mighty days. Nowhere else in all the world is there such a chance for the triumph on a gigantic scale of the great cause of democratic and popular government."[14]

The core aim of progressive thought in the late nineteenth century was to replace corruption and amateurism in government with efficiency, expertise, and the highest standards of excellence. "We who stand for the cause of progress," Roosevelt announced, "are fighting to make this country a better place to live in for those who have been harshly treated by fate; and if we succeed it will also really be a better place for those who are already well off."[15]

America would become great when the best-trained and most competent officials—those "whose veins thrill with abounding vigor"—ran cities, states, and federal agencies, according to Roosevelt and other progressives. Widespread expertise and personal integrity would boost American production, power, and social peace. This approach embraced the possibilities—and necessities—of good, even "gigantic," government.[16]

In the last decades of the nineteenth century, many members in Congress agreed, especially because presidents had long exploited their powers of appointment to fill executive agencies with political friends and favor-seekers, rather than the best-qualified candidates. Andrew Jackson had pioneered the use of the "spoils system" to transform the government in his image, and other presidents, including Lincoln, had distributed patronage appointments to placate allies and buy off potential adversaries. The nineteenth-century presidency was a patronage institution, where the executive derived influence over society from the friends he employed in expanding government offices. "I have more pegs than holes to put them in," Lincoln famously commented, and so he, like other presidents, funded the creation of more government holes.[17]

As reports on corruption filled the nation's multiplying newspapers, it was no longer possible to deny that the spoils system had resulted in incompetent employees running the government. The number of people on the federal payroll had swollen from 20,000 during Andrew Jackson's presidency to 53,000 after the Civil War, and 131,000 in 1884; in less than fifty years, the staff of the executive branch had increased by more than 600 percent. The effectiveness of the federal government did not grow in parallel with the vast expansion of its payroll. On the contrary, bloated federal offices often functioned to serve the employees, not the citizens demanding service.[18]

A growing number of businesspeople and reformers wanted to make government more effective and less beholden to powerful patrons. As early as 1867, the National Manufacturers' Association proposed legislation requiring that federal employment be based on merit, not favoritism. Thomas Jenckes, a Republican from Rhode Island, led the charge in Congress for civil service reform. After a number of stalled efforts, in 1883 Congress passed the Pendleton Act, which created a new Civil Service Commission to investigate and redesign federal employment practices. The act encouraged competitive examinations for office and rigorous evaluation of performance; it discouraged political appointments and lifetime tenure. Above all, the Pendleton Act made the progressive demand for "good administration" fundamental for future thinking about the purposes of government in the United States.[19]

Theodore Roosevelt jumped at the opportunity to be a part of this transformation. After serving in the New York State Assembly, he moved to Washington, D.C. in 1889 to work as one of the new civil service commissioners. His six years in this role deeply influenced his rapid rise to the presidency and his reimagining of executive leadership. Roosevelt arrived in the nation's capital committed to expert governance, and he quickly developed a deep disdain for those—in agencies like the US Postal Service and the War Department—who resisted. He saw them as backward, unpatriotic, and ultimately threatening to the growth of the nation. Roosevelt came to believe that firm directives and public shaming from the Civil Service Commission, and eventually the president, were necessary to free government from the stranglehold of self-serving mediocrities.[20]

"My four months in Washington have made me more than ever a most zealous believer in the merit system," Roosevelt wrote to a prominent Boston newspaper editor in August 1889. "I do not see how any man can watch the effects of the spoils system, both upon poor unfortunates who suffer from it and upon the almost equally unfortunate men who deem that they benefit by it, without regarding the whole thing in its entirety as a curse to our institutions."[21]

Roosevelt's zealous effort to end the spoils system helped create more "merit" positions in the executive branch. Converting patronage jobs to merit involved a requirement of proven qualification, often by competitive examination, and a guarantee of job protection, even if the party in power changed. Emphasizing merit, the number of federal employees with high school and even college degrees rose during Roosevelt's tenure on the Civil Service Commission. It became harder to hire less qualified people because of the public scrutiny surrounding government employment. By the end of the nineteenth century more than half of the appointments in the executive branch were based on merit. Increased professionalism was evident in many agencies, especially the State Department, the War Department, and the US Postal Service.[22]

About half the federal government, including numerous cabinet secretaries, remained within the grasp of patronage appointments. That fact continued to frustrate Roosevelt and fellow progressives. Too many citizens viewed the executive branch as a source of jobs for favorites, not an incubator of creative policy. The federal government of the late nineteenth century remained lethargic, inefficient, and often quite corrupt. It was not a leader of reform or social improvement. That was evident in the personalities of the "dud presidents."

As a civil service commissioner seeking to transform government, Roosevelt failed, but he failed gloriously. Roosevelt raised attention to the corruption of government, and he identified himself as a leading advocate for fairness, talent, and effective performance. Already, he was *the* national figure—more than his fellow commissioners, or even Presidents Benjamin Harrison and Grover Cleveland—who championed the creation of a modern, progressive civil service.

Returning to New York City as a police commissioner, and then assuming the role of assistant secretary of the US Navy under President William McKinley, Roosevelt promoted an image of himself as the great reformer of government institutions. The reality often fell short, but his efforts were genuine and his accomplishments were real, if smaller than he admitted.

ROOSEVELT'S SELECTION AS WILLIAM McKINLEY'S VICE PRESIdential running mate in 1900 reflected his stature as a reformer and his national fame. McKinley envisioned a less active presidency than Roosevelt, but he shared the New Yorker's goal of making government more effective at supporting a rapidly expanding society. Fighting a war in 1898 against the declining Spanish Empire in Cuba, Puerto Rico, and the Philippines, McKinley sought to remove sources of instability from the Western Hemisphere and expand American market access in Asia. The Philippines would provide a powerful base for trade and influence around China; seizing Cuba and Puerto Rico insured American economic and military dominance in the Caribbean. In these regions, McKinley and his secretary of state, John Hay, feared encroachments by Britain and Germany. The world was getting too small for the rising powers, including the United States, and McKinley agreed with the advocates of "forward" American efforts to seize overseas beachheads for trade and security.[23]

Roosevelt was all about "forward" policies. He advocated for war against Spain, and he used his position as McKinley's assistant secretary of the navy to promote his views. He connected war with personal vigor and public devotion. Attacking the rich and self-satisfied yet again, he reminded listeners at the recently created Naval War College: "If we forget that in the last resort we can only secure peace by being ready and willing to fight for it, we may someday have bitter cause to realize that a rich nation which is slothful, timid, or unwieldy is an easy prey for any people which still retains those most valuable of all qualities, the soldierly virtues." Referring to the scramble for territory among European empires—as well as the legacies of Washington, Jackson, and Lincoln—he announced: "This Nation cannot stand still if it is to retain its self-respect, and to keep undimmed the honorable traditions inherited from the men who with the sword founded it and by the sword preserved it."[24]

For Roosevelt, war sustained his progressive vision. It provided an opportunity to prove American sophistication and manliness, and an avenue for spreading those qualities to "backward" societies. In his worldview, fighting Spain was part of his broader crusade to combat corruption, patronage, and unqualified leaders. Helping to build new independent societies, under American tutelage, reinforced the reforms Roosevelt advocated at home: expert governance, rational management of resources, industrial development, and tough individualism.

Demonstrating the "strenuous life" during fighting in Cuba and the Philippines would encourage the same in the United States, giving more influence to the men, like Roosevelt, who were self-consciously "in the arena."[25]

Hoping to make his mark, Roosevelt left his desk as assistant secretary of the navy at age 39, rustling together his own volunteer cavalry regiment, dubbed the "Rough Riders." They included an awkward mix of about one thousand Ivy League graduates, professional athletes, cowboys, miners, former soldiers, land prospectors, and even American Indians. Many had never seen battle; others had seen little else.

Roosevelt, who had never been a soldier but who now called himself "Colonel," organized his ragtag posse into a military unit. Although the main battle they fought, charging up San Juan Hill on 1 July 1898, was neither a military necessity nor a glorious victory, it solidified the image of the Rough Riders and Roosevelt as courageous fighters. They attacked the Spanish soldiers, Roosevelt later explained, not merely to win a battle, but to eradicate Madrid's baneful influence and bring American individualism, productivity, and rationality ("Americanism," as he called it) to former colonies.

Roosevelt also seized the opportunity to prove his skills as a leader. "I was not reckless," he recounted in exaggerated terms, "but with a regiment like this, and indeed I think with most regiments, the man in command must take all the risks which he asks his men to take if he is going to get the best work out of them." Roosevelt placed himself in the dangerous parts of the battlefield, where the action was most violent, unpredictable, and also exhilarating. Looking back many years later, he remembered: "San Juan was the great day of my life."[26]

AFTER A SHORT AND LARGELY UNEVENTFUL TWO YEARS AS GOVER-nor of New York, in March 1901 Roosevelt became the vice president of the United States. McKinley found the former Rough Rider irresistible as a running mate. Roosevelt was now the most prominent progressive in the country; he was also one of the most successful professional politicians. Except for his brief stint as commander of the Rough Riders, he had done nothing else.

As with previous (and later) vice presidents, Roosevelt felt constrained and ignored. For the first time, his professional responsibility—to follow the president's lead—conflicted with his progressive impulse to push, bully, and cajole. For the first time, Roosevelt had a disciplining boss, and it rattled a man whose appeal derived from his flamboyance and ceaseless challenging of banal authority. "You know," he wrote fellow Rough Rider, Leonard Wood, "the Vice-Presidency is an utterly anomalous office (one which I think ought to be abolished)." He mused about himself as a "politician whose day has passed; who by some turn of the kaleidoscope is thrown into the background; and who then haunts the fields of his former activity as a pale shadow of what he once was; or else who finds himself adrift in the hopeless position of the man who says he can do anything but who therefore can do nothing."[27]

McKinley's shocking assassination on 14 September 1901 lifted the constraints on Roosevelt, unleashing him to lead the nation as he had long hoped, and as no president had done before. "It is a dreadful thing to come into the Presidency this way," Roosevelt wrote, "but it would be a far worse thing to be morbid about it. Here is the task, and I have got to do it to the best of my ability." Clearly relishing the opportunity, despite the tragedy that made it possible, Roosevelt confided: "It is only a beginning, but it is better to make a beginning good than bad."[28]

ROOSEVELT BEGAN FAST. "UNDER OUR CONSTITUTION," HE ADMITTED, "there is much more scope for such action by the State and the municipality than by the nation." But, Roosevelt believed, "the National Government can act." He would turn the executive into the reformer-in-chief.[29]

His initial reforms focused on increasing federal regulations over large corporations ("trusts"), requiring more transparency about their decisions, increasing protections for forests and other federal lands, adding federal support for railways and other infrastructure, and strengthening the US military. He defended restrictions on immigration and police actions against alleged anarchist terrorists, and at the same time demanded investments in education and the uplift of disadvantaged communities, including African Americans and American Indians. He supported high tariffs to protect domestic industries, and he advocated for more treaties of "reciprocity" with other nations, encouraging increased foreign trade.

It was an ambitious agenda, especially for a man thrust into the presidency only a few weeks earlier. Roosevelt drew on more than a decade of his own progressive activism. His agenda was personal, and it reflected his impatient, bullying personality. Now that he was the national executive, he wanted to be *the* national policy-maker.

Although many of his programs were not new, they all included a newfound emphasis on leading American society from the office of the president. He would drive the main reform engine. Roosevelt called for cooperation from Congress, but he put himself in the clear lead, defining a new balance of power in favor of the federal executive. "When the Constitution was adopted, at the end of the eighteenth century," Roosevelt explained, "no human wisdom could foretell the sweeping changes, alike in industrial and political conditions, which were to take place by the beginning of the twentieth century. At that time it was accepted as a matter of course that the several States were the proper authorities to regulate." Referring to the development of commerce in particular, he declared: "The conditions are now wholly different and wholly different action is called for. I believe that a law can be framed which will enable the National Government to exercise control."[30]

When he spoke of the "National Government," Roosevelt meant himself. His reforms looked out from the Executive Mansion, which Roosevelt renamed the "White House." None of his proposals included major changes in the structure of governing institutions. Daily practice mattered for Roosevelt, and he intended from his first day as president to make the national executive the dominant actor in all parts of American life. This was a truly radical idea, resisted in the abstract by men like Mark Twain and even McKinley's closest aide, Mark Hanna, but made a reality by force of Roosevelt's personality and policy vision. Although his presidency claimed lineage stretching back to Lincoln, Jackson, and Washington, it was in fact a new model for the nation's executive—"modern" in the eyes of Roosevelt's many supporters, "dictatorial" according to his numerous critics.[31]

At 42, the youngest president in American history, Roosevelt often thought of himself as a dictator—a benevolent dictator (or "elective King") who would use his energy and expertise to improve democracy. This attitude was common among many progressives who believed that brains and virtue could improve a messy democratic process. Roosevelt and his fellow progressives were enthusiastic to expand executive power if it served the public, as they believed it would.[32]

The new president took on big business and the defenders of excess wealth he had long despised. Lincoln never did anything like this. If Roosevelt had a historical analogue for this domestic battle, it was Jackson. Roosevelt, however, did not seek to empower the downtrodden as Old Hickory had done, but to educate and regulate the elite on his own terms.

Roosevelt believed that the free market had allowed the biggest businessmen to grow too big, to become something akin to "barons of the twelfth century." The president would cut them down to size, allowing them to continue their productive work, but within limits set by the federal government to protect the public interest. "We had come to the stage," Roosevelt later wrote, "where for our people what was needed was real democracy," enforced by a powerful president against "the tyranny of a plutocracy." This was classic progressive language, taken in part from William Jennings Bryan and the populists. Roosevelt matched the tenacity of Bryan and other activists who never reached the White House.[33]

He immediately confronted the most powerful financier in America, J. P. Morgan. The New York banker provided much of the capital for the Northern Securities Company, a "trust" that consolidated the major railroad corporations in the northwestern region of the United States. The consolidation of these railroads facilitated price-fixing and other collusive practices, often at the cost of small businesspeople and farmers. Northern Securities was not the largest trust in the country, nor was it the only one financed by Morgan, but it was a dominant actor west of the Great Lakes. If you did business in that region, you had to use the rail lines owned by Northern Securities; they had a virtual monopoly.[34]

Roosevelt ordered his reluctant attorney general (and former railroad lawyer), Philander Knox, to prosecute Northern Securities under the Sherman Anti-Trust Act, which had been dormant since its passage by Congress in 1890. The Department of Justice sued Northern Securities in the Minneapolis federal court in 1902. The case made its way to the Supreme Court two years later, where the justices ruled five-to-four in favor of the federal government and its newly asserted authority to break up interstate trusts that limited economic competition. Echoing Roosevelt and writing for the majority on the Supreme Court, Justice John Marshall Harlan explained: "The combination here in question may have been for the pecuniary benefit of those who formed or caused it to be formed. But the interests of private persons and corporations cannot be made paramount to the interests of the general public."[35]

Roosevelt's commitment to break up the trusts and assert presidential power over the economy made this fundamental shift in American anti-monopoly policy possible. It would not have happened if McKinley had survived the assassin's bullets. Roosevelt followed his own rhetoric, seeking to clean out corruption, empower experts, and open opportunities for men "in the arena"—particularly the businesspeople, farmers, and other citizens who did not want to be held hostage by a railway monopoly. He made himself the prosecutor of misused wealth and distorted power, and he personally challenged influential figures to live up to the progressive ideals that he espoused. Roosevelt was not attacking inequality, but privilege, degeneracy, and what he saw as elite backwardness (he called men like Morgan "aristocrats"). Dismantling monopolies, Roosevelt contended, would allow for more merit, more vitality, and more growth. He made this a personal mission for his presidency.[36]

THE SAME LOGIC MOTIVATED ROOSEVELT TO MEDIATE, AS NO president had before, between the owners and workers in America's coal mines. In 1894 President Grover Cleveland had used his office to protect order and defend property owners during the Pullman railroad strike. For Cleveland and his predecessors, the president had a duty to act as a policeman during domestic disputes.

When more than 140,000 miners in Pennsylvania left work demanding higher wages, Roosevelt remade the role of the president. He inserted himself as a negotiator in 1902, shaping a settlement on behalf of workers, including thousands of immigrants. He did this by drawing on the expertise of labor activists, including progressive journalist Jacob Riis. Roosevelt met frequently with union leaders and business owners, he solicited the opinions of experts, and he contemplated a range of policy scenarios. Above all, he took personal responsibility for this domestic labor problem, asserting executive power over production, wages, and even private property in the name of the national interest. He had very limited constitutional authority for his actions, but that did not matter to him, or to most Americans.

Roosevelt recognized that coal, quite literally, fueled early twentieth-century America. The strike that began in the spring of 1902 led to higher coal prices, which slowed economic growth. It also risked triggering heating shortages that winter. Roosevelt understood that other industries—oil, the railroads, manufacturing—looked to the labor strife around the coal mines as a sign of what was to come for them.

To the frustration of the mine owners, Roosevelt expressed sympathy for the workers who labored underground in difficult conditions for low wages. He had read enough progressive literature to understand the poor circumstances of many workers, and he believed that higher wages would encourage better living conditions and more patriotic citizenship. Roosevelt wanted mine workers to have the opportunity to improve themselves and to see their jobs as more than the drudgery that limited aspirations in their communities. Unlike other presidents, Roosevelt deeply respected the manual labor of the mine workers, and he made sure they knew that.

Of course, the president also respected the private property and business investments of the mine owners and their financial backers. Roosevelt met frequently with them, and he worked sincerely to understand their position. Men like J. P. Morgan and many others had a lot invested in the mines, and they faced increasing pressure to dig more coal at lower cost. Most important, the mine owners feared labor unrest that would jeopardize their businesses, and for that reason they opposed the demands of the United Mine Workers Union. The precedent the strikers were setting was too dangerous; mine owners did not believe the union had a right to exist. They saw it as an anarchist, or even socialist, institution.

The mine owners wanted the support of the president for a military solution to the strike. This was the model from Cleveland's time in office. Roosevelt refused and forced the owners and workers to accept a presidentially appointed arbitration commission that included five men: a military engineer, a mining engineer, a judge, an expert in the coal business, and an "eminent sociologist" (who was actually a labor leader). This was another classic progressive solution to a social problem: relying on an impartial and representative expert panel to adjudicate a dispute. Roosevelt leaned heavily on J. P. Morgan to coerce the mine owners into accepting the commission, which they eventually did in late October 1902.

The commission spent five months examining the mines in Pennsylvania, holding public hearings, and interviewing more than five hundred people—including workers, union organizers, and family members. In a stunning move, on 22 March 1903, the commission announced its recommendation that the mine workers should receive their requested 10 percent pay increase, as well as guarantees of a workday not exceeding nine hours. As Roosevelt predicted, the commission argued that better pay and work conditions would improve health and safety for the entire industry. The commission did not force the mine owners to recognize the United Mine Workers Union, but the workers' demands had received unprecedented attention. It was now impossible to deny their representation in future negotiations.

Roosevelt left no room for the mine owners to reject the arbitrated agreement. They risked not only alienation from a sometimes-vengeful president, but also a barrage of other possible pressures from a more active federal government. The mine owners accepted the settlement because Roosevelt made it the least bad alternative for them. To their surprise, he had legitimized the demands of the workers and used his executive office to promote the interests of labor, not just the protection of business and property. No other president had interceded like this before.

Business interests remained influential, but they confronted a newly empowered counterbalance in labor and an unprecedented arbitrating force in a president who injected himself personally into that role. Roosevelt used his executive power to promise fairness for previously ignored actors. His progressivism motivated him to see the expansion of presidential involvement in the economy as a mechanism for strengthening democracy, capitalism, and the overall prosperity of the republic.

ROOSEVELT VIEWED THE NATION AS AN ORGANIC BODY, EQUALLY dependent on its strongest and weakest elements. The president was more than a father figure or a national defender; he was a personal arbiter for the constituent parts. This executive responsibility meant improving life for all citizens—workers, farmers, racial minorities, and business owners. It also meant expanding opportunities for ambitious citizens to act in pursuit of their own interests and the public good. A progressive president used his power to insure cooperation between individuals and the broader nation.

In this context, Roosevelt was the first president to think of the executive as a provider, as well as a protector, of the public "welfare." He used the word more forcefully than any of his predecessors, and he presented it as one of the purposes of strong executive power. "The welfare of each of us is dependent," Roosevelt announced, "upon the welfare of all of us."[37]

He famously promised to help each citizen get a "square deal": "Among ourselves we differ in many qualities of body, head, and heart; we are unequally developed, mentally as well as physically." "Far and away," Roosevelt explained, "the best prize that life offers is the chance to work hard at work worth doing; and this is a prize open to every man."[38]

No other president had promised citizens a "deal" before. Washington had offered fatherly guidance, Jackson had provided popular access to power, and Lincoln had defended an expanded vision of freedom. None of them had given citizens anything directly. Now Roosevelt pledged to contribute to the public welfare through a series of executive initiatives.

He began by breaking up trusts (like Northern Securities) and defending worker rights (as he did for the United Mine Workers). And then, in his second term as president, Roosevelt went much further, launching a series of aggressive initiatives to protect less advantaged citizens, farms, and businesses against the biggest actors in the American economy.

Roosevelt started with the land. More than any president before him, he used the power of the presidency to create public lands that would guarantee men and women the opportunity to remake themselves, as he had done himself, growing from a sickly boy into a confident leader. Public lands would provide areas free from the dominance of big businesses and large labor unions, where individuals could breathe, pursue adventure, and, most of all, think and improve themselves. The public lands would become a foundational resource for the men and women whom Roosevelt wanted to empower "in the arena" of an urbanizing national behemoth. Building on the frontier-expanding efforts of Andrew Jackson and others, Roosevelt turned the presidency into a frontier-conserving institution, protecting resources and freedoms for those pressured (and often coerced) by more powerful actors. The expanding frontiers of public land, driven by the chief executive, were the setting for every citizen to get his or her square deal.

The president was tenacious in turning land over to the public for perpetuity. By executive act he designated more than 200 million acres of land (more territory than the current state of Texas) for the improvement of citizens. They were to have equal access, regardless of income or background. They were to use the land for their enjoyment, their growth, and their experience of the "strenuous life."

To manage the new public lands on behalf of the people, Roosevelt created a new executive agency in 1905: the US Forest Service. Gifford Pinchot served as its first chief, and he reported directly to the president. They were long-time friends, fellow progressives, and committed, in Pinchot's words, to putting the land into the "service of man." This meant preserving access and also using the land, through dam development and other technologies, to generate energy resources for citizens with diverse needs.[39]

Roosevelt and Pinchot worked to preserve pristine forests and rivers, while they also supported prosperous lumber mills, factories, and towns. They used government resources and regulatory laws (often issued as executive orders, signed by the president) to insure the maximum benefits for the largest number of citizens. They pursued "progress" through preservation and production, balanced by enlightened executive leadership. "There is an intimate relation," Roosevelt extolled, "between our streams and the development and conservation of all the other great permanent sources of wealth. It is not possible rightly to consider the one without the other."[40]

"Good laws," the president elaborated, "can do much good; indeed, they are often indispensable. There is urgent need that we should have honest and efficient legislation and honest and efficient action by those whose province it is to put the legislation into effect." The president and his new Forest Service would cultivate the honesty, efficiency, and foresight to turn land to value for each and every citizen. Great leaders around the White House would make good laws.[41]

ROOSEVELT WENT BEYOND LAND REFORM AND TRUST-BUSTING. As the central piece of his square deal, he pressured fellow Republicans and opposition Democrats in Congress to pass legislation that would control the rates that railroad companies—the largest corporations in the country—charged to move people and products across the land. Tighter regulation of shipping and industry was a long standing proposal from progressives, many of whom had initially looked to state and local governments for action. Roosevelt nationalized the idea, using a more energetic presidency to push protections for small producers and consumers across the country, while at the same time allowing large corporations to grow and prosper.

Under the Hepburn Act, passed in 1906 and named for Iowa Congressman William Hepburn, the federal government would now determine "just and reasonable maximum rates" for railroad charges. The executive branch, following Roosevelt's progressive leadership, used the new legislation to review railroad company accounts and practices, open them to public comment, and supervise related industries, including the rapidly multiplying oil pipelines across the country.

The Interstate Commerce Commission (ICC), initially created in 1887 but weak until Roosevelt's presidency, served as the expert investigator and enforcer of the new regulations. The president appointed the five individuals who served on the ICC, and although he had little direct control over their actions, they worked as part of his larger executive branch, responding to the general guidelines he issued for enforcing the laws of the land. As a powerful presidentially appointed administrative body, the ICC extended the reach of the man in the White House. The president became a price-setter for producers and consumers, taming the free market as never before.[42]

Washington, Jackson, and Lincoln never aimed to transform the public regulation of industry, as Roosevelt did, and they never achieved as much in this or any related domestic policy area. Roosevelt's progressive achievements were truly unprecedented; they re-made the national executive. For all of their continued limitations, the Hepburn Act and the ICC opened the door for a century of similar regulatory efforts, through presidentially appointed expert commissions, in communications (the Federal Communications Commission, created in 1934), aviation (the Civil Aeronautics Board, created in 1940 and replaced by the Federal Aviation Administration in 1958), and product safety (the US Consumer Product Safety Commission, created in 1972), among many others.

Today, Americans can rely on safe and affordable communications, air travel, and consumer products because of Theodore Roosevelt's decisive expansion of presidential power into domestic regulation. Not only that, but his square deal laid the foundation for the New Deal and much that has come after it. This was an unimaginable trajectory, even for the most active and successful presidents who preceded the nation's first progressive executive.[43]

PROGRESSIVE LEADERSHIP DID NOT NECESSARILY IMPLY PEACE-making. Roosevelt was a skilled negotiator, but he associated force as much as diplomacy with effective presidential action. In a competitive global setting, rife with promising partners and dangerous adversaries, Roosevelt perceived military power as an absolute necessity for security, prosperity, and justice. The United States could not dominate the world, and Roosevelt affirmed John Quincy Adams's famous warning against going abroad "in search of monsters to destroy." Roosevelt believed the United States had to develop enough power to enforce a balance between competing nations, encouraging cooperation and deterring aggression. Rising international capabilities would allow the United States to become, in Roosevelt's words, "more and more the balance of power of the whole world." [44]

Roosevelt was the first commander-in-chief to think globally. He sought to expand the American armed forces, particularly the US Navy, which could counteract efforts by other nations—especially Germany, Russia, and Japan—to grab territory and oppress occupied citizens. Roosevelt favored an approach in the tradition of British imperial policing, which was designed to maintain stability in important regions; he prepared for the United States to replace Britain as global "balancer" where necessary. As president, he intervened through military and non-military action far from American shores, negotiating with other powerful nations, and prioritizing order and access above democracy and justice. In contrast to the more inwardly focused presidencies of Washington, Jackson, and Lincoln, Roosevelt believed that the American executive had to wield a "big stick" to manage multiplying sources of international conflict. His was the first imperial presidency. [45]

Roosevelt made construction and deployment of American warships a priority. The United States had never possessed a world-class navy, generally favoring a smaller merchant marine to protect commercial shipping instead. With the exception of the Civil War, Americans sought to keep their military forces small, divided (the Constitution separated war-making between the departments of war and navy), and close to home. The president was commander-in-chief, but there was not very much to command. The leaders of foreign powers—in England, France, Germany, Japan, and elsewhere—looked upon the United States as a weak, sometimes irrelevant, international actor.

Roosevelt changed that. He naturally looked to the navy because it was the branch of the military he knew best. He also associated the sea with the "strenuous life." Throughout his presidency, Roosevelt promoted investments in what he called the "surest guaranty of peace"—which to him meant "a first-class fleet of first-class battleships." Washington and Jackson were army men, even if the armies under their executive command were not large; Roosevelt was the first to define a navy-focused presidency.[46]

Alfred Thayer Mahan, a somewhat obscure US Navy captain who wrote *The Influence of Sea Power Upon History*, became a spokesman for Roosevelt's strategic vision. Mahan helped promote a large navy as necessary for American growth, not just defense, which made it difficult for critics in Congress to oppose. He gave historical legitimacy to the president's advocacy of the "strenuous life," but now on the water.[47]

For all their eloquence, however, Mahan's and Roosevelt's aspirations exceeded what was possible. The US Navy remained inferior to its British, German, and French peers during Roosevelt's presidency (and until after the First World War). Still, Roosevelt changed the terms of debate and the role of the commander-in-chief. Moving well beyond territorial defense and the protection of shipping, he used the nation's enlarged naval capabilities to display America's emerging power. Although he did not threaten war, Roosevelt militarized the growing American presence abroad. He also gave American foreign policy a more aggressive edge, bringing potential power to allies and adversaries alike.

Between December 1907 and February 1909 the president sent a fleet of sixteen modern battleships and escort vessels around the world: to Brazil, Chile, Australia, Japan, China, the Philippines, and other distant ports of call. Roosevelt had the ships painted bright white—the "Great White Fleet"—to symbolize the purity of American power. In typical bombast, he compensated for past inferiorities by flexing newfound muscle, and promised peace for all friends who respected American power.

On the triumphant return of the fleet to the Atlantic coast, the president proclaimed to the sailors: "Other nations may do as you have done, but they'll have to follow you." The United States was now a self-proclaimed international leader; the respect for the president's power had increased abroad and at home. The nation's commander-in-chief had more obvious "bullying" authority, although his bark remained greater than his bite.[48]

ROOSEVELT PERCEIVED HIS INTERNATIONAL POLICIES COMPLEmenting his reform agenda at home; this foreign-domestic reform connection created a model for future presidents, especially his cousin Franklin. Theodore Roosevelt pursued peace through strength overseas, more avenues for American profit and security, and an expansion of "civilizing" forces. His international vision combined elements of nationalism, internationalism, and imperialism. It was realistic in its emphasis on national interests, but it was also idealistic in its desire to bring progress to the world. Roosevelt believed that just as the smartest and strongest citizens could improve American society, they could do the same for other peoples and cultures, especially those who were still "backward" in his view. Roosevelt redefined the purpose of the presidency with his mix of international realism and idealism.[49]

The most important example of Roosevelt's worldview emerged during a war between Japan and Russia. Fighting in the Pacific and on the Asian mainland in 1904 and 1905, Japan seized control of the Korean peninsula, Port Arthur on the Yellow Sea, parts of resource-rich Manchuria, and a number of disputed islands in the Sea of Japan. The war between Japan and Russia contributed to the fall of the last Chinese imperial dynasty and the decades-old European spheres of influence around China, negotiated primarily between Britain, France, Russia, and Portugal. In the early twentieth century, East Asia was on the verge of a larger civil war with global implications.[50]

Roosevelt inserted himself into this conflict, approaching the Japanese leadership about negotiating a settlement that would bring the fighting to an end and secure their victories. Although wary of growing Japanese power in Asia, Roosevelt also had deep respect for the accomplishments of the island nation, and he generally held Russian society in much lower regard. The president worked hard, however, to include the tsar and his government in the negotiations, promising that an agreed peace would help preserve the Romanov family's power over Russia, at least a little longer.

Roosevelt convinced the monarchs in Tokyo and St. Petersburg to send their closest foreign policy advisors to the seaside town of Portsmouth, New Hampshire, where they could negotiate in secrecy. The delegates arrived in early August 1905, and they met throughout the month. Roosevelt played a personal role in the negotiations, using his charm and wit to encourage the attendees to forge a compromise. He created a shared "spirit" of Portsmouth among the belligerents, now seeking a mutually beneficial settlement.[51]

The Portsmouth Treaty, signed on 5 September 1905, gave Japan permanent control of the valuable territories it had conquered, including the entire Korean peninsula and the southern part of Manchuria. Japan now dominated trade in the region through its occupation of Port Arthur and the railway connecting this sea landing with the Manchurian hinterland. A few decades later, the Japanese would use this strategic position to attack the mainland of China. At Roosevelt's insistence, the Japanese withdrew their demands for a cash indemnity from Russia to cover the costs of the war. This was a crucial concession to the tsar's near bankrupt treasury.[52]

After signing the treaty, the tsar continued his military and industrial modernization program, especially in northern Manchuria. Russia invested heavily in postwar railway building, furthering work on the Trans-Siberian rail line, completed in 1916. Japan became the dominant power around the Korean peninsula, but Russia maintained its strength in the wider landed region. Roosevelt envisioned these circumstances as a rough balance of power that could promote lasting stability and increased American access to the region for trade.

The American president had mediated what he believed was a peace where "each power will be in a sense the guarantor of the other's good conduct." He expected the United States to maintain friendly and profitable relations with both Tokyo and St. Petersburg. He also hoped that the increased stature of the presidency would expand American leverage in other regions of conflict, particularly in North Africa and in Venezuela, two areas where Roosevelt also sought, with less success, to mediate between aggressive foreign powers.[53]

Roosevelt believed that the American president had the power and distance from imperial conflicts to become the world's chief diplomat. For a time, he managed this feat, and he created a foundation for his successors to do the same. Roosevelt rejected what had been the traditional American aversion to great power politics, held by Washington, Jackson, and Lincoln alike. Roosevelt's diplomatic internationalism did more than anything before his time to globalize the American presidency.

For his efforts, Roosevelt received the Nobel Peace prize in 1906, becoming the first American to win the award. The Nobel committee praised Roosevelt's work to build peace through arbitration, compromise, and negotiation in areas of dangerous conflict—while ignoring his frequent bluster and bullying. The committee acknowledged the American presidency as an office with unique diplomatic possibilities.

Accepting his award in Oslo in May 1910, by which time he had left office, Roosevelt sought to define his legacy. He emphasized his—and his nation's—combination of strength and negotiation, righteousness and compromise. He described his efforts as the pursuit of the "strenuous life" through active, even muscular, peace-making. All of his accumulated thoughts about politics and the presidency, as well as force and democracy, came together in his explanation of what peace meant in global terms:

> We must ever bear in mind that the great end in view is righteousness, justice as between man and man, nation and nation, the chance to lead our lives on a somewhat higher level, with a broader spirit of brotherly goodwill one for another. Peace is generally good in itself, but it is never the highest good unless it comes as the handmaid of righteousness; and it becomes a very evil thing if it serves merely as a mask for cowardice and sloth, or as an instrument to further the ends of despotism or anarchy. We despise and abhor the bully, the brawler, the oppressor, whether in private or public life, but we despise no less the coward and the voluptuary. No man is worth calling a man who

will not fight rather than submit to infamy or see those that are dear to him suffer wrong. No nation deserves to exist if it permits itself to lose the stern and virile virtues; and this without regard to whether the loss is due to the growth of a heartless and all-absorbing commercialism, to prolonged indulgence in luxury and soft, effortless ease, or to the deification of a warped and twisted sentimentality.[54]

Roosevelt went on to propose a new international institution to help enforce his vision of peace. He called upon the leaders of the great powers, including the United States, to "form a League of Peace, not only to keep the peace among themselves, but to prevent, by force if necessary, its being broken by others." As he explained, "Each nation must keep well prepared to defend itself until the establishment of some form of international police power, competent and willing to prevent violence as between nations."[55]

Roosevelt was not the first to propose a "League of Peace" among the most powerful states. The idea dated to the Congress of Vienna in 1815, and Roosevelt noted the influence of the Hague Peace Conferences in the late nineteenth and early twentieth centuries. For the first time, however, Roosevelt placed the American presidency at the center of this effort. He saw the international "League" as a natural outgrowth of his progressive reforms at home—breaking old corrupt and degenerate monopolies. Most of all, Roosevelt perceived American leadership in a "League" of civilized states as a foundation for future American security and prosperity.[56]

Roosevelt's internationalism set an enduring precedent for the American presidency (but not for the Congress and other parts of American society). His successors—Presidents William Howard Taft and Woodrow Wilson—pursued similar forms of internationalism. Both supported what became the League of Nations after the First World War. Both defined the United States as an international arbitrator among the major powers. Even future presidents who expressed misgivings about American international leadership—including President Herbert Hoover—defended Roosevelt's enduring call for American participation in cooperative efforts "to secure peace within certain definite limits and on certain definite conditions."[57]

Roosevelt made the president into an international peacemaker for the next century. He enhanced the presence of American ideas, arms, products, and other influences across the globe, on a scale unthinkable for prior leaders of the nation. Roosevelt globalized the American presidency, with very mixed results.[58]

ONE OF THE PERNICIOUS LEGACIES OF ROOSEVELT'S INTERNA-tionalism originated in his hierarchical worldview. His prejudices, which mirrored those of American society at large, justified inequalities in power, wealth, and voice in political decision-making. They excluded many "backward" peoples from "great power" cooperation, and they rationalized exploitation, empire, and even mass killing. Roosevelt embodied the progressive urge to improve less developed societies and races, but his concept of improvement reflected the paternalism of elites who felt themselves authorized to dictate how "lesser" peoples should live. As Roosevelt strove to make the United States an equal actor with European and Japanese counterparts, he asserted American superiority over others, especially in Central and South America. Roosevelt's internationalism encouraged American militarism south of the border, and it also made the American president into a frequent Latin dictator. Roosevelt's successors would carry forward his assumptions and behavior patterns within the Western Hemisphere.[59]

Well-traveled and conversant in German and French (as well as some Italian), Roosevelt believed the world's "civilizations" were interdependent but unevenly developed. He used the term "civilization" as other learned cosmopolitans did at the time: to encompass culture, economy, and leadership. It carried racial and regional assumptions—favoring light-skinned Europeans over dark-skinned Africans—but had more to do with learning and governance than inherited characteristics. For Roosevelt, civilization meant discipline, unity, knowledge, and strength. Civilized peoples knew who they were, worked together, had advanced ideas, and were able to wield power for their purposes. As a term, civilization included common virtues, shared purposes, and collective muscularity—in spirit and in bodies. Although nations and empires mattered enormously to Roosevelt, he believed that the sources of power resided in the conjunction of traditions, ideas, practices, and institutions that distinguished one group of people from another.[60]

American perceptions that the residents of the Philippines were "uncivilized" underpinned Roosevelt's justification for invasion and occupation of the archipelago after 1898. Similar views drove his efforts to enforce American dominance in the Western Hemisphere. As he called for cooperation in Europe and Asia, he demanded direct American rule closer to home. He saw hemispheric dominance, often through the military, as part of the frontier-expanding and civilizing role of the progressive presidency.

Building on the Monroe Doctrine, which in 1823 had asserted an American prohibition on new European colonies in the Western Hemisphere, Roosevelt expanded the writ of the president to enforce favorable conditions for the United States in Latin America. That often meant direct military intervention in places, including Cuba and the Dominican Republic, as well as demands for American-led arbitration in, most notably, Venezuela. Throughout the region, from Mexico to Argentina and Brazil, Roosevelt asserted American power, often neglecting concerns about sovereignty and democracy; Roosevelt's primary goal was to protect the interests of the United States. He wanted to expose the region to the disciplined, productive, "strenuous life" of American civilization, but he did not trust that this would happen without external American control. Roosevelt feared that the selfish and degenerate qualities he criticized within American society would predominate more easily in less "civilized" areas due to a combination of harmful local traditions and exploitative foreign influences, especially the European imperial powers.[61]

In his December 1904 State of the Union message, Roosevelt claimed exclusive presidential "civilizing" powers in the Western Hemisphere. This was an effort to protect American interests, push progressive reforms, and undermine domestic objections to expansionist policies. "It is not true," Roosevelt wrote, "that the United States feels any land hunger or entertains any projects as regards the other nations of the Western Hemisphere save such as are for their welfare. All that this country desires is to see the neighboring countries stable, orderly, and prosperous." To Roosevelt and other progressives, these last three words had specific meaning: "If a nation shows that it knows how to act with reasonable efficiency and decency in social and political matters, if it keeps order and pays its obligations, it need fear no interference from the United States."

The causes for decisive action arose, according to Roosevelt, when nations geographically close to the United States did not follow these strictures.

> Chronic wrongdoing, or an impotence which results in a general loosening of the ties of civilized society, may in America, as elsewhere, ultimately require intervention by some civilized nation, and in the Western Hemisphere the adherence of the United States to the Monroe Doctrine may force the United States, however reluctantly, in flagrant cases of such wrongdoing or impotence, to the exercise of an international police power.
>
> …Our interests and those of our southern neighbors are in reality identical. They have great natural riches, and if within their borders the reign of law and justice obtains, prosperity is sure to come to them. While they thus obey the primary laws of civilized society they may rest assured that they will be treated by us in a spirit of cordial and helpful sympathy. We would interfere with them only in the last resort, and then only if it became evident that their inability or unwillingness to do justice at home and abroad had violated the rights of the United States or had invited foreign aggression to the detriment of the entire body of American nations.[62]

Observers referred to this statement—combining a dogmatic definition of "civilization" with an assertion of unilateral American power—as the "Roosevelt Corollary" to the Monroe Doctrine. Roosevelt expanded the meaning of President James Monroe's warning against renewed colonialism in the Western Hemisphere. For most of the nineteenth century, the United States had no mechanism for enforcing Monroe's words, relying instead upon cooperation from the British Navy. Now, with Roosevelt's announcement, the president pledged to use the nation's enlarged navy (and army) to enforce American-supported laws and expectations through direct military intervention.

Roosevelt declared that the United States had the right to act as an "international police power" in the Western Hemisphere.

The president did not hesitate to implement his words. By late 1903 he had already dispatched American warships to the Caribbean waters northwest of Colombia, encouraging the citizens of the Panamanian isthmus to declare their independence. The US Senate had passed legislation authorizing the construction of an artificial canal through Panama, providing a navigable channel between the Atlantic and Pacific Oceans that would save more than 7,000 miles for ships traveling between the East and West coasts of the United States. The initial plan was to work with the Colombian government, which controlled Panama, but when the Colombian government rejected the American proposal, Roosevelt intervened to separate Panama from Colombia and coerce the new (and vulnerable) state into serving his "civilizing" purposes.

On 18 November 1903 Secretary of State John Hay signed a treaty with the American-approved diplomatic representative of Panama, Philippe-Jean Bunau-Varilla, granting the United States control of a ten-mile wide zone for canal construction. The Roosevelt administration agreed to pay the Panamanian state $10 million for the land, plus an additional $250,000 each year. Most important, the United States guaranteed the independence of Panama in return for the right to build and operate the desired canal.[63]

Through this deal, President Roosevelt transformed the landscape of Central America by force of arms and money. He trampled the expressed claims of the Colombian and other governments in the region. Although Roosevelt believed that the canal would bring valuable economic activity to the region for "civilizing" purposes, he clearly acted to place American needs above those of others. The canal was a bold act of American "policing power" that Roosevelt justified in December 1904. The Roosevelt Corollary advocated what looked to many like American imperialism in the name of "civilization."[64]

FOLLOWING MORE THAN A DECADE OF ARDUOUS LABOR AND ADvanced engineering, the Panama Canal opened in August 1914, a triumph of Roosevelt's vision for the presidency, even if he was, by this time, no longer the nation's chief executive. The ambition to acquire the land and remake it on a monumental scale was evidence of Roosevelt's active, bullying leadership. Neither the founders nor any of his other predecessors had imagined a presidency with such power and scope. Roosevelt's vision for the office is the first that looks familiar to us today.

The Roosevelt presidency added direct action and aggressive problem-solving to the dignity of Washington, the populism of Jackson, and the eloquence of Lincoln. Roosevelt's presidency was more powerful and more focused on specific national needs than any before. Roosevelt's presidency was also more global and local at the same time. He combined force with diplomacy, and elite leadership with conspicuous attacks on aristocracy and monopoly. Ever since Roosevelt left office, the nation and its executive have been more committed to mastering the world and spreading American influence.

Roosevelt's successors never looked back. Woodrow Wilson, despite his profound enmity toward his rival, presided over the opening of the Panama Canal. Wilson continued to expand the progressive ambitions of Roosevelt's presidency in regulating the economy through the creation of the Federal Reserve and defending "civilization" abroad through participation in World War I and the Versailles Settlement. In the interwar years, Secretary of Commerce and then President Herbert Hoover used the executive to protect domestic industries and open foreign markets.[65]

Roosevelt's presidency defined the policy agenda of the progressives who followed him. They were unique figures in their time. They transformed a sleepy post-Civil War America into a dynamo driven, above all, by a forceful and dynamic president—a true chief executive for national affairs.

Theodore Roosevelt was the first progressive president, and his cousin Franklin would soon move the office beyond progressivism to embrace a broader definition of the public welfare. Theodore made the president a master of complex policies; Franklin turned policy mastery into public nurturing, especially in hard times.

Theodore Roosevelt's advocacy of the "strenuous life" created a most strenuous presidency. He increased the speed, range, and impact of the nation's executive as a catalyst for domestic and international change. His presidency took on massive new responsibilities, from breaking up trusts and mediating strikes to negotiating foreign settlements and building a two-ocean canal. Theodore Roosevelt was a progressive, but he was also hyper-interventionist in all areas of policy. There was so much of him, and he affected nearly every major issue of his day.

Future presidents would be expected to do the same. Few would have Theodore Roosevelt's energy and skill; even fewer would have his vision of a better nation for all. Theodore Roosevelt's progressive presidency made Franklin Roosevelt's New Deal presidency possible, and necessary.

CHAPTER 6

National Healer

I can recall walking eastward on the Chicago Midway on a summer evening...drivers had pulled over, parking bumper to bumper, and turned on their radios to hear Roosevelt. They had rolled down the windows and opened the car doors. Everywhere the same voice, its odd Eastern accent, which in anyone else would have irritated Midwesterners. You could follow without missing a single word as you strolled by. You felt joined to these unknown drivers, men and women smoking their cigarettes in silence, not so much considering the President's words as affirming the rightness of his tone and taking assurance from it.

Saul Bellow, 1983[1]

A Russian-Jewish immigrant who came to the polyglot city of Chicago—bursting at its seams with young, ambitious strivers—Saul Bellow did not initially look to the American president for inspiration or assistance. The prosperous white Christian men of marble who had run the country were distant, dull, and largely irrelevant for an ethnic Chicagoan struggling to survive in one of the world's most competitive, crowded, violent cities.

Bellow remembered President Herbert Hoover's inauguration with the contempt of a street-side tough. "I knew what he looked like. His hair was parted down the middle, he wore a high collar and a top hat that looked like Mr. Tomato on the College Inn juice bottle. Full and sedate, he was one of those balanced and solid engineering-and-money types who would maintain the secure Republican reign of Silent Cal [President Calvin Coolidge], the successor of the unhappy Harding [President Warren Harding]."[2]

Bellow remembered how foreign the entire presidential spectacle seemed to a newly Americanized arrival who thought of democracy in terms of daily struggle. The real-lived Chicago—"a sprawling network of immigrant villages smelling of sauerkraut and home-brewed beer, of meat processing and soap manufacture"—was far removed from the "stale" national politics that did not mean much to Bellow, his buddies, or most of those around them. Immigrants in Chicago and other growing cities voted in elections, as they were told by their local bosses, but they did not expect much in return, especially from the elites in the White House. National politics was just another scam.[3]

The crash of the stock market on 29 October 1929 revealed as much. Those who had worked hard and saved for their families lost everything. Those who had climbed the competitive ladder of success fell fast and hard. Even families with inherited wealth found themselves living in threadbare circumstances. If getting rich had been a scam from the start, then losing it all was cruel justice. The hard times unmasked the hypocrisy and hubris of those who lived on high.

"The Great Depression was a time of personal humiliation for those who had worked and lived in respectable prosperity," Bellow remembered, "but for the young this faltering of order and authority made possible an escape from family and routine." Bellow was one of thousands to ride the nation's trains as a hobo, joining the swelling ranks of migratory workers living without security, but also without rigid rules. Presidents and other national leaders mattered less and less to this tramping world. Herbert Hoover—the "great engineer"—did not pull any of the gears that mattered for Bellow and his friends on the road.[4]

THE CAUSES OF THE GREAT DEPRESSION WERE ROOTED IN A rapidly growing population and an expanding economy. Bellow's Chi-

cago was ground zero for these changes. The gargantuan meat processing and soap manufacturing on the shores of Lake Michigan integrated
the work of millions of bankers, farmers, factory workers, and consumers across multiple continents. The scale of what Bellow perceived as an
economic "scam" (what others called the "market") drowned the scam-
mers themselves. There was no effective scammer-in-chief (or "executive") who could understand it all and maintain control.

Booms and busts had been common in prior decades, but this time
was different. The amount of wealth lost, the rapidity of its disappearance, and the number of people affected exceeded any previous experience. The spiraling decline that followed made it difficult for even the
most sophisticated observers to avoid panic. The more you had, the more
you lost. Every self-preserving reaction seemed to contribute to spreading devastation. In the past, powerful figures (like the banker J. P. Morgan) had stepped forward to bolster the market through new injections
of capital; now, no one had enough money or influence to turn things
around. The market was too vast, too multilayered. For those alive at the
time, it felt like citizens were trying to swim against an onrushing river.
The current carried even the strongest individuals downstream.

Beyond the spiraling economic devastation, the deepest problem was
intellectual. Many of the citizens who lost their jobs, their homes, and
their basic means of sustenance did not understand what was happening.
How could all the money dry up? How could prosperous communities in
North America and Europe become so poverty stricken? Local farmers
and businesspeople had not done anything wrong. They had continued to
cultivate their land and trade their goods. They had, for the most part, been
good stewards of the capital invested in their communities. The problem
came from somewhere else, but they did not understand where or why.

The system of trade and exchange across continents had become so
complex that no one really understood what drove the precipitous
economic decline. This was true of the most learned analysts, including the famous English polymath, John Maynard Keynes. Months
before the crash he had predicted continued growth in wealth and
leisure time for ordinary citizens, who would, Keynes anticipated, feed
and clothe their families working fewer hours each day. The opposite
was the case in the 1930s.[5]

For leaders of all kinds, the Great Depression was an existential challenge. How could they lead when they could not comprehend the drivers of current difficulties? Most officials abandoned hopes of "solving" the problem and turned instead to tactics aimed at stopping, or at least slowing, the bleeding. In Germany, Italy, and Japan this entailed redoubled government efforts to seize scarce resources from domestic owners and foreign populations. In the Soviet Union, Josef Stalin forced citizens, frequently at the cost of their lives, to give nearly everything they owned to the state. Both the fascists and communists dispossessed wealth from minority groups and political dissenters. These were regimes that trampled freedom for short-term sustenance.

President Herbert Hoover resisted these dangerous tendencies. A successful businessman who had risen through hard work from his poor, orphaned childhood, Hoover conceived of leadership as arbitration and guidance. He saw himself primarily as an engineer who could steer different parts of the economy to work together. The director of the American Relief Administration in Europe after the First World War, and then US Secretary of Commerce in the 1920s, Hoover had done precisely that. He had heroically fed starving citizens in Belgium and Russia by convincing Midwestern farmers to send their surplus grain to Europe, with the help of US shipping companies and American philanthropists, many of whom traveled to manage food distribution in foreign countries. American aid, delivered in "Hoover bags," kept millions of people alive, even in communist-led Russia.[6]

Hoover saw his role as encouraging and enforcing agreements that served the interests of as many Americans as possible. He sought to connect powerful actors and motivate them to do good for society by doing well for themselves. He believed that the enlightened, savvy leader could create positive outcomes through targeted incentives and well-managed associations. In his roles as international businessman, philanthropist, and public servant, Hoover proved that he excelled at these tasks. He was widely viewed as a prophet of progressive, scientific leadership, a successor to Theodore Roosevelt.[7]

Elected in November 1928, Hoover entered the White House with high hopes that his brand of progressive leadership would increase

American prosperity. It had the opposite effect, often for reasons out of his control. The steep decline that began after the stock market crash depleted the capital from the economy that Hoover planned to mobilize for new business deals. The confusion and despondency of the biggest economic actors diverted them from the opportunities for cooperation that Hoover had extolled. Fear motivated flight from the innovation and investment that the president promoted.

Panic among business leaders, stockholders, and the public at large triggered a "race to the bottom." Investors sold their stocks and converted their wealth into cash. Ordinary families withdrew their money from banks and placed it, quite literally, in their mattresses. Anticipating a decline in consumer demand, business leaders cut production and fired workers. Despite the agricultural and industrial surpluses of prior years, food and factory goods quickly disappeared from stores as businesses halted production and distribution. The United States and much of the world entered a deflationary tailspin where prices went down and people stopped making and selling things. Factories closed, stores shut, and farms foreclosed when their owners could not pay their mortgages or buy new supplies.

There were few deals for Hoover to negotiate. Encouraging cooperation between groups became impossible as everyone focused on immediate needs. This was the psychology behind bank runs. Once people lost trust in the stability of basic institutions, they started to anticipate the worst. Convinced that long-secure banks would not return money to depositors, citizens demanded a withdrawal of all deposits (a "bank run"), causing the very collapse of the banks that they had feared.

President Hoover was unprepared for what he confronted. He had mastered the work of guiding a stable and predictable system of economic exchange to produce more, for more people. He had experience shaping public and private incentives for bringing groups together. These tasks depended on increasing the resources available to all actors. Hoover had thrived in settings where he could distribute wealth and build trust between people. The devastation of the Great Depression undermined public trust, and it made Hoover's efforts at deal-making and mediation seem terribly insufficient. His progressive ideas of management did not address the shortages of money, nourishment, and hope in Bellow's Chicago and other parts of the country.

Franklin Roosevelt emerged as a national figure during this crisis of economy and leadership. Hoover (born poor) was a pioneering businessman; Roosevelt (born rich) devoted his life to politics. He lived and breathed the networking, maneuvering, and campaigning that determined power in large public organizations. He loved interacting with people—hearing their stories, telling his own, and charming listeners into following him. He was not a deep analytical thinker, like Hoover, but he had an eye for the big issues that captured attention and influenced decisions. Roosevelt learned to surround himself with people who could help him talk through tough and pressing matters. Once he made a decision, he persuaded, cajoled, and sometimes manipulated naysayers into supporting his efforts. He led by words and by feel—and he learned to do this for everyone, from advisors in his office to citizens listening far away.

Roosevelt was different from any leader Saul Bellow had ever seen or heard before. He empathized with struggling citizens, he connected with urban ethnics, and he resonated with poor farmers. He used the new technology of the radio to connect with citizens, to talk directly to them, and to persuade them. Roosevelt imagined a united public linked through the radio, and he gave it substance with his words. That is what Bellow and so many others felt as they heard the president's "odd Eastern accent" and listened intently.

He was familiar and strange at the same time; paternal but not oppressive. His voice, his attitude, his confidence, and his identification with diverse citizens made him the greatest national healer American society had seen. He did not offer a quick surgery, but promised continuing positive work on behalf of the ailing patient. Roosevelt seemed to understand boys like Bellow, and he offered them an outstretched hand of partnership uncharacteristic for leaders before his time.

Franklin Roosevelt came from one of the most elite American families, and he modeled his career on his heroic namesake.

He never worried about making a living because his doting mother, Sara, continued to support him, even when he became president of the United States. In the White House, Roosevelt still collected his allowance from his mother until her death in 1941.

The scion from Hyde Park had what one of his advisors called an "unconquerable confidence," which came from the fact that he was always financially secure and surrounded by affection. He was never unsure about his own exceptional background and personality. He was not ordinary in any way, and he knew it. From a very early age, Roosevelt believed that he was destined to lead his country, like cousin Theodore.[8]

Franklin understood the presidency through the experiences of "Uncle Ted," as he frequently called him. Franklin studied his leadership carefully, at close range. Eleanor Roosevelt, Franklin's wife, was Theodore's niece. On 17 March 1905 "Uncle Ted" gave Eleanor away at her wedding with Franklin. Everyone understood that this was a political family, and Franklin was the heir to the family vocation. Elihu Root, former secretary of war and one of the leading figures in the Republican Party, famously commented on the ambitions of the Roosevelt men: "Whenever a Roosevelt rides, he wishes to ride in front."[9]

Franklin internalized the grandeur of his family, but he was very different from "Uncle Ted." If Theodore was an excitable bully, Franklin was a calm, almost nonchalant, conversationalist. The younger Roosevelt preferred to listen and charm. Theodore loved to fight; Franklin was conflict averse. Both men believed in the power of a strong presidency, but Franklin was convinced that the leader had to use a gentler touch than his frequently rough cousin. Politics for Franklin was about bringing antagonistic groups together, and the president had to use the full force and resources of the government to encourage that behavior, giving the greatest number of citizens an opportunity to participate.

This attitude defined Franklin from the moment he began his political career. Josephus Daniels, the prominent North Carolina newspaperman and Democratic Party activist, described meeting Franklin in 1912, when it was clear that the young Roosevelt (then 30 years old) was the "coming man" of contemporary politics. Daniels explained that Roosevelt was one of the "most charming and handsomest young men I have known in my life." He "possessed a spontaneity and gaiety, as well as good looks, fine bearing, and sterling qualities." Daniels viewed the young Roosevelt as a much more congenial version of his famous cousin.[10]

Roosevelt took advantage of his name, but immediately cut an independent figure for himself. Theodore's side of the family was Republican, closely connected to the large business families of New York City. Franklin's branch, reared ninety miles north amid the landed estates in Hyde Park, was attached to the Democratic Party and its skepticism of city-dominated corporations. Hyde Park Democrats also opposed the urban ethnic bosses who dominated the party, especially those in New York City's infamous Tammany Hall. Roosevelt successfully ran for state senator in 1910, pledging to support progressive legislation that would bring economic assistance to farmers and small town merchants. He criticized the "machine politicians" who had long exploited state political offices to serve the interests of business elites and immigrant Irish, Italian, and Central European constituencies.

In the New York legislature Roosevelt fought to maintain state ownership of water and other resources for the public good. He also attacked the rampant corruption of many office-holders. Although Roosevelt was hardly a radical, he saw a vital role for government in regulating society and promoting opportunities for all citizens. This position emerged from his personal disdain for money-obsessed businessmen. He was not an entrepreneur or a striver, but a secure aristocrat who viewed public service as a calling. Roosevelt's ambition was to secure love, not profit, from the broad community of American voters. He echoed "Uncle Ted" in his commitment to the common interest above all.[11]

Roosevelt's mission was to make government a source of support for citizens. He understood how important financial security was to his own life, and he believed that others should have the same. He did not envision a society with equality of talent or outcomes; he knew that was not possible, or even desirable. His elite status reflected the common belief, at the time, that some are born better than others. Acknowledging what many people called the "natural" inequalities within human society, Roosevelt desired a common foundation on which all individuals and families could build, in their own ways. Amid inequality, he wanted to increase the opportunities for citizens to rise from their different starting points.

Social and economic mobility was the core of the American dream for Roosevelt. He saw safety and security as higher values than wealth and material achievement. Safety and security allowed citizens the chance to rise through hard work. Wealth and other material resources, he believed, were more the outcomes than the sources of mobility. Perhaps that was because wealth was a given for him and material achievements were not necessary. Safety and security, however, required the assistance of others, even for those who seemed to have it all. The First World War and Roosevelt's personal ordeal with polio reinforced that point. Even the wealthiest citizens could lose everything.

Roosevelt defined mobility as an individual quality that emerged through cooperation with other people. To rise, a citizen needed to work with others, benefiting from their assistance and at the same time contributing to the greater good. Although the Anglo-American constitutional tradition defined rights, including property, in individualistic terms, Roosevelt recognized that the presumption of democracy was that no man is an island. Human beings improved themselves and their society, he believed, when government helped them to help each other.

His personal connection to the ordinary citizen mattered more for Roosevelt than philosophical or legalistic deliberations on policy. He spent nearly all of his waking hours surrounded by diverse people—labor leaders, Jewish immigrants, business owners, intellectuals, and especially his poor Hudson Valley constituents. He listened to their concerns about the loss of control over their farms and small businesses in the face of increasing market pressures. Even before the Great Depression, he sought to maintain the capitalist economy by using government to restore some control to ordinary citizens. He was not an economic or social expert who offered clear solutions to the concerns of his constituents. Instead, Roosevelt relied on his empathy and his efforts to manage public institutions so that they could address citizens' needs. The role of state government, in particular, was crucial for Roosevelt, insuring access to basic resources—including water, food, shelter, and electricity. He wanted to create a level playing field so everyone had a chance.

As Hoover focused on the fundamentals of the American economy, Roosevelt emphasized the public welfare. Elected governor of New York in 1928, Roosevelt gave the clearest articulation of his political philosophy in a speech on 1 January 1929, ten months before the stock market crash upended the prosperity of the era. He challenged the everybody-can-get-rich attitude that was so popular among ambitious New Yorkers: "Our civilization cannot endure unless we, as individuals, realize our personal responsibility to and dependence on the rest of the world. For it is literally true that the 'self-supporting' man or woman has become as extinct as the man of the Stone Age." And he reminded listeners: "Without the help of thousands of others, any one of us would die, naked and starved."[12]

ROOSEVELT UNDERSTOOD THE FUNDAMENTAL CHALLENGE OF mid-twentieth-century politics better than anyone else: citizens needed government to help manage the growing complexity of the economy and society. Government had to become more than a referee and a mediator, in Hoover's terms. It had to give citizens some leverage over the global market forces that increasingly affected their lives. Government would protect freedom, in this context, by regulating economic and social change more rigorously to serve the interests of citizens. Political leaders, in Roosevelt's eyes, would have to direct expanding state and federal activities for this purpose. They would also have to invent new ways for government to function.

Expanding Washington's power had its dangers. That was evident in the fascist and communist societies, where the regimes repressed dissent and any deviation from the will of the dictators. The preservation of democracy required continued limits on the expansion of government. In particular, American citizens demanded freedom from interference in their life choices. Market forces were a primary source of local intrusion; citizens did not want to create a more threatening intruder in the form of a meddling central government. The challenge was to devise new forms of government that tamed the market and empowered local freedoms. Citizens wanted stability and control, without sacrificing liberty or property. They looked to their elected leaders to reconcile the contradictions inherent in this task. Democratic government had to become more active in people's lives, while remaining limited in its infringements on basic rights.

Although Roosevelt did not have a detailed plan, he recognized the needs around him. "Public assistance" did not mean handouts. Rather, it entailed using government resources to help people navigate treacherous conditions and enhance their life choices—securing a job when unemployed, raising children in a crowded city, or paying a mortgage on a family farm. These were private transactions, but the government had a growing role to play in insuring their integrity and accessibility. Citizens needed to know that they were not getting cheated, and they needed some help making sure they were not left out, especially during hard times.

Unlike its fascist and communist rivals, the US government responded to economic and social complexity by expanding the definition of personal freedom. This was a crucial part of Roosevelt's pioneering leadership. He believed that individual choices were ever-more constrained by impersonal forces, and he saw collective action, through government, as a counterweight. State and federal officials would not "take over" local businesses. Nor would they play guardian for families. Roosevelt's vision of government was the same as his vision of community. Citizens depended on collective efforts to keep everyone safe and secure so that individuals could then make free choices about their lives. Community safety required more than just law enforcement; it involved forward-looking investments in roads, schools, libraries, hospitals, and other centers for those in need. Roosevelt was independently wealthy, but his early career focused on political activity within communities—Groton, Harvard, and Hyde Park. He saw the federal government as a large community organization, and he characterized the president as a community leader.

This was a radical shift from Hoover and others who expected a business executive, a prophet, or a warrior in that office. Roosevelt was none of these things. He was a joiner, an organizer, and a community-builder. Roosevelt brought people together and he encouraged them to work in unity. He motivated and encouraged. He rarely dictated and he never claimed personal superiority. He was a healing president, not a forceful *Führer*.

AT THE START OF ROOSEVELT'S CAREER, URBAN SOPHISTICATES and suffering citizens smelled a scheme in his cooperative style, but soon enough they recognized something different. More important than the substance of Roosevelt's policies was his authenticity—his ability to build trust with millions of citizens who had reason to disbelieve. Although he looked and sounded different than most Americans, Franklin Roosevelt conveyed an understanding of their lives. He identified with those he never met or heard, and more important, they identified with him. That was why, as Bellow recounted, the men and women driving on the highway pulled over to hear Roosevelt's words and share his message.

Citizens did not just listen; they connected with their president as never before. He was part of their community, and their community grew and deepened around him. Even a cynical Chicago immigrant boy felt connected to the other people hearing the president. Roosevelt grasped their problems and offered collective hope for improvement, and perhaps even redemption.

Roosevelt's candor and directness began with his inaugural address. Unlike Hoover, he spoke in simple terms about current difficulties and he was clear about what he intended to do: "Our greatest primary task is to put people to work. This is no unsolvable problem if we face it wisely and courageously. It can be accomplished in part by direct recruiting by the Government itself, treating the task as we would treat the emergency of a war, but at the same time, through this employment, accomplishing greatly needed projects to stimulate and reorganize the use of our natural resources."[13]

These words represented neither the hesitant verbiage of bureaucracy nor the boisterous feel-good language of empty patriotism. Roosevelt employed a pragmatic vernacular of problem-solving. Like Lincoln, he chose ordinary words that everyone could use and understand. He avoided vacuous boasts and empty promises. Roosevelt's main message was that he planned to lead through "unity" and "action"—the two most common words in his inaugural address and his subsequent statements. These were also the words that characterized what Roosevelt aptly called the "temper of our people."[14]

Many citizens attributed their political awakening to Roosevelt and the programs he created to nurture their communities. Bellow became a successful author (later winning the Nobel Prize for Literature), employed during 1938 and 1939 by the Writers' Project of the Works Progress Administration (WPA), funded directly by the president. Many, if not most, of Bellow's contemporaries who attained fame from poor urban origins could say the same—they connected to American society in new ways through Roosevelt, and his programs opened new pathways for them in life.[15]

Like no other national executive before him (or since), Roosevelt helped turn wayward youth into college-educated professionals with a sense of public service and hope for the future. He reached recent immigrants and African Americans, factory workers and farm hands. Roosevelt's broad identification with citizens empowered them to change their lives. Some citizens, especially from minority backgrounds, remained left out, but Roosevelt's presidency reached deeper into American society than ever imagined by Washington, Jackson, Lincoln, or even "Uncle Ted."

THERE WERE, OF COURSE, MANY OPPOSED TO ROOSEVELT'S programs, and his vision, from the very start. He seized extraordinary presidential powers—"dictatorial powers," in the estimation of Hoover and other Republicans—to support experimental efforts. "I am prepared under my constitutional duty," Roosevelt explained, "to recommend the measures that a stricken Nation in the midst of a stricken world may require." Echoing Lincoln's argument for actions "otherwise unconstitutional" to protect the Union, Roosevelt explained what he would do if the other branches of government resisted: "I shall ask the Congress for the one remaining instrument to meet the crisis broad Executive power to wage a war against the emergency, as great as the power that would be given to me if we were in fact invaded by a foreign foe."[16]

From his first months in office his famous "hundred days"—Roosevelt moved the presidency from its exalted pulpit to a more informal station. He used "emergency" powers to steer the daily hopes and actions of citizens, going above and around traditional institutional barriers. The radio was his most direct and effective instrument, reaching citizens at home and in their cars. The president used the newest communications technology to stretch across the geographical and institutional distances separating citizens from the leader of what was now a very large country—in population, more than thirty times larger than the nation George Washington had led.

Through his words and policies, Roosevelt showed ordinary Americans that they could help themselves, and he would aid that process. He inspired the broad morale of the public as no other president had before. His was a democratic power that violated most of the images of elite, heroic authority embodied by his predecessors, including Jackson and Lincoln. Franklin Roosevelt increased the direct power of the president over ordinary citizens, just as he increased the power of citizens over their own lives.

That was the secret of his leadership—tying his power to the power of ordinary people, and expanding both together. Fellow Democrat Andrew Jackson had destroyed much of the federal government, especially the National Bank, to free citizens from restriction. Roosevelt, in contrast, expanded the federal government to free citizens from suffering. Roosevelt created local opportunities through a powerful national presidency that inspired possibilities unimaginable before. He combined Andrew Jackson's focus on non-elites (the "people's presidency") with Theodore Roosevelt's emphasis on government regulation (the "progressive presidency") to create the "New Deal."

The New Deal drew on Theodore Roosevelt's "square deal" and Andrew Jackson's militant populism. "I pledge you, I pledge myself," Franklin Roosevelt famously announced, "to a new deal for the American people. Let us all here assembled constitute ourselves prophets of a new order of competence and of courage. This is more than a political campaign; it is a call to arms. Give me your help, not to win votes alone, but to win in this crusade to restore America to its own people." The New Deal aimed to serve the "men and women, forgotten in the political philosophy of the Government of the last years" who sought, above all, a "more equitable opportunity to share in the distribution of national wealth."[17]

Roosevelt broke tradition with his New Deal, promising to make the president—far beyond the imaginations of all his predecessors—a deliverer of opportunity to every citizen, including immigrants and minorities. The executive would not only promote national goals; he would now manage programs that created jobs for citizens, relief for the poor, and investments in the improvement of local communities. The president would become local provider as well as national leader.

Franklin Roosevelt's New Deal language spoke less of the missionary goals articulated by Abraham Lincoln and Theodore Roosevelt, and much more of the ordinary needs the president planned to serve: "What do the people of America want more than anything else? To my mind, they want two things: work, with all the moral and spiritual values that go with it; and with work, a reasonable measure of security—security for themselves and for their wives and children. Work and security— these are more than words. They are more than facts. They are the spiritual values, the true goal toward which our efforts of reconstruction should lead."[18]

Roosevelt made the president a protector of each American's basic welfare. Washington, and even Lincoln, would have found the ambition fantastical; Franklin Roosevelt made it seem natural. He amplified the expectations, reach, and tone of the American presidency in just about every way—and set them impossibly high for his successors.

Roosevelt offered few easy solutions in his speeches and he never claimed imminent success in turning around the Great Depression. Quite the contrary, his appeal came from his frank acknowledgement of citizens' suffering and his ready admission that improvement was difficult. His modesty gave him credibility from the crowded streets of Chicago to the parched farms of Dust Bowl Kansas. Roosevelt was not a know-it-all with ready answers. He was not a bragging warrior, promising to overpower all demons.

National healing came from Roosevelt's leadership of a process that displayed understanding and empathy for "fellow Americans," and showed a willingness to try different things that could begin to make life better. Instead of a grand plan, Roosevelt offered to roll up his sleeves with other citizens as they worked together to find common ways forward. He pledged to implement new programs, assess how they worked, and do more of what worked, less of what did not. The outcomes were important, but the process mattered most of all.

Citizens felt they were no longer acting in isolated communities, but were part of what Roosevelt called a common national effort. This was the main point of the president's "fireside chats," broadcast into people's homes in the evening. The president pledged to explain complex policies "for the benefit of the average citizen." He believed that he "owed this" to all Americans. "I know that when you understand what we in Washington have been about I shall continue to have your cooperation as fully as I have had your sympathy and help."[19]

Roosevelt promised success through unity and understanding. Although he was largely confined to the White House, he joined citizens in voice and sentiment within their local communities. He was a leader who they felt labored alongside them, even as he spoke with a funny accent. Roosevelt healed in the old fashioned way: he did not diagnose miracle drugs; he made house calls and he dispensed slow, incremental, but optimistic remedies. He was more nurse than doctor, more trusted father figure than genius reformer. Roosevelt was a president who seemed to care more than any before, and that made all the difference for cynical boys like Saul Bellow.

We have not seen a president who could touch the down-and-out, as well as the rich and successful, with the same facility since Roosevelt's time in office. He greatly expanded the democratic reach of the presidency, as he also set near impossible expectations for his successors.

As late as 1932, the American president was a leader of still limited means. For all of Theodore Roosevelt's rhetoric about progressive reform and international power, the national executive had few administrative resources at his disposal. President Herbert Hoover had a personal staff of three secretaries, a small cabinet of agency heads, and a military that was not prepared for conflict on any serious scale. Hoover was an ambitious thinker, with a vision of international trade and rule of law, but he ran a government that was small, weak, and severely limited in its capacity for influence—both at home and abroad. The ineffective government responses to the collapse of the world economy illustrated this point. The American president was more bystander than leader during the first years of the Great Depression.[20]

As he proclaimed in his inaugural address, Franklin Roosevelt was determined to make the president a more effective leader across society. "We must act and act quickly," he asserted. Yet he quickly confronted limitations. Ambition and rhetoric were not enough. [21]

Roosevelt appointed a cabinet of secretaries for the Treasury Department, the State Department, the War Department, and other agencies. He also distributed patronage jobs—spoils, in the terms of Andrew Jackson's era. Nonetheless, Roosevelt's ability to make federal, state, and local institutions bend to his will was constrained by their distance from his oversight, their ability to avoid accountability, and, most important, the very complexity of the issues involved. How could a president in Washington, D.C. require a state budget director to follow his preferences and how would he even know that they were being followed? How could the national executive implement policies that involved regulatory and legal details few experts could fully understand? How could a distant president diminish the resistance of local officials? Civil servants who objected to Roosevelt's priorities often simply ignored him, waiting him out as they had prior leaders of empty ambition.

Max Weber, the great early twentieth-century German sociologist, identified this institutional logjam as the modern condition of bureaucracy. To lead, he argued, powerful figures had to persuade through their charisma and they had to create alternative routines for institutions that traditionally resisted change. This process was always hard, but it grew in difficulty as societies became larger, the issues more complex, and the governing professionals less closely connected. If Andrew Jackson faced resistance from the Bank of the United States, and Abraham Lincoln could not get his early generals to fight, Franklin Roosevelt contended with many more banks, generals, and other institutions and bureaucrats—most of whom he could not even identify. Issues surrounding the economy, preparedness, and basic governance were much harder to pin down than they had been in a smaller, less diverse America of the past. As Weber predicted, size and complexity in government encouraged powerful reform rhetoric from leaders, but it made the implementation of change from the top nearly impossible.[22]

In his first days as president, Roosevelt battled with the bureaucracy. He learned quickly that he had to negotiate and compromise. He could not rule by order of the president, even when he had the majority of the American people behind him. The White House simply had too few enforcers and the American system placed too many checks on presidential power. Resistance emerged immediately from Congress, the Supreme Court, state offices, and even the Treasury and other departments that reported to the Oval Office. Balanced budget orthodoxies and attachments to the gold standard and high tariff trade policies, for instance, motivated powerful figures across the government to challenge, constrain, and sometimes disobey presidential demands. From the beginning, Roosevelt had to expend enormous energy not only making big decisions, but protecting them from destruction at the hands of officials opposed to his policies.

Roosevelt recognized that his power was dependent on a combination of persuasion and bargaining. The president had to convince followers, including those in government, that he had morality, justice, and necessity on his side. He also had to offer rewards to those who faithfully executed his policies—resources, prestige, and autonomy to pursue their own goals. More than any of his predecessors, Roosevelt understood that if he wanted to achieve policy changes in a stagnant and complex society, he had to increase his leverage with diverse actors who could, and did, oppose him.[23]

The best way to expand bargaining power in a modern bureaucracy, Weber predicted, is to expand administrative capabilities. That is precisely what Roosevelt did. Prior presidents rose above the machinery of government, relying on charisma, personal credibility, and bullying, when necessary. In military affairs and international diplomacy presidents tended to dig a little deeper into the details, but for the domestic matters that occupied the majority of their time in office, they emphasized politics over policy. Presidents negotiated power, not the microelements of program development—most of which occurred within the states, and sometimes within federal agencies, far from White House view.

Roosevelt turned the Executive Mansion into the national control tower, managing the economy and other elements of social development as no president contemplated before. That is why his opponents called Roosevelt a dictator. In reality, he was what scholars have labeled the first "administrative president."[24]

ENTERING OFFICE AS THE ECONOMY AND THE NATION'S BANKING system were in free fall, with hints of labor unrest across the country, Roosevelt seized on the crisis to create a web of innovative administrative capabilities. He began with the Emergency Banking Act, approved by desperate members of Congress on 9 March 1933, just five days into the new presidency. The House and the Senate voted overwhelmingly for the bill before White House drafters completed the final text. Most representatives did not even have a chance to read what they were voting for. Convinced that the country needed exceptional presidential efforts to save the economy, they gave Roosevelt new powers to direct the banks, the currency, and the modes of exchange. He became a dominant national economic actor on a scale never imagined by Washington, Lincoln, or Theodore Roosevelt. Despite their shared Democratic party affiliation, Jackson would have found Roosevelt's new centralizing powers an affront to democratic principles.

The Emergency Banking Act intended to protect democracy from the chaos of bank runs, deflationary spirals, and severe economic depression. Along with the Bank Holiday, which temporarily closed all financial institutions after an unprecedented (and constitutionally questionable) presidential order, the Emergency Banking Act created executive powers to protect the money of depositors. Even more extraordinary, the legislation gave Roosevelt the authority to require citizens to exchange their personally held gold for government-printed dollars. In other words, the president requisitioned the property of citizens and replaced it with paper—showcasing images of prior presidents, of course. "I am," Roosevelt coyly admitted, "keeping my finger on gold."[25]

For about a century—dating back to the Coinage Act of 1834, signed by President Jackson—gold had served as the foundation for American currency. The gold standard guaranteed that there was a pot of precious metal, with seemingly stable value, behind each sheet of monetary paper. The Jacksonians favored the gold standard because it took the control of currency value away from the banks, and Republicans after the Civil War liked it because it protected the value of investments in railroads, ships, and factory products. The gold standard allowed a consistent supply of credible "sound money."

Franklin Roosevelt used the same phrase, but he replaced gold with presidential authority. He wanted to expand the supply of capital in a depressed economy by printing more money, absent additional gold. During his first days in office, Roosevelt sent the new money to banks that could not repay their depositors. He recognized, of course, that there were limits, beyond which citizens would not trust the value of the new paper. He also confronted experts, including Chairman of the Federal Reserve Paul Warburg, who warned of inflation.

"Sound money" for Roosevelt now meant presidentially managed money. Roosevelt's solution was to identify the presidency with the dollar. As late as March 1933, there were many kinds of money circulating—gold certificates, national bank notes, federal dollars—and the White House played little role in managing them. These currencies had value only because people believed there was gold behind them, somewhere. Roosevelt not only seized the gold, he seized the money. He made the federal dollar the standard currency, replacing most other currencies through the Emergency Banking Act and subsequent measures.

If citizens trusted the president, they would trust the money he printed. If the president increased the money supply carefully, that would put more capital into circulation for the economy, and encourage trust among businesspeople and consumers. Most important, if citizens felt the benefits of Roosevelt's presidential dollars, especially through job growth, they would not miss their gold. Roosevelt understood that Americans valued their livelihoods more than their gold, and they would use dollars that a president managed to improve their conditions. In a decade, after the Second World War, the entire world would rebuild around US dollars.

Replacing gold with dollars was Roosevelt's first and perhaps boldest move. He drew on the thinking of John Maynard Keynes, in particular. He also exploited the American desperation for hope and action, as his inaugural address promised, amid so much fear and disorientation. Presidential control of money, and much of the economy, gave people focus and direction. It also provided a foundation for rebuilding the trust needed to inspire citizens for shared sacrifice. When confronted by critics of his allegedly dictatorial approach to the economy, Roosevelt mused about the presidentially managed currency: "How do I know that's any good?" The answer: "The fact that I think it is, makes it good." That message made more sense to struggling boys like Saul Bellow, who wanted to believe in their president, than the old explanations given by Wall Street bankers about gold and inflation. [26]

Roosevelt made the president the manager, guarantor, and trust-builder for money in a cash-starved economy. Nowhere does the Constitution describe an executive role in day-to-day economic matters; the founders never anticipated that such a role might be necessary. Herbert Hoover's aloofness during the Depression was in line with the approaches of Washington, Jackson, Lincoln, and Theodore Roosevelt. Franklin Roosevelt placed the presidency in every purchase and exchange of currency by citizens and businesses alike. Just as he entered people's cars and homes through the radio, he inserted himself into their wallets through the dollars he printed.

Roosevelt made the president the nation's "money czar," as his critics correctly understood. Citizens and presidents have retained those expectations ever since. Leaders are judged, as never before, on how well they manage and "grow" the economy. Roosevelt created unrealistic expectations in many areas, but perhaps nowhere more so than in the economy. [27]

By increasing the supply of money in circulation, Roosevelt hoped to stimulate more economic activity. He sought to raise prices, especially for farm products, whose prices had been depressed since the middle of the 1920s. Due to technological advances and more extensive land cultivation, American farmers grew more crops than ever before. Their costs of planting increased, but their revenues did not keep pace because the surplus of foodstuffs reduced prices. As a consequence, many farmers found themselves without sufficient cash to cover their costs. Debt levels increased, and especially after October 1929, foreclosures on farms multiplied across the countryside.

Excessive planting and a series of droughts in the lower middle plains of the country (especially Kansas, Oklahoma, Texas, and New Mexico) contributed to giant sand storms and sudden crop failures—the "Dust Bowl." Debt and drought forced multi-generation farm families to become landless transients wandering, with all their possessions, for food and work. They were, in the words of John Steinbeck, "Americans who have gone through the hell of the drought, have seen their lands wither and die and the top soil blow away; and this, to a man who has owned his land, is a curious and terrible pain."[28]

Roosevelt reached out directly to suffering farmers. He did not have an easy solution to their twin challenge of debt and drought, but he provided federal financial assistance on an unprecedented scale. After the Emergency Banking Bill, the president sent Congress a Farm Relief Bill, officially titled the Agricultural Adjustment Act. Passed by Congress on 10 May 1933, the legislation created the first federal agency, under presidential control, to subsidize farming across the country.

The Agricultural Adjustment Administration (AAA) paid farmers to stay on their land by giving them money to grow less. In some cases it paid for the destruction of crops and livestock. The goal was to reduce farm costs and simultaneously raise crop prices, allowing producers a better chance of accruing sufficient revenue for their families. The AAA also hoped that reducing excessive crop cultivation would allow the parched topsoil in Dust Bowl areas to improve.

Historians diverge over the effectiveness of these policies, but they agree that the policies represented a new presidential role. The executive could now use monetary flexibility to inflate food prices and transfer more wealth to cash-poor landowners. The AAA and other agencies, especially the Department of Agriculture, emerged as powerful regulators of what was grown and how much it cost. Food and farming, formerly the exclusive authority of state and local governments, became federal turf under Roosevelt's emergency measures.[29]

In 1936 the Supreme Court challenged this expansion of federal power, ruling in *United States v. Butler* that the AAA was unconstitutional. Roosevelt, however, found other ways to maintain his subsidies through alternative legislation and various federal agencies. Spending the new money he printed, by the late 1930s he became the farmer-in-chief. To this day, federal subsidies to farm communities largely determine what is grown in the United States, how much it costs, and who profits. Large agrarian corporations, not family farmers, do most of the farming in the United States, and they work hand in hand with Congress and the president to determine which food products reach consumers at lowest cost. The Roosevelt presidency saved thousands of farmers by creating a highly regulated, subsidized, and managed market—dominated by national economic goals, not nutritional wisdom. [30]

THE PRESIDENT SHOWED MORE WISDOM AND EFFECTIVENESS IN addressing the fundamental problem of joblessness, especially in cities like Chicago. Speaking to the nation on 24 July 1933, Roosevelt explained: "For many years the two great barriers to a normal prosperity have been low farm prices and the creeping paralysis of unemployment. These factors have cut the purchasing power of the country in half. I promised action." The AAA and the departure from the gold standard boosted farm prices. The president embarked on even more far-reaching and diverse "industrial recovery acts" to put people back to work. [31]

The first and most important of these acts was the Federal Emergency Relief Act, passed by Congress and signed by Roosevelt on 12 May 1933. It created a parallel agency to the AAA, the Federal Emergency Relief Administration (FERA). Led by Roosevelt's close advisor, Harry Hopkins, FERA federalized and expanded direct relief to unemployed citizens. In the past, only state and local governments provided aid to suffering citizens. That was true even during the Civil War, when the main federal benefit program was veterans' pensions, not family assistance. The federal government left the sustenance of citizens, even during acute economic crises, to the states. Hoover had expanded federal loans to states to help with these efforts, but he did not provide any direct help to citizens.

Roosevelt used FERA to reach out to unemployed men and women, as he had with destitute farmers. Building on the work of the Temporary Emergency Relief Administration he had created (with Hopkins) for New York State, the president channeled new money to poor families throughout the country. In Saul Bellow's Chicago, for example, one-third of the working-class population received federal assistance by the end of 1933. During the next two years, FERA and related federal agencies provided more than 80 percent of the aid sent to residents in the city. Much of that assistance went to recent immigrants, like Bellow's family, as well as African Americans and other minorities. FERA reached widely, across diverse communities, as no federal agency other than the army had before. This was indeed a "war" against the emergency, as Roosevelt repeatedly claimed.[32]

No wonder citizens who previously paid little attention to the president now listened carefully to his words. Before Roosevelt's presidency, direct federal assistance did not exist; the federal government was not a welfare organization. Few states or cities had the resources to make a meaningful difference in their residents' lives. A former governor, Roosevelt understood the limits of the states. He put citizens in Chicago and other communities on the federal "dole," giving them a reason to feel "saved" from starvation by their president.[33]

The federal dollars that began to arrive in local communities created a dialogue between citizens and Washington, D.C. that did not exist before. The explosion of letters to the White House captured this phenomenon, as did the personal comments about Roosevelt as a "family" member from citizens with no blood connection. Direct federal assistance nurtured a relationship between citizens and government that was focused on the public good.[34]

If Theodore Roosevelt was the first progressive president, promoting ambitious national reform goals, Franklin Roosevelt became the first welfare president, bringing public assistance directly to suffering citizens. Roosevelt's welfare policies made boys like Bellow feel more connected to the country, more "American." As a consequence, citizens participated more in public institutions, and they showed a willingness to sacrifice for common purposes. Racism and selfishness remained powerful dividers, but Roosevelt encouraged cooperation as no president had before. Despite limited economic means, citizens who felt connected to their federal government showed a willingness to leave their communities and traditions, and undertake new activities for national and self-improvement.

Laborers long ignored (and frequently repressed) by the country's elites now felt included in the national narrative.[35]

That was the ethos of the Civilian Conservation Corps, the Civil Works Administration, the Works Progress Administration, and hundreds of other federal public works agencies created in this dynamic Depression era. As president, Roosevelt built a messy, expensive, and inefficient maze of federal offices, each sponsoring "make work" opportunities for citizens in different, and sometimes contradictory, ways. The point was to put the millions of unemployed Americans to work, and to do it fast. Harry Hopkins famously said: "Hunger is not debatable."[36]

ROOSEVELT SPENT MORE MONEY AND ADMINISTERED MORE WELfare programs than any other president before. His welfare expenditures exceeded all of his predecessors combined. During his twelve years as president—more than any other national executive in American history—he built the modern administrative presidency. His duration in office and the continuation of his programs long after he died testify to his enduring impact.

Roosevelt often overreached, as when he tried unsuccessfully to "pack" the Supreme Court with more of his appointees in 1937. Over time, his programs did noticeably less to inspire the same confidence and dynamism as earlier efforts. Nonetheless, Roosevelt constructed a modern national welfare state, with federal machinery, using the White House as the headquarters—the brain for the growing New Deal body. He acted as chief strategist and engineer, articulating the goals and coordinating the different actions, incorporating diverse ideas and pursuing multiple pathways at the same time.[37]

Roosevelt healed the nation by connecting with ordinary people and making them feel he was helping them, or at least trying. His presidency was less White House bound than any before, even though he could not walk. He was ubiquitous and tenacious, like Theodore Roosevelt, but Franklin backed his words with the money, jobs, and other opportunities he sent to towns and farms around the country. No president had ever done anything like this before. Roosevelt was the modern executive who saw beyond the chaos, and now made house calls.

George Washington had traveled around the countryside, but he did not dispense resources as Roosevelt did. Jackson protected frontier settlers from interference, but Roosevelt brought their descendants direct help. Lincoln might be the best analogue for Roosevelt. Lincoln unified a country divided by slavery, but where Lincoln depended on a destructive army and a unifying political vision, Roosevelt employed the promise of new opportunities and the resources of expanding federal programs. Lincoln fought to unify with new presidential war powers; Roosevelt invested in prosperity with new federal administrative powers. If Lincoln was *the* nineteenth-century president, Roosevelt was *the* twentieth-century American leader.

Lincoln's presidency anticipated Roosevelt's. The latter had to contend with the collapse of the American (and world) economy, but they both spent much of their presidencies at war. In retrospect, Roosevelt's ability to respond creatively to the Great Depression and echo Lincoln's war performance is truly exceptional. No other president faced the same range of existential challenges. As a consequence, no other president had so many opportunities to change the basic structure of American society, and vast sections of the modern world. Roosevelt turned the darkest of times into the brightest of new hopes. He was not only the first welfare president, but, by 1944, the first global president, influencing more parts of the world than any previous American executive. He pioneered the New Deal and then globalized its reach.[38]

Like Lincoln, Roosevelt anticipated the coming of a horrible war, and he did all he could to forestall American participation, even though he knew it was probably unavoidable. Still mired in the lingering unemployment of the Great Depression, Americans were reluctant to spend their limited treasure on foreign conflicts. Roosevelt understood that any war the United States entered had to be a war of necessity, imposed on the country after all alternatives had been explored. Congress, and especially public opinion, placed severe constraints on the president's war-making powers. He was the commander-in-chief, but not the dominant decision-maker for sending the nation's sons into battle.

By 1937, if not earlier, Roosevelt recognized that rising fascist power, particularly in Japan and Germany, posed a threat to American democracy on the same scale as the Great Depression. Indeed, the two phenomena were intimately connected. Economic despair and political disillusion in the 1930s motivated millions of citizens in Europe and Asia, and some in the United States, to support strongmen who promised salvation through strength. Fascist leaders blamed "outsiders"—Jews, Chinese, Slavs, and Americans, among many others—for dividing their societies and holding them back. Relying on a strong expansionist military, fueled by dictatorial control over the economy, fascists promised to win back the land, wealth, and respect that suffering Japanese and German citizens deserved—their rightful "place in the sun."[39]

ROOSEVELT'S PREOCCUPATION WITH THIS GATHERING STORM explains, in part, his missteps on court-packing and other domestic policy issues at the time. His October 1937 speech in Chicago was uncharacteristic in its alarm and its challenge to the inward focus of most Americans. Roosevelt began by drawing a contrast between "our peace" and the "very different scenes being enacted in other parts of the world." The president described a "reign of terror and international lawlessness," saying that: "Nations claiming freedom for themselves deny it to others. Innocent peoples, innocent nations, are being cruelly sacrificed to a greed for power and supremacy which is devoid of all sense of justice and humane considerations."

This mayhem mattered to Americans, Roosevelt contended: "Let no one imagine that America will escape, that America may expect mercy, that this Western Hemisphere will not be attacked and that it will continue tranquilly and peacefully to carry on the ethics and the arts of civilization." The forces of militancy were too great and their demands insatiable. Americans had no choice but to bolster and extend their defenses.

Roosevelt said multiple times that he was determined "to keep out of war," but he warned: "We cannot have complete protection in a world of disorder in which confidence and security have broken down." He called for cooperation among the peace-loving nations of the world to limit the growth of fascist aggression. Most famously, Roosevelt referred to conflict in Europe and Asia as an "epidemic of physical disease."

When an epidemic spreads, Roosevelt reminded listeners, "the community approves and joins in a quarantine of the patients in order to protect the health of the community against the spread of the disease."

Short of war, the United States had to cooperate with other states to separate, contain, and ultimately starve out the belligerent nations. That was the most prudent defense, and it required more active, forward measures, according to the president. These measures included economic sanctions against aggressors and coordinated military preparations with allies. Roosevelt wanted to avoid a repeat of the First World War, not by staying out of the next global conflict, but by trying to prevent it in the first place. He did not speak of overthrowing fascists; he wanted to quarantine them. Roosevelt's successors would call this policy "containment."[40]

Despite the power of Roosevelt's logic, the First World War lingered as a traumatic memory. In addition to the widespread death and destruction, the First World War left behind heavy debts and festering animosities among the belligerents. In the United States many mainstream politicians, including Senator Harry Truman, alleged that war profiteers had driven the country into a distant conflict for personal gain. When Roosevelt delivered his "quarantine" speech he knew he was speaking against widespread public sentiment to stay out of foreign conflicts. Beginning in 1935, Congress passed a series of Neutrality Acts that restricted American trade and travel with any country at war. Roosevelt tried to translate his domestic clout into public support for cooperation with threatened allies and limited American military preparations, but he made little headway.

The president was severely constrained in his ability to combat aggressors Americans preferred to ignore. He commanded a still small, ill-funded, and unambitious diplomatic-military apparatus. American isolationism reflected the nation's focus on its domestic needs and its institutional bias in that direction. The growth in presidential power from Washington to Roosevelt occurred, with a few exceptions, at home and not abroad. The New Deal president was a national, not an international, executive.

The loud and vituperative criticisms of Roosevelt's "quarantine" speech reminded the president of the constraints he faced. The *Chicago*

Tribune, a consistent advocate of isolationism, claimed that listeners to the president received an unnecessary "world-hurricane of fright." With some justification, the editors accused Roosevelt of provocations that would make it difficult to avoid war, despite contrary public demands: "Does not Mr. Roosevelt's policy invite the coming of the day when he, too, may have no alternative but resort to arms?" Other critics diagnosed a conspiracy, where the president "hit upon the idea of becoming aggressive internationally to divert attention from mounting domestic problems."

Roosevelt always had domestic opponents, most of whom he had effectively marginalized. In foreign policy, his critics had the upper hand. Senator Hiram Johnson from California summarized the public consensus after the speech, when he explained: "We want no union with welching nations who will…tell us we must lead mankind to save the world."[41]

Roosevelt had enough trouble saving the American economy; he did not seek to "save the world." In the weeks after his Chicago speech, the president backtracked from his language about quarantining fascism. He remained convinced, however, that Japanese and German aggression undermined the international openness and cooperation necessary for the New Deal to succeed. Roosevelt's fears materialized in a matter of months, when Japanese bombers sunk an American gunboat, the USS *Panay*, as it tried to evacuate American civilians (mostly merchants, missionaries, and educators) from the war-torn Chinese city of Nanking. The Japanese apologized for the incident, which resulted in the deaths of three American sailors, but they showed no willingness to curtail their aggressive actions in East Asia. The world observed a similar dynamic in Nazi behavior in the Rhineland, and soon Czechoslovakia as well.[42]

Roosevelt deferred to the public's isolationist sentiment, but he still resolved to prepare for likely international conflict. As with his domestic programs, Roosevelt showed more concern for solving problems than observing constitutional limitations. He believed the president should serve the public welfare above all, and he expanded the power of the office accordingly, often despite tradition and even law to the contrary.

Speaking to Congress in 1939, as he pressed for authority to assist anti-fascist forces in Europe, Roosevelt explained: "Our policy must be to appreciate in the deepest sense the true American interest. Rightly considered, this interest is not selfish. Destiny first made us, with our sister nations on this hemisphere, joint heirs of European culture. Fate seems now to compel us to assume the task of helping to maintain in the western world a citadel wherein that civilization may be kept alive."[43]

In response to pressure from the president, and expanding warfare in Europe and Asia, Congress granted Roosevelt a number of exceptions to neutrality legislation—all with the intention of staying out of war. These congressional measures included: permission in 1939 to sell non-war materials to belligerents ("cash and carry"), approval in 1940 to trade fifty US Navy destroyer ships to Britain in exchange for eight military bases in the Western Hemisphere ("destroyers for bases"), and authorization in 1941 to "lend" war materials to friendly countries abroad ("lend-lease"). Roosevelt sold each of these measures as an alternative to American participation in war, but he knew that each brought the country closer to direct involvement.

That was, by this time, Roosevelt's goal. He used his persuasive and administrative powers to push the country out of neutrality. Lend-Lease is perhaps the clearest example of how he did this. At the end of 1940, six months after the fall of France, Roosevelt went on the radio to shape public opinion about the war. He began by equating assistance to Britain, China, and eventually the Soviet Union with New Deal commitments to suffering Americans. "We met the issue of 1933 with courage and realism," Roosevelt reminded listeners. "We face this new crisis—this new threat to the security of our nation—with the same courage and realism. Never before since Jamestown and Plymouth Rock has our American civilization been in such danger as now."

Roosevelt described in detail how the fascist powers refused to compromise, how they built huge military capabilities and conquered their neighbors, and most frightening, how they could threaten American territorial security. The president warned: "Frankly and definitely there is danger ahead—danger against which we must prepare. But we well know that we cannot escape danger, or the fear of danger, by crawling into bed and pulling the covers over our heads."

The New Deal had called on citizens to experiment and innovate, and Roosevelt now recommended the same for contending with foreign enemies: "We must be the great arsenal of democracy. For us this is an emergency as serious as war itself. We must apply ourselves to our task with the same resolution, the same sense of urgency, the same spirit of patriotism and sacrifice as we would show were we at war."

Roosevelt was once again the problem-solver-in-chief, now asking Americans to join together in a collective act of global problem solving. "American industrial genius," he elaborated, "unmatched throughout all the world in the solution of production problems, has been called upon to bring its resources and its talents into action. Manufacturers of watches, of farm implements, of linotypes, and cash registers, and automobiles, and sewing machines, and lawn mowers and locomotives are now making fuses, bomb packing crates, telescope mounts, shells, and pistols and tanks. But all of our present efforts are not enough. We must have more ships, more guns, more planes—more of everything. And this can only be accomplished if we discard the notion of 'business as usual.'"[44]

The president maintained the fiction that arming friendly nations was an alternative to war. His most impressive moment walking this tightrope came during one of his press conferences in late 1940. "I have read a great deal of nonsense in the last few days by people who can only think in what we may call traditional terms about finances," Roosevelt recounted, deploying his well-rehearsed condemnation of New Deal critics.

> Suppose my neighbor's home catches fire, and I have a length of garden hose four or five hundred feet away. If he can take my garden hose and connect it up with his hydrant, I may help him to put out his fire. Now, what do I do? I don't say to him before that operation, "Neighbor, my garden hose cost me $15; you have to pay me $15 for it." What is the transaction that goes on? I don't want $15—I want my garden hose back after the fire is over. All right. If it goes through the fire all right, intact, without any damage to it, he gives it back to me and thanks me very much for the use of it. But suppose it gets smashed up—holes in it—during the fire; we don't have to have too

much formality about it, but I say to him, "I was glad to lend you that hose; I see I can't use it any more, it's all smashed up." He says, "How many feet of it were there?" I tell him, "There were 150 feet of it." He says, "All right, I will replace it." Now, if I get a nice garden hose back, I am in pretty good shape.[45]

Roosevelt's garden hose analogy made intervention in Europe and Asia sound neighborly and self-protecting. Of course, a good country should loan a hose to neighbors to stop a fire before it spreads. Of course small steps to help friends fight dangerous threats were wise, even cost-effective.

The president made forward actions sound defensive, and he deployed American capabilities—money and materiel—without declaring war. Washington, Jackson, and Lincoln never had the resources or reason to act similarly. Theodore Roosevelt aspired to be a global power broker, and he supported American participation in the First World War, but he never contemplated presidential intervention on this scale without a domestic war consensus.

Franklin Roosevelt became the first war-making president because he converted New Deal reach at home to war-making powers abroad, ahead of congressional and public opinion. He was more than just commander-in-chief; he was also now a dispatcher of mass power abroad. He defined foreign threats and defensive necessities, and his pre-war maneuvers constrained efforts by others, especially Congress, to avoid war. Roosevelt pioneered presidential war powers through a combination of public communication about emerging threats and manipulation of expanding American military and economic capabilities. From 1939 to 1941 the president sent aid to Britain in its conflict with Germany, and he simultaneously escalated economic sanctions on Japan. By the summer of 1941, the United States (the world's largest oil exporter) had restricted Japan's access to energy supplies, as it increased aid to China and other neighboring countries. At home, the president organized federal oversight of war production with cooperation from industry and labor leaders, he instituted a selective service draft to register young men for military conscription, and he declared a national state of emergency.[46]

The nation's founders never intended the president to have such broad powers. Roosevelt, however, saw these powers as essential for performing his stated duty, like Lincoln, of protecting the "peace, the integrity, and the safety of the Americas." Future leaders would agree with Roosevelt's judgment, providing strong support for expansive war-making powers in each post-World War II presidency. Roosevelt was the first president to defy constitutional limits on foreign intervention, and he set the mold for those who followed. Just as he had come to dominate domestic policy, he did the same in foreign policy, leaving Congress and other parts of the US government far behind.

Roosevelt still regarded a declaration of war from Congress as necessary, eventually. His successors would jettison that constitutional requirement as well. Roosevelt was the first to act as a global imperial president, and he was the last to ask Congress for formal authorization to do so. Roosevelt's exceptional use of presidential war-making powers became normal—even insufficient—for the next generation of national executives.

THE JAPANESE ATTACK ON PEARL HARBOR WAS NOT A TOTAL surprise to the president and his closest advisors, even if Roosevelt was horrified by the event itself. Like Lincoln in early 1861, Roosevelt anticipated an enemy act of war, especially from the Japanese, who were chafing under American sanctions. The president only underestimated the boldness of the Japanese, expecting them to attack the American bases in the Philippines, not the huge US naval installation in Pearl Harbor, Hawaii—more than 3500 miles from Japan.[47]

The destruction on 7 December 1941—four US battleships sunk, four damaged, 188 US aircraft destroyed, and 2,403 Americans killed—made war finally unavoidable. "Hostilities exist," Roosevelt explained to Congress. "There is no blinking at the fact that our people, our territory, and our interests are in grave danger." Although this was not how Roosevelt hoped to begin full American participation in the war, with such grave devastation to the US Navy, he was relieved that the limits on his war powers had been lifted, at last. He could now pursue vigorous anti-fascist efforts in the open, further expanding the power of the presidency at home and abroad. Like Lincoln after the attack on Fort Sumter, Roosevelt placed the resources of the country under his command to fight a total war aimed at the unconditional surrender of the enemy. Germany and Italy declared war against the United States on 11 December, followed by immediate reciprocal responses from Congress and the president.[48]

"We are now in this war," Roosevelt told listeners over the radio. "We are all in it—all the way. Every single man, woman, and child is a partner in the most tremendous undertaking of our American history. We must share together the bad news and the good news, the defeats and the victories—the changing fortunes of war." And Roosevelt began with an honest appraisal of the bad news: the destruction of Pearl Harbor, the American retreat from the Philippines, and the Japanese attacks on Guam, Wake, and Midway islands.

The president asked Americans to draw confidence from the preparations they had made under his leadership: "Precious months were gained by sending vast quantities of our war material to the Nations of the world still able to resist Axis aggression. . . . That policy has been justified. It has given us time, invaluable time, to build our American assembly lines of production. Assembly lines are now in operation. Others are being rushed to completion. A steady stream of tanks and planes, of guns and ships, and shells and equipment—that is what these eighteen months have given us."

To achieve victory in what Roosevelt anticipated would be a "long war," he needed to direct resources from the White House. He would exceed even Lincoln's exercise of presidential power over domestic affairs. Roosevelt reached deeper into American society to fight a larger, more distant war than any of his predecessors imagined.[49]

The president's strategy, based on the model of the New Deal, was to win the war by harnessing the enormous productive capacities of the United States to feed, clothe, and arm more people than anyone else. A string of new executive agencies, especially the War Production Board (WPB), allowed the president to match resources with military needs, just as Roosevelt had used earlier federal programs and agencies, including the Works Progress Administration (WPA), to match resources with economic needs. The acronyms, powers, and purposes—although unprecedented—were familiar, and even comforting, for Americans who had lived through the New Deal.

Even more than in the 1930s, during the Second World War Roosevelt took control of the American economy. His agencies, not business owners or the market, determined what was produced, where, and how. The federal government placed orders with factories, provided the capital, and then purchased the goods. The federal government also required businesses and workers to follow labor laws that determined pay, work hours, and workplace conditions—including non-discrimination against women and minorities in some instances. Factory life was far from egalitarian, but presidential war directions broke down, at least temporarily, many previous barriers to African American and female participation in the workforce. Roosevelt made the war a lever for bringing citizens together to fight fascism, even if it meant abandoning long-held prejudices, including those held by Roosevelt himself.

THERE WERE LIMITS TO INTEGRATION, AS THERE HAD BEEN during the New Deal. Although Roosevelt created a civil rights division in the Justice Department in 1939 and signed Executive Order 8802 in 1941 to outlaw racial discrimination in defense industries, he continued to target minority groups for differential treatment. Roosevelt appealed to many minority groups, especially African Americans, for electoral support, but he affirmed the prejudices of Jim Crow voters too. That was his electoral strategy, running for minority and traditional white votes at the same time. Roosevelt was a politician above all, and he did play to certain derogatory public attitudes—some of which he shared. Most notoriously, he refused to support anti-lynching congressional legislation that would have outlawed vigilante violence against African Americans, but also antagonized Southern Democratic voters. The New Deal and war president was still a racist president.

On 19 February 1942 Roosevelt revealed the racial component of his leadership. Despite opposition from many of his close advisors, he signed Executive Order 9066, authorizing the War Department to create internment camps for citizens deemed threatening to the national war effort. As a consequence, another new federal agency, the War

Relocation Authority (WRA), forced more than 100,000 American citizens of Japanese descent, as well as a smaller number of German and Italian descent, into federal incarceration. For more than three years, the US government held these citizens without due process, taking them away from their homes, their work, and their communities. By personal order, the president put thousands of innocent people in prisons. Even Lincoln never dared go so far in his efforts to defeat the Confederacy.

Roosevelt knowingly denied citizens their basic rights because he feared their possible role in espionage—despite no evidence—and he hoped to bolster public confidence at their expense. Many Americans felt more secure when these minorities were locked away. For all his other civil rights advances as part of the New Deal and the war effort, internment of the Japanese proved that Roosevelt was not using his expanded powers to prioritize equality or fairness for all groups. He brought more Americans together for common purpose than any previous president, but he continued to exclude and scapegoat certain vulnerable groups when doing so served his larger purposes.[50]

Japanese internment was not Roosevelt's only wartime failure. Throughout the war, as throughout the Depression, the United States failed at more things than its challengers—en route to bigger breakthroughs than anyone else. The failures were necessary for the breakthroughs. Roosevelt could tolerate the failures, as the dictators could not, and he doubled down where he saw emerging possibilities, even as the fascists stuck to their traditional ways. Roosevelt was iterative and pragmatic, avoiding the absolutes that imprisoned other regimes in unbreakable patterns of aggression. Roosevelt used his war powers to pursue an evolving mix of American strategies in different theaters. Nowhere was this more evident than in the building of the atomic bomb, which gave the United States a new source of leverage—not a "trump card," as some wrongly claimed—to induce Japanese surrender.[51]

Initiated in secrecy by Roosevelt in 1942, the Manhattan Project was yet another New Deal-style program that used federal resources to mobilize scattered and diverse citizens, including numerous immigrants.

Through the Manhattan Project, the president spent more money on government-sponsored science than any previous American leader, creating an entire scientific city in Los Alamos, New Mexico that employed more PhDs than any university or business. Roosevelt placed the vast project under his direct authority, through US Army General Leslie Groves. Most significant, Roosevelt ordered the project to serve a specific public need—winning the war with a new, more powerful weapon. The Manhattan Project extended the New Deal model for fighting the Second World War, and it also created the template for "big science" research in the second half of the twentieth century.[52]

The atomic bomb was not just the "absolute weapon," as described by an observer after the war-ending explosions in Hiroshima and Nagasaki; it was also the ultimate New Deal weapon against fascism. The United States developed the first atomic bombs for the same reason that it won the war: it had more resources than any competitor and it had a powerful president who skillfully mobilized those resources for common purpose, encouraging innovation and cooperation as he also pushed his power into new areas of American life. The fascist countries were more centralized and they could also mobilize resources effectively, but they could not innovate and adjust. Roosevelt's inefficiency contributed to early American difficulties in the war, when elements of American society were working at cross-purposes. The country ultimately benefited from the president's support for multiple initiatives and his willingness to get behind new projects, like the atomic bomb, that promised substantial benefits at home and abroad. Roosevelt invested more resources in more things than his counterparts, and he experimented more extensively to find the projects that would yield desired results.[53]

Before his death in April 1945, Roosevelt was still tinkering toward victory. He planned to use the atomic bomb and other pieces of America's gargantuan arsenal to end the war on favorable terms. The president directed American production, he controlled the weapons, and he decided when to use them. He drew on the work of millions of citizens, but he did not consult with them or Congress before making monumental decisions. When Roosevelt's sudden successor, Harry Truman, ordered the dropping of the atomic bombs on Japan in August 1945, he was taking the final step on Roosevelt's long journey since 1933 to place the fate of the nation, and now the world, in the president's hands. From Truman's time to our own, every president has struggled with the almost inhuman responsibility of American leadership in a nuclear age. The president possesses the power to annihilate that predecessors could never imagine.

Roosevelt's war presidency created the superpower presidency. No one, before Roosevelt or since, has been ready for this responsibility. The New Deal and the Second World War gave the president life-and-death powers over countless citizens, at home and abroad. Roosevelt managed those powers to serve the public welfare, defend the nation, and heal its people. He died, in part, from the personal toll. Presidents after Roosevelt could barely keep up with the demands his model of leadership generated.

GEORGE WASHINGTON'S FIRST STATE OF THE UNION ADDRESS in January 1790 captured the uneasy balance between the unifying national authority of the president and the control over daily policy by Congress and the states. Roosevelt's most enduring State of the Union, delivered more than 150 years after Washington's, showed how the long line of presidents in-between had seized much of policy for themselves. Roosevelt's famous words to the nation in January 1941 embraced the rising presidential ambitions over that time.

He described "a world founded upon four essential human freedoms."

> The first is freedom of speech and expression—everywhere in the world.
>
> The second is freedom of every person to worship God in his own way—everywhere in the world.
>
> The third is freedom from want—which, translated into world terms, means economic understandings which will secure to every nation a healthy peacetime life for its inhabitants—everywhere in the world.
>
> The fourth is freedom from fear—which, translated into world terms, means a world-wide reduction of armaments to such a point

and in such a thorough fashion that no nation will be in a position to commit an act of physical aggression against any neighbor—anywhere in the world.[54]

The Four Freedoms defined Roosevelt's purpose as a New Deal and war president. They justified his uses of expansive powers and his imposition, repeatedly, of White House influence where it had never been so strong before. The process began with a jumble of new financial, employment, and welfare agencies in the 1930s. The process continued into the 1940s with a new generation of agencies devoted to rearmament, production, and security. Washington, D.C. became a year-round national management headquarters, replacing the seasonal swamp that served as a small town capital before Roosevelt. The government grew in the service of the Four Freedoms, and the president acted as its driver, taking the reins from the more cumbersome and divided Congress.[55]

The Second World War erased the traditional domestic focus of American presidents, and it carried them far from home in pursuing the Four Freedoms. Roosevelt not only traveled around the US frequently, he also ventured abroad more than any of his predecessors. Although he was wheelchair bound, Roosevelt flew to meet allies and participate in regional gatherings. The president made monumental decisions in these meetings without consulting Congress or the states. He used his influence to shape the emerging contours of postwar societies, especially in Europe and Asia.

Roosevelt's promotion of the Four Freedoms helped define a new international system. The war ended and the United States was the only large democratic country left standing, prepared to reconstruct the devastated nations in line with the Four Freedoms. These straightforward principles became the motivators and the content for a new American internationalism expressed through the United Nations, regional alliances, and occupation regimes in Europe and Asia. The president's stature grew as the opportunities for spreading the Four Freedoms multiplied in the last stages of the war.[56]

German and Japanese surrender gave way to Russian-American tensions because Roosevelt's vision threatened the power of a Soviet government that had also won the war, but at much higher cost than the

United States. More than 25 million Russians perished during the Second World War; fewer than half a million Americans died. Soviet leader Josef Stalin had to fortify himself and his regime against the juggernaut that the New Deal and the war had created in what was, just a few years before, an American nation trying to isolate itself from the wider world. The Soviet Union, and other postwar American adversaries, feared the increasing power commanded by the president.[57]

Roosevelt did not create the Cold War between the United States and the Soviet Union; on the contrary, he did all he could to smooth relations and avoid conflict. And he might have succeeded had he lived, but the president who commanded atomic weapons, the most productive economy, and a gargantuan bureaucracy of surrogate actors was almost inevitably threatening to a communist regime intent on preserving itself against foreign influences. President Truman had little opportunity to allay Stalin's concerns about how American power might be used. The Soviet dictator entertained exaggerated fears of foreign aggression after the war, but his reading of American presidential power was largely accurate. Stalin ruled by force with little resistance, but also limited resources. Roosevelt, and then Truman, governed with continued resistance, but unmatched resources for pursuing their aims.[58]

At the time of his death, Roosevelt had restored the American economy and nearly defeated fascism on two continents. He bequeathed growing military and economic capabilities to his successors. With each new weapon and program—from the atomic bomb to the Marshall Plan and Point Four development aid—the president increased his influence and shaped the postwar international system. No other figure had more global impact than the American president after 1945.

Roosevelt made it possible for figures like Harry Truman and Dwight Eisenhower to "lead the free world." Since George Washington's time Americans had identified themselves as a society apart from the "Old World"; they now defined themselves as *the* nation-builders, reformers, and defenders of "developing" societies. If the American president was one of many powerful international figures before Roosevelt entered the Oval Office in 1933, when he died the president had risen as an executive without parallel—directing more financial, human, and institutional capital than all of his peers combined. He was as close to a true leader of the world as anyone has come, before or since.[59]

THE ROOSEVELT PRESIDENCY WAS A LEVIATHAN, "CIVILIZED," IN Saul Bellow's words, by the character of the man in charge and the constitutional structure he worked within. Roosevelt's personal commitment to decency, democracy, and cooperation disciplined the powers he harnessed for the benefit of millions of citizens. Many people, however, remained left out. Roosevelt's critics represented groups that did not share the benefits, and also recognized the danger in the powers the president had amassed. Charles Beard, a distinguished historian and commentator, resisted what he viewed as the overweening and often unchecked powers of a president who dominated the economy, war, and many other elements of society. Such a president looked more and more like a dictator than the dispassionate and distant figure embodied by Washington. Roosevelt carried the presidency far from its eighteenth-century origins, which made it more attractive to citizens like Bellow, but also more threatening to principled democrats, like Beard.[60]

The critics were prescient. Roosevelt built the postwar presidency, the one we still have today, and he was the last to master it. His successors would find themselves struggling to manage an office that more often managed them. Extraordinary power not only corrupts, it encourages distraction, hubris, narcissism, and excess. Good men followed Roosevelt in the presidency, but none of them accomplished nearly as much, even though each worked equally as hard, if not harder. The problem for Roosevelt's successors was too much power, too much responsibility, and too much temptation. Roosevelt was the last great president because the office was still small enough for him to control it, just barely. After him, the continued increase in presidential power exceeded executive capacity. The office grew to serve suffering humanity in the mid-twentieth century, but it ultimately became impossible in its scale and scope. That was the dilemma that undid Roosevelt's deeply frustrated successors, and the citizens who elected them.

Roosevelt spent more of his twelve years in the presidency responding to crises than leading in new and dynamic directions. In his best moments, he turned crises into opportunities for creativity, but that was not always the case, and it was increasingly difficult as war followed depression. From skill and experience, Roosevelt still found a way to preserve space for some strategic leadership. That space shrunk during his time in the White House, and it nearly disappeared for those who came after him.

The presidency became a lonely office in the twentieth century because it conveyed an image of overwhelming power, but possessed a diminished capacity for creative action. Presidents faced ever-growing demands on their attention, their resources, and their sympathy that they simply could not meet. They found few openings for reflection amid the onslaught of foreign and domestic responsibilities.

For all his warmth and empathy, Roosevelt felt the isolation of excessive responsibility, and he anticipated the dismay of his all-powerful but overburdened successors. "Someday you may well be sitting here where I am now as President of the United States," he said in conversation with Harry Hopkins. "And when you are, you'll be looking at that door over there and knowing that practically everybody who walks through it wants something out of you. You'll learn what a lonely job this is." [61]

Global power and personal isolation go hand in hand, weakening the ambitious leaders who have struggled with both since Roosevelt's presidential reign. In trying to do so much for so many, the postwar president could no longer maintain close connection with anyone other than himself. Like the doctor who cares more for cures than patients, the Cold War president became a powerful technician pursuing policies that no longer healed.

PART II
Fall

CHAPTER 7

Frustrated Frontiersmen

Franklin Roosevelt opened his presidency by counseling against fear; John F. Kennedy began by proclaiming a new tough-minded idealism: "Let every nation know, whether it wishes us well or ill, that we shall pay any price, bear any burden, meet any hardship, support any friend, oppose any foe to assure the survival and the success of liberty."[1]

Kennedy substituted flagrant displays of courage for the modesty of early postwar America. His "Camelot" entourage condemned the lack of creativity in Roosevelt's successors, promising a return to the energetic experimentation of the New Deal. Kennedy advisor Arthur Schlesinger, Jr. captured the restlessness of many citizens living under the competent but often uninspiring presidencies of Harry Truman and Dwight Eisenhower. "Our urgent need today," Schlesinger wrote, "is for a new conviction of national purpose and a new sense of national identity." He predicted, "The essential difference between the fifties and sixties will lie rather less in ideas or programs than in the *spirit* which informs our action. . . . What we most need is a new will—a new sense of vision and a new sense of resolution."[2]

The Kennedy presidency became an instrument for renewing Roosevelt's New Deal spirit in a Cold War context of American wealth instead of poverty, and foreign intervention instead of isolation. "We were activists," another Kennedy advisor recounted. "We thought the world could be changed. We thought one man could make a difference. You know, this is the Kennedy thesis. We believed that individual effort could

181

change the world; that one man's efforts did make a difference. Pragmatic, idealistic, activist. This was an interventionist administration."[3]

The "deal" in Roosevelt's New Deal was about helping those who had been left out—the "forgotten" men and women in a suffering society. "Deal" meant compromise, cooperation, and collective sacrifice. For a nation that had emerged from depression and world war but now confronted discontent at home and nuclear danger from a communist enemy, Kennedy promised more than "deals." He promoted achievements that would help the country break out of current stalemates and inspire the best in citizens. Kennedy looked forward to a "New Frontier" that would build upon the New Deal for a competitive and frequently frightening Cold War. With the emergence of new nations from collapsing empires in Asia and Africa, and the rise of more active minority populations within the United States, the president faced wider demands on his power than ever before.[4]

By the late 1950s, citizens at home and abroad looked to him as more than just a national figurehead. He was the self-proclaimed leader of the "free world." People expected him to promote continuous improvement in the lives of diverse communities. He was the chief advocate of democratic development and the chief source of assistance (economic and military) for that goal.

In this context of heightened expectations, the president had to be a visionary. To explain how he was using the incredible resources at his disposal and how he was integrating the needs of different peoples, the president had to paint a compelling picture of an American-led world that promoted freedom and prosperity. He had to make the American-led world appear benevolent and inevitable, but also perilous and unprecedented, demanding strong and direct leadership from Washington. The "spirit" of history seemed to move in the American direction, and the president was the necessary pilot for that process. Roosevelt had first promoted this perspective with his call for a world governed by the "Four Freedoms," but Truman and Eisenhower had not matched his eloquence or vision. Kennedy intended to offer both, surpassing his predecessors.

Like Roosevelt, Kennedy was an activist, but his vision was more ambitious, unilateral, and militant. Roosevelt's New Deal was conscious of limits, at least beyond US borders; Kennedy's "New Frontier" denied most limits. Roosevelt hedged his bets, juggling contradictory options. Kennedy barreled forward, using the presidency to push Americans steadfastly into new challenges and opportunities. He chose the metaphor of settling new territory, rather than compromising on old land.

Accepting the Democratic Party nomination for president in Los Angeles, Kennedy connected his leadership with expansion, growth, and idealism: "I stand tonight facing west on what was once the last frontier. From the lands that stretch three thousand miles behind me, the pioneers of old gave up their safety, their comfort and sometimes their lives to build a new world here in the West." Kennedy continued, "Today, some would say that those struggles are all over—that all the horizons have been explored—that all the battles have been won— that there is no longer an American frontier. But I trust that no one in this vast assemblage will agree with those sentiments. For the problems are not all solved and the battles are not all won—and we stand today on the edge of a New Frontier—the frontier of the 1960s—a frontier of unknown opportunities and perils—a frontier of unfulfilled hopes and threats."[5]

ONLY FORTY-THREE YEARS OLD AT THE TIME OF HIS INAUGURATION (just 279 days older than Theodore Roosevelt, still the youngest president in history), Kennedy thought of himself as a pioneer. Although he came from a wealthy and well-connected family, Kennedy was an Irish Catholic, and thus an outsider to the main lines of ethnic and religious power in the United States. His youth also set him apart from the middle-aged lawyers and businessmen who dominated American leadership circles. Kennedy represented a new generation of leaders—defined by expertise and will—who promised to bring renewed energy to the American dream through enlightened leadership.[6]

Echoing Theodore Roosevelt, Kennedy embodied the ambitions of restless, highly educated American men who self-consciously lived the "strenuous life." They had served in the Second World War and had found success in their careers, but they felt frustrated by the limited creativity of Truman and Eisenhower. The first two postwar presidents appeared too traditional, too unsophisticated, and often too modest. As Kennedy and others saw it, they underperformed, given all that they could have achieved.[7]

Strength of mind and body went hand in hand with freedom for Kennedy and his followers. Risk-taking was essential for achievement. Charisma and sex appeal supported ambitious claims of American purpose. Articulate and made for television, Kennedy was a new kind of global American president. He was a glamorous celebrity who promised a spark of "magic" for postwar America, and the wider world.[8]

DESPITE KENNEDY'S CHARISMA, FRANKLIN ROOSEVELT WAS STILL the lodestar of American leadership. He did not yet have a statue in Washington, D.C., but the modern city was his monument. Neither Abraham Lincoln nor Theodore Roosevelt would have recognized Franklin Roosevelt's Washington, a city of imperial pretensions, with its massive government buildings testifying to the new global power of the nation and its federal government. Roosevelt's presidency had dragged the country from depression and isolation to growth and world leadership. Kennedy's advisors reminded him how different his inauguration day in 1961 was from Roosevelt's in 1933, but they also looked back to the New Deal presidency because it set so many of the expectations and demands for what was now the world's most powerful office.[9]

The new president did not confront a single crisis, like the Great Depression, but rather a series of challenges that pulled his administration in multiple directions. Unlike Roosevelt, Kennedy struggled to establish priorities and pursue them consistently. This became the pattern for every postwar president, especially after Kennedy. Strong presidential power, at home and abroad, coupled with vast expectations, triggered a proliferation of foreign and domestic demands. Cold War presidents were always overstretched presidents. Each ambitious administration, seeking to solve big problems, found itself overwhelmed and tied in knots.

Two years into office, Kennedy reflected on this difficulty: "The American Presidency," he wrote, "is the center of the play of pressure, interest, and idea in the nation; and the presidential office is the vortex into which all the elements of national decision are irresistibly drawn.

And it is mysterious because the essence of ultimate decision remains impenetrable to the observer—often, indeed, to the decider himself."[10]

Washington, Jackson, and Lincoln never viewed the presidency as the "center" for "all the elements of national decision." And they never described presidential decision-making as "mysterious" or "impenetrable." Theodore Roosevelt strove to make the presidency more central for reforming American society, but the office remained distant from most citizens. Franklin Roosevelt moved the office into what Kennedy called "the center of the play of pressure, interest, and idea in the nation." Kennedy inherited that condition of presidential centrality, as the range of postwar presidential responsibilities grew at home and across the globe.

Even after two years in the White House, he remained defensive. Like Roosevelt, he commented on the "loneliness" of the office, despite the constant barrage of "divergent advice and clamorous counsel." "A wise President," as Kennedy put it, "gathers strength and insight from the nation. Still, in the end, he is alone."[11]

In the frenzy of White House policy-making, the president was isolated from the issues of daily economy and security that his power most deeply affected. He received extensive information—Kennedy speech writer Theodore Sorenson described him as "drowning in paper"—but the president saw less of the lives behind the memos. The country (and much of the world) now came to the White House, and that volume of demand profoundly restricted the executive's ability to reflect, connect, and empathize with the millions of people he touched. Power at this level depersonalized what had been a profoundly personal office.[12]

Kennedy was the first of many presidents to feel lost in his own power. His frequent sadness, unlike Roosevelt's unbreakable joviality, reflected the frustrations of the postwar presidency. Despite the public image of carefree charisma, Kennedy described himself as "always on the edge of irritability." Reading the frequent criticisms of his leadership, he exclaimed: "If they want this job they can have it tomorrow." Being president was not all it was cracked up to be, even in Camelot.[13]

KENNEDY'S EXCITING NEW FRONTIER WAS QUICKLY LOST IN MANaging smaller clogged roadways. His first hundred days, like Roosevelt's, were filled with crises, but the demands were fragmentary and often contradictory. The Kennedy crises encouraged energetic reactions from his advisors, but also a departure from a coherent focus on core national interests. The president quickly found that his daily actions did not match his priorities. The crises set his agenda. Trying to do more than his predecessors, he often found himself accomplishing less.

This was especially true for foreign policy, where the administration deployed resources, particularly in Cuba and Southeast Asia, that achieved little, and often undermined American purposes. The challenge was not too little presidential power or experimentation, but too many demands on the executive, and his ambition to solve all problems. Fearing inaction in the face of communist advances, the president responded too often with interventions that increased instability and openings for the adversary, while draining American lives and treasure. Ironically, these outcomes were often precisely what Kennedy and his advisors predicted, but they felt pressured to act nonetheless.

A giant superpower could not sit back and claim an absence of good options when its ambitions were so great. This reasoning motivated the ill-fated invasion of the Cuban Bay of Pigs in April 1961 and covert deployments of American military force to South Vietnam at the same time. Gloomy prognostications about the nature of American allies and the capabilities of American military assets surrounded each decision. Kennedy was pessimistic from the start. He approved action, and predictable failure, in Cuba and South Vietnam because he felt domestic and international pressure to do something. He had all this power, and he had to use it. If he couldn't do something to stop communists in Cuba and Vietnam, how would he stand strong elsewhere?[14]

The experience of German and Japanese appeasement in the 1930s hung over Kennedy's head (the infamous "Munich Analogy"), as did the pretension of American invincibility. It was easier for Kennedy, Lyndon Johnson, and every successive president to intervene and hope for the best, rather than admit to limitations. Global power induced global activism, even when it undermined American interests.[15]

Roosevelt, of course, faced enormous pressures during his presidency, but he did not address the sheer range of simultaneous challenges that Kennedy now confronted. The United States was a far less dominant country in the 1930s, and demands for American action were therefore more limited. The profound suffering of the Great Depression disciplined Americans against expecting too much; the limited horizons of the time contributed to popular skepticism about foreign interventions. Roosevelt felt constrained by the isolationist impulse, not the pressure to intervene that characterized the Cold War. The continued growth of presidential power, from the 1930s to the 1960s, reversed assumptions about how that power should be used.[16]

Roosevelt needed a long time to prepare the country for war against fascism, and his responses to civil rights agitation at home were hesitant, at best. Still, overall, Roosevelt's achievements created expectations of ever greater and faster presidential involvement to insure citizen welfare and security against a wide variety of dangers. Kennedy contributed to these rising expectations with his ambitious New Frontier rhetoric, but that rhetoric also entrapped him in hyper-action, and ultimately, policy overload.

The volume of crises was just too much for Kennedy's "best and the brightest," whose immense talents could not keep up. Unemployment remained high (near 7 percent of the eligible workforce) and growth was slow, but the administration also faced concerns about rising debt. Civil rights marchers in the South and "Freedom Riders" from the North pressured Kennedy to use his executive power to break the civil rights logjam in Congress, but the president also received warnings of increased violence if he encouraged more agitation in Southern counties. Kennedy tried to reduce the risks of nuclear confrontation, even as he increased the US nuclear arsenal to counter Moscow's conventional advantages. Kennedy had to assure allies that American security commitments were credible, just as he had to show that he was serious about negotiations and disarmament. And this was only a partial list of the president's daily policy menu—bursting with options that overwhelmed the man at the head of the table.

Most vexing, the president tried to place the United States firmly on the side of countries emerging from colonialism, but he still saw a need to intervene in these areas, often undermining popular governments, to prevent the spread of communist influence. The latter pressure took the president farthest afield from his geopolitical priorities, as he spent much of his time in office debating policies for Congo, Algeria, British Guiana (later Guyana), Laos, Cuba, and, of course, South Vietnam. Those were not the regions that would determine the future of the United States, and they were not the places where an ambitious executive intended to define his presidency. But in making the United States the leader of the free world, Roosevelt had forced his successors to maintain that posture.[17]

From his first days in office, Kennedy was unmoored from the issues he intended to build his presidency around: American growth and containment of Soviet power. He was the first in a line of postwar presidents to discover that executive responsibilities were now so extensive, they had become self-defeating. The crises ruled the president more than he ruled the crises. He and his advisors were in constant reactive mode from each civil rights protest and congressional budget battle to each nuclear weapons development and communist advance in a distant country. "There was too little time to plan, to think," David Halberstam observed. "One could only confront the most immediate problems and get rid of them piecemeal but as quickly as possible, or at least postpone any action."[18]

Roosevelt had operated on a broad policy canvas too, but he kept his focus on jobs at home and defeating fascism abroad. Kennedy managed too many responsibilities and commitments to maintain a similar focus. The urgent and immediate crowded out the strategic for Kennedy, as it never did for Franklin Roosevelt, Theodore Roosevelt, or Abraham Lincoln. Kennedy's youthful energy and ambition only contributed to the fragmenting pressures on American power.[19]

CONSTANT CRISES WERE ONLY ONE PART OF THE CHALLENGE. Kennedy also inherited a gargantuan government bureaucracy, evident in the sprawling growth of Washington, D.C. as the hub for federal agencies. To implement the New Deal, Roosevelt had created numerous bureaus—including the Securities and Exchange Commission (SEC), the Social Security Administration, and the Federal Deposit Insurance Corporation (FDIC), among many others. They occupied the ubiquitous barracks-like buildings hastily constructed along the crowded streets running through the once seasonal swamp-town turned year-round city of directors, administrators, secretaries, coordinators, and countless assistants.

Although the new executive agencies allowed the president to manage the economy and American society as never before, they also protected permanent commitments he had to fulfill and habitual routines he had to follow. Roosevelt created the agencies for his purposes in the 1930s and 1940s, but they matured to set the purposes for future presidents. By the 1960s they had become organized constituencies, with active stakeholders who made it increasingly difficult for an executive to consider closing them or departing from their priorities. The federal agencies were tools of modern government policy that came to define everyday content and practice. Schlesinger complained that they "remained in bulk a force against innovation with an inexhaustible capacity to dilute, delay, and obstruct presidential purpose. Only so many fights were possible." Bureaucrats would often win by wearing down their busier and more distracted boss.[20]

The agencies had real power, beyond their ability to obfuscate and delay. The rational behavior of bureaucracies encouraged popular belief in their capabilities. They provided the services—grants, safety measures, and pensions that Americans now demanded. The bureaucracies also measured problems and defined success, with their control over information and their mobilization of "expert" opinion. Kennedy confronted not only overwhelming demands on his power, but ubiquitous measures of performance derived from bureaucratic analysis: the gross domestic product (GDP), the consumer price index (CPI), and the nuclear balance, among others. These measures created imperatives for action, despite presidential priorities, especially if the numbers tracked in the wrong direction.[21]

Of course, the numbers were never "real"; they were bureaucratic approximations that created perceptions the president had to address. Measures of slow economic growth and increasing poverty in 1961, for example, forced Kennedy to prioritize those issues over investments in education, health care, and other social needs. The same was true for foreign policy, where measures of growing communist strength, including the nuclear balance, pushed the president to prioritize anti-communist actions in Cuba and Vietnam, rather than a broader promotion of democracy and international stability. Bureaucracies made facts, and presidents had to act accordingly.

Roosevelt defined the meaning of the Great Depression and the Second World War by using the radio to explain certain facts in a coherent and compelling way to ordinary citizens. The president chose the facts that mattered most and he constructed a narrative to justify his policy priorities around them. His apparent authority and narrative sincerity made his words persuasive for skeptical listeners, like Saul Bellow. Roosevelt's narrative resonated with the experiences of citizens, and explained complex local challenges. Max Weber had argued that state power turned on the monopoly of violence; Roosevelt proved that the near monopoly of facts mattered just as much.[22]

Kennedy did not command anywhere near the same narrative authority as Roosevelt, despite his magnetism and eloquence. Kennedy's charming of news reporters was not sufficient either. The growth of federal agencies and their public reporting capabilities created a more competitive space for narrative and fact. The president simply could not control how Americans thought about the challenges they faced, as Roosevelt did during the Banking Crisis of 1933 or the days after the Pearl Harbor attack. Although the "bully pulpit" had a bigger bully, he no longer spoke with the same public authority.

Arthur Krock, one of the most respected reporters in Washington, D.C. since the 1920s, observed how Kennedy and his successors struggled with increasing difficulty to set their own headlines, and escape the story lines promoted by others—including "experts" and interest groups—occupying authoritative positions around government. "Historians," Krock predicted, "will differ on whether the political philosophy and the economic and military direction of any nation have changed more fundamentally than those of the United States in a comparable period of time—1933 to 1967," when Krock wrote these words. "Among these changes are a Federal union almost replaced by a mass Federal democracy controlled by an alliance of politicians and special interest groups," rather than the traditional elected figures— Hoover, Roosevelt, and Eisenhower—Krock had covered throughout his long journalistic career.[23]

Kennedy tried to focus on his strategic priorities, but he failed because there were too many easily accessible and seemingly "factual" measures of reality for citizens to find on their own—often as reported in local newspapers. Federal agencies studied numerous issues, they gained credibility as experts, and they cut complex problems into simple assessments of growth or decline, improvement or regression. The bureaucratic measures colored, and often undermined, the reality that Kennedy had hoped to make from his imagined, but soon forgotten, New Frontier.

Kennedy never controlled the framing of his program in the way that Roosevelt did. He never effectively mobilized the enormous power at his disposal to pursue a coherent domestic or international agenda. He never stimulated the imagination of Americans in the ways that Roosevelt's rhetoric opened a new world for suffering citizens. Kennedy's eloquence and image were seductive, but not uplifting, because alternative information undermined his strongest claims.

Where was the New Frontier for a country that seemed to be going in so many directions at once? How could people serve their country when there were so many different public definitions of what the country was about? American politics in the 1960s centered on many things—civil rights, consumerism, anti-communism, democratization, and development—in many places, well beyond the fifty states. Despite the Cold War, the country lacked a truly unifying challenge.[24]

Built for the Great Depression and the Second World War, the presidency Kennedy inherited was not ready for the diffusion of superpower responsibilities. Arthur Krock described this shift. His lamentations about "mass Federal democracy" reflected his frustration that so many more people pulled at the government—postwar Lilliputians tying down the impressive and growing Gulliver of New Deal creation. The public agencies, organizations, and citizens' groups empowered by Roosevelt held down Kennedy, rather than helping him to fly high.[25]

THE TIES ON THE PRESIDENT ARE EVIDENT IN HIS DAILY CALendars, which constitute the best available day-to-day record of executive leadership since the early twentieth century. Franklin Roosevelt's calendars were informal, recorded by hand, and populated with a small number of daily appointments. Roosevelt had short ceremonial meetings (usually in the early afternoons) and longer policy discussions (usually in the late afternoons and evenings, often including dinner). He met with a wide variety of people, most of whom had a connection to New Deal or World War II policy matters. Roosevelt's daily calendar reveals an executive with focus, flexibility, and some spontaneity. He has time to acquire new information, discuss it with numerous people, and then carefully decide on his chosen course of action. A day in the life of Roosevelt's presidency, even after a traumatic event like the Japanese attack on Pearl Harbor, seems humane—even "slow" by later standards.

Roosevelt's long-time advisor, Samuel Rosenman, recounted the president's well-paced and purposeful work routine:

> He had breakfast in bed at about eight, during which he read papers, talked with his immediate staff, and laid out the work for the day. Then about ten in the morning to the [Oval Office], where he worked without stop, with lunch at his desk, until five in the afternoon. Then home for a swim and some tea, frequently with visitors on official or political business. Dinner was often with one or more friends, public officials or official guests, seldom alone. After dinner—except for a rare social evening—he was wheeled into his study, where he continued to work on papers, speeches, bills; he even carried memoranda and reports to bed; frequently he continued to discuss business with me or others after getting into bed. And he always had to read several late newspapers before finally turning out the light.[26]

Roosevelt worked hard, but he protected opportunities for deep engagement with people and issues, and he carved out time for reflection and creativity. He was never frantic, and rarely rushed. He was in control, even in the immediate aftermath of horrible, unexpected events.

Presidents Truman and Eisenhower had their daily calendars typed, reflecting more formality, pre-planning, and staff management of the president's time. They also had slightly more meetings per day, on average, and fewer long, late-day meetings than Roosevelt. Truman

343

Monday

DECEMBER 8

APPOINTMENTS		APPOINTMENTS
8.00		2.15
8.15		2.30
8.30		2.45
8.45		3.00
9.00 At White House		3.15
9.15		3.30
9.30		3.45
9.45		4.00 Vice President + Members
10.00		4.15 of Congress, signing
10.15		4.30 War Resolution Against Japan
10.30		4.30 Hon. Norman Davis
10.45		4.45 Mayor LaGuardia
11.00		5.00
11.15		5.15
11.30		5.30
11.45		5.45
12.00 Left for Capitol		6.00
12.15		6.15
12.30 Deliver Message to Congress		6.30
12.45		6.45
1.00 (Lunch)		7.00
1.15		7.15
1.30		7.30
1.45		7.45
2.00 Russian Ambassador Maxim Litvinoff		8.00
		8.15

SOURCE FOR PAGES 193-194: Franklin Delano Roosevelt Presidential Library, Hyde Park, New York.

11 55 To Doctor's Office 12 05

12 05 To Capitol to deliver message to
joint session of Congress, Yc by Mrs. R.,
both aides, Capt. + Mrs. James R.,
Mr. Harry Hopkins, Judge Rosenman,
Mr. Hamlin, Miss Tully, Mrs. Dorothy Brady,
Miss Thompson, Mr. Robt. Sherwood, Mrs. Helm
Ambass. Phillips, + Mrs. Stephen Early 12 55

12 55 To Doctor's Office 1 20

1 20 Lunch - Mr. Harry Hopkins, Mr. Robt. Sherwood,
Judge Samuel Rosenman + Miss Grace Tully

3 54 To Office; 6 55 From Office via Doctor's

7 30 Dinner - List

12 20 Retired

Mrs. Roosevelt

9 00 To Civ. Defense Office 11 55

12 05 See Above

12 55 To Civ. Defense Office 5 45

(1 05 Lunch - Sm. Din. Rm. - List (13)) 3 00

(4 20 Meeting of group to hear Mrs. Mary Bethune List 5 20)

6 30 Dinner - Miss Thompson + Mr. Lash 7 10

7 10 To Airport enroute Los Angeles, Yc by
Miss Thompson + Mr. Lash .

Houseguests

4 45 Capt. Elliott Roosevelt, Major G. B. Dany +
Lt. Gerald Keely arrived

6 30 Mr. Joseph Lash 7 10

and Eisenhower were earlier to rise and to bed than their somewhat nocturnal predecessor. Nonetheless, their workdays were not that different from Roosevelt's. They both protected time for close attention to a small number of domestic and foreign issues—with adequate opportunity for discussion, reflection, and relaxation. Both Truman and Eisenhower valued time away from the office—often in Key West, Florida, for the former, and at Augusta National Golf Club for the latter. They were in control of their time and their relatively small staffs. Their executive lives looked like those of business leaders around the country, many of whom were Eisenhower's closest friends and golf buddies.

Kennedy wanted to run his presidency in similar ways. He was ambitious, but he was not a workaholic. He enjoyed many diversions, and he needed extensive time in his schedule for a variety of medical treatments. Kennedy valued conversation, he sought diverse opinions, and he hoped to define his presidency through achievements on big domestic and international issues. Roosevelt was the model for him and his advisors—all of whom came of age admiring the great man.[27]

Yet as Kennedy's daily calendar reveals, he departed immediately from that model. The effort to follow Roosevelt, as Richard Neustadt (Kennedy's advisor on executive organization) suggested, produced a very different result. Making the president ubiquitous—Neustadt's advice was to "oversee, coordinate, and interfere with virtually everything"—created a bias to quick action, rather than deliberative consideration. It also fed unrealistic expectations, stretching the president too thin, and encouraging frequent arbitrariness. The vast multiplication of issues between Roosevelt's time and Kennedy's meant that the latter could not cover all the topics knowledgably and efficiently. Delegation and prioritization were essential, and clarity of purpose was therefore more important than direct management. As recounted in his calendars, too much of Kennedy's time was spent managing messes, not leading where he wanted to go.[28]

Kennedy had far more meetings than any of his predecessors, and these were dominated by people who worked for him and had similar backgrounds ("the best and brightest"), not the broader range of people and opinions that Roosevelt imbibed at his informal conversation table.

Kennedy talked with more people, but they were more of the same, and they moved quickly from one issue to another because they already knew the answers. They solved problems and resolved issues very professionally; they did not experiment, as Roosevelt's more spontaneous work-style allowed.

Kennedy also spent more time entertaining visiting leaders and diplomats than any previous president. This behavior reflected, in part, the president's interest in foreign affairs and high society. More significant, however, was the rise of new nations in former imperial territories and the expanding American presence around the world. Roosevelt, Truman, and Eisenhower thought very little about Africa, and they spent even less time wining and dining its dignitaries, unless they worked for the British or French governments. By 1961 the proliferation of independent states and increasing American concern about the spread of communism crowded the president's calendar with more leaders to charm, persuade, and often assist. Ceremonial duties diminished the president's previously available deliberative policy time. More media events at home, particularly on television, had a similar effect. All the new talking made it harder to find time for serious thinking in the White House.[29]

THE FRENETIC PACE OF THE KENNEDY PRESIDENCY CONTRASTED sharply with the slower, more deliberative Roosevelt years. This was evident during the most shocking day of Kennedy's tenure—his "Pearl Harbor." On 16 October 1962 President Kennedy's national security team briefed him on evidence that the Soviet Union had secretly begun assembling nuclear missiles in Cuba, capable of irradiating the United States within a few minutes. Although the United States maintained a massive numerical superiority in its nuclear arsenal, no adversary had ever brought so much destructive power so close to the homeland. Kennedy and his advisors were indignant at Soviet aggression, and determined to force the removal of the missiles.

"I don't think we've got much time on these missiles," Kennedy concluded near the end of an hour-long discussion squeezed into a tightly scheduled day of meetings with congressmen, foreign princes, businessmen, journalists, and various others. "We can't wait two weeks while we're getting ready to roll. Maybe we just have to just take them out, and continue our other preparations if we decide to do that. That may be where we end up. I think we ought to, beginning right now, be preparing to. Because that's what we're going to do *anyway.* . . . We're going to take out these missiles."[30]

What became known as the Cuban Missile Crisis preoccupied the thinking of the president and his closest advisors for the next two weeks. Yet unlike Roosevelt after the Pearl Harbor attack, Kennedy could not devote maximum time and energy to this world-changing challenge. Beginning on 16 October 1962, his calendars recount a breakneck marathon of other crises, commitments, and obligations. They reveal that Kennedy had to work more hours, greet more people, and manage larger meetings than Roosevelt—just to keep up with all of his presidential responsibilities. Kennedy struggled to find time to deliberate with his closest advisors about a crisis that could trigger nuclear war. Despite the enormous stakes, superpower conflict in Cuba received less day-to-day presidential priority than the events surrounding world war a generation earlier. The comparison between Roosevelt's and Kennedy's calendars is illuminating (see pages 198-200).

The calendars for Kennedy's days before and after 16 October 1962 looked very much the same. Meetings and ceremonies trumped policy priorities. Busyness discouraged deliberative focus. The president was everywhere and therefore less present anywhere than his predecessors, even as he worked more hours and charmed countless people.

Scholars of the Cuban Missile Crisis, particularly those who correctly praise Kennedy's prudent judgment, miss this point. Although the Executive Committee spent the two weeks of the crisis in intense discussions, the president still allocated most of his time to many other things—a degree of executive distraction not seen before in such an intense moment.

Kennedy's fractured attention had serious policy effects. Going back to the failed April 1961 American-sponsored invasion of the Bay of Pigs in Cuba, military and strategic advisors had created a series of "facts" and processes that foreshortened the president's options. They defined the Soviet Union and Cuba as aggressive allies who necessitated

TUESDAY, OCTOBER 16, 1962

9:25 am	The President arrived in the office.
9:30 - 9:48 am	Commander and Mrs. Walter M. Schirra, Jr. Walter, III and Suzanne
9:50 - 9:54 am	Mr. Edward McDermott
10:00 - 10:26 am	(Congressman Ross Bass) OFF THE RECORD (Tennessee)
10:26 - 10:30 am	(Hon. C. Douglas Dillon) (Hon. Henry Fowler) (Hon. Myer Feldman)
10:33 - 11:15 am	The President met with the members of the Panel on Mental Retardation in the Fish Room.
11:15 - 11:46 am	Hon. Charles E. Bohlen U. S. Ambassador to France
11:50 - 12:57 pm	OFF THE RECORD MEETING RE CUBA (The Vice President) (Hon. Dean Rusk) (General Maxwell Taylor) (Hon. Roswell Gilpatric) (Hon. Edwin Martin)
1:03 pm	The President departed the office and went to the Mansion.

1:00 pm	LUNCHEON at the White House in honor of His Royal Highness Hasan al-Rida al-Sanusi, Crown Prince of the United Kingdom of Libya:
	The President
	H. R. H. The Crown Prince of the United Kingdom of Libya, Hasan al-Rida al-Sanusi
	H. E. Waniis al-Qadhaafi
	  Minister of Foreign Affairs
	H. E. The Ambassador of Libya
	  Dr. Mohieddine Fekini
	H. E. Yunis Bilkhair
	  Minister of Defense
	The Honorable Fathi al-Khoja
	  Master of Cermonies of the Royal Household

(continued)

SOURCE FOR PAGES 198-200: John F. Kennedy Presidential Library, Boston, Massachusetts.

1:00 pm   LUNCHEON list continued from previous page:

The Honorable Abdullah Sikta
    Director of the Development Council
The Honorable Khaliifa Muusa
    Under Secretary of Finance and Director-General
    of Customs
The Honorable Ahmad al-Hamaali
    Federal Director of Press and Publications
Mr. Abu al-Qaasim al-Ghamaary
    Private Secretary to His Royal Highness
Colonel Idris Issawi
    Deputy Chief of Staff, Libyan Army
Colonel Raasim al-Naaili
    Aide-de-Camp to His Royal Highness

The Vice President
Hon. George Ball, Under Secretary of State
Hon. Adlai E. Stevenson
Senator Benjamin A. Smith, II
Hon. J. Wesley Jones
Hon. Angier Biddle Duke
Hon. McGeorge Bundy
Hon. G. Mennen Williams
Hon. Edmond C. Hutchinson
Hon. Eugene R. Black
Hon. George W. Mitchell
Mr. Henry J. Tasca
Mr. Henry C. Alexander
Hon. Lewis Clark
Mr. James O. Donnell, II
Mr. Boyd France
Dr. Jerome H. Holland
Mr. Alfred Jacobsen
Dr. Majiid Khaddouri
Mr. Leonard F. McCollum
Mr. Clark R. Mullenhoff
Mr. Michael Ross
Mr. Robert Roth
Mr. M. A. Wright

TUESDAY, OCTOBER 16, 1962   Page 3

3:57 pm   The President returned to the office.

4:04 - 4:10 pm   (Mr. Samson Field)   OFF THE RECORD
                     (Chairman, Board of Directors, The Printing
                     Company of America)
                 (Mrs. Jim Akin)

4:25 pm   The President departed the White House and motored
                 to the Department of State Auditorium.

4:35 - 4:50 pm   ADDRESS BY THE PRESIDENT before the National
                 Foreign Policy Conference for Editors and Radio-TV
                 Public Affairs Broadcasters at the Department of State
                 Auditorium.

4:58 pm   The President returned to the White House.

5:00 - 6:00 pm   H. R. H. Hasan al-Rida Sanusi
                     Crown Prince of the United Kingdom of Libya
                 H. E. Waniis al-Qadhaafi, Minister of Foreign Affairs
                 H. E. Dr. Mohieddine Fekini, Ambassador of Libya
                 H. E. Yunis Bilkhair, Minister of Defense
                 Hon. John Wesley Jones, U. S. Ambassador to Libya
                 Hon. G. Mennen Williams
                     Assistant Secretary for African Affairs
                 Mr. Camille Noffel, interpreter
                 Mr. William Witman, II
                     Director, Office of Northern African Affairs

6:30 pm   (11:50 am meeting resumed):
                     (The Vice President)   OFF THE RECORD
                     Hon. Dean Rusk)
                     (General Maxwell Taylor)
                     (Hon. Roswell Gilpatric)
                     (Hon. Edwin Martin)

7:55 pm   The President went to the Mansion.

                 (OFF THE RECORD, the President and Mrs. Kennedy had
                 Dinner with the Joseph Alsops)
                     The President and Mrs. Kennedy
                     Mr. and Mrs. Philip Graham
                     Ambassador Charles Bohlen
                     Ambassador Herve Alphand
                     Mrs. Thomas Bryadon
                     Sir Issah Berlin

forceful resistance at all points. They promoted a strong consensus that Cuba was particularly threatening to the United States, requiring efforts to overthrow Fidel Castro's regime, long before the Soviet missiles arrived. American aggression might have, in fact, encouraged Soviet leader Nikita Khrushchev to send the missiles in the first place. Most significant, Kennedy's advisors repeatedly chose to prepare military options and discount diplomatic alternatives, pushing him to choose the former over the latter.

After the debacle at the Bay of Pigs, Kennedy understood that he had to make a more personal effort to push back against the assumptions of his advisors, interrogate the evidence, and widen the options presented to him. That shift in process required enormous time and energy, and a willingness to confront repeated resistance and foot-dragging from self-assured officials in Defense, State, and other agencies. The president's extensive responsibilities did not allow him to confront these bureaucratic tendencies consistently, as the Cuban Missile Crisis proved.

The discussion at the first hastily prepared meeting moved in predictable directions—Kennedy's advisors assumed aggression by the adversary, they pushed the president to act quickly, and they showed a clear preference for military force. When Secretary of State Dean Rusk suggested that Soviet leader Nikita Khrushchev might have been reacting against Washington's "substantial nuclear superiority," the conversation quickly turned to Americans' reactions to the news of the missiles, not Soviet motives or areas of possible compromise. There was little time for empathizing with, or at least understanding, the adversary.[31]

In addition to its superior nuclear stockpile, the United States also deployed nuclear weapons around the Soviet Union, in Turkey and Western Europe. But everyone at Kennedy's table (including the president himself) found it easy to focus on Cuba, not the broader context. Weighing the costs of action to protect America's overwhelming strategic advantage versus the benefits of possible inaction, or alternatives, required much more introspection and careful thought. Time and competitive pressures in the nuclear age discouraged critical analysis of this kind.[32]

Much of the first and later Cuban Missile Crisis meetings centered on whether air strikes should target the missiles alone, the wider base facilities, or the entire island. No one questioned whether air strikes were a good idea, although Kennedy had misgivings. The president carried the unique burden of making decisions that could trigger a nuclear war—and that was an outcome he wanted to avoid, if at all possible. The enormity of presidential power in the nuclear age created pressures to act, but it also disciplined against moves that might lead to Armageddon. Every president after Roosevelt lived with that nightmare—caused by fears of too little force ("appeasement") or too much ("provocation").[33]

After the first meeting on 16 October 1962, Kennedy had to interrogate his advisors closely to find the correct balance between force and diplomacy. He often missed the mark because he wanted to appear strong to observers at home and abroad, and his bureaucracy reinforced that ambition. Allowing the missiles to remain in Cuba, even temporarily, created more uncertainty for analysts than removing them with direct American force.

The bias in policy planning tilted toward invasion. Everyone around the table admitted they could not be certain of Soviet reactions, but they believed they could destroy the missiles and that they should show maximum toughness. Kennedy never reversed that bias, even as he knew he exaggerated American capabilities and underestimated enemy reactions, which was often the case in these deliberations during the Cold War. Presidential advisors to a strong and self-righteous superpower fall into an almost unavoidable hubris of power. Roosevelt and his advisors never had enough power, relative to their adversaries, to overestimate themselves quite so much.

Kennedy had, perhaps, learned from Roosevelt, despite many contrary pressures. Kennedy's modesty during the Cuban Missile Crisis is the most striking part of the record. After twenty-one difficult months in office, he saw the biases in the information he received, the constraints on his understanding of distant actors, and, most important, the limits of his power to affect change, despite appearances to the contrary. He resisted a quick and illusory "solution" to the crisis. He was deeply skeptical of simple answers to the complex problems surrounding Soviet power, Cuban nationalism, and American security.

The president prolonged the deliberations about Cuba, he pursued a series of half measures (especially a quarantine of Soviet shipping), and he experimented with various diplomatic overtures. All the way through, he struggled to make time for asking hard questions. He confronted increasing pressure to act, rather than think.

Thanks to Kennedy's personal efforts—often concealed from members of the Executive Committee—Soviet and American leaders reached a war-avoiding compromise on 28 October 1962, almost two weeks after Kennedy learned about the missiles in Cuba. Soviet Premier Khrushchev agreed to withdraw his weapons, in exchange for a public American pledge not to invade the island. Kennedy also secretly promised to withdraw US missiles stationed in Turkey. The problem of a communist Cuba was not solved for the United States, and Fidel Castro's regime would remain a threat to American regional interests for the next three decades, but Kennedy had found a way to contain the danger while also preserving the image of American strength. By resisting military action and making concessions, the president exerted control over events that at first appeared to be spiraling beyond his grasp. He achieved more by doing less—running against all the expectations and pressures of presidential power.[34]

THE CUBAN MISSILE CRISIS WAS REMEMBERED AS A HEROIC moment, which in some ways it was, yet Kennedy and other presidents could neither treat it as an enduring victory nor a replicable model. If anything, the precarious and difficult path to success in defusing the crisis pointed to the challenges of doing something similar ever again. On the brink of potential nuclear war, Kennedy forced himself and his advisors to give the crisis intensive attention, despite competing priorities. The president was terribly overstretched, physically and mentally, and he could not keep this up for long. Nor could his overburdened successors.[35]

The agreement that removed Soviet missiles did not point to a clear way forward. How would the United States pursue its anti-communist agenda in Latin America with Castro's Cuba intact, receiving continued aid from the Soviet Union? How would Washington and Moscow manage their rivalry to prevent future crises of this sort in Berlin and other areas of conflict? The division of Berlin remained a source of recurring incidents from 1948, when Soviet leader Josef Stalin temporarily closed road access to the western half of the city, through the days before the Cuban Missile Crisis, when Moscow and Washington continued to threaten one another with war over control of the former German capital. The withdrawal of Soviet missiles from Cuba was a huge relief for everyone involved, but it was merely a temporary respite for a long-term illness that sapped presidential energy and continued to imperil the United States. Although American leaders had even greater military power after 1962, the security and prosperity of the United States did not increase. If anything, Americans grew more anxious and insecure about their future.[36]

No president, including Kennedy, could expect to devote the personal time and energy exerted during the Cuban Missile Crisis to the long list of equally vexing domestic and international crises: Berlin, Vietnam, the disputed Chinese-Indian border, civil rights in the United States, and poverty at home and abroad. Each of these challenges was prominent during the Missile Crisis, and observers of each issue expected a powerful president to act decisively. Kennedy did not have the time to manage so much complexity and detail, especially as the demands on the president continued to grow. The Cuban Missile Crisis was the beginning, not the end, of permanent crisis decision-making in the White House.

Ever more overloaded after those fateful thirteen days, Kennedy did not convene another Executive Committee meeting, but instead avoided weighty decisions. He simply could not take the time to make effective policy choices, so he stalled, hedged, and ultimately, did very little. The year after the Cuban Missile Crisis was replete with new conflicts and indecision from a hesitant executive. Civil rights leader Martin Luther King, Jr. and French president Charles de Gaulle were among those who expressed frustration with an American president who seemed stymied, distracted, and often despondent. The ambitions of the New Frontier had given way to the realities of a giant, charismatic American Gulliver, tied down by proliferating Lilliputian crises, sapping his impressive strength.[37]

THE PRESIDENT COMMANDED MORE POWER THAN EVER BEFORE, but he possessed less freedom in his actions, especially when it came to the main source of that power: the military. In his final speech as president, and his last public advice to Kennedy, Dwight Eisenhower famously warned about the "military-industrial complex": "This conjunction of an immense military establishment and a large arms industry is new in the American experience. The total influence—economic, political, even spiritual—is felt in every city, every State house, every office of the Federal government. We recognize the imperative need for this development. Yet we must not fail to comprehend its grave implications. Our toil, resources and livelihood are all involved; so is the very structure of our society."[38]

Having served almost fifty years in the military and the presidency, Eisenhower understood the organizations he described better than almost anyone else. He also had deep regrets about his own inability, after many failed efforts, to limit the "unwarranted influences" over executive decision-making. Despite his experience and prestige, he never succeeded in merging the four postwar military services (to keep the total military small), reducing the nuclear arms race, or curtailing the growth of the federal budget. His attempts to tighten spending on lucrative military, business, and welfare projects always gave way to demands he could not resist. His opponents exaggerated threats to justify their programs, oversold the value of their services, and mobilized powerful constituencies that even the hero of the Second World War had to respect.[39]

Kennedy understood the power of military and industrial interests from his own time in government and his proximity to his businessman father. Like Eisenhower, his recurring frustration during his presidency was not Congress, where he maintained effective working relationships, but the military. From the failed Bay of Pigs invasion of April 1961 through the frightening days of the Cuban Missile Crisis and beyond, Kennedy found that the uniformed services acted as Eisenhower predicted: encouraging more weapons, more spending, and more militarization in response to every crisis. The military cultivated powerful supporters who embraced its fierce anti-communism and the local jobs that came with new bases and new federal purchases of materiel.

The tensions between the president and the armed services began when Kennedy demanded tighter control and wider options for the possible uses of nuclear weapons. His deputy secretary of defense, Roswell Gilpatric, remembered that from the first days of the Kennedy administration, the president's closest civilian advisors "became increasingly horrified over how little positive control the president really had over the use of this great arsenal of nuclear weapons." The military held close command over deployment plans and routines for launching weapons. They needed presidential approval, but the Single Integrated Operational Plan (SIOP) left few options for the executive other than approval or disapproval, and even that might not be possible in the event of a break in the chain of command due to an enemy attack.[40]

The military chiefs resented Kennedy's efforts, through Secretary of Defense Robert McNamara, to enforce civilian control. They saw Kennedy and his advisors as lightweights, and acted with only slightly disguised disdain for the White House. Kennedy's unwillingness to use more force, as recommended by military leaders during deliberations on Cuba, Berlin, Laos, and Vietnam, deepened negative attitudes toward the president. Kennedy sent forces to all of these places, but always less than the military demanded. He hedged his commitments with diplomatic overtures and compromises, as evidenced during the Cuban Missile Crisis. His political prudence looked "weak" to the strongest peacetime military in American history.

Deputy Secretary of Defense Gilpatric recounted the tension between the president and the military. He described a briefing Kennedy received on nuclear war:

> We had Lieutenant General [Samuel E.] Anderson of the Air Force, who wasn't one of the brightest generals, and he was utterly unsuited for this kind of role. He had been head of the Air Defense Command, Continental Air Defense Command, and when he got to the point where there were no more spots for him, he was given this job. And with [Chairman of the Joint Chiefs of Staff] General [Lyman] Lemnitzer sitting there, he put on this, you know, this horrendous portrayal of what would happen in the event of a nuclear strike [against the United States by the Soviet Union]. And it was just done, you know, as though it were for a kindergarten class. . . . And he wouldn't speed it up; he wouldn't accept questions; he just stuck to his

script. And finally, Kennedy got up and walked right out in the middle of it, and that was the end of it. And we never had another one.[41]

No president since Lincoln had worse relations with the military than Kennedy. And in Lincoln's case, the officers below General George McClellan showed respect, often admiration, for the president. Kennedy faced deep hostility from many levels of the military because it had become what it never was before: a power center with unmatched resources, personnel, prestige, and political reach. The president commanded the military, but it also commanded him, as evident from the creeping militarization of American policies around the world from the 1960s to the present.[42]

Seasoned commanders in the military services resented the highly educated, privileged political elites who questioned their judgment. They saw themselves as the true guardians of American security. Although they followed the law, they resisted presidential leadership wherever they safely could. For this reason, the nation's enormous military capabilities were never coordinated effectively with Kennedy's policies in any of the Cold War crisis zones. Too often, an overworked and under-informed president had to choose among limited options that really served goals, and strategic ends, other than his own. The same problem would plague Kennedy's successors—the heavy burden of a peacetime military-industrial complex that Eisenhower lamented and the nation's founders never imagined.

LYNDON BAINES JOHNSON LEARNED AS MUCH, AFTER KENNEDY'S assassination in Dallas on 22 November 1963. Unlike Kennedy, Johnson was acutely conscious of how constrained his power would be from the start—because he had not been elected president and did not have strong supporters in the executive branch. Johnson inherited all the resistance to presidential power that Kennedy elicited, without the prestige and New Frontier aura of his youthful predecessor.

Johnson had one area of advantage over Kennedy: Congress. He focused on using the legislature as no executive had since Franklin Roosevelt. Johnson was, in fact, the first Senate majority leader to become president. (Only one Speaker of the House, James Polk, had become president.) The majority of American presidents, with few exceptions, had little national legislative experience. Washington and the two Roosevelts never served in Congress. Lincoln served only two years in the House of Representatives, and Jackson served one year in the House and a little more than three years in the Senate. Kennedy's fourteen years in the House and Senate more than doubled the combined national legislative experience of the others.

Johnson's twenty-four years in Congress, including six as Senate majority leader, made him a historical anomaly as president of the United States. He was the rare executive who made his name forging compromises among various local representatives, and writing those compromises into law. Johnson defined his political philosophy in terms of legislative compromise, not steely command over a nation and its people. "The very purpose of Congress," he wrote, "is to arrive at national decisions by bringing together some 531 individuals, representing 170 million individuals, to achieve consent on the way the nation should go. Were we bound by rigid dogmas, whatever their name, there would be no more cause for assembling Congress than bringing the Soviet Presidium together. We are not so bound, and it is part—a great part—of my own philosophy that the Congress reaches a very dubious decision when its choices are made solely by head counts of the partisan division."[43]

Johnson rejected rigid partisan ideology for what he called "national interest solutions." That meant crafting laws to encourage development and opportunity for the greatest number of citizens. "Our nation," Johnson wrote while Senate Majority Leader, "is possessed of certain resources—resources of nature, resources of position, and resources of the human mind. Without conquest or aggrandizement, we cannot add to these basics. Thus whatever we are to be, we must build from those things at our disposal."[44]

A poor boy from the Texas hill country, Johnson referred repeatedly to the success of the New Deal in bringing education, jobs, and electricity to struggling citizens from all backgrounds. The New Deal turned the lights on for Johnson and so many others, and he viewed politics as precisely that process of providing the necessary resources to develop each region of the country. To lead was to legislate with federal dollars, according to Johnson. It meant raising up the poor and needy with the outstretched arms of a powerful federal government. Johnson's most moving speech, delivered to the nation in March 1965, elaborated on this vision of politics as public improvement:

> This is the richest and most powerful country which ever occupied the globe. The might of past empires is little compared to ours. But I do not want to be the President who built empires, or sought grandeur, or extended dominion.
>
> I want to be the President who educated young children to the wonders of their world. I want to be the President who helped to feed the hungry and to prepare them to be taxpayers instead of tax-eaters. I want to be the President who helped the poor to find their own way and who protected the right of every citizen to vote in every election. I want to be the President who helped to end hatred among his fellow men and who promoted love among the people of all races and all regions and all parties. I want to be the President who helped to end war among the brothers of this earth.[45]

During his time in Congress, Johnson helped set agency goals, budgets, and regulations. He helped write the legislation governing the postwar American military, economic, and social infrastructure. Johnson was most adept at turning legislative rules to his purpose, convincing Congressmen to vote his way, and getting himself and others reelected, repeatedly, by voters who wanted benefits for their communities ("pork") and cared little for procedure or policy detail. He delivered resources and votes, together.[46]

Traveling around Texas today, one can still see the imprint of Congressman and Senator Johnson in the large interstate highways, the rice and other farm subsidies flowing to desert areas, and the proliferation of military bases and related facilities in a region distant from foreign threats. Johnson was the consummate legislator of the twentieth century, building his power by working with representatives from all parts of the country to procure maximum benefits for each district and state, especially his home state. He was neither an ideologue nor a charismatic public figure, but a pragmatist who brought his fellow politicians together to serve the material needs of their constituents, or at least the ones who voted for them. He was more populist than principled, more about creating beneficial federal programs for various groups than managing their efficiency and implementation.[47]

Franklin Roosevelt was his hero, and Johnson emulated Roosevelt's New Deal policies, even as he lacked Roosevelt's charisma and management skills. Johnson worked the aisles, the cloakrooms, and the phones. He was a formidable one-on-one presence. He was, however, far less comfortable in front of crowds, or on the radio and television. Around the table with fellow power brokers he reigned supreme; surrounded by diverse and unpredictable groups of bureaucrats, experts, foreigners, and citizens, he struggled to connect. His unmatched legislative acumen did not translate into the executive presence of Roosevelt or even Kennedy, and Johnson knew it. It was one of the reasons he hated, and feared, the Kennedys so much.

THE VICE PRESIDENCY, EVERY BIOGRAPHER OF JOHNSON OBSERVES, was the worst time in his political career. He was emasculated by the Kennedys and his departure from the Senate, his beloved home court. Johnson lost his legislative power and he became an appendage to the executive, spending most of his time traveling to far-away places, like Vietnam, at the president's behest. Listening to recordings of Johnson in Kennedy administration meetings, his awkwardness and uncertainty are painfully evident. For the first time in his political career, he was part of an executive team, not the chief deal-maker. The discussions focused on the complexities of implementing policy; Johnson felt less authoritative than the administration's experts, and he perceived that his legislative skills were little valued in the White House.

The problem went beyond his stormy relations with the Kennedys. Johnson simply had not made the transition from legislator to executive. Few men before Johnson had moved from the crowded caucuses of congressional compromise to the more detailed work of executing policy among a complex swirl of domestic and international stakeholders. If congressional legislation involved mixing different ingredients for a stew, executive work was making fine wine—nurturing fruit through complex climactic conditions was crucial, and delicate. Johnson mastered the messy Senate stew, but he was out of place in the refined White House vineyard.

After Kennedy's death, when Johnson suddenly became the leader of the free world, the master legislator returned to what he knew best. From the first hours after the assassination, he made the president into the legislator-in-chief. Engaging in simultaneous telephone conversations, as only he could, Johnson managed the Congress from the Oval Office. Like in his pre-White House days, the new president laid out an ambitious legislative agenda, and he used his well-honed skills of persuasion and coercion to move votes his way. He counted the votes and converted the naysayers with promises of pork for their districts and reprisals if they resisted.

Johnson's daily calendar from 11 March 1965 shows how his merger of legislative and executive functions changed the presidency. The contrast with Roosevelt and Kennedy is striking, despite the fact that both Kennedy and Johnson viewed Roosevelt as a model. In postwar America, the aspiration to Roosevelt-style ubiquity—"oversee, coordinate, and interfere with virtually everything"—turned each president's ambitious legislative agenda into a near pathological, and sometimes self-defeating, enterprise.

By the time Johnson took office, the president simply had too many responsibilities, from war in Southeast Asia and nuclear arms control in Europe to economic management and civil rights reform at home. Trying to serve as chief legislator and chief executive turned an inhuman job into an impossible leap of folly. From the start, Johnson wore himself and everyone around him out. He tried to make too many decisions—some he handled well, some he neglected because of distraction. Thoughtless decisions made in haste produced long-term problems that undermined his agenda, and ultimately destroyed his presidency.

ON 11 MARCH 1965, WHEN JOHNSON BEGAN TO PUSH FOR A sweeping Voting Rights Act, we see his potential as a master legislator and the signs of his early demise as an overburdened, and hyperactive, executive. Johnson was trying to run the world from the Oval Office, as presidential responsibilities seemed to demand, but the world was running him. He was going in too many directions at once. Civil rights reform and unending war in Vietnam represented the highs and lows of presidential promise for Johnson, but they were part of the same dynamic. Unprecedented power encouraged rapid problem-solving in all areas—just as Johnson extolled as a senator. Although direct presidential action worked well for some long-standing issues (especially those Johnson knew well), it backfired for others (where Johnson was less familiar).

The power to do extraordinary things with federal resources—building a "Great Society," as Johnson called it—was also the power to fail greatly, blowing up entire villages needlessly. Johnson and his supporters never accepted that the two went hand in hand, but they did, from the early months of his first full term to his embarrassing withdrawal from possible reelection just three difficult years later. The calendars show how presidential power made Johnson a giant, as it also brought all of his ambitions crashing down, fast and hard.

Flush from an overwhelming electoral victory in November 1964 that exceeded even Roosevelt's reelection in 1936, President Johnson began 1965 with more support, from the public and Congress, than any of his postwar predecessors. Few presidents won as big as Johnson did in 1964, with more than 60 percent of the popular vote. [48]

Always impatient for success, Johnson intended to capitalize on his victory, pushing immediately to transform domestic and international politics. His calendars show that he worked harder and longer in pursuit of these goals than Kennedy or Roosevelt. 11 March 1965 was only one of numerous days when he devoted hours to discussing the details of civil rights, medical insurance for the elderly, education funding, immigration law, and foreign policy with his friends in Congress. One newspaper reporter commented: "Rarely has one man so dominated Washington as President Johnson now does." He acted "like an orchestra leader; a beachmaster on an invasion front, a traffic-control superintendent at a busy railroad front."[49]

THE WHITE HOUSE

PRESIDENT LYNDON B. JOHNSON

DAILY DRAFT

Date March 11, 1965

The President began his day at (Place) White House

Entry No.	Time In	Time Out	Telephone Lo	Telephone LD	Activity (include visited by)	Expenditure Code
	9:36					
		9:00				
	8:59a			t	McGeorge Bundy	
C	9:16a			t	Robert Anderson in New York City	
	9:55a			t	George Reedy	
	10:15				Bill Moyers	
C	10:35a			t	AG Katzenbach	
	11:00a			t	George Reedy	
	11:20a				Rufus Youngblood – USSS	
	11:30a			t	Lee White	
C	12:12p					
					John Bogle	
					Mildred Brown · Whittier Sengstacke –	
					C. C. Dejoie John Sexton –	
					Carlton Goodlett Frank Stanley –	
					Percy Greene J.S. N. Tross –	
					Emory Jackson Frank Thomas –	
					T. C. Jervey Howard Woods –	
					John Kirkpatrick Thomas Young –	
					Eleanor or Lofton	
					Frank Mitchell	
					John Murphy	
					Marjorie Foster	
					Longworth Quinn	

SOURCE FOR PAGES 213–218: Lyndon B. Johnson Presidential Library, Austin, Texas.

At one time during the afternoon two of the demonstrators left because they had gas to go to the bathroom -- they had been served coffee during the morning hours. At another point the demonstrators got up -- as if to leave and headed toward an exit, but when they noted that no one was there to see them, they stopped and took up their seated places just outside the theater.

THE WHITE HOUSE

PRESIDENT LYNDON B. JOHNSON
DAILY DIARY

The President began his day at (Place): White House

Date March 11, 1965

Day Thursday

Time In	Out	Telephone	Activity (include visited by)
1:30			Gerri Whittington was asked also to join the group -- for pics that were taken and to participate in the meeting
			The President also gave away folders of his Inaugural address and the State of the Union address.
2:12			(Cecil took pics -- and after the meeting, the Press went in) To the office -- w/ Marvin Watson and JV (Note: JV asked that someone fr. th e office go into to take notes on the meeting still in progress.)
2:15		t	Bill Moyers (p)
2:20p			Theodore "Ted" Sorenson in the lounge
2:25p		f	George Reedy
2:35p	2:50		National Newspaper Publishers Association went to the Oval Office to join the President and to say goodbye to him.
			He gave told members of the group
2:50	3:00p		No longer of Ted Sorenson
			Staff members: Lee White, Jack Valenti, Bill Moyers, Cliff Alexander, during which time the President briefed White, Moyers and Alexander on how to go to talk to the demonstrators -- the 3 left for the mansion at
3:30	3:32	f	Bill Moyers 3:15p
3:45			Jack Valenti

SEE TRAVEL RECORD
FOR TRAVEL ACTIVITY

Page No.: 2

THE WHITE HOUSE
PRESIDENT LYNDON B. JOHNSON
DAILY DIARY

Date: March 11, 1965
Day: Thursday

The President began his day at (Place): White House

Entry No.	Time In	Out	Telephone Lo	LD	Activity (include visited by)	Expenditure Code
	3:56		t		Jack Valenti (pl)	
	4:00		f		George Reedy	
	4:06		t		Jack Valenti (pl)	
	4:07	4:17			Bill Moyers and Cliff Alexander	
		4:30			Jack Valenti, George Reedy, and Lee C. White - RE: Civil Rights problems	
					— in Selma, Alabama and sit-in demonstrators in the East Wing of the Mansion	
	4:24				Agent Rufus Youngblood joined -- RE: same as above -- but mainly concerned	
					with sit-in demonstrators in the White House -- Agent Youngblood said that	
					their were mainly of student age -- not over 25 years of age, and that at the	
					beginning there were 6 white students and 6 Negro students -- at this point	
					2 had left -- The problem concerned -- was not that the students were of	
					a violent nature, but that it was a "touchy" problem of "throwing" them out	
					since the closing time of the White House tours was 12:00 noon.	
	4:35		t		George Reedy (pl)	
	4:36		f		George Reedy	
	4:42		t		Bill Moyers (pl)	
	4:44			LD	Acting Attorney General Nicholas Katzenbach	
	4:53				rm -- asking to get Agent Rufus Youngblood to come in again.	
			t		Marvin Watson	

SEE TRAVEL RECORD
FOR TRAVEL ACTIVITY

Page No.: 3

THE WHITE HOUSE
PRESIDENT: LYNDON B. JOHNSON
DAILY DIARY

Date __March 11, 1965__

Day __Thursday__

The President began his day at (Place) __White House__

Entry No.	Time In	Time Out	Telephone Lo	Telephone LD	Activity (include visited by)	Expenditure Code
	4:55	5:00			Agent Rufus Youngblood (see page 8)	
	4:56		t		Bill Moyers (pl)	
	5:00		t		George Reedy (pl)	
	5:04		t		Bill Moyers (pl)	
	5:12		t		Attorney General Nicholas Katzenbach	
	5:20				Lee White, Jack Valenti, Marvin Watson -- Agents Youngblood and Johns, and George Reedy) In the Oval Office viewing the live televised conference of AG Katzenbach with the Press -- The Attorney General stated the Administration's viewpoints along w/those of the Justice Department. He was asked questions concerning the riots in Selma, and the legislation from the White House on Voter's Rights that will be sent to the Hill sometime next week. The President was intently watching the telecast -- with his chair pulled up directly in front of the set, and leaning over to get a "good, close look". The staff assistants and SS Agents were watchi'ng and listening in the background.	
	6:00				Departed the White House and motored to the Sam Rayburn Office Building on the Hill for what was a scheduled 5:00 pm OFF THE RECORD dedication of the "Albert Thomas Gymnasium". Even though the President was an hour late, the group was still gathered. (Jack Valenti had called in earlier to Congressman Oren Harris (Ark.) asking him to hold the people until the President came)	
					Accompanying the President were:	
	6:06				Arrived at the Office Building and was met by:	

REMARKS BY THE PRESIDENT

SEE TRAVEL RECORD
FOR TRAVEL ACTIVITY

Page No.: 4

THE WHITE HOUSE
PRESIDENT LYNDON B. JOHNSON
DAILY DIARY

Date __March 11, 1965__
Day __Thursday__

The President began his day at (Place)

Entry No.	Time				White House — Activity (include visited by)	Expenditure Code
	In	Out	Lo	LD		
		6:32			Returned to the Office... and into the office.	
		6:40			George Reedy	
		6:41			In midr's -- looked through pics on gw's desk -- and sa'd that he heard that someone in the WH had tied themselves to a rail, so that they wouldn't be moved from the East Wing -- (this response came from watching the TV that was on in midr's office -- John Chancellor's news report fr. the WH on the sit-ins in the WH)	
c		6:42			To the Mansion w/ MW -- for CONGRESSIONAL RECEPTION -- last of the series of 10, 151 guests	
		6:45p			To Red Room for a receiving line and w/ Mrs. Johnson and picture taking with each guest	
		7:20p			To East Room for briefing The President opened the briefing with remarks on the Selma, Alabama situation, and told th group that because of that situation, he had asked the Attorney General to be present for the briefing. The Attorney General spoke to the group solely on the civil rights problem, and clearly def ned all remarks which he delivered in his 5:45 press conference this afternoon. There was extensive questioning by Cong. John Bell Williams of Mississippi and the Congressman from Selma who is a Republican.	
					Kermit Gordon delivered his summary of the budget problems. He was questioned extensively and acidly, according to Claude Desautel, on his article in the January Saturday Review of Literature where he said that there were too many farmers --by Republican farm Congressmen.	
					The Vice President spoke briefly	

SEE TRAVEL RECORD

THE WHITE HOUSE
PRESIDENT LYNDON B. JOHNSON
DAILY DIARY

Date _March 11 1965_

Day Thursday

The President began his day at (Place) ___The White House___

Entry No.	Time In	Time Out	Telephone f or t	Lo	LD	Activity (include visited by)	Expenditure Code
						on the phone.	
						Secretaary McNamara delivered remarks on the Defense Budget and the	
						Vietnam situation	
						Secretary Rusk spoke on the Vietnam Situation and world problems.	
						While the Secretary of State had the floor, the President and the Vice President	
						left to make two telephone calls	
	9:25p		t			Mrs. James C. Reeb, Birmingham, Alabama (wife of the former D.C. Minister	
						who had died in Selma, Alabama at the hands of white protestors to the	
						civil rights efforts in Alabama)	
	9:35p		t			Mr. Reeb (father of the above named minister), Birmingham, Alabama	
						The President, Mrs. Johnson, and the Vice President talked on these calls	
						The President returned to the East Room and joined the briefing	
						still in progress.	
	9:40p					To State Dining Room for refreshments -- and joined the ladies	
	10:16p					To second floor	
	10:37					Mrs. Lawson, USSS - at Northeast Gate	
	10:50					" "	
	11:30p					Retired	

SEE TRAVEL RECORD

218

Johnson had already signed the Civil Rights Act in July 1964 that banned the long-standing practice of racial discrimination in public settings. The Civil Rights Act forced the integration of American society—in schools, workplaces, parks, and restaurants—just as activists had long demanded. It was a victory for the civil rights movement, as well as Lyndon Johnson. It showed the president's determination to move fast and achieve big things, beyond even the expectations of Kennedy's New Frontier.[50]

In early 1965 Johnson sought another civil rights act, this one guaranteeing the right to vote for all citizens, especially minorities who faced pervasive barriers to political participation in many parts of the country. Johnson responded to intensive pressure on this issue from civil rights activists marching through Selma and other Southern cities where they faced determined opposition—often expressed in the most hateful terms—from white citizens fearful that they would lose political control over their communities if voting was truly opened to all adults. Southern governors, especially Alabama's George Wallace, provoked violent defenses of segregation from white citizens as they also appealed to the president for help in maintaining public order. Wallace warned Johnson of impending "revolution."[51]

Johnson acted decisively to assert his authority, promote voting rights, and also protect order. He pushed Congress to pass legislation—the Voting Rights Act—that simultaneously reinforced the rule of law and guaranteed voting access for long-denied citizens. According to the legislation that the president signed on 6 August 1965, the federal government had to certify ("pre-clearance") that counties with historical barriers to voter registration had indeed removed those barriers. Federal officials could register voters directly, as the Constitution had never allowed before, and they had a right to monitor elections in areas suspected of voter suppression. For the first time in US history, every county across the land had to, in Johnson's words, "open its polling places to all of its people. . . . It is nothing less than granting every American Negro his freedom to enter the mainstream of American life: not the conformity that blurs enriching differences of culture and tradition, but rather the opportunity that gives each a chance to choose."

As he used his power to expand the range of freedom for long-denied groups, the president tried to show understanding, even sympathy, for those who resisted. "It is difficult to fight for freedom. But I also know how difficult it can be to bend long years of habit and custom to grant it," Johnson admitted. "There is no room for injustice anywhere in the American mansion. But there is always room for understanding toward those who see the old ways crumbling. And to them today I say simply this: It must come."[52]

With his signature on both the Civil Rights and Voting Rights Acts, Johnson had done more for racial inclusion in American society than any president since Lincoln. He had lifted some of the lingering burdens of slavery. Johnson had also given new meaning to freedom and justice in postwar society, making access to public places and voting rights essential to basic citizenship. He was particularly proud of that monumental accomplishment.

Progressive legislation, however, increased the demands on the president, as he was now responsible for enforcing the new laws in many increasingly hostile parts of the country, including Johnson's native South. In addition, civil rights activists were not satisfied with the two acts. They demanded more attention to stubborn racial barriers, including job, housing, and education discrimination. Johnson's promises of freedom and justice committed him to do more—much more—in pursuit of these ideals.[53]

He confronted intensifying demands from contradictory constituencies, including New Left activists, Black Power advocates, and an emerging New Right. All of these groups, and others, looked to the president, holding Johnson accountable to his expanding promises. As the president tried to manage diverging coalitions in Washington, it became increasingly difficult for him to please any of his multiplying critics. Legislative horse-trading could not cover for the fact that the president was now requiring people to change how they behaved in their schools, their offices, and even their churches. He was also asking activists to accept compromises that increased equality for citizens, but still fell short of full inclusion. Within a year of passing the Voting Rights Act, Johnson lost the support of key Southern Democrats, like Arkansas Senator J. William Fulbright, and prominent civil right activists, especially Martin Luther

King, Jr. Conservatives in Congress who opposed the president's civil rights legislation also regrouped and mounted organized opposition.[54]

THE PRESIDENT'S PROBLEM WAS NOT ONLY DIVERGENT EXPECTA- tions on civil rights, but the war in Vietnam, another matter that creeped into his calendar, especially after he sent 3500 US Marines to South Vietnam on 8 March 1965. They were the first American combat soldiers deployed to the conflict, which was soon seen as "Johnson's War." The president was never optimistic about the alli- ance he inherited with a corrupt and largely incompetent, but firmly anti-communist, government in Saigon. American military advisors in Indochina, dispatched by Eisenhower and Kennedy, had become sitting ducks for repeated attacks by communist forces seeking to control the whole country. "It's the damn worse mess I ever saw," Johnson's close friend, Senator Richard Russell, warned. "It look like the more we try to do for them, the less they willin' to do for them- selves. There's no sense of responsibility there on the part of any of their leaders. . . . I don't see how we're ever gonna get out without fightin' a major war with the Chinese and all of 'em, down there in those rice paddies and jungles."[55]

Johnson ruefully agreed with Russell's analysis, but he worried that if he withdrew from Vietnam, the communists would "chase you into your own kitchen." He feared what Eisenhower had called a series of "falling dominoes," triggered as communists moved from one new ter- ritory to another, grabbing ever-more vital areas and growing stronger, as had the Germans and Japanese in World War II. Johnson did not want to be labeled an "appeaser" or a "quitter." He wanted to stand strong against the communists, as Kennedy apparently had during the Cuban Missile Crisis. "I don't see what we can ever hope to get out of this. . . and I don't think that we can get out," Johnson sadly concluded as early as May 1964.[56]

The force and money at the disposal of the president allowed him to wage war without asking Congress for a declaration. Unlike Lincoln or Roosevelt, Johnson was never "in" or "out" of the war that defined his presidency. Instead, he deployed the extraordinary resources at his command, including as many as five hundred thousand Americans in 1968, to keep the communists from winning. The president supported extensive economic development efforts in South Vietnam, costing Americans billions of dollars, but he was not naïve. The limitations of the Saigon government were evident, and Johnson never expected it to sustain itself. South Vietnam was like George Wallace's state of Alabama: Johnson did not want to own it and he did not want to see it fall into chaos either. The president sought to preserve a non-communist order and improve circumstances on the ground in South Vietnam, where possible.[57]

JOHNSON'S INCREMENTAL ESCALATION OF AMERICAN MILITARY commitments reflected his ambition to do more of everything: fight communists, support allied governments, pursue civil rights at home, and maintain "law and order"—a phrase Johnson was the first to use. He also wanted to avoid all dangers of warfare with the Soviet Union and China, and all risks of alienating voting groups at home, including Southern whites. In this sense, Johnson echoed Kennedy's undisciplined New Frontier—hyperactive on many fronts—perhaps with even more energy and determination, and certainly with less eloquence.[58]

Johnson was spread so thin that he barely slept. His calendars show longer and longer days, ceaseless meetings and phone calls, and debilitating routines. Instead of reexamining assumptions and thinking strategically, Johnson and his advisors obsessed about managing proliferating crises. Presidential meetings devolved into ever-more granular discussions of long-standing problems. The pressure was too intense to think beyond the immediate matter. The fear of failure, evident from Johnson's first discussions of Vietnam, made it impossible to succeed, or at least move on.

Most debilitating was Johnson's inability to explain what he was doing. He had good reasons for all of his actions, and he shared them, but he failed to tell a compelling story to the American people about why he was using his enormous powers as he was. Abraham Lincoln defended the Union and Franklin Roosevelt promoted jobs for destitute

Americans, but it was never clear how Johnson's many actions cohered in a single narrative. What was Vietnam about? The president never gave a persuasive answer. After the passage of the Voting Rights Act, it was not clear what Johnson's proliferating pieces of legislation amounted to, in the broadest sense. What role did he see for a more active government? How would it redefine the meaning of democracy and the relationship between citizens and leaders? What would a "Great Society" look like for ordinary citizens?

Johnson was not as naturally eloquent or even poetic as some of his predecessors, but that was not the fundamental problem. A politician who based his career on cajoling elected officials to support controversial legislation did not have the ability to persuade the more diffuse audience of the American public. He was unpersuasive because his policies were a mix of so many different plans, projects, and promises that they often contradicted one another, and rarely pointed in a single direction. That was the source of public confusion and frequent opposition to the Vietnam War. It was also the motivation for civil rights activists to criticize Johnson after 1965 in growing numbers. People did not know what he was about, and from his daily calendars it appears that he often forgot himself.

Less than four years after his landslide victory in the 1964 election, the president's grand ambitions had become self-limiting. One of his closest friends sadly remembered the civil rights and anti-war protests that convulsed the White House in 1968: Johnson "could not go anywhere." His presidency had become "disastrous."[59]

POWER DEFINED KENNEDY AND JOHNSON MORE THAN THEY defined it. They departed from their priorities because they felt they had to. Their presidential power elicited expectations, commitments, and hubris that drove their daily behavior. Instead of pursuing fundamental interests, they reacted to pressures and perceived weaknesses. Instead of setting an international agenda, they each followed priorities set abroad and in the streets. Kennedy and Johnson extolled the presidential power they so deeply craved, but they suffered the profound frustration of feeling that their long-sought power, once exercised, was not all it was cracked up to be—not even close. For each man, the presidency was a deeply unhappy, disillusioning experience.

Abraham Lincoln, Theodore Roosevelt, and even Franklin Roosevelt were less powerful, possessing fewer capabilities with fewer expectations. They each expanded the office they inherited, but were not subsumed by crisis. The earlier presidents did not lose perspective and they did not neglect their priorities. They tamed and focused their power for their articulated purposes. They were more in control because they did not try to control too much, even as they addressed some of the biggest challenges in American history.

Kennedy and Johnson chased new frontiers, bringing remarkable talent, energy, and idealism to the presidency. But those qualities are not enough, and in fact they became debilitating. Kennedy and Johnson were unable to rise above their crises and congested calendars. Their presidencies mark a turning point when the power of the modern executive grew almost unmanageable, and certainly unsatisfying—for leaders and citizens alike. The frustration of these presidents had become the frustration of ordinary Americans too.

CHAPTER 8

Leading Actor

Ronald Reagan's entire presidency turned on the chaotic, world threatening events of 1983. Fifty years after Franklin Roosevelt struggled to alleviate the spiraling suffering of citizens during the Great Depression, Reagan promoted calm among advisors and adversaries as the Cold War inched dangerously toward Armageddon. "In the morning," Reagan recorded in his personal diary on 10 October 1983, "I ran the tape of the movie ABC is running on the air November 20. It's called 'The Day After.' It has Lawrence, Kansas wiped out in a nuclear war with Russia. It is powerfully done—all $7 million worth. It's very effective and left me greatly depressed." Reagan concluded with words he repeated in his diary and his public statements for the remainder of his presidency: "My own reaction was one of our having to do all we can to have a deterrent and to see there is never a nuclear war." A month later he described a briefing about American nuclear war plans as a "most sobering experience."[1]

He had not started his presidency, or his political career, that way. Raised in the small town of Dixon, Illinois, during the Depression, Reagan came of age with deep appreciation for Franklin Roosevelt's leadership and the New Deal. Roosevelt's programs had, in fact, saved his family when Reagan's father—a hard-drinking shoe salesman—lost his job, like millions of other Americans. The Works Progress Administration employed both Reagan's father and his older brother, allowing them to sustain the family amid rural poverty.

Young Ronald Reagan, then a student at nearby Eureka College, was moved by Roosevelt's connection to ordinary citizens. Roosevelt was the first politician Reagan remembered as an inspiration and a role model. He was also one of the last men Reagan praised at the end of his presidency: "All across the Nation, millions of new voters looked at this President who was filled with confidence in the future, faith in the people, and the joy of the democratic rough-and-tumble, and they said to themselves maybe someday they, too, would like to serve the Nation in public life. I was one of those millions. Franklin Roosevelt was the first President I ever voted for, the first to serve in my lifetime that I regarded as a hero, and the first I ever actually saw; that was in 1936, a campaign parade in Des Moines, where I was working as a radio announcer."[2]

Inspired by Roosevelt's radio voice—"I remember how a light would snap on in the eyes of everyone in the room just hearing him, and how, because of his faith, our faith in our own capacity to overcome any crisis and any challenge was reborn"—Reagan pursued his own career in radio, and eventually in motion pictures. He arrived in Hollywood in 1937 as a bright-eyed idealist, hoping that he could inspire fellow Americans with uplifting stories on the movie screen. To the end of his life he tried to do the same; his presidential diary is filled with enthusiasm for epic tales of American selflessness, accompanied by disdain for "realistic" depictions of vanity, corruption, and illicit behavior. "Ran a movie…It was a comedy (Jane Fonda, Dolly Parton, and Lilli Tomlin) 'Nine to Five.' Funny—but one scene made me mad. A truly funny scene if the three gals had played getting drunk but no they had to get stoned on pot. It was an endorsement of Pot smoking for any young person who sees the picture."[3]

These comments reveal the conservative temperament that drove Reagan to abandon Roosevelt's Democratic Party and embrace the postwar Republican Party of Dwight Eisenhower and, later on, Barry Goldwater. As an actor in Hollywood, and then the leader of the most powerful actors' union (the Screen Actors Guild), Reagan encountered radicals of many varieties who questioned the American political and economic system. Some were communists critical of inequalities and committed to cooperation with the Soviet Union, despite its obvious threat to American security. Some were social democrats, advocates of higher taxes, larger government programs, and expanded civil rights. Some were isolationists demanding an American withdrawal from the wider world and a focus on local needs. All of these groups, and others, challenged Reagan's view of the essential benevolence of American domestic and international policies. As he saw it, they called for major changes in government that would limit the individual freedoms of citizens, especially upwardly mobile professionals in growing industries, like Hollywood.

Reagan judged criticisms of the American system as betrayals of Roosevelt's New Deal legacy. He understood the New Deal as a patriotic effort to preserve capitalism by empowering individuals and increasing their opportunities for success with new federally supported projects, industries, and technologies. As someone who had benefited directly from a variety of these programs (especially through his father), Reagan viewed the efforts of Democrats after Roosevelt as distortions of the great man's legacy. He perceived postwar government growth as a hindrance for his continued professional and personal progress. Reagan benefited, and believed many Americans benefited, from free markets that the New Deal preserved, but that postwar labor, welfare, and anti-poverty regulations constrained. He criticized President Lyndon Johnson's "Great Society" as an unacceptable and counterproductive intrusion of "greater government activity in the affairs of the people."[4]

"I have spent most of my life as a Democrat," Reagan explained in 1964, but "I recently have seen fit to follow another course.... No nation in history has ever survived a tax burden that reached a third of its national income. Today, 37 cents out of every dollar earned in this country is the tax collector's share, and yet our government continues to spend 17 million dollars a day more than the government takes in." The New Deal had lifted Reagan out of poverty, but now the tax burden and government regulation were holding him, and other children of the New Deal, back. The beneficiaries of government intervention in the 1930s chafed under the burdens of those policies extended by postwar presidents, including Democrats (Truman, Kennedy, and Johnson) and one Republican (Eisenhower). Reagan's shift to the Republican Party was a result of the New Deal's successes, as he himself admitted, and his desire to escape its excesses.[5]

The growing size and intrusive power of government had, according to Reagan, undermined the freedom that was at the core of New Deal policies. He favored what he viewed as "small government support" for citizens, which he associated with Franklin Roosevelt (as well as Theodore Roosevelt and Abraham Lincoln), against "big government control," which he associated with social welfare policies run by faceless bureaucrats. Reagan interpreted high taxes, strict work regulations, and forced efforts at changing community behavior—especially around race relations—as restrictions on the freedoms the New Deal was meant to preserve. Influenced by Senator Joseph McCarthy, Vice President Richard Nixon, and other tenacious anti-communists, he perceived postwar Democrats as weak in their cautious action against communists abroad and their sympathizers at home.[6]

Reagan turned to the Republican Party because he believed it was most committed to his understanding of the New Deal as a program rooted in individual freedom, national security, and preservation of American communities, like his hometown of Dixon, Illinois. Moreover, the Republican Party firmly rejected the radicalism, including pot smoking, that Reagan viewed as a threat to his Norman Rockwell image of a wholesome American society. Leaving Hollywood to become an official spokesperson for General Electric products (including dishwashers, refrigerators, and washing machines), he emerged as a leading Republican voice for individualism and traditional family values. Communism, excess government, and an emerging counterculture were the adversaries that Reagan pushed against.

He brought his message to thousands of General Electric employees, shareholders, and consumers, as well as hundreds of thousands of television viewers. From 1954 to 1962 Reagan hosted "General Electric Theater," broadcast each Sunday evening. He also traveled to Rotary clubs, business associations, and college campuses promoting what he called the "New Right." Speaking in 1957 at the commencement for his alma mater, Eureka College, the former New Deal devotee advocated a renewal of what he described as imperiled freedoms: "There are many well-meaning people today who work at placing an economic floor beneath all of us so that no one shall exist below a certain level or standard of living, and certainly we don't quarrel with this." But, Reagan warned, "look more closely and you may find that all too often these well-meaning people are building a ceiling above which no one shall be permitted to climb and between the two are pressing us all into conformity, into a mold of standardized mediocrity."[7]

Reagan entered politics to fight against what he perceived as the creeping mediocrity of postwar America, a mediocrity that threatened his own advancement as a high-tax-paying, upwardly mobile citizen. Mediocrity meant the enforcement of "ceilings" that limited opportunities, the confiscation of personal resources, the departure from traditional community (including religious) values, and the tolerance of radical criticisms at home and communist threats abroad. Mediocrity meant restriction and radicalism for Reagan, not the freedom, opportunity, and tradition that he revered in his small town New Deal upbringing.

Reagan was only one of thousands of other small town Midwesterners who had moved to California after the 1930s in search of jobs. He ran for governor in 1966, appealing to these transplants and many others as a candidate not of Roosevelt's "forgotten men," but of postwar America's "over-regulated" citizens. Reagan promised to reduce the size of state government, cut its spending, and free citizens and businesses for more growth. To restrain civil rights and anti-war protests that had become common, particularly around universities, Reagan pledged to restore order. Abroad, he called for Americans to stand up against communists, and to be more vigilant about acts of Soviet-sponsored infiltration.[8]

The governor's office has been the most common stage for presidential aspirants, and that was true for Reagan. His mixed but popular record in the largest state gave him many advantages as a national candidate. His vocal support for Republican candidates, especially Barry Goldwater in 1964, solidified his standing within his new party. He challenged Republican leaders in the early 1970s, Presidents Richard Nixon and Gerald Ford, to do more to reduce government at home and increase American strength abroad. Reagan wanted California and the United States to be unleashed from limitations, often self-imposed, on wealth and power.[9]

"Right now," Reagan asserted in a 1975 radio speech, "business is more regulated in America by government than it is in any other country in the world where free enterprise is still permitted. If we had less regulation we could have lower prices. Government has grown so big in these last four decades that not even the office of management and budget in Washington knows how many boards, agencies, bureaus, and commissions there are." He elaborated, "We pay higher prices growing ever higher, because government continues to spend more than it takes in and because too much money is chasing too few goods and services. There could be more goods and services available for us to buy if government would lift some of the paper burden from the back of our industrial system." Reagan's economic analysis was simple, direct, and compelling for citizens who felt government was getting in the way, rather than helping them to get ahead.[10]

GOVERNMENT HAD BEEN THE ANTIDOTE TO FEAR FOR ROOSEVELT and the engine of achievement for Kennedy and Johnson. Reagan redefined government as the chief hindrance to freedom. Reversing Kennedy's famous inaugural promise to "pay any price and bear any burden," Reagan used his presidential inauguration, in January 1981, to argue the opposite: "Government is not the solution to our problem; government is the problem. From time to time we've been tempted to believe that society has become too complex to be managed by self-rule, that government by an elite group is superior to government for, by, and of the people. Well, if no one among us is capable of governing himself, then who among us has the capacity to govern someone else?"[11]

Reagan worked as president to strip away regulations, enabling citizens to act with greater freedom. This effort began with race, still a fundamental issue for many Southern voters who opposed the forced integration of Lyndon Johnson's Civil Rights and Voting Rights Acts, as well as subsequent federal requirements for affirmative action, school busing, and redistribution of tax revenues. Reagan expanded his assault on federal interventions when, in August 1980, he visited the Neshoba County Fair, near the site in Philadelphia, Mississippi, where three civil rights workers (James Earl Chaney, Andrew Goodman, and Michael Schwerner) were brutally murdered sixteen years earlier by local law enforcement and members of the Ku Klux Klan—who were often one and the same.

No presidential candidate had spoken in Neshoba, yet Reagan saw an opportunity to fuse his criticisms of federal excesses with local racism. Reagan's speech gave carefully coded solace to thousands of residents who resented the intrusion of non-white citizens in their communities, their schools, and their places of work. The racism of the 1980s was not as violent or explicit as a generation earlier, but it remained deeply embedded in Southern (and in some Western and Northern) criticisms of crusading Washington bureaucrats who disrespected ordinary hard-working, God-fearing Americans.

These were the people whom Franklin Roosevelt had reached with his New Deal promises of jobs and security. Kennedy and Johnson had lost them in what felt like programs that spoke more to elites and racial minorities. Reagan believed that many Americans, especially white, middle- and lower-income Americans, had been left behind. In Neshoba, he framed his presidency as a new pledge of hope for the ordinary men and women who wanted space to live in freedom, without condescending federal intrusions. Reagan renewed Roosevelt's expressions of empathy for poor white citizens by accepting race separation and inequality. He did not justify racism, but reiterated racist criticisms of civil rights programs pursued by the federal government.[12]

"We've had the New Deal," Reagan told fair-goers in Neshoba, "and then Harry Truman gave us the Fair Deal, and now we have a misdeal   In more recent years with the best intention, they have created a vast bureaucracy, or a bureaucratic structure bureaus and departments and agencies—to try and solve all the problems and eliminate all the things of human misery that they can. They have forgotten that when you create a government bureaucracy, no matter how well intentioned it is, almost instantly its top priority becomes preservation of the bureaucracy."

Echoing the leaders of the Old Confederacy, Reagan tied himself to that past: "I believe in states' rights; I believe in people doing as much as they can for themselves at the community level and at the private level. And I believe that we've distorted the balance of our government today by giving powers that were never intended in the Constitution to that federal establishment. And if I do get the job I'm looking for, I'm going to devote myself to trying to reorder those priorities and to restore to the states and local communities those functions which properly belong there."[13]

"States' rights" in Mississippi meant rebuffing federal integration efforts, as everyone in attendance understood. Reagan did not devote one
word to the infamous murders that had occurred just sixteen years earlier, still under FBI investigation. He was going to make his presidency
about restoring respect and freedom for ordinary white families, like his
own, who felt neglected and attacked in the years after Franklin Roosevelt's time in office.[14]

REAGAN WAS TRUE TO HIS WORD. HE BEGAN HIS PRESIDENCY
with an ambitious program of tax breaks, spending cuts, and reductions
in business, civil rights, and labor regulations. He argued that returning
more private capital to the economy and reducing costs of production
would stimulate growth. Reagan also supported the Federal Reserve's
efforts, under Chairman Paul Volker, to boost interest rates for the purpose of curbing what had been very high rates of inflation in the late
1970s. Reagan's goal was to stimulate jobs by freeing business growth.[15]

The president's proposed economic program promised "a new beginning for the economy…based on the premise that the people who make
up the economy—workers, managers, savers, investors, buyers, and sell-
ers—do not need the government to make reasoned and intelligent
decisions about how best to organize and run their own lives." Reagan
envisioned a national executive who did not dispense direct aid, but
protected stable and predictable markets driven by the choices of individual producers and consumers. "Decisions to work, save, spend, and
invest depend crucially on expectations regarding future government
policies. Establishing an environment which ensures efficient and stable
incentives for work, saving, and investment now and in the future is the
cornerstone of the recovery plan."[16]

Reagan would not interfere with market priorities, as presidents
since Franklin Roosevelt had done. Reagan proudly proclaimed that his
laissez-fair approach was a "dramatic departure from the trends of recent years." He echoed Andrew Jackson's populism more than the economics favored by presidents from Washington and Lincoln to
Theodore Roosevelt, Franklin Roosevelt, John F. Kennedy, and Lyndon
Johnson.

The major exception to Reagan's Jacksonian views on economy was defense spending. Here Reagan echoed Theodore Roosevelt more than the Tennessee frontiersman. The military was "the only department in our entire program that will actually be increased over the present budgeted figure," he announced. As Reagan tried to cut expenditures for housing and education, he boosted defense spending, particularly for nuclear weapons systems. During his first three years in office, Reagan raised annual expenditures for defense from $134 billion to $210 billion. He thus devoted an additional 1 percent of the country's entire economic output (gross domestic product) to the military, a level of defense spending not seen since the Vietnam War.[17]

Reagan believed that postwar spending in the United States had weakened the country by drowning free enterprise in a sea of domestic programs as it deprived defense needs abroad. He used his presidency to reverse that equation. Renewed strength internationally would weaken competitors, open up markets, and enable a confident and stable space for individuals to innovate at home. Aggressive anti-communism, in particular, would protect the American-led capitalist system from infiltration and inspire more entrepreneurship. Defense spending promoted the opportunities, the president believed, that limited government enabled.

Reagan articulated this perceived connection between strength and freedom in his address to the British Parliament during the summer of 1982. He and Prime Minister Margaret Thatcher shared a bond over their belief that fighting communism abroad and big bureaucracies at home was part of a single struggle—"a crusade for freedom." "We have not inherited an easy world," Reagan observed. "If developments like the Industrial Revolution, which began here in England, and the gifts of science and technology have made life much easier for us, they have also made it more dangerous. There are threats now to our freedom, indeed to our very existence, that other generations could never even have imagined." The greatest danger was obviously nuclear war, but the president pointed to other concerns as well: "There is a threat posed to human freedom by the enormous power of the modern state. History teaches the dangers of government that overreaches—political control taking precedence over free economic growth, secret police, mindless bureaucracy, all combining to stifle individual excellence and personal freedom."

Speaking in a country with a large and powerful Labor Party, Reagan acknowledged "that among us here and throughout Europe there is legitimate disagreement over the extent to which the public sector should play a role in a nation's economy and life." He accepted no divergence, however, in the need for powerful military capabilities to protect the freedoms of citizens on both sides of the Atlantic. "Our military strength," he explained, "is a prerequisite to peace, but let it be clear we maintain this strength in the hope it will never be used, for the ultimate determinant in the struggle that's now going on in the world will not be bombs and rockets, but a test of wills and ideas, a trial of spiritual resolve, the values we hold, the beliefs we cherish, the ideals to which we are dedicated."[18]

As a former labor negotiator during his days leading the Screen Actors Guild, Reagan was serious about negotiating "from strength" with the Soviet Union. A stronger, more confident United States would allow the president to demand more concessions from foreign leaders on arms control, open trade, and human rights. He recognized he could not get everything he wanted by force alone, but force was necessary to create a favorable negotiating environment for his side.

Reagan's national security directives embodied this approach. In January 1983 Reagan signed a document alerting all parts of the government that "the US must convey clearly to Moscow that unacceptable behavior will incur costs that would outweigh any gains. At the same time, the US must make clear to the Soviets that genuine restraint in their behavior would create the possibility of an East-West relationship that might bring important benefits for the Soviet Union."[19]

Reagan wanted to talk with Soviet leaders and, like Roosevelt during the Second World War, he sought to identify shared interests, but he insisted that the deals negotiated come largely on American terms: "The US will not seek to adjust its policies to the Soviet internal conflict, but rather try to create incentives (positive and negative) for the new leadership to adopt policies less detrimental to US interests. The US will remain ready for improved US-Soviet relations if the Soviet Union makes significant changes in policies of concern to it; the burden for any further deterioration in relations must fall squarely on Moscow. The US must not yield to pressures to 'take the first step.'"[20]

The president criticized his predecessors for reaching out prematurely and yielding too much. Reagan claimed that prior leaders, including Richard Nixon and Henry Kissinger, had negotiated from weakness, not strength, allowing Moscow to improve its international position. Reagan aimed to reverse what he perceived as Soviet gains by making the American president the world's leading negotiator, with unprecedented muscle behind his words and the most dynamic, free people within his borders: "US policy must have an ideological thrust which clearly affirms the superiority of US and Western values of individual dignity and freedom, a free press, free trade unions, free enterprise, and political democracy over the repressive features of Soviet Communism." Confidence at the negotiating table would force the other side into strategic concessions, according to Reagan, when accompanied by military superiority and domestic prosperity.[21]

The biggest concession Reagan wanted was to eliminate nuclear weapons. Although he rapidly increased the US arsenal to affirm American military strength, he dreaded the deployment of these capabilities that could destroy the entire world. Reagan's personal anti-nuclear sentiment dated back to at least 1979, when he visited the North American Aerospace Defense Command (NORAD) near Colorado Springs, and learned that the United States possessed no effective defense to counter nuclear weapons launched against the nation's territory, even if launched accidentally. "We have spent all that money and have all that equipment," Reagan reportedly said, "and there is nothing we can do to prevent a nuclear missile from hitting us." Despite the extraordinary power possessed by the president, he could only choose to retaliate or wait when confronted with a nuclear attack on the United States. Either way, hundreds of thousands or millions of Americans would die. Reagan was unsatisfied with the absence of better options throughout his presidency.[22]

American nuclear defense relied on "mutually assured destruction" (MAD)—deterring any adversary from striking the homeland with a promise that the attacker would suffer more grievous destruction from America's overwhelming second-strike capability. In the context of nuclear deterrence, peace depended on all actors recognizing the retaliatory Armageddon they would endure after an attack, and the need to back down. This is what appeared to happen during the Cuban Missile Crisis, when both Nikita Khrushchev and John F. Kennedy restrained the belligerence of their advisors. Soviet and American leaders clearly understood that a nuclear first strike, or even a serious provocation, was an act of national (and very likely, global) suicide.[23]

Reagan was not satisfied with a peace that depended on the permanent vulnerability of American territory. To him, the safety of mutually assured destruction and nuclear deterrence was illusory. It ran against all of Reagan's instincts about protecting freedom from fear and government control. "We have allowed ourselves to believe in the MAD system," Reagan chided a reporter. "We have to see what now, with the least lead time, will allow us to come back to a position where we cannot, in the next few years, reach a point at which the Soviet Union could deliver an ultimatum and our only response would be pushing the button."[24]

Strategic experts condemned Reagan's naïveté. Mutually assured destruction guaranteed stability by dissuading attackers, former Secretary of Defense Robert McNamara claimed. Henry Kissinger had also agreed, as evidenced by his negotiation of the Anti-Ballistic Missile (ABM) Treaty in 1972, which limited the number of missile-defense systems the two superpowers could deploy to neutralize a potential nuclear strike against their territory. The risk according to McNamara and Kissinger was that if one side believed it could survive a nuclear strike, it might have an incentive to attack first and destroy as much of the adversary's capabilities as possible—"winning" a war with limited damage at home. To dissuade any possible recourse to nuclear weapons, the experts argued, the prospect of conflict had to be truly suicidal for all participants.[25]

Reagan's efforts to break out of a deterrence mindset and pursue unilateral defense frightened those who had managed and studied nuclear issues since the Second World War. One prominent observer called Reagan a "nuclear hawk" because he wanted to create an American nuclear advantage. It sometimes appeared that the president and his advisors understated the risks of an unbalanced system and the irrevocable damage that even a partially defended nuclear strike would bring on civilians. Many Soviet and European observers were shaken by Reagan's belligerence.[26]

Reagan took these criticisms seriously, particularly when they encouraged voters to view his tough rhetoric with alarm. He reiterated his pledge to pursue peace through negotiations in every speech, even ones where he called the Soviet Union an "evil empire." His controversial speech in March 1983 that condemned Moscow for seeking "world revolution" and abandoning morality included an important (but often ignored) commitment to negotiate for nuclear disarmament: "I intend to do everything I can to persuade them [the Soviet leaders] of our peaceful intent, to remind them that it was the West that refused to use its nuclear monopoly in the forties and fifties for territorial gain and which now proposes a 50-percent cut in strategic ballistic missiles and the elimination of an entire class of land-based intermediate-range nuclear missiles." Reagan asked listeners "to resist the attempts of those who would have you withhold your support for our efforts, this administration's efforts, to keep America strong and free, while we negotiate real and verifiable reductions in the world's nuclear arsenals and one day, with God's help, their total elimination."[27]

The president was actually quite sophisticated in his integration of strength and negotiation. He sought to reassure Americans and the nation's allies, as he also aimed to intimidate foreign adversaries. He stuck to his belief that an expansion of freedom and ingenuity at home would contribute to stronger defense. Artificial government-mandated "freezes" on nuclear defenses (like the ABM Treaty) undermined both freedom and security, Reagan believed, by curtailing citizen initiative. They created the "ceilings" and "mediocrity" that Reagan abhorred. Instead, he doubled down on his faith that more competition, more openness, and more ingenuity in weapons development—as in other areas—would improve America's ability to get what it wanted, short of war.

THESE PRINCIPLES, AT THE CORE OF REAGAN'S POLITICS FOR DEcades, provided the foundation for what became his most surprising and unprecedented effort to change the world. Still, it was consistent with Reagan's long-term vision of American society, nurtured in the aftermath of Roosevelt's New Deal and postwar debates about national policy. Reagan's "Strategic Defense Initiative" (SDI) embodied his view of the president as a catalyst for the innovations of free citizens and a referee for basic order—a "leading actor" in promoting opportunities that served a public mission and protected private enterprise.[28]

Just two weeks after labeling the Soviet Union an "evil empire," on 23 March 1983 Reagan addressed the nation on TV and radio. "What if free people," Reagan asked, "could live secure in the knowledge that their security did not rest upon the threat of instant US retaliation to deter a Soviet attack, that we could intercept and destroy strategic ballistic missiles before they reached our own soil or that of our allies?"

Admitting this was a "formidable, technical task, one that may not be accomplished before the end of this century," the president placed faith in the ingenuity of American scientists. This was a worthy expenditure of precious government resources, Reagan explained, unleashing free enterprise to address a big problem and promising security for all Americans: "Isn't it worth every investment necessary to free the world from the threat of nuclear war? We know it is."[29]

Invoking Franklin Roosevelt's support for the Manhattan Project, Reagan did not claim special expertise or detailed knowledge of how his vision would reach fruition. Instead, he described what he believed was possible and necessary, he warned against fearful cynicism, and he pledged his support for the creativity of others. He would not manage the project; he would promote it and mobilize resources for it. The president saw himself as a leading actor for "changing the course of human history," if he could get others with more specific talents to experiment in pursuit of a world freed from nuclear dangers.

Roosevelt had spoken in similar terms for combating poverty and fascism. Unlike Kennedy and Johnson, who emphasized government as the key actor for positive change, Reagan placed the onus on his listeners, expecting them to respond as a result of new incentives rather than regulations or requirements. His language was similar to Roosevelt's in its emphasis on volunteerism and patriotism above all. "I call upon the scientific community in our country, those who gave us nuclear weapons, to turn their great talents now to the cause of mankind and world peace, to give us the means of rendering these nuclear weapons impotent and obsolete."

Reagan's Strategic Defense Initiative was controversial from the moment he announced it. Strategic experts and foreign observers argued that SDI would shake the stable balance of terror between the United States and the Soviet Union, allowing Washington to consider a successful nuclear first strike, confident that American defenses could thwart Soviet retaliation. Reagan seemed intent on tearing up a decade of arms control agreements (especially the ABM Treaty) that limited defensive systems and preserved parity between Moscow and Washington. The president clearly sought a unilateral American advantage. He did not even confer with his closest allies, including British Prime Minister Margaret Thatcher, who were uniformly skeptical of his plans.

Scientists and engineers doubted that an effective defensive system was viable in the first place. Intercontinental missiles traveled at very high speeds and altitudes; they were difficult to intercept. In 1983 the Soviet Union possessed more than 30,000 nuclear warheads that it could deploy on thousands of missiles. The clear advantage favored the offense, and SDI would encourage adversaries to build more missiles to overwhelm defensive efforts. Arms control advocates rejected Reagan's claim that strategic defense would lead to nuclear reductions. The safest strategy for the Soviet Union would be to build more nuclear weapons, not fewer, in response.[30]

Research since the end of the Cold War has shown that this was what the Soviets did. Most startling, Moscow invested in a "dead hand" system that would automatically launch an overwhelming nuclear retaliation against the United States. Soviet engineers designed this system to counter what they perceived as Reagan's aggression. The president's talk of defense sounded threatening in Russia, and it motivated more militarism.[31]

SDI frightened Soviet leaders because they knew they could not keep up with American technology. Their economy emphasized mass production, not innovation. Their digital capabilities, necessary for any such system, were far behind those of the United States. Although the United States never managed to create a nuclear shield, even more than thirty years later, the vision inspired other technologies, including ground based limited counter-missile systems. Scholars continue to debate whether these benefits outweigh the hundreds of billions of dollars expended on strategic defense since 1983, and the ways it provoked adversaries.

For all its mixed results, SDI embodied Reagan's aspiration for his presidency: to support free enterprise at home that would increase national security. Reagan married traditional values of self-sufficiency and individual freedom with modern technologies of science and war. He was not concerned with the details, but the vision and the promise. The postwar presidents had suffocated hopes for idealistic change in the complexities of bureaucracy, regulation, and expert authority. Reagan painted a picture in words, well performed on radio and television, that renewed hope, idealism, and what his campaign handlers famously called "morning in America."[32]

Reagan freed the presidency from sinking in excessive day-to-day responsibilities, focusing executive leadership on a few simple, deeply-held, and widely shared aspirations. He returned the presidency to mission over management. That was the source of his early success, but also the trap for his later shortcomings, which required major policy adjustments.[33]

THERE WERE TWO REAGAN PRESIDENCIES. DESPITE HIS EARLY promise, everything came apart for the self-confident actor in late 1983. He knew his lines and his role, but the story around him changed. By the middle of the decade his presidency looked very different from what he and those who initially supported him expected.

To call it a reversal is too strong, but to see consistency is also inaccurate. Reagan's transformation was caused by the growth of the presidency and the historical trajectory since the New Deal. Even though this "anti-government" executive wished otherwise, it turned out that he had to choose intervention and control more often than free markets and moral clarity. His willingness to go off his own script, despite the criticisms of close advisors, showed that the actor understood the circumstances of his office and the nature of his times better than many political operatives who claimed his legacy.[34]

Reagan's policy shifts reflected his ability to adjust on stage while remaining true to his character and values. His shifts also showed how the multiplying domestic and international responsibilities of the late twentieth-century presidency defined the executive as much as he defined the office. Reagan's enduring strength as a president was not his ideological obstinacy or his policy steadfastness, as some have argued, but his flexibility. Reagan echoed Roosevelt in his skillful responsiveness to various audiences, even as he struggled with the complex commitments that entangled Kennedy and Johnson.

Members of Congress passed Reagan's large tax cuts during his first years in office, but they refused to reduce spending on social services, agriculture, business subsidies, infrastructure, and various other programs. Republicans, including Reagan, supported many of these expenditures, even as the president demanded smaller budgets. It was much easier to advocate less spending than to find acceptable cuts. The president was more successful in reducing the enforcement of regulations through the executive agencies he controlled, than he was in reducing spending through an appropriations process where his powers were limited. The president's programmatic interests (especially in defense) required him to trade off with the demands of other elected officials.

During Reagan's first three years in office, annual non-defense expenditures rose from $457 billion in 1980 to $598 billion in 1983. The rate of non-defense spending growth was slower than the expansion in military spending, but it still represented a major increase. Overall, federal spending grew from 21 percent of the nation's gross domestic product when Reagan took office to almost 23 percent as he entered his fourth year. The annual shortfall in government revenue (the budget deficit) more than doubled due to the combination of lower taxes and increased spending. Most astonishing, between 1980 and 1984 the total federal debt ballooned from less than $1 trillion to more than $1.5 trillion—almost 40 percent of the gross domestic product. The federal debt would rise to more than 50 percent of the gross domestic product before Reagan left office.[35]

These truly astonishing numbers revealed how the Reagan administration's policies inflated government spending and debt-taking, rather than the opposite. If anything, the federal government became *more* intrusive in the economy, interfering with the freedom and entrepreneurship that Reagan had espoused so eloquently. In 1985 the president's young budget wizard (and former Michigan congressman), David Stockman, resigned. He renounced what he criticized as corruption by a combination of actors, Republican and Democrat, who sold out the vision of smaller government for a heavily indebted system that gave away money to all groups, especially the rich and well-connected.

Stockman echoed Andrew Jackson's attack on elite financial manipulators facilitated by a president who did not anticipate the consequences of cutting taxes without the firm spending ceilings, particularly for defense, that he abhorred. Stockman did not doubt Reagan's sincerity, but he observed firsthand a stunning "lapse into fiscal indiscipline on a scale never before experienced in peacetime." As he recounted, "Ronald Reagan had been induced by his advisors and his own illusions to embrace one of the more irresponsible platforms of modern times." Stockman criticized the president for believing he could "alter the laws of arithmetic. No program that had a name or line in the budget would be cut; no taxes would be raised. Yet the deficit was pronounced intolerable and it was pledged to be eliminated."[36]

Reagan saw the numbers himself. Although he would not accept increased taxes, and he could not eliminate congressional spending authority, he searched for ways to curtail federal debt and spending, even in his aggressive defense budget. Reducing commitments abroad was, in fact, one way to accomplish this goal. The president would continue to talk tough, but he would now emphasize efficiencies, burden sharing, and even cooperation with adversaries to reduce costs. If a strong international defense was meant to protect freedom at home, the economics of peace became more attractive for Reagan in 1983.

Opinion polls taken by the White House confirmed this insight. American voters had two main worries: war and economic decline. Voters attributed both, in part, to Reagan's belligerence and his low tax, high spend policies. To defend his presidential agenda, Reagan had to show he really wanted peace and reductions in costly American commitments. This was more than a re-election imperative for the president; it was crucial for his effort to restore confidence in what he believed was a demoralized nation. After talking with his pollster Richard Wirthlin in October 1983, Reagan noted, "there is a deeply buried isolationist sentiment in our land." Like previous presidents, he had to address these concerns as he simultaneously sought to stand strong abroad and increase the global reach of the American economy.[37]

INTERNATIONAL AFFAIRS IN LATE 1983 UNDERMINED REAGAN'S nascent peace efforts. A series of events, loosely related to one another, shook the White House, and the president in particular. They dominate his personal diary during what he repeatedly refers to as an uncomfortably "hectic" time: "Everyone talks about what should or should not be done but they don't know the real facts." Although words of exasperation were rare from Reagan, they appear most often in this difficult period, as he struggled with the limits of his power as president.[38]

During his first years in the White House Reagan had tried to keep his daily schedule light, with fewer meetings than his predecessors, and more time to write letters, work on speeches, and escape the Oval Office. He preferred quiet evenings with his wife, Nancy (they would often watch movies together) to the late-night work sessions of Kennedy and Johnson. The events of late 1983 forced Reagan out of his more relaxed routine, leaving him scattered and over-scheduled like his predecessors. He found it difficult to get his bearings as one crisis after another came before him. He also began to feel alone—the paradox of having such a large staff and so few friends—especially when Nancy was not around.

During the weekend of 22-23 October 1983, when the president had planned to enjoy a quiet visit to the Augusta Country Club in Georgia, he was awakened two mornings in a row, at 4:00 a.m. on Saturday and then at 2:30 a.m. on Sunday. The first time was to authorize an invasion of the Caribbean island of Grenada, where a Cuban-supported coup triggered American worries of communist advances there and in the rest of the region. The coup leaders in Grenada had assassinated the island's popular prime minister, and they had imposed a form of martial law that Reagan officials viewed as the first step toward a broader Caribbean revolution. Scholars have since criticized the Reagan administration's exaggeration of the communist threat in Grenada, but at the time the president and his closest advisors were deeply alarmed. They perceived growing Cuban and Soviet aggression in Central America, and they were committed to showing strength in response. Reagan's diary records that in the early morning hours of 22 October, he authorized "an outright invasion" to defeat the coup leaders and protect "six other Caribbean nations, including Jamaica and Barbados."[39]

Following a series of failed US Navy Seal reconnaissance missions, almost two thousand American troops invaded Grenada on 25 October, accompanied by approximately 300 soldiers from regional partners. The invasion force easily secured the island, although its operations were embarrassingly disorganized; many units lacked basic navigation and communications preparations. On 27 October, US air units fired inadvertently on a brigade of American soldiers, wounding seventeen, one of whom later died. The mishaps that accompanied the American invasion of this tiny, undefended island belied the president's boasts about increasing military strength. As an official US Army history of the operation later revealed, this was a "'no-notice' joint-force contingency operation," and the results showed that despite increased defense spending, the US Army was unprepared for "work in a joint environment with its Air Force, Navy, and Marine counterparts."[40]

Members of Congress reacted by passing the Goldwater-Nichols Act, which required more integration among military services. International leaders, including British Prime Minister Margaret Thatcher, condemned the decision to invade Grenada and the subsequent military operation. The president's decision was popular at home, but it raised new concerns about the effectiveness of his leadership. Had he really made the United States stronger? The "isolationist" voices he feared in the United States grew louder; events in Grenada gave them a new platform.

On the morning of Sunday, 23 October 1983, as American forces prepared to invade Grenada, an Iranian suicide bomber drove a truck filled with explosives into the US Marines barracks in Beirut, Lebanon, near the embattled city's airport. The attack caused the building to collapse, crushing and suffocating 241 Americans inside. Just a few minutes later, a second truck detonated a suicide bomb near the barracks for French forces in Beirut, killing 58 paratroopers.

Reagan's diary recorded: "About 2:30 in the morning awakened again: This time with the tragic news that more than 100 Marines in Beirut had been killed by a car bomb driven by a suicide driver. . . . We all believe the Iranians did this bombing just as they did with our embassy last April." The president was referring to an earlier suicide bombing in Beirut that killed 63 people, including 17 US citizens.[41]

Reagan had deployed American soldiers to Beirut in the summer of 1982 as part of a multinational force seeking to restore order amid a civil war that was tearing the once prosperous country apart. Syrian, Israeli, and Iranian-backed groups were fighting for control over the city, giving rise to new local paramilitary groups and new forms of religious extremism. Working with the United Nations, the Reagan administration hoped to use a show of force to stabilize the situation and avoid a widening regional conflict. In fact, the American military presence only further inflamed the fighting and motivated a series of attacks on US troops in the region, and soon beyond it. In Beirut, Americans became a target for extremist groups that viewed (and continue to view) a more assertive United States as a repressive, anti-Islamic force. The bombing of the US Marines barracks was the beginning of a new era of anti-American terrorism in the Middle East.

The Reagan administration was unprepared to meet this threat. The president and his closest advisors had assumed that increased American military strength would deter attacks on US interests. Reagan also believed that American promises of freedom would attract more followers across the globe. The events in Beirut and the wider region challenged these assumptions. Right or wrong, thousands of citizens in the Middle East viewed American power as offensive and threatening, and they were more motivated than ever before to bring violence upon Americans in response. The terrorism of the early 1980s was an extension of localized conflict in the Middle East against the United States and its perceived influence in the region. American strength did not bring peace, but just the opposite.

REAGAN OBSERVED A SIMILAR DYNAMIC IN EUROPE. HIS EFFORTS to expand American nuclear and conventional capabilities, including the deployment of intermediate range nuclear missiles in Western Europe, brought the United States and the Soviet Union closer to nuclear war than at any time since the Cuban Missile Crisis. Both superpowers were rapidly adding to their European-based military forces, increasing their espionage activities, and spreading belligerent propaganda. Observers worried that Washington and Moscow had entered an arms race "spiral"—a replay of the lead-up to the First World War. With more weapons pointed in both directions, escalation became easier (and less politically risky) than backing down and hoping for the best.[42]

During the autumn of 1983 tensions peaked. On 1 September two Soviet fighter jets scrambled from their base in northeastern Russia to intercept an unidentified airplane that had strayed over the Kamchatka peninsula. The Reagan administration frequently sent spy planes along this route, so the Soviet pilots assumed that the aircraft was the same. When the aircraft did not respond to visual warnings, one of the Soviet fighter jets shot it down.

The aircraft was, in fact, a civilian 747 jet, flown by Korean Air Lines from JFK International Airport in New York to Seoul, South Korea. After refueling in Anchorage, Alaska, the aircraft had inadvertently flown about 200 miles off course, over Russian territory. Soviet Air Forces failed to contact the civilian pilots by radio, and they did not give the aircraft a chance to get back on course. More than a decade later, one of the Soviet fighter pilots recalled: "I wondered what kind of plane it was, but I had no time to think. I had a job to do. . . . My orders were to destroy the intruder. I fulfilled my mission."[43]

The result of that mission was 269 civilian deaths, including 61 Americans. Among others, the passenger list included a member of Congress, Georgia Representative Larry McDonald, an outspoken Democratic critic of the Soviet Union. Voice recordings later revealed that the pilots and passengers were unaware of the danger, and the aircraft was not destroyed instantly. Instead, the damaged plane drifted for about twelve minutes after it was shot, falling to the ocean, where many injured passengers drowned.

Reagan labeled the attack the "Korean airline massacre." It was an immediate shock to citizens in the United States and the wider world. Observers interpreted the attack as an escalation in the Cold War, another step toward direct warfare between Moscow and Washington. Thousands of civilian aircraft were vulnerable in the same way. Would the United States retaliate against a Soviet passenger jet? Would the Soviets take the same action again? Where would the retaliation end?

Reagan recognized the severity of the situation, and he responded with very strong words, returning to his characterization of the Soviet Union as an "evil empire": "This was the Soviet Union against the world and the moral precepts which guide human relations among people everywhere. It was an act of barbarism, born of a society which wantonly disregards individual rights and the value of human life and seeks constantly to expand and dominate other nations."

The president called for new sanctions to isolate the Soviet Union, reparations to compensate suffering families, and a further buildup in American military forces. He closed his angry address to the nation by quoting one of Abraham Lincoln's most famous speeches, given on the eve of the Civil War: "Let us have faith that right makes might, and in that faith let us, to the end, dare to do our duty as we understand it." Everyone understood the threat of war in these words.[44]

And the United States prepared for nuclear war in the weeks after. In early November American and NATO forces simulated a full-scale nuclear attack on the Soviet Union. The exercise ("Able Archer 83") exceeded all previous war games in scope. The allied armies moved 40,000 soldiers across Western Europe, including more than 15,000 US troops airlifted overseas for this simulated battle. To prevent enemy surveillance, they conducted many of their operations with radio silence and encrypted messaging. The top US military and political authorities, including high-level White House and Pentagon officials, moved to secure locations in North America and practiced the procedures for launching nuclear and chemical weapons.[45]

Soviet leaders thought these actions might be more than just a simulation. The Soviet general secretary, an elderly and ill Yuri Andropov, told his advisors that he feared Reagan had gone mad, seeking to end the Soviet Union (and much of human civilization) with overwhelming force. A retrospective study of highly classified evidence for President George H. W. Bush in 1990 confirmed that the Soviets were indeed convinced Armageddon had arrived, or it was dangerously close.[46]

Reagan's CIA director and former campaign manager, William Casey, briefed the president about what had quickly become one of the most dangerous war scares of the Cold War. Casey described "a rather stunning array of indicators" showing unexpected Soviet war preparations: "The Soviets have concluded that the danger of war is greater and will grow." Casey cited "lowered Soviet confidence in their ability to warn of sudden attack." American strength had increased Moscow's vulnerability, which also increased Moscow's incentive to act first: "These perceptions, perhaps driven by a building US defense budget, new initiatives in continental defense, improvements in force readiness, and a potentially massive space defense program may be propelling the Soviet Union to take national readiness measures at a deliberate pace."

Despite his prior advocacy for more American pressure on Moscow, Casey believed Soviet leaders were legitimately and dangerously spooked. "The military behaviors we have observed involve high military costs in terms of vulnerability of resources for the sake of improved national military power, or enhanced readiness at the price of consumer discontent, or enhanced readiness at the price of troop dissatisfaction. None of these are trivial costs, adding thereby a dimension of genuineness to the Soviet expressions of concern that is often not reflected in intelligence issuances."[47]

Reagan was visibly shaken. He found it "really scary." His national security advisor, Robert McFarlane, recounts that the president inquired how the Soviets could believe that he wanted to start a nuclear war: "Do you suppose they really believe that?" Reagan asked. "I don't see how they could believe that—but it's something to think about."[48]

Reagan's efforts to build up the US military and challenge Soviet misdeeds were designed to bring peace, not war. But now he recognized that his "tough guy" act had gone too far, and had even become counterproductive. The aftermath of very trying events in late 1983—from Beirut and Grenada to the Korean Airliner and the NATO war exercise—convinced Reagan that he had to approach his role in a new way.

His primary goal of enhancing freedom and fighting communism had not changed. His belief in American strength and benevolence remained firm. What changed was Reagan's understanding of how his words and actions were interpreted by others. An actor by profession, he cared deeply about the reception of his ideas. Being correct was not enough. Reagan wanted to connect with audiences and encourage behavior favorable to the United States. The events of late 1983 taught him that he had failed to connect, and he had motivated many of the wrong reactions.

His handwritten diary entries for this period are particularly revealing because they show a remarkable empathy for Soviet fears and a renewed commitment to persuade and connect by other means. Reagan had a sincere message of peace, and he was now going to share it through more direct contact with Soviet leaders: "[Secretary of State] George Shultz and I had a talk mainly about setting up a little in house group of experts on the Soviet Union to help us in setting up some channels. I feel the Soviets are so defense minded, so paranoid about being attacked that without being in any way soft on them we ought to tell them no one here has any intention of doing anything like that. What the h—l have they got that anyone would want."[49]

Reagan later reflected on this moment in his memoirs: "During my first years in Washington, I think many of us in the administration took it for granted that the Russians, like ourselves, considered it unthinkable that the United States would launch a first strike against them. But the more experience I had with Soviet leaders and other heads of state who knew them, the more I began to realize that many Soviet officials feared us not only as adversaries but as potential aggressors who might hurl nuclear weapons at them in a first strike." Intent on correcting that misperception, Reagan wrote, "I was even more anxious to get a top Soviet leader in a room alone and try to convince him we had no designs on the Soviet Union and the Russians had nothing to fear from us."[50]

The president never used the phrase "evil empire" again. He now called for "constructive cooperation" instead. In January 1984 he startled listeners (and antagonized hardliners in his own party) with a speech that, as he wrote in his diary, "left the door open to the Soviets": "Neither we nor the Soviet Union can wish away the differences between our two societies and our philosophies, but we should always remember that we do have common interests and the foremost among them is to avoid war and reduce the level of arms." Reagan called for limiting the use of force in international disputes, reducing nuclear and conventional arms, and establishing a "better working relationship" between long-standing adversaries.[51]

Reagan understood this represented an about-face for him, and he courageously extolled the shift as necessary: "Living in this nuclear age makes it imperative that we do talk. Our commitment to dialog is firm and unshakeable."[52]

Just four months earlier Reagan had quoted Lincoln's justification for conflict on the eve of the Civil War. Now he closed his speech with a statement resembling President Kennedy's call for reconciliation after the Cuban Missile Crisis: "Let us also direct attention to our common interests and to the means by which those differences can be resolved."

Reagan offered a parable to explain his change in perspective:

Just suppose with me for a moment that an Ivan and an Anya could find themselves, oh, say, in a waiting room, or sharing a shelter from the rain or a storm with a Jim and Sally, and there was no language barrier to keep them from getting acquainted. Would they then debate the differences between their respective governments? Or would they find themselves comparing notes about their children and what each other did for a living?"

People want to raise their children in a world without fear and without war. They want to have some of the good things over and above bare subsistence that make life worth living. They want to work at some craft, trade, or profession that gives them satisfaction and a sense of worth.

If the Soviet Government wants peace, then there will be peace. Together we can strengthen peace, reduce the level of arms, and know in doing so that we have helped fulfill the hopes and dreams of those we represent and, indeed, of people everywhere. Let us begin now.[53]

Reagan was true to his new words. After early 1984 he did more than any president since Franklin Roosevelt to pursue a working relationship with Soviet leaders. Like Roosevelt, he remained wary of Soviet intentions and he continued to build American strength, especially through his Strategic Defense Initiative. Reagan had reached out to Soviet leaders before, but now he followed his personal messages with additional overtures. He sent a series of emissaries—including Secretary of State George Shultz, Vice President George H. W. Bush, former National Security Advisor Brent Scowcroft, and Senate Majority Leader Howard Baker—to meet with Soviet officials, emphasize America's peaceful intentions, and encourage cooperation. He curtailed what had been almost daily efforts to embarrass and provoke Soviet leaders. Most significant,

Reagan committed himself to major arms reductions. The president went further than any American leader before him (Roosevelt, of course, had died before the first atomic bomb was tested): "I support a zero option for all nuclear arms. As I've said before, my dream is to see the day when nuclear weapons will be banished from the face of the Earth."[54]

For Soviet leaders, Reagan's overtures were credible because he expended political capital to pursue them. He elicited growing criticism from hardline anti-communists in the United States, many of whom worked for his administration. Some of the most vocal Republicans opposed any discussions with communists. Even foreign allies who supported negotiations with the Soviets, including British Prime Minister Margaret Thatcher and West German Chancellor Helmut Kohl, dissented from Reagan's desire to eliminate all nuclear weapons, which they perceived as an essential element of their national defense. Reagan's public willingness to challenge these important groups and defend his peace efforts encouraged observers in Moscow to take him seriously.

A new generation of Soviet leaders, many of whom had traveled in the West and recognized the severe economic and technological deficiencies in their own society, had reason to reciprocate. They resented Reagan's previous condemnations of the Soviet Union, his advocacy of what they perceived as an unjust economic system, and, most of all, his assertion of American global supremacy. Nonetheless, the Soviet figures who came to be known as the "new thinkers" in the second half of the 1980s needed an American partner to justify reductions in international tensions and military expenditures, allowing their government to focus on development at home.[55]

Mikhail Gorbachev, who ascended to Soviet general secretary in March 1985, became the vessel for this transformation. He was a true believer in communism who hoped to strengthen the Soviet Union by eliminating corruption, encouraging innovation, and empowering the best leaders. To do these things, which he later called "Perestroika" ("Restructuring"), he sought to reduce the influence of the military and security services. Gorbachev wanted to make the Soviet Union a central part of what he envisioned as a "common European home."[56]

He grabbed a hold of Reagan's overtures with a zeal that surprised the president himself. Beginning with their first summit meeting in

Geneva in November 1985, the two former adversaries met more frequently than any previous pair of American and Soviet leaders since Roosevelt and Stalin. Like those earlier war-time conferences, the Reagan-Gorbachev summits allowed them to forge a strong personal connection and discuss fundamental strategic questions. Their meetings produced the most significant nuclear cutbacks to that time, and a general reduction in global tensions between the most powerful states. In the fall of 1986 the two leaders almost reached agreement on the unthinkable: Reagan's proposed "zero option" for the elimination of all nuclear weapons.[57]

In May 1988 Reagan became the first American president since Richard Nixon to visit Moscow, meeting with Soviet leaders and citizens who no longer viewed him as a foreign adversary, but instead as a potential ally. Walking amiably with Gorbachev inside the walls of the medieval Kremlin fortress, a reporter asked Reagan if he still believed the Soviet Union was an "evil empire." "You are talking about another time, another era," he replied, as the Soviet leader beamed.[58]

When Gorbachev visited the United States six months later, the thaw in the two nations' formerly belligerent relations was again evident, particularly on the streets of New York City. Bankers, business owners, office workers, and students (including this writer) lined Lexington Avenue to greet the leading communist figure in the world, now a rock-star symbol for peace and reform.

Reagan's change of script after 1983 had helped to shift the larger Cold War narrative. This was his greatest presidential success, even if it contradicted his earlier anti-communist belligerence. Reagan defended his vision of freedom by working closely with the leader of the regime that most opposed his vision. Reagan and Gorbachev, like Roosevelt and Stalin, never agreed on economic principles—the American remained an advocate of capitalism, and the Russian a critic.

Out of necessity, Reagan used his presidency to re-direct the world away from the possibility of war. He pushed a large government bureaucracy that he abhorred to exert more control, not less, over the forces and habits that encouraged conflict. Like his early hero, Franklin Roosevelt, Reagan used his executive powers, formal and informal, to regulate a dangerous world. He reached out to adversaries, he experimented with new overtures, and he took risks for peace, despite the obvious ideological inconsistencies. Reagan's foreign policy after 1983 made the president a leading actor for negotiating the end of the Cold War.

REAGAN'S REMARKABLE TRANSFORMATION AND HIS SUCCESSFUL efforts to negotiate with Soviet leaders restored a heroic veneer to the American presidency. Reagan proved that a powerful, open-minded executive could change the world. He also showed how unpredictable and unplanned presidential leadership was. More than almost any other national executive before him, Reagan had to reverse his rhetoric and actions in response to dangerous circumstances, and overcome stiff resistance, while remaining true to his values and goals. Transformation on that scale required a willingness to recognize failure, learn, and adjust. It took great courage, and some luck.

In part because this shift required so much presidential attention, Reagan could not lead similar policy transformations in other areas. Most of his programs at home and abroad did not achieve their aims; many caused great harm to the country.

Reagan's efforts to foster economic growth through reduced taxes and regulations landed the nation in a quagmire of debt and widened income inequality. Despite his repeated pledges to reduce borrowing, the federal government's indebtedness almost tripled during his presidency from less than $1 trillion in 1981 to just under $3 trillion in 1989. The annual federal budget deficit almost doubled from $105 billion to $198 billion. This rate of debt increase had not occurred since Franklin Roosevelt's presidency, and it revealed that Reagan's programs had actually expanded the size of the federal government, with new spending on benefits for the elderly, agricultural subsidies, and of course, the military. Steep tax cuts on high earners and corporations reduced the revenue needed to cover these expenses. Rising indebtedness reflected exactly what Reagan had promised to prevent: more government intrusion in the economy and heavier obligations on the backs of citizens, who ultimately bore the responsibility of paying off the national debt.[59]

US economic growth had reached a healthy 4 percent annual rate by the end of Reagan's presidency, but the mix of high spending and low tax policies meant this growth disproportionately benefited former high tax earners and chosen recipients of government assistance. The tax cuts and spending increases of the Reagan years boosted some groups, who gained surplus capital, at the expense of many others, who became deeply indebted. This kind of economy created more of a bubble than a stable route to prosperity. It also increased polarization among citizens.[60]

More than anything, the oldest US president before the election of Donald Trump[61] helped the oldest Americans to live better than all other groups. Minorities and low-skilled workers experienced economic stagnation, and often decline. And for the first time since the nineteenth century, citizens under age 18 began to suffer higher rates of poverty than any other group. During the 1980s more than one in five children had inadequate access to food, shelter, and schooling. The young did not benefit from Reagan's tax breaks or spending priorities.[62]

Overall, more Americans fell into poverty during Reagan's presidency than moved into prosperity, or at least modest comfort. Despite Roosevelt-like government spending, the results were the opposite. Many of the gains from the New Deal and Lyndon Johnson's Great Society were reversed. Sixty percent of American households (in the lowest and middle income groups) saw little or no gains in wealth, and many experienced decreases in health. Education levels in the country stagnated, limiting the opportunities for poor citizens to improve their earning chances.[63]

Although Reagan claimed otherwise, it was hard to argue that Americans became freer during his presidency. The weight of the evidence indicates that some already privileged citizens (mostly white males) increased their wealth, but most Americans became more debt-saddled and stuck in jobs with long hours and limited pay. Increases in gross domestic product during the Reagan years came predominantly from people working longer hours, rather than from innovation. More than at any time since the Great Depression, American citizens were chained to stagnant jobs, personal debt, and crumbling public institutions. They might have won the Cold War, but the majority did not believe they were winning in the economy. That frustration persisted among the millions who felt left behind, into the next century.[64]

AMONG THOSE EXCLUDED FROM THE NARRATIVE OF FREEDOM Reagan put forward were people afflicted with a scary disease: Acquired Immunodeficiency Syndrome (AIDS). The virus (known as HIV) that caused AIDS began to appear in the United States in the early 1980s. It slowly debilitated the patient's immune system, leaving the individual's body incapable of fighting off common bacteria or viruses. AIDS sufferers often died from pneumonia or another usually non-fatal illness as their bodies slowly shut down.

By the end of the 1980s, more than 100,000 Americans had perished from the disease, and millions came to live in fear of it. Transmitted through body fluids, AIDS impacted the gay and drug-using communities worst of all. Citizens across the country worried about the fatal possibilities from intimate contact with strangers. Concerns about AIDS killed the casual sex culture of the 1960s and 1970s, and encouraged discrimination against suspected carriers. In particular, fear of AIDS inflamed public hatred of gay men. To many Americans, their "lifestyle choices" imperiled all of society.[65]

Reagan understood the tragedy of AIDS firsthand. In 1985 his long-time friend and fellow actor, Rock Hudson, died of the disease. Yet as panic spread about how heterosexuals were allegedly at risk, and as acts of discrimination became common across the country, Reagan said very little. He did not speak out against hatred of homosexuals or other exaggerated and misplaced fears. He did not express sympathy with the sufferers. Most significant, he did not offer major federal support for medical efforts to cure the disease or curtail its spread within gay communities.

When US Surgeon General C. Everett Koop advocated programs for "safe sex," Reagan joined criticisms of what he and many other Americans saw as encouragement of licentious behavior. The president asserted that "the primary responsibility for avoiding AIDS lies with the individual." Voicing his conservative values, he advised all citizens to "abstain from sex until marriage." Gay and lesbian individuals could not marry at the time, so Reagan's comment appeared to deny their existence. The wholesome boy from Dixon refused to address what he did not want to see.[66]

Public health officials, activists, and local leaders blamed Reagan for callously allowing so many citizens to suffer. Before dying from the disease himself, the journalist Randy Shilts published an exposé, *And the Band Played On*, that documented how national figures looked away from the crisis. Another prominent writer compared AIDS to genocide and presidential passivity to a war crime. "ACT-UP," an AIDS advocacy group formed in 1987, mobilized tens of thousands of young people to wear stickers and carry signs saying "Silence=Death."[67]

The criticisms of Reagan's leadership were well founded. The president spoke out strongly against the suffering under communism, and he mobilized citizens to pursue peace with the Soviet adversary after 1983—yet he could not find the same empathy for AIDS victims, and he failed to adjust his thinking to overwhelming evidence about how the disease was harming the country. Part of the problem was Reagan's prejudice toward the LGBTQ community—a prejudice shared by many other Americans at the time. Part of the problem was his insulation from the issue and what the disease looked like up close.

For all the power that the presidency commands to reach citizens at home and abroad, Reagan's failed leadership during the AIDS crisis captures how difficult it has become for the national executive to see beyond his existing commitments and prejudices. Reagan had too many other concerns, and he gave them priority. Reagan and his closest advisors did not have the interest or time to think about the issue with the depth it deserved. In not acting, of course, they were also responding to conservative constituencies that did not want the president to "condone" homosexual lifestyles or premarital sex. For an overcommitted and uncertain president, sticking with existing policies seemed most appealing for this and many other issues, including poverty.

The more powerful and ambitious the president, the harder it is to change course. That was true for Kennedy, Johnson, and Reagan. As they took on new responsibilities and confronted an incredibly complex array of challenges, they lost the flexibility that Franklin Roosevelt had exercised so well. Executive leadership became more stubborn in the face of failure, rather than responsive. That posture played well on television, and it conserved time for other matters. Changing direction took more effort. Staying the course was efficient—even as tens of thousands of Americans died.

REAGAN'S PRESIDENCY ENDED IN SCANDAL. COMMITTED TO SEcuring the release of American hostages held in Lebanon after 1983, members of Reagan's National Security Council secretly and illegally sent weapons to a hostile government in Tehran, in return for help with freeing the Americans. Iran paid for the weapons (between $10 million and $30 million), and the White House diverted that money to the Contra rebels fighting a socialist government in Nicaragua. The diversion of money violated explicit congressional prohibitions on military aid to the Nicaraguan insurgency.[68]

The arms-for-hostages-for-anticommunist-assistance triangle was a complex undertaking that revealed the frustrations the Reagan administration felt from the limits on its congressionally authorized power. The Iran-Contra affair also revealed the difficulties presidents have controlling their own staffs. The organizers of the scheme, particularly Lieutenant Colonel Oliver North and Admiral John Poindexter, followed what they believed were the president's intentions, and they had his consent. The most careful study of the topic reveals that despite the obvious illegality, "the president approved every significant facet of the Iran arms deals, and he encouraged conduct by top aides that had the same aim and outcome as the diversion—to subsidize the Contra war despite the congressional prohibition on US aid." According to CIA officials who met with him, Reagan was "obsessed" with getting the American hostages released and stubbornly committed to helping the Contras overthrow socialists in Nicaragua.[69]

Without him fully realizing it, Reagan's strong beliefs empowered zealous staff members, including North and Poindexter, to push beyond the legal boundaries of their authority. If they were working on behalf of the president's goals, as they claimed, traditional assumptions about transparency and accountability seemed less important. Congress, the law, and other restraints looked like nuisances for an administration committed to getting big things done. Reagan did not flaunt the law personally, but he helped enable the law-breaking.

By Reagan's time, it was no longer possible for the president to closely follow all the domestic and international programs under his purview. This represented a shift from the experimentation of Franklin Roosevelt's New Deal presidency. Roosevelt empowered various agencies and other actors, but the range of activities was still small enough that he could require direct accountability. He also designated multiple figures of responsibility for each project, encouraging them to compete and bring him different information, to get a fuller picture of activities. Roosevelt enforced presidential accountability.[70]

Even if he had tried, Reagan could not have maintained the same direct control over the larger, more complex, and more international government bureaucracy that he led. His expansion of the military and related activities greatly increased the reach of US agencies. Reagan delegated authority and reduced oversight in the hopes of empowering his subordinates and pursuing multiple agendas. He wisely avoided the micromanagement and near-authoritarian impulses that limited creativity, and often effectiveness, under his predecessors. That was the enduring lesson of Lyndon Johnson's failure in Vietnam for Reagan and others who lived through that agonizing war with a maniacal president.[71]

The irony was that Reagan's effort to avoid single-minded commitments opened the presidency to policy indiscipline—too many interventions without careful strategic consideration. The sale of weapons to Iran undermined the administration's priority of reducing violence and the spread of Islamic extremism in the Middle East. The diversion of money to the Contras gave further life to an insurgency that was ineffective, at best, and often responsible for worse human rights violations than the socialist regime it opposed. The Contras pushed potential regional supporters of the United States to back the Nicaraguan socialists (the Sandinistas), out of fear for how much more harmful the Contras and other paramilitary groups would be in power. The entire Iran-Contra operation was a strategic blunder, even before American citizens became aware of it.

The revelation of this sordid affair by a Lebanese magazine in November 1986 triggered a series of congressional hearings that rivaled the

Fulbright hearings on the Vietnam War in the late 1960s and the Watergate hearings on Richard Nixon's impeachment in 1974. Members of Congress accused the president of breaking the law, and they grilled officials about their activities. Citizens watching the hearings on television became convinced that their government was lying to them, that it was incompetent, and that it was not serving their interests. Reagan's best defense, like Lyndon Johnson's and Richard Nixon's, was that he was acting with good intentions and he did not know about the flagrant abuses committed by those who worked for him. "I hadn't been fully informed," the president told Americans, but now he "sought to find the answers." Those were not the words of a strong and effective leader.[72]

REAGAN REMAINED PERSONALLY POPULAR, ESPECIALLY FOR HIS SUCcess in bringing peace with the crumbling Soviet Union. Perceptions of the American presidency as an office, however, reached a new low. Even more than after Lyndon Johnson's and Richard Nixon's terms in office, citizens no longer trusted the president or believed he could solve big problems. [73]

The American president's powers, and the expectations around those powers, had continued to grow since Franklin Roosevelt's time in office, but Kennedy, Johnson, and Reagan had all experienced frustrating constraints. They fed rising expectations of the presidency, and they fell short of their inflated promises. They were overwhelmed by the range of issues before them and the complexity of the problems they confronted. Cuba, Vietnam, AIDS, and Iran-Contra unmasked a sinking, not a commanding, president.

The post-Roosevelt presidents found it difficult to match their power with their purposes. The federal government was too massive and too fragmented. Superior American power could not reverse Fidel Castro's Cuban revolution, free Southeast Asia from communism, create debt- and tax-free prosperity, or eliminate poverty and disease. Although American power appeared transformative, its efficacy was marginal, at best.

The gargantuan scope of American power was, in many ways, self-limiting. The president could use guns and dollars to pursue his goals, but for all his firepower and wealth, he could not control outcomes. His immense capabilities sparked resistance and counter-moves. His immense capabilities also encouraged more and more requests for assistance. The president had so much power, but it was never enough.

Reagan learned that lesson better than most of his predecessors during the crises of late 1983. He adjusted his policies with remarkable rapidity once he recognized that saber-rattling was making the United States less secure. The courageous president abandoned his most belligerent behavior and reached out to the Soviet Union to rectify his misuse of power. This was Reagan's finest moment—and it showed the promise of a flexible and adaptive executive.

He did not do the same for the economy, AIDS, the Middle East, or Nicaragua. In each of these areas, Reagan held tightly to his faith in individual freedom, markets, and small government. When his policies contributed to diminished freedom and distorted markets, he did not change direction. He faced strong pressures to stay the course. Powerful presidents are rarely flexible because their power is attached to established practices and assumptions.

Reagan helped end the Cold War, but the Cold War also ended him. He was hyper-interventionist at home and abroad, despite his calls for less government. He spent more on defense and select social programs, despite his demands for frugality. And he encouraged higher expectations for executive performance, not less. He created a more powerful presidency to make his case for a less powerful federal government.

Reagan never resolved that contradiction. His enduring popularity reflects his ambition to scale back the excesses of the New Deal. Yet the appeal of his presidency centered on his ability to do more of the same. Presidential rhetoric was anti-government, but the late twentieth-century presidency was a creature of big government. That trend has only continued, to the dismay of Reagan's successors.

CHAPTER 9

Magicians of Possibility

The lives of recent American presidents began with missing fathers. "All my life," Bill Clinton admitted in his memoir, "I have been hungry to fill in the blanks, clinging eagerly to every photo or story or scrap of paper that would tell me more of the man who gave me life." Clinton never met his father, who died in a car crash, weeks before his birth in Hope, Arkansas.[1]

Barack Obama met his father briefly as an adolescent, but barely knew him when he, too, died in a car crash. "At the time of his death," Obama remembered, "my father remained a myth to me, both more and less than a man. . . . I think probably the most important thing was his absence." Obama struggled early in life to fill that void. Like so many other black teenagers in postwar America, he came of age without a black male role model.[2]

Confronted very early by the uncertainties about their past, Clinton and Obama grew up fast. They had to be self-reliant because their mothers were often away and their grandparents could not keep up. They had to provide stability for younger siblings born to different fathers. Most of all, they had to show strength and self-control when frequently confronted by insults, slights, and, in the case of Clinton, an alcoholic and abusive stepfather. They both rose above these challenges to become the leaders of their families at a young age.[3]

They did so on the margins of American society, in the rural South and the distant island of Hawaii. (Obama also spent four years living in

Indonesia before he turned ten.) They saw American power from the outside in, as it affected communities far from New York wealth and Washington influence. They were talented provincials, with problematic backgrounds, to say the least. No one, except their mothers, anticipated they could ever become national leaders. Election to the presidency seemed as improbable as a trip to Mars, or at least the moon.

CLINTON AND OBAMA SAW THE DARK SIDE OF AMERICAN LIFE up close. Many of their peers had similarly troubled family histories, living on the edge of poverty, ill health, and violent death. Most of their peers had ambitions that barely extended beyond their immediate circumstances.

The later lives of the two presidents were unfathomable in their youth, as they remain inexplicable for their peers. Even when recognized for their extraordinary talents, Clinton and Obama seemed destined to live within the limits of the circumstances of their births, their communities, and especially their families. Too much was working against them—poverty, prejudice, and, of course, the traditional business and cultural elites who remained unaccepting of them until they had reached the presidency, and often not even then. They each had important early mentors—including Senator J. William Fulbright for Clinton and some of Chicago's leading liberals for Obama—but these were the exceptions. Most powerful people underestimated these powerless young men.

Clinton and Obama came of age just as upward mobility for men like them was becoming more difficult. In the last quarter of the twentieth century, where you were born and how much your father earned strongly predicted how far you could climb. Fatherless rural or African American boys were two of the least mobile groups—they experienced limited income growth and their early mortality rates remained high. To become president from where Clinton and Obama started was more improbable than the rise of Andrew Jackson or Abraham Lincoln, who were born into a society where poor white boys really did become rich landholders with remarkable regularity. That was not the case in the more stratified society of the late twentieth century, when social and financial capital came to matter more than individual talent and ambition.[4]

THE COMMUNITIES CLINTON AND OBAMA GREW UP IN DID NOT match the American dream of prosperous families living in idyllic, suburban settings. From an early age, however, neighbors recognized something different in these two young men. They were unusually perceptive and emotionally mature. Despite their broken families, Clinton and Obama were comfortable among diverse people and in unfamiliar places. They were high achievers and natural leaders, at the top of their classes and successful in many areas. From a young age, Clinton and Obama were brilliant generalists who could do nearly everything well (with seeming ease), but never chose to be the best at any single thing. They were confident and capable, not necessarily disciplined or devoted.

Their self-confidence encouraged complaisance, especially when it came to studying, which they often left to the last minute before examinations and other deadlines. (They would show the same uncanny ability to perform well on short notice throughout their careers.) Self-confidence also allowed these poor boys to pursue goals well beyond their means. They were not revolutionaries, but they were involved in making change. Clinton started as a student politician; Obama began as an activist in Chicago after college.

Their idealism, evident early in each man, drove their actions. Clinton and Obama felt deeply connected to their modest surroundings; each was part of the "neighborhood gang." Though popular in their communities, Clinton and Obama were not satisfied. Their absent fathers left them exposed, but also convinced that families could be more secure, communities could be more prosperous, people could have more opportunities. Clinton and Obama did not see these images as abstract hopes. Each man embodied faith in progress, and each denied the fatalism that shadowed tragedy in their earliest years.

With loving mothers and grandparents who instilled an unbreakable sense of possibility in their fatherless sons, Clinton and Obama strove to conquer the limits society had placed upon them. They wanted to make good, to be loved and respected by the people who doubted them. They revered, sometimes worshipped, their mothers, and sought to protect the women who had protected them. Clinton dedicated his memoir to his mother, "who gave me a love of life." Obama dedicated one of his books to "my mother—whose loving spirit sustains me still." The absent fathers shadow the Clinton and Obama memoirs; the loving, sacrificing mothers shine through as sources of affection, confidence, and motivation to push forward.[5]

And push both Clinton and Obama did. As a high school student, Clinton eagerly traveled to the White House with the Boys Nation leadership group, and he positioned himself ahead of his friends to meet President John F. Kennedy. (A resulting photograph is the most famous of Clinton's early years.) In middle school, Obama returned to Hawaii from Indonesia with his mother so that he could enter the best available school, the Punahou School in Honolulu. Both he and Clinton worked hard enough to earn scholarships to elite colleges—Occidental in Los Angeles and Georgetown in Washington, D.C.—that were beyond the reach of most of their peers, and unthinkable for most members of their families. Clinton went a step further, winning a Rhodes Scholarship that took him to Oxford University and into the global elite. Obama's rise was no less vertiginous, taking him to Columbia University and then Harvard Law School. Although they sometimes tried to hide it, Clinton and Obama were ambitious climbers.[6]

To climb from where they started, they needed help. Clinton and Obama learned early to flatter powerful figures, elicit assistance, and take advantage of opportunities. Clinton had close friends among good ole boys, businesspeople, and the best and brightest in Hot Springs, Arkansas, where he attended high school. Obama was well liked and highly regarded among the various mixed race communities in Honolulu, including those who hung out on the basketball courts and regularly smoked marijuana. Clinton and Obama used their talents to build bridges of various kinds that supported their ambitions.[7]

That was the secret of their success from their earliest years to their remarkable White House ascendance. They had so few advantages, but so much talent, and an uncommon touch with diverse groups. They were charismatic in their ability to move people with their words and actions. They never blended in; you always knew they were there.[8]

Throughout their lives, Clinton and Obama cultivated a colorful mix of supporters. They boosted themselves to the top on the strength of their likeability, as well as their intellectual and physical presence. They learned to persuade, charm, and love—rather than intimidate, cajole, and domineer as other male figures around them did. The influence of their mothers made them, in this sense, uniquely feminine among rising male talents. For a country where women and people of color became the majority of the electorate, these two men feminized and blackened the presidency.

IT TOOK THE EYE OF A NOVELIST TO DESCRIBE THE APPEAL, BORN of unlikely life stories, in the backgrounds of Clinton and Obama. In 1998 Toni Morrison identified Clinton as "our first black president," even though his skin was white. When Barack Obama campaigned a decade later to become the first African American president, Morrison emphasized his wisdom, not his black skin.

"In thinking carefully about the strengths of the candidates," she wrote, "I stunned myself when I came to the following conclusion: that in addition to keen intelligence, integrity and a rare authenticity, you exhibit something that has nothing to do with age, experience, race or gender and something I don't see in other candidates. That something is a creative imagination which coupled with brilliance equals wisdom." She went on: "Wisdom is a gift; you can't train for it, inherit it, learn it in a class, or earn it in the workplace—that access can foster the acquisition of knowledge, but not wisdom." Unique talents and trying experiences cultivated a special charisma in Barack Obama and Bill Clinton. [9]

Morrison was channeling the wonder many felt about these men and the American presidency two centuries after George Washington invented the role. Clinton and Obama were the historical children of the first executive and the changes in American society since his time. Their lives captured the promises of mobility, openness, and diversity in American power, as well as the enduring challenges of inequality, discrimination, and resentment. Their rise to the White House promised a more representative and innovative leader for some; it threatened a more radical and disruptive executive for others. That was why Clinton and Obama were simultaneously loved and hated—like other famous outsiders-turned-heroes in American history: Frederick Douglass and Muhammad Ali, among many others. [10]

The uncommon intelligence and inescapable "blackness" of the two presidents was substantive. It made their leadership into something different from anything else before. They rose through mainstream education, commerce, and politics—like all previous presidents—but they identified more closely than any of their predecessors with the citizens who were left out, the men and women who were born near the bottom of society. That was their fatherless, poor story on the margins of America, as much as their incredible, talented, courageous climb to the heights of national influence. They were elite and common simultaneously, insider and outsider, white and black, American and "other." They were not warriors who stood above other men, as Jackson did, and they lacked Lincoln's ability to float eloquently over a landscape filled with death. Clinton and Obama came from the crowd, buried deep within the mix of daily life, part of the "Bubbas" who frequented McDonald's, in Clinton's case, or the kids who played full-contact basketball under streetlights, in Obama's experience.

They didn't inspire the downtrodden through a pandering or angry populism, but with a hopeful promise to make other fatherless children into college graduates, business owners, professionals, and even presidents. They would raise others up, help them climb high mountains without bringing them low. They promised achievement, development, and, ultimately redemption—when the low become the high.

That was the Clinton and Obama story, and it became the theme—struggle, aspiration, and continued challenge—defining the American presidency at the end of the twentieth century. These two presidents had a magic quality in their ability to rise from difficulty, and they opened countless imagined possibilities for different citizens.

Their apparent magic was threatening for conservative opponents (including President George W. Bush), who defended an older white, traditional America. Their magic was also insufficient for radical followers who wanted rapid and far-reaching change. Clinton and Obama were slow and steady reformers who moved deliberately but cautiously—challenging the conservative holdouts and disappointing the impatient radicals. Their moderation made them appealing to voters between the extremes. It was not just a political strategy; it was who they were.

Obama captured this deliberate approach to change in his reflections on the civil rights movement. Commenting on his own election to the presidency, he explained: "We are here today because we know we cannot be complacent." The president rejected cynicism, but he did not advocate quick formulas for progress. He reminded listeners: "Securing the gains this country has made requires the vigilance of its citizens. Our rights, our freedoms—they are not given. They must be won. They must be nurtured through struggle and discipline, and persistence and faith."[11]

Struggle, discipline, persistence, and faith were the qualities that allowed Clinton and Obama to climb. Most citizens, however, only became familiar with these figures once they reached the top of the mountain. Observers did not really understand how they got there. Seeing their lives from the apex, not the valley, the climb looked easy—an inspiration for some to overestimate their talents, and a prod for others to see dirty, racist conspiracies.

Exuberant supporters—especially young and diverse voters—expected these two talented men to right long-standing wrongs, ending decades of inequality and discontent. Clinton promised to focus on "the economy, stupid," as if it were a problem that a smart leader with the correct values could somehow "fix." Obama ran on a compelling slogan: "Yes, we can." Willpower would drive out prejudices and tear down fences, building a more peaceful and inclusive society, or so his campaign videos claimed.[12]

Exaggerated fears of each president grew in parallel with the exaggerated hopes. Business leaders, Christian evangelists, and conservative rural citizens believed that the fixes the new presidents promised would upend their already tumultuous lives. If Reagan had promised them a familiar "morning in America again," Clinton and Obama seemed to offer an exotic "new America" where they would be left out and lose their inherited privileges. The heroic qualities of Clinton and Obama looked villainous to some who clung to an older, whiter country that they believed was slipping away. Clinton managed to appeal to many white rural and working-class voters through his acceptance of conservative cultural positions surrounding faith-based politics, opposition to gay marriage, and tough penalties on crime. But he and Obama sided more often with the proponents of change, embracing greater secularism, tolerance, and public assistance. Many citizens with limited mobility feared change that empowered new up-and-comers, who were also new competitors. The politics of hope for fast-risers triggered a politics of resentment among those (perhaps larger in number) who were stuck, or sinking.[13]

During the lifetimes of Clinton and Obama, the United States had become more racially diverse, more global, and more unequal at the same time. Well-educated, healthy, networked citizens did better than ever before. The less educated and less connected, particularly middle-aged white male factory and farm workers, fell behind. The rise of Clinton and Obama was possible because of this bifurcation, even though they promised to fix it. They were products of the deepening social divide they hoped, and failed, to heal.[14]

The two presidencies evoked some of the most visceral responses in the history of the office. The inherited order of power in American society was at stake. Clinton and Obama's supporters looked to the president to boost their possibilities. Opponents hoped to preserve what they had. The elections in 1992 and 2008 (and 2016) challenged traditional authority as much as the civil rights movement and Reconstruction had in the past. Citizens clinging to their hard-earned positions in American society stood against would-be presidents who embodied social change.

Obama understood how his presidency contributed to this dynamic of intensifying social conflict deep within the country, and he could never get past it. "A President who looked like me was inevitable at some point in American history," he said, at the end of his time in office. "It might have been somebody named Gonzales instead of Obama, but it was coming. And I probably showed up twenty years sooner than the demographics would have anticipated. And, in that sense, it was a little bit more surprising. The country had to do more adjusting and processing of it. It undoubtedly created more anxiety than it will twenty years from now, provoked more reactions in some portion of the population than it will twenty years from now. And that's understandable."[15]

PRESIDENTS ALWAYS HAD DETRACTORS, BUT CLINTON AND OBAMA elicited notably extreme emotional responses, magnified by a twenty-four-hour news cycle and, in Obama's case, a social media landscape that encouraged sensational appeals to the prejudices of viewers. Unsubstantiated accusations that Clinton murdered his former deputy White

House counsel and racist fabrications that Obama was born in Africa circulated for years, seeming to gain veracity from sheer repetition.

The metastasizing slanders, rumors, and other attacks crowded out serious policy discussion. Politics centered more on the personal, and its contested meanings for different citizens, than ever before. Although the public images of Washington, Jackson, Kennedy, Reagan, and others mattered, their personalities and daily behaviors were never dissected and distorted in the same detail—and with such immediacy for millions of viewers. Citizens heard more about the intimate lives of recent presidents than ever before.

Debates about health care, economics, and national security devolved into screeds about who could be trusted and who could not. Condemnations of "death panels," "socialist radicals," and "apologists for Islamic extremism" dominated the opposition to the presidents, rather than detailed analysis of their very moderate plans. Counterresponses against "racists," "capitalist fat cats," and "war-mongers" characterized much of the rhetoric from presidential defenders, including Clinton and Obama themselves. Instead of substantive debate about the needs of the country, modeled on the progressive or New Deal eras, personal invective and innuendo defined public deliberation. Even politicians with the skills of the two Roosevelts would have drowned in these conditions. Clinton and Obama barely stayed afloat.

The destructive focus on the personal undermined leadership. Executives, especially in a democracy, cannot sit atop the mountain and condescend to a restive population below. George Washington understood that, and spent much of his presidency reaching out to citizens he knew he had to win over to his new position. Yet Washington also understood that he could not be just "one of the crowd." The presidency required special respect and admiration if it was to succeed in unifying the people. Andrew Jackson achieved a mix of commonness and presidential distinction through his military record. Lincoln and the two Roosevelt presidents used their remarkable command of language to bolster the dignity of the office. In their best moments, Kennedy, Johnson, and Reagan did the same.

The public's intimate knowledge of Clinton and Obama's lives—in part encouraged by them during their personal journeys to the White House, and then magnified by the modern media—diminished any room for the executive to lead from the heights. He was now down and dirty with every other man, and that made it especially difficult to lift citizens to greater goals, particularly when the issues were so complex. Their controversial lives, and the public obsession with those controversies (real and fabricated), diminished the majesty of the office. The president had received special respect, even in the most partisan times, before Clinton and Obama. Under them, the office lost its dignity because they did not match the assumed portrait of the president, and their supporters and opponents could not agree on a new image. Instead, partisans attacked one another, questioned each other's legitimacy, and undermined leadership at all turns.

The dangerous irony was that the public diminishment of leaders increased the popular appetite for someone who could still rise above the contemporary mess—someone who could "save" us. The presidency looked all the more magical in its possibilities because the daily practice had become so ugly. Dissatisfied with the presidency as deconstructed by the modern media, citizens looked for a figure who could somehow rise up and make it all better—someone who mastered a range of complex issues in detail, brought different groups together, crafted creative policy options, and implemented them with an iron will.

In their most hubristic moments—especially when campaigning— Clinton and Obama seemed to offer that amazing symphony of skills. In reality, neither they nor anyone else could meet these expectations, especially under conditions of intimate scrutiny and unceasing public attack. The expectations skyrocketed as the space for accomplishment disintegrated. Clinton and Obama's failure to do the impossible deepened public disappointment. Their personal flaws became the explanation for public dissatisfaction, and voters searched with greater anger for better candidates. Voters did not confront their overinflated expectations, their too intimate dissection of leaders, or the limitations of the best executives in the full-contact melee of contemporary politics. The problem was much bigger than the men in office.

CLINTON AND OBAMA BROUGHT UNIQUE BACKGROUNDS AND IM-pressive capabilities to the White House, and they offered promising visions for a more inclusive country. Their talents were, however, not nearly enough to satisfy supporters or disempower the groups that stood against them. Just the opposite: their presidencies were frequently beaten down by a divided audience that they had cultivated in their extraordinary rise from insignificance to global predominance.

By the time they entered office, the responsibilities of the president had grown to Everest-like dimensions. Clinton and Obama had climbed from low valleys, where most of their contemporaries remained stuck in their discontent. From the top of the world, leadership was more perilous than ever before. The air was thin and the scrutiny was intense. There was only one direction to go—down, fast and hard.

They tried to defy gravity, and for a while it looked like they could. Supporters and opponents largely agreed that Clinton and Obama were potentially transformative figures. Their talents, backgrounds, and incredible rises affirmed that point. Their records of winning people over—especially in their unlikely elections to the presidency—proved their power. The problem was that the expectations for these powerful men continued to rise when they entered the White House, giving them the aura of near invincibility. Clinton promised to remake the American economy for left out groups—a policy greeted with enthusiasm by the disadvantaged and resisted by the well heeled. Obama offered a vision of a post-racial America—an attitude that motivated diverse young voters, but alienated an older and whiter core of citizens.

Clinton and Obama encouraged simultaneous utopian and dystopian expectations that grossly exaggerated the real possibilities for new policy. "Change" was easier to promote than to practice from the White House. Clinton and Obama were neither the national saviors their supporters desired, nor the ingenious villains their critics condemned. In fact, their understanding of national policy was often quite limited. Neither had extensive foreign policy or military experience (unlike George Washington or Franklin Roosevelt), neither mastered the workings of the federal government (unlike Theodore Roosevelt), and neither devoted years to the study of a particular policy issue (slavery for Abraham Lincoln; the Soviet Union for Ronald Reagan). Clinton and Obama defined themselves by their flexible and quick-adapting minds, but those qualities did not substitute for deep thinking about how to shift the behavior of a massive government and a sprawling, diverse country. Serving as the governor of a small poor state and the junior senator from a middle-sized state did not prepare either man for pushing big change through a national democracy filled with countless legal barriers and institutional bottlenecks. On entering the presidency, they were not ready to pursue utopia, or even a New Deal.

The circumstances did not allow for a new president to act with the transformative scope of Franklin Roosevelt. The daily presidential agenda was too full and fragmented. Like John F. Kennedy and Lyndon Johnson, Clinton and Obama were harried, overstretched, and reactive executives. They rarely had time to think beyond their minute-to-minute meetings, where they confronted an ever-increasing barrage of crises, demands, and obligations. They had too little time and too few resources to pursue most of their plans. Their days were dominated by events—from wars in Yugoslavia and Somalia to repeated mass shootings in the United States and allegations of police brutality—that made it difficult to stay focused on the change they promised. Although they remained committed to their ambitious agendas, they were too busy defending the existing order to build a new one. Their presidencies were filled with smart moves, but few strategic breakthroughs.

A fairly typical day from Clinton's first months as president reveals how the range of issues—even non-crisis issues—left him little time to focus on what mattered most. The constant "briefings" show reaction, not forward-thinking policy. The range of meetings—from congressional leaders to Coretta Scott King, President Jean-Bertrand Aristide, and the American Ireland Fund—capture the fragmentation of the president's time and the constant need to please domestic and foreign groups. Like Lyndon Johnson, and unlike Franklin Roosevelt, Clinton's days were filled with break-neck sprints, not a deliberative policy marathon to a chosen destination.[16]

The same was true for Obama. The consequence was limited accomplishments, frequent haste, and emerging fatigue, rather than big and enduring New Deal-style transformations. From the beginning, these enormously energetic and talented men were running on tracks they did not choose, control, or really care about. Tactical brilliance crowded out strategic focus.

SCHEDULE OF THE PRESIDENT
FOR
TUESDAY, MARCH 16, 1993
FINAL DRAFT

tba   **JOG**

8:45 am-   **BRIEFING**
9:15 am   **OVAL OFFICE**
          Staff Contact: Tony Lake

9:15 am-   **BRIEFING** for Bipartisan Leadership Meeting
9:30 am   **OVAL OFFICE**
          Staff Contact: Howard Paster

9:30 am-   **BIPARTISAN LEADERSHIP MEETING**
10:15 am   **CABINET ROOM**
          Staff Contact: Howard Paster
          POOL SPRAY at beginning of meeting

10:30 am-   **MEETING**
10:45 am   **OVAL OFFICE**
          Valeriy Zorkin, President of Russian Constitutional
          Court
          Staff Contact: Tony Lake
          CLOSED PRESS

10:45 am-   **PHONE AND OFFICE TIME**
11:45 am   **OVAL OFFICE**

11:45 am-   **WESTERN SENATORS MEETING**
12:30 pm   **ROOSEVELT ROOM**
          Staff Contact: Howard Paster
          CLOSED PRESS

12:30 pm-   **MEETING**
12:45 pm   **OVAL OFFICE**
          Mack McLarty, George Stephanopoulos, Marcia Hale,
          Bruce Lindsey
          Staff Contact: Marcia Hale

as of 03/15/93 7:05pm

SOURCE FOR PAGES 273-274: William J. Clinton Presidential Library, Little Rock, Arkansas.

12:45 pm- 1:00 pm	**BRIEFING** for Aristide meeting **OVAL OFFICE** Staff Contact: Tony Lake
1:00 pm- 3:30 pm	**LUNCH, PHONE AND OFFICE TIME** **OVAL OFFICE**
3:30 pm- 3:50 pm	**MEETING** **OVAL OFFICE** Mrs. Coretta Scott King Staff Contact: Dan Wexler **CLOSED PRESS**
4:00 pm- 4:45 pm	**MEETING** **OVAL OFFICE** President Aristide Staff Contact: Tony Lake **CLOSED PRESS**
4:45 pm- 5:00 pm	**QUESTIONS** and **PHOTO OP** by press pool with President Aristide **OVAL OFFICE** **POOL PRESS**
5:30 pm- 6:15 pm	**HISPANIC CAUCUS** **ROOSEVELT ROOM** Staff Contact: Karen Hancox **POOL SPRAY** at beginning of meeting
6:40 pm	**THE PRESIDENT** departs White House en route Capitol Hilton [drive time: 5 minutes]
6:45 pm	**THE PRESIDENT** arrives Capitol Hilton
6:45 pm- 7:30 pm	**AMERICAN IRELAND FUND RECEPTION** **CAPITOL HILTON** 10001 16th Street Attire: Black Tie Remarks: David Kusnet Background: Joan Baggett Staff Contact: Marcia Hale **NOTE:** The President will attend reception only **OPEN PRESS**

as of   03/15/93   7:05pm

Their adversaries had a clearer mission. Clinton and Obama confronted a stubborn, "by any means necessary" opposition. Reminiscent of Andrew Jackson's presidency, they faced partisans—in this case, conservative Republicans—who prioritized defeating them above the needs of daily governance or even the integrity of American democracy.

At the end of his presidency, an exasperated Obama described the partisan opposition, especially in Congress: "What has been true for some time is that if I proposed something that was literally word for word in the Republican Party platform, it would be immediately opposed by eighty to ninety percent of the Republican voters. And the reason is not that they've evaluated what I said. It's that I said it." Republican leaders, particularly Senate Majority Leader Mitch McConnell, never denied this assessment; in fact, they promoted it to mobilize their confederates.[17]

Opposing Clinton and Obama, and everything they stood for, was a priority in itself. It became a source of pride for the Republican opposition, and a litmus test for proving one was a "true conservative." Party leaders defined compromise with Clinton and Obama as appeasement of evil—analogous to appeasement of fascism or communism in previous generations. Many respected Republican moderates, including House Speaker John Boehner and Senator Richard Lugar, lost their jobs amid the upheaval. Other highly regarded Republican moderates, especially Senator John McCain, lurched to the right to save themselves.[18]

Partisanship and a virulent political attack culture prohibited legislative compromise. Repeated government shutdowns, due to disagreements over the federal budget, illustrated the debilitating obstructionism of the period. Clinton's presidency marked an escalation in partisan warfare that continued under George W. Bush and reached an apex by the end of Obama's presidency, when it pervaded almost all elements of American government.

Republican obstructionism was about policy, power, and identity. Clinton and Obama's opponents resented their non-traditional backgrounds, their remarkable rise, and the people they brought along with them. Although moderate in temperament, Clinton and Obama seemed radical because their lives and sympathies challenged the economic, cultural, and political status quo. They were outsiders who never lost their outsiderness; they were the poor boys at the rich man's country club.

You could see it in the outraged faces of their opponents and the extreme language they used as they accused Clinton of moral depravity and Obama of being un-American. Instead of debating policy, opponents denounced the policy-maker.

MOTIVATED BY AN UNCOMPROMISING COMMITMENT TO REDUCE taxes and protect a traditional white America, men like Georgia Congressman Newt Gingrich and Mississippi Senator Trent Lott killed major White House programs aimed at health care reform, environmental protection, and economic assistance for poor citizens, especially minorities, women, and children. They made themselves into a permanent veto on policy change, using congressional measures like the filibuster more than ever before in American history. They also tried to manipulate the legal system to intimidate and, in Clinton's case, impeach the president.

The brazen attempts to stop Clinton and Obama's policy agendas shook the foundation of American democracy. Moving big policy through Congress always required some cooperation among the parties, as occurred, for instance, when President Ronald Reagan and the Democratic Speaker of the House of Representatives, Thomas "Tip" O'Neill, negotiated tax cuts in 1981. No such "grand bargain" was possible when Gingrich and Lott, and their successors during Obama's presidency, refused to compromise. They feared that giving the presidents any major achievement would empower the larger forces of change in the country they wanted to resist.

The "blackness" of Clinton and Obama would darken white America, the Republicans anticipated, if these presidents established a governing paradigm on the model of Theodore Roosevelt's Square Deal, or Franklin Roosevelt's New Deal, or even Lyndon Johnson's Great Society. The Republicans fought to prevent White House policy on any scale, from executives whose programs and personal histories they deemed illegitimate, heretical, and ill-conceived. Presidential politics became more religious war than policy debate.[19]

In this overheated context, partisan gridlock grew worse than it had been in at least a century. Disciplined Republican opposition to presidential policy preferences, regardless of content, became the norm. To Clinton and Obama's immense frustration, they were unable to push through major policies regarding economic inequality, environmental protection, infrastructure development, or education reform. The one major exception was the Affordable Care Act, passed by Congress without a single Republican vote, and signed into law by President Obama on 23 March 2010. Republican congressmen and governors immediately began to undermine the legislation.

Overall, Clinton and Obama's legislative accomplishments were infrequent and small. Their executive orders had limited scope because they lacked the legislative permanence and financial commitment of congressional legislation. Their successors reversed many of them with ease. Checks and balances became stagnation and do-nothingism when the party that lost the White House barricaded itself to deny presidential advances anywhere across the policy landscape.

These circumstances deepened public cynicism about politics in the United States. Citizens perceived their elected representatives, including congressmen and the president, as corrupt and untruthful for their inability to follow through on campaign promises for major change. It looked to many observers like the politicians really did not want to get anything done. They had resources and talent, but apparently no will. The potential, particularly for Clinton and Obama, was so great. How could they fall short?[20]

Both Republicans and Democrats were responsible for the deep partisanship of the period, but the Republicans were most unified and uncompromising in their opposition during the Clinton and Obama presidencies. Voters, however, did not draw distinctions, expressing disdain for politicians in both parties. They voted consistently for those who promised to break the logjam with a mix of ideological zealotry and extreme actions, from repeated filibusters to government shutdowns to personal bullying tactics.

Unlike Franklin Roosevelt and Lyndon Johnson, who cultivated some bipartisan support in Congress, both Clinton and Obama spent much of their presidencies searching for ways of getting around

Republican obstructionism. After early failed efforts, they each gave up on finding support across the aisle. Stuck in the partisan whirlwind surrounding the presidency, Clinton and Obama found that their persuasive talents worked best when they were preaching to their partisan choir.

The big ideas about reform that animated Clinton and Obama's hopes and drew on their personal backgrounds did not seem feasible when the opposition was so sharp. The two presidents had the ambition to pursue their own progressive and New Deal agendas, but they did not believe it was possible in their time. They had the ability to communicate with the eloquence of Lincoln and the clarity of Roosevelt, but they doubted a divided country would listen.

As a consequence, they rejected ambitious reform agendas and high-minded policy goals in favor of careful steps. They walked slowly, and sometimes surreptitiously, through a landscape filled with landmines of opposition. For all their achievements, they were not ready for the continuous warfare of the contemporary American presidency. No one else, past or present, would have been prepared for the impossible leadership challenges of the early twenty-first century.

GRADUALISM—SLOW, PATIENT, STEP-BY-STEP EFFORTS TO "NUDGE" change—rather than rapid transformation on the model of Franklin Roosevelt, guided Clinton and Obama. This approach was tedious and uncertain, but it also contributed to some enduring achievements. It was modest, of necessity, and selective.[21]

Elected in an era free from the Cold War, but also mired in recession and ethnic conflict around the globe, President Bill Clinton sought to focus his presidency on improving economic conditions for American citizens. "It's the economy, stupid," his campaign manager, James Carville, famously exclaimed. Entering the White House in 1993, President Clinton had a clear domestic agenda, but few concrete international goals. He intended to increase jobs and growth at home, using foreign policy primarily for those purposes, and avoiding foreign distractions wherever possible. He wanted to stimulate the existing economy and give more citizens benefits from its growth. He would not try to change the fundamental dynamics of investment, production, and consumption in an unequal, capitalist international economy.

Clinton succeeded in stimulating growth with targeted spending, new market openings, and attraction of foreign investment to the United States. He worked more closely with industry than any of his immediate predecessors, and he increased the power of the Department of Commerce and the US Trade Representative to sell American products abroad. He made himself business leader-in-chief, surpassing even Ronald Reagan's efforts in this area. Clinton's uncanny ability to charm people and direct them to support his goals worked very well with business figures at home and abroad, and many of their political representatives.

Republican concerns about Clinton's spending did not dissipate, despite robust economic growth. If anything, economic growth fueled increased domestic pressure to slash remnants of Roosevelt's New Deal and Johnson's Great Society, which now seemed unnecessary and wasteful to opponents. Clinton's closeness to business leaders empowered the free market advocates who made these arguments. Despite their differences on many policies, the president's friendship lent prestige to figures who opposed his initial efforts to make the economy more equal.

Bowing to Republican pressure, Clinton disciplined American budgeting to reduce the nation's annual deficit spending. He rejected significant increases in assistance for the poor, abandoning his prior commitments. For welfare payments going to unemployed adults, he tied federal aid to stricter work requirements. Clinton limited his economic policies to job creation and growth in Gross National Product (GNP), neglecting many concerns about equity, sustainability, and especially help for the most needy. Clinton sacrificed those additional economic needs, and core Democratic Party positions, to keep his push for jobs and growth going.[22]

By the second term of his presidency, the nation was running an annual budget surplus for the first time in almost thirty years. Some observers called Clinton a "new Democrat" for managing the economy like a fiscal conservative. Clinton's mix of market openings and welfare austerity increased aggregate wealth, and also inequality. He abandoned

Roosevelt and Johnson's commitment to a progressive economic system, in favor of trying to lift all boats at the same time. Clinton mended many deficiencies in the economy he inherited, but he did not transform or significantly reform it.[23]

THE SAME WAS TRUE FOR FOREIGN AND ENVIRONMENTAL POLICY under Clinton, and later Obama. The two presidents scaled back big goals of spreading democracy or ending global warming for more modest commitments to reinforce international stability and reduce harmful human effects on the environment. They used American force frequently—in Somalia, the former Yugoslavia, and throughout the Middle East—but they avoided on-the-ground troop commitments, ambitious nation-building efforts, and especially large military conflicts. They were multilateral and cautious. Clinton and Obama were much more comfortable as global policemen preserving world order, rather than war leaders pursuing liberation from "evil empires."

Foreign civil wars dominated the Clinton years. The new president had criticized his predecessor, George H. W. Bush, for doing too little in the face of atrocities, but he was not much more active. Clinton was hesitant to intervene (even in cases of genocide), half-hearted in most of his actions, and often ineffective. From his first days in office, he was uncertain about how to match American power with a defense of democracy and human rights. He sometimes seemed unwilling to try. Clinton was often distracted with domestic issues, impatient with international complexities, and even indifferent to foreign events. His closest advisors had high regard for his capabilities, but were deeply frustrated with Clinton's indiscipline around foreign policy.[24]

In Yugoslavia, Serb and Croat militias widened their ethnic cleansing efforts, as the White House failed to orchestrate an effective multilateral response until late in Clinton's second term. In Somalia, the president inherited a humanitarian intervention, under United Nations direction, that exposed US Army Rangers—deployed as protectors for aid workers—to urban guerilla warfare that resulted in eighteen American combat deaths in October 1993, and few positive results despite the high cost. Clinton ordered the withdrawal of US troops, abandoning the region to terrorists, some of whom later joined Al Qaeda and the Islamic State (ISIS).[25]

Scarred by the events in Somalia, six months later President Clinton refused to deploy American troops when Hutu militias in Rwanda killed more than 500,000 Tutsi and Hutu citizens. United Nations peacekeepers helplessly watched the genocide. Observing these events in horror as a young journalist, Samantha Power explained, "American leaders did not act because they did not want to. They believed that genocide was wrong, but they were not prepared to invest the military, financial, diplomatic, or domestic political capital needed to stop it."[26]

A president who identified closely with the poor and disadvantaged could not bring himself to deploy American power to protect African families slaughtered in cold blood. Clinton later apologized, but he had been fearful of risking American lives, even for worthy purposes, once he entered the presidency. Any American deaths would be his responsibility.

Clinton was constrained by his own power, and the potential costs of failed action. He sought small, careful responses (and non-responses) for genocidal problems. A powerful presidency seemed weak indeed.

Barack Obama shared Samantha Power's criticism of Clinton. He read her Pulitzer Prize-winning book about genocide, *A Problem From Hell*," and boosted her into a high-ranking White House position, later US Ambassador to the United Nations. Although he was elected in part because of President George W. Bush's disastrous and unnecessary war in Iraq, Obama sought to avoid Clinton's passivity in the face of foreign atrocities. Influenced by his own background and his conversations with Power, Obama advocated the use of force to protect weak and vulnerable communities.

"We will not eradicate violent conflict in our lifetimes," he admitted when receiving the Nobel Peace Prize in December 2009. "There will be times when nations—acting individually or in concert—will find the use of force not only necessary but morally justified. . . . [M]ake no mistake; Evil does exist in the world." Obama continued, "To say that force may sometimes be necessary is not a call to cynicism—it is a recognition of history; the imperfections of man and the limits of reason."[27]

In practice, Obama emphasized democratic alliances and the rule of law. He wanted to be the leading promoter of both. He spoke from the heart when he criticized the alternating militarism and passivity of privileged citizens facing injustice at home and abroad. There was a strategic middle ground that called for the deployment of American power to build institutions, allowing people to govern themselves in lawful ways. Obama sought to civilize the world without conquering it.

The president envisioned a broader and more creative foreign policy, freed from an instinctual reliance on overwhelming American military power, which had proven less effective than it first appeared. He wanted more diverse partnerships and intelligent persuasion, less physical posturing and self-righteous certainty. Obama's international outlook mixed American muscle and dollars with advocacy for democratic ideals, assistance from friends, and openness to change—even from old enemies. Despite his limited foreign policy experience, Obama had a more thoughtful worldview than Bill Clinton (or George W. Bush), born, in some ways, of his own international background.[28]

The new president did not rule out military conflict, but he preferred targeted force, with discrete purpose. He sought to tame war with law, and where possible, end American military conflicts (especially in the Middle East) that undermined the values of the nation and its allies. That was his rationale for withdrawing from Iraq, where he believed the US invasion in 2003 had imperiled America's global standing, brutalized its politics, and overburdened its economy. He "surged" American forces in Afghanistan to defeat the remnants of Al Qaeda and the Taliban, but the goal there was to withdraw quickly and limit the costs of continuous fighting. Obama wanted to replace foreign occupations with multilateral nation-building, and he hoped to return resources to American society, suffering from a debilitating recession at home. "America could best serve the cause of freedom," Obama wrote, "by concentrating on its development, becoming a beacon of hope for other nations and people around the globe."[29]

He began by banning torture, drawing down American forces in Iraq, and pledging to close the prison at Guantanamo Bay—acts of war ordered by his predecessor, George W. Bush. Obama made one of his first major foreign trips to Egypt, not Israel, where he redefined the American image abroad. Instead of dividing the world between those "with us" and those "with the terrorists," he gave a speech about enduring connections across religious and ethnic lines. Obama called upon listeners "to join together on behalf of the world that we seek—a world where extremists no longer threaten our people, and American troops have come home; a world where Israelis and Palestinians are each secure in a state of their own, and nuclear energy is used for peaceful purposes; a world where governments serve their citizens, and the rights of all God's children are respected. Those are mutual interests. That is the world we seek. But we can only achieve it together."[30]

Obama's words echoed some of Clinton's "soft" policies, but the new president was more willing to use lethal force. He initiated a rapid increase in targeted killings of terrorists through a mix of aerial drone strikes and US Special Forces operations, including the famous 2 May 2011 raid on Al Qaeda leader Osama bin Laden's compound in Pakistan. Obama's lawyers worked hard to create new legal authorizations to justify targeted killings, even as they claimed the country was returning to more vigorous due process protections. The president wanted more diplomatic and military tools for law enforcement and peace promotion overseas, not permanent war or occupation. He expanded the global policing powers of the president, as he also reduced the number of actions justified by war.[31]

More than Clinton, Obama returned to the liberal internationalism of Franklin Roosevelt. Like Roosevelt, Obama was deliberative. He sought to win over challengers and achieve his aims, short of armed conflict. Obama had thought deeply about the prior sixty years of American foreign policy, and the recurring experiences of international crisis. He endeavored to avoid wars wherever possible, to manage the use of force tightly, and to make certain that the full range of American resources were matched to clear and important political aims. Obama wanted to erase the militaristic Cold War mentality that he saw in the Global War on Terror. He made a compelling case for dialing back military action, and dialing up diplomacy and persuasion, even in a world filled with anti-American aggressors. His vision of the presidency was militarily restrained and politically active.

OBAMA'S LIBERAL INTERNATIONALISM ACHIEVED MANY THINGS. He reversed more than fifty-five years of Cuban-American hostility, turning an embarrassing source of anti-American hostility in the Western Hemisphere into an opportunity for American trade and travel. Even Obama's most vocal Republican adversaries, including Texas Governor Greg Abbott, embraced this move.

More controversial, President Obama negotiated and then implemented a comprehensive agreement with ten international signatories that halted Iranian nuclear weapons development for at least a decade. Despite strong Republican opposition in Congress, the president used all of his available influence to craft an enforceable framework for verifying that Iranian nuclear facilities were closed and incentivizing broader cooperation. As part of the deal, the United States returned Iranian money seized after 1979, and it dropped some of the sanctions that crippled Iran's economic growth.

The full effects of the Iranian nuclear deal remain uncertain, but President Obama succeeded—as his predecessors did not—in opening possibilities for cooperation between Washington, Tehran, and other allies around regional and global issues. He increased American leverage in Iran by giving the United States greater access to their people, as well as their leaders. He used the many dimensions of American presidential power to create promising, but certainly not guaranteed, policy opportunities. Although the nuclear deal had its critics, it is hard to deny that it was preferable to an imminent nuclear crisis, and probable war, between Israel and Iran.[32]

THE MOST OBVIOUS FAILURE OF OBAMA'S FOREIGN POLICY WAS Russia. The eight years of his presidency witnessed the poisoning of what were still optimistic ties between the United States and Russia in 2008, and a return to Cold War hostilities—perhaps even worse. By the summer of 2016, Russia was following the old Soviet script of challenging

NATO forces in Europe, invading neighboring states (Ukraine, and especially the Ukrainian province of Crimea), aiding Middle Eastern strongmen (Bashar al-Assad in Syria), harboring spies with valuable American secrets (Edward Snowden), and attacking American information networks (cyber-warfare). Russian President Vladimir Putin went a step beyond where Soviet leaders had feared to tread, intervening directly in an American election to support a candidate (Donald Trump) strangely susceptible to the Russian leader's influence. Marrying traditional KGB tactics to cyber-warfare and social media savvy, Putin helped to create a Manchurian Candidate bent on weakening American power from within.[33]

The rise of the Islamic State (ISIS) was another failure. With the withdrawal of American soldiers from Iraq and Afghanistan under Obama, a new terrorist organization emerged. It was led by poorly educated Islamic leaders who were radicalized in American-run prisons, where they also formed resilient criminal networks. Released into collapsing societies, they organized a media-savvy transnational organization that mobilized followers to overturn Western power and build an alternative state. They used terror to intimidate enemies and they ran proto-state institutions in the Middle East to sell oil, collect taxes, and finance attacks. Amid civil war in Syria, ISIS established pockets of power. ISIS incubated terrorism in the Middle East, and as far away as Belgium, France, and Somalia. It spread fear across the globe, with even wider reach than Al Qaeda and other predecessors.[34]

Obama's attempts at Middle East peace-building clearly did not work. His military de-escalation in the region contributed to the rise of ISIS, despite American successes in killing Al Qaeda leaders through targeted drone attacks and Special Forces operations. Without a war-fighting army in the region, the United States left a vacuum that the most extreme and violent groups filled. ISIS exploited the resentments of many Sunni Muslims and the absence of another group capable of enforcing order. Obama's liberal internationalism failed to stop a Middle Eastern descent into Hobbesian "state of war" conditions, including public executions, forced migration, and genocide.

Despite continuous urgings, the president did not intervene to stop the horror brought by ISIS because he did not see a way out of a new conflict. Like Clinton, he watched passively as a militant regime, this time in Syria, massacred hundreds of thousands of civilians, forcing more into exile. The United States did little to help with the immigration crisis, and it failed to open its doors widely to refugees, accepting far fewer than smaller states in Western Europe. President Obama's personal commitment to the disadvantaged did not translate into effective assistance—or anything else—for those most in need.

He started to sound like Clinton too. In a set of interviews with journalist Jeffrey Goldberg, he confessed to presidential limits: "There are going to be times where either because it's not a direct threat to us or because we just don't have the tools in our toolkit to have a huge impact that, tragically, we have to refrain from jumping in with both feet."[35]

These were wise but deeply unsatisfying words from the most powerful man in the world. President Obama had pledged to use the tools of his office—military, economic, and diplomatic—to protect suffering groups. He wanted to be more active than Clinton, less hyperactive than Bush, and more strategic than both. He turned out looking ineffectual, weak, and largely reactive. Obama's foreign policy created new openings in Iran and Cuba, it cut American losses in Iraq and Afghanistan, and it maintained general stability for the United States in Europe, Latin America, and Asia. These achievements were modest, at best, and they left a sense of doom hanging over the international system as Obama left the White House amid accumulating evidence of Russian aggression, even within the American electoral process.

A crowded and complex international landscape had rendered hollow the towering promises of an ambitious American president. The range of divisive issues and powerful adversaries exploded the global vision of democracy and law that Obama brought to the job. If anything, the most transformative result of his presidency was the shocking revolt against nearly all global activities in the "Brexit" vote for Great Britain to leave the European Union in the summer of 2016, followed by the US election of Donald Trump later the same year.

Trump's battle cry to "build a wall," fortressing white America, rejected everything in Clinton and Obama's dreamlike embodiment of diversity, internationalism, and slow, steady change. The black presidents' rise seemed so fantastic and illusory, as it came apart so fast, at the center of American power. The presidency was too big, and ultimately too demanding, even for these unusually able and precocious men. Perhaps no one could master the modern presidency.

Millions of voters understood that, on some level. They chose a brash personality who rejected the entire history of the office, to blow it all up. Trump was the president as destroyer. He banished the slick, swarthy magicians who had promised to do the impossible for an eager American (and global) audience. When the most talented figures failed, the "real man" took over. Many voters obviously did not see an alternative. The impossible presidency produced a truly impossible president.

EPILOGUE

New Beginning

B y the start of the twenty-first century, the inhuman demands of the office made it impossible to succeed as president. Public expectations for rapid achievements grew as the possibilities for enduring accomplishments, even on a modest scale, declined. The issues were too diffuse and difficult for any single leader to integrate them in a coherent narrative, beyond daily crisis management. The pressure to react quickly and globally left little space for thought and creativity about policy, or much of anything else.

Every failure became an immediate global headline for repeated, extreme condemnation. Even the most promising leaders were exposed for all their warts and weaknesses. They could never recover. They could never catch up and get ahead of the pressures, oppositions, and lies. Great men slowly faded into a shadow of their inspiring life stories.

Presidents had been heroes in the past; they became targets of derision by the second half of the twentieth century. Presidents who oversold their policies and underperformed contributed to this dynamic, as did public impatience and misunderstanding about how policy is made. A healthy skepticism about leaders is valuable for democracy, but contemporary cynicism and anger tear the necessary fabric for experimentation and cooperation. Policy requires many hands working together, not cutting each other's throats.

It was impossible to lead as president in 2016, and voters recognized that. They elected an anti-leader, Donald Trump, whose main qualification was that he had never served in public office and had no desire to act like a traditional public servant. Every other president before him had precisely these experiences. Trump promised to be a disrupter, a deal-maker, and a tough guy taking on what he called a "rigged" system, a "swamp" of government.

"Blowing up the system" was perhaps an understandable reaction to public discontent. Millions of voters who chose this path believed government had failed, and they wanted to bring the president down. They no longer believed the office could produce a Washington, a Lincoln, a Roosevelt, or even a Reagan. And they were probably correct.

Disruption, however, is not a long-term strategy. It is an anti-strategy. American prosperity has always depended on good governance and leadership, as this book has shown. Attacks on the very possibility of governance will never "make America great," and the fall of the presidency imperils any future rise of the United States. The election of 2016 should inspire renewed discussion of the presidency—its historical sources and future potential. What will the presidency of the twenty-first century look like? This is a time for new beginnings.

After Donald Trump, improved national leadership will require remaking the office, the larger governance of the United States, and the expectations of the public. The inherited presidency is no longer the correct presidency for the twenty-first century. Nor is Trump's anti-presidency a constructive alternative. The United States needs a new burst of institutional reform, not just endless debate about who should be president.[1]

The long rise and short fall of the nation's highest office opens an opportunity to redesign it for a new world. Living through a profound crisis of leadership in the United States, Americans can reimagine and then recreate a powerful democratic presidency, as prior generations have, in their best moments.

There are several possible pathways forward. First, the presidency has grown too large in its responsibilities and its expectations—well beyond the imaginings of the founders and generations of Americans before the Second World War. The obvious lesson is that the office needs new boundaries. What are the vital national interests presidents should address and what are the powers they should have in those areas? The list of issues should be limited and the powers should match national needs.

As this book shows, the presidency has grown in ways that neither serve national interests nor match power to those purposes. A serious redesign of the office to make its form follow vital functions—and fewer additional, non-necessary roles—will empower presidents to achieve more in areas that matter most (including national security), and avoid issues that should not come to their office (especially divisive cultural debates). Clearer definitions of presidential responsibilities will also make it easier for voters to identify the appropriate qualifications and choose candidates poised for success. Asking the president to do less can indeed allow him or her to accomplish more.

Presidential achievements have always depended on effective communications with various groups: members of Congress, foreign leaders, and especially American voters. The founders based their thinking about democracy on the assumption that leaders, including the president, could engage in a reasoned, fact-based discussion with the public about the nature of American policy. They recognized the many challenges that came with a large population of widely varying backgrounds and interests, but they believed that the best proposals would win broad support in what they envisioned as a rigorous marketplace of ideas. Presidents from George Washington to Franklin Roosevelt placed great emphasis on their words because they valued public discussion and hoped it would unify a divided nation behind wise governance.

A second pathway for presidential reform involves public communications aimed at this same goal of enlightening, rather than alienating, citizens. The 2016 election revealed how various factors—including new media—have shattered the nation's ability to conduct a reasoned public discussion of policy. Instead of serious, fact-based debate, an increasingly segmented media landscape encourages citizens to receive information that confirms their biases, often without attention to contrary facts or perspectives. In the highly individualized social media space, the absence of traditional editorial standards means that information circulates as truth with very little accountability to evidence. This "false news" phenomenon is not entirely new, but it now pervades public discussion of policy. Politicians, journalists, and intellectuals spend much of their time "correcting" false information, not debating the real challenges confronting the country. The contrast with the rigorous fact-based dialogue envisioned by the founders, and later generations, could not be greater.

Presidents need to work from some agreed facts when making policy. Otherwise, they are driving blind. Although ideology is unavoidable in policy-making, presidents must be cold-eyed realists in their focus on the needs of the nation. No one else is elected to serve this vital role.

Restoring facts to public discussion requires the president to return to his public educational role—something Washington, Lincoln, and the Roosevelts took very seriously. Escaping partisanship and "false news" demands consistent efforts to explain policy through diverse channels. This involves support for institutions that offer serious, fact-based information to a broader public. These institutions have traditionally included schools and universities, public information services (especially public radio and television), and other public service organizations (the Federal Reserve and the Congressional Budget Office, for example). They report to the entire country, and they are scrutinized for their objective efforts. We need more sources of serious research and dissemination in our society, and they should receive public funding to maintain their rigor and independence, rejecting the moneyed and partisan interests that distort many private "think tanks."[2]

Strengthening these public institutions, and inventing new ones, would give presidents a better chance at building consensus for their priorities. Strengthening these institutions would also give citizens a firmer foundation for determining who is best suited to represent their interests in office. Democratic leadership requires a vibrant fact-based public sphere, and trusted anchors for informed policy discussions. Theodore Roosevelt meant precisely this when he referred to the "bully pulpit," which he hoped would educate and motivate the public, not peddle myths and lies.

In a smaller eighteenth- and nineteenth-century country, it was easier for well-informed citizens to assess facts. Presidents debated difficult issues from trade and taxes to slavery, expansion, and war. But they generally agreed on the basic facts with their adversaries. Andrew Jackson and his opponents did not disagree on whether the Bank of the

United States regulated the American monetary system, they differed on whether it should do that. Similarly, Abraham Lincoln and Confederate leaders did not disagree about whether slavery existed, but whether it should expand and continue to dominate parts of the American economy. Restoring agreement on basic facts will not end conflict, but it will allow presidents to focus on the issues that really matter for the future prosperity and safety of the nation.

This is intensive work, requiring extraordinary energy, patience, and determination from a president already overloaded with countless other demands. The third pathway for reform might involve a more institutionalized division of responsibilities between a president and perhaps a prime minister—both of whom would be elected by the American people at different intervals. The founders wanted a single executive, but they never anticipated the range of challenges and responsibilities the modern office holder would confront. A single executive for an enterprise as gargantuan and labyrinthine as the United States has become anachronistic.

Dividing domestic and international authorities, as the French political system does, or dividing policy leadership from head of state responsibilities, as in the German constitution, would allow presidents more of a chance to lead. A separation of roles would open some time in the president's crowded calendar for deeper deliberation around key issues. A division of roles would also create more opportunities to focus and innovate, rather than just react.

The growth of the United States, and the challenges of a more tightly connected world, demand more of every president. The men (and one day, women) in office can no longer keep up. Some institutional division of responsibilities at the top seems necessary for sustaining the office. A single executive is just no longer practical.

THE CONTEMPORARY PRESIDENT, LIKE OTHER EXECUTIVES, IS RUNning ever faster on a policy treadmill, where just keeping up is a form of progress, and changing direction is likely to cause a damaging fall. Instead of imagining something better, presidents just keep running. They often forget why.

History has brought us to this difficult moment when we must recognize that our inherited assumptions and practices no longer serve the nation (and the world) as well as they once did. The presidency has always been in flux, from its initial uncertain creation by the founders through a Civil War, a Great Depression, and much more. Its genius is its ability to change. And the twenty-first century is a time when the office must be remade again. History does not offer clear recipes, but inspiration and hope. The presidency is defined by the people in and around it, not the ink on constitutional parchment.

Imagining a new presidency is necessary for a country that remains "the last, best hope of earth." In another time of crisis, Abraham Lincoln reminded Americans that we "hold the power and bear the responsibility," if only we will seize it. The people still make the presidency, and they can make it less impossible.[3]

ACKNOWLEDGMENTS

Writing a book about the history of the presidency during so much presidential turmoil has been quite an adventure. It has reminded me of the precariousness of everything we perceive as permanent. That is why history matters—it gives us a context for understanding change, possibility, and, yes, danger. Leadership in a democracy is vitally important, but it is stunningly difficult. At the very least, we have an obligation to try and understand it.

Understanding comes from research, observation, thought, and people most of all. Books are extended conversations, and there are many smart and helpful voices behind the words written by this author. Many of those voices were, in fact, wiser than this author, and therefore, as always, the flaws are all mine. Writing a book about the presidency is indeed a humbling experience.

As is convention, I usually close my book acknowledgments by thanking my wife and kids. This time they go at the top of the list, where they belong. This is yet another book dedicated to them because none of it would be possible without them. My wife, Alison Alter (now Austin City Councilwoman Alison Alter), is my love, my partner, my moral loadstar, and my inspiration. I write about leaders; she is one. And she is always there with me.

Our kids, Natalie and Zachary, are truly extraordinary. (Of course we are biased, but these are still facts.) Together, they bring a sparkle of discovery into every day. Natalie has taught me to be more empathetic, tactile, and forgiving in my approach to research and life. She is a born leader who never puts herself ahead of others. Zachary has taught me to ask deep unconventional questions, to follow surprising stories, and to feel words, not just use them. He is one of the most powerful thinkers I have ever met, and his love of knowledge for its own sake inspires me.

So many others contributed their knowledge too. My research assistants at the University of Texas at Austin—Jordan Shenhar, Mrinalini Shah, and Abigail Griffin—helped me to dissect how presidents spend their time through a close analysis of their calendars. They also taught me lots of cool stuff about Excel and PowerPoint. Numerous graduate students and faculty at the University of Texas at Austin Department of History, the Lyndon B. Johnson School of Public Affairs, and other institutions offered valuable feedback on various parts of this book. I cannot thank them all, but I would like to single out for special thanks: Barry Bales, Brian Balogh, Bill Brands, Hal Brands, Karl Brooks, Seth Center, Robert Chesney, John Cisternino, Vaneesa Cook, Jack Cunningham, Augusta Dell'Omo, Charles Edel, Joshua Eisenman, Jeffrey Engel, Gregory Fenves, David Fields, Bryan Frizzelle, James Galbraith, Adi Gordon, Michael Granof, Udi Greenberg, Ray Haberski, John Hall, Mark Hand, Robert Hutchings, Andrew Johns, Ronald Johnson, Peniel Joseph, Sarah Kaiser-Cross, Michael Kimmage, John Lewis Gaddis, Benjamin Griffin, William Hitchcock, Daniel Hummel, William Inboden, Jacqueline Jones, Paul Kennedy, Christine Lamberson, Mark Lawrence, Melvyn Leffler, Mitchell Lerner, James Martin, James McKay, Simon Miles, Jennifer Miller, Kazushi Minami, Scott Mobley, Steven Oreck, Craig Pedersen, William Powers, Varun Rai, Marc Selverstone, Debbie Sharnak, William Taubman, Benjamin Valentino, Miha Vindis, Dustin Walcher, Vanessa Walker, and Emily Whalen.

In addition to my historical research, I have benefited enormously from the feedback of numerous contemporary business and government leaders. These include the hard-working and inspiring students in the Executive Master in Public Leadership Program (EMPL) at the LBJ School, where I am fortunate to serve as academic advisor and a course instructor. These students are true pioneering leaders! Other leaders who have helped me to understand the issues include: Gordon Appleman, Adam Blum, Talmage Boston, Harral Burris, Robert Campbell, Josiah Daniel, Mark Eaker, Julius Glickman, Jeanne Klein, Michael Klein, Livingston Kosberg, Jim Kurtz, Steven Olikara, David Schiff, Andrew Seaborg, Andrew Thompson, and some others I should not name.

Steven Schragis has probably heard me talk about this book more than anyone else. He has organized countless opportunities for me to lecture to large audiences about it, and he has taught me a lot about what it means to make history an accessible source of public enlightenment (and entertainment too). Steven helped with the book's title and many other parts.

Andrew Wylie, my agent, helped me to conceptualize this book. Lara Heimert, my editor, helped me to bring it to fruition. Lara's close reading of the manuscript fleshed out some of the most important arguments, and refined the overall organization of the book. She is brilliant and lots of fun to work with. Dan Gerstle painstakingly improved every line of the book. His detailed edits were the best I have ever received, and I am very grateful.

One last thing: I am the child of immigrants—from India and Russia. I am grateful that I have the opportunity to live and work in a vibrant, inclusive, diverse democracy. It needs repair. And this is my effort to help, in some small way. I thank all the other concerned citizens who do much more to keep our society free. They are the true leaders, and we need more of them!

NOTES

INTRODUCTION

1. See Niccolo Machiavelli, *The Prince*, trans., Harvey Mansfield (Chicago: University of Chicago Press, 1998); J.G.A. Pocock, *The Machiavellian Moment: Florentine Political Thought and the Atlantic Republican Tradition* (Princeton: Princeton University Press, 1975).

2. "Thomas Jefferson to Thomas Leiper, 12 June 1815," in *The Papers of Thomas Jefferson*, Retirement Series, vol. 8, *1 October 1814 to 31 August 1815*, ed. J. Jefferson Looney (Princeton: Princeton University Press, 2011), 531–34.

3. See Arthur Schlesinger, Jr.'s highly influential book on the distortion of American leadership: *The Imperial Presidency* (Boston: Houghton Mifflin, 1973). For a similar argument about how the pursuit of wealth and power distorted American corporate leadership, see Rakesh Khurana, *Searching for a Corporate Savior: The Irrational Quest for Charismatic CEOs* (Princeton: Princeton University Press, 2002).

4. The presidencies profiled in this book are, by necessity, selective and interpretive. I have focused on the presidents whom I deemed most transformative and revealing for the evolution of the office over more than two centuries. Although I cover ten presidents in depth, there are, of course, many other presidents who merit close study. This book emphasizes depth over breadth, examining key moments in the transformation of the presidency. Another book, with a different analytical focus, might choose other presidents to profile.

5. On this point, see James Goldgeier and Jeremi Suri, "Revitalizing the US National Security Strategy," *Washington Quarterly* 38 (Winter 2016), 35–55.

6. Franklin Roosevelt quoted in Robert E. Sherwood, *Roosevelt and Hopkins: An Intimate History* (New York: Harper and Brothers, 1948), 3.

7. Lyndon B. Johnson Presidential Recordings, Conversation with Governor George Wallace, 18 March 1965, WH6503.09, Miller Center Presidential Recordings Program, http://millercenter.org/presidentialrecordings. My transcription from the original recording. I have tried to preserve the original dialects and speech patterns in my transcription.

8. See Richard E. Neustadt, *Presidential Power: The Politics of Leadership from Roosevelt to Reagan* (New York: John Wiley & Sons, 1960, expanded and revised edition 1990). See also Matthew J. Dickinson, *Bitter Harvest: FDR, Presidential Power, and the Growth of the Presidential Branch* (New York: Cambridge University Press, 1996); William G. Howell, *Thinking about the Presidency: The Primacy of Power* (Princeton: Princeton University Press, 2013), esp. chapters 1, 6–7.

9. See Jeffrey Goldberg, "The Obama Doctrine," *The Atlantic* (April 2016), 70–90.

10. See Jeffrey K. Tulis, *The Rhetorical Presidency* (Princeton: Princeton University Press, 1987), esp. 145–204.

11. On the disappearance of great presidents after Franklin Roosevelt, and the need to lower expectations, see Aaron David Miller, *The End of Greatness: Why America Can't Have (and Doesn't Want) Another Great President* (New York: Palgrave Macmillan, 2014).

12. Paul Kennedy has famously identified this tendency to overstretch as a recurring phenomenon in all powerful states, including the United States. See Paul Kennedy, *The Rise and Fall of the Great Powers* (New York: Random House, 1987). For an application of this analysis to American policy-making, especially since the Second World War, see Peter Beinart, *The Icarus Syndrome: A History of American Hubris* (New York: Harper Perennial, 2010).

13. For more detailed analysis of how leaders use and misuse history, see Richard E. Neustadt and Ernest R. May, *Thinking in Time: The Uses of History for Decision-Makers* (New York: Free Press, 1986); Ernest R. May, *"Lessons" of the Past: The Use and Misuse of History in American Foreign Policy* (New York: Oxford University Press, 1975); Hal Brands and Jeremi Suri, eds., *The Power of the Past: History and Statecraft* (Washington, D.C.: Brookings Institution Press, 2016).

CHAPTER 1

1. Abolitionism in the late eighteenth century has generated a very large literature. One of the best books remains: David Brion Davis, *The Problem of Slavery in the Age of Revolution, 1770–1823* (Ithaca: Cornell University Press, 1975).

2. Letter from James Madison to Thomas Jefferson, 17 October 1788, in *The Papers of James Madison Digital Edition*, J. C. A. Stagg, ed. (Charlottesville: University of Virginia Press, 2010), document available online: http://rotunda.upress.virginia.edu.ezproxy.lib.utexas.edu/founders/JSMN-01-11-02-0218 [accessed 06 Jan 2015].

3. See the classic, but still valuable works: R. R. Palmer, with new forward by David Armitage, *The Age of Democratic Revolution: A Political History of Europe and America, 1760–1800* (Princeton: Princeton University Press, 2014, originally published 1959–64); Eric Hobsbawm, *The Age of Revolution, 1789–1848* (London: Weidenfeld and Nicolson, 1962). For a wider and more recent analysis of this period, see David Armitage and Sanjay Subrahmanyam, eds., *The Age of Revolutions in Global Context, c. 1760–1840* (New York: Palgrave, 2010).

4. For a good analysis of seventeenth- and eighteenth-century social contract theory, see Christopher W. Morris, ed., *The Social Contract Theorists: Critical Essays on Hobbes, Locke, and Rousseau* (New York: Rowman and Littlefield, 1999).

5. See the classic and still valuable study: Friedrich Meinecke, *Die Idee der Staatsräson in der Neueren Geschichte* (Munich: R. Oldenbourg, 1925). See also Harvey C. Mansfield, Jr., *Taming the Prince: The Ambivalence of Modern Executive Power* (New York: Free Press, 1989), 151–78.

6. Alexander Hamilton, "The Duration in Office of the Executive," Federalist 71, 18 March 1788, available at: http://avalon.law.yale.edu/18th_century/fed71.asp.

7. Alexander Hamilton, "The Executive Department Further Considered," Federalist 70, 18 March 1788, available at: http://avalon.law.yale.edu/18th_century/fed70.asp.

8. Samuel Adams quotation in Gordon S. Wood, *The Radicalism of the American Revolution* (New York: Random House, 1991), 400; Thomas Jefferson, "Autobiography," 6 January 1821, available at: http://avalon.law.yale.edu/19th_century/jeffauto.asp. See also Thomas Jefferson to John Adams, 28 October 1813, in *The Adams-Jefferson Letters: The Complete Correspondence between Thomas Jefferson and Abigail and John Adams*, ed. Lester

J. Cappon (Chapel Hill: University of North Carolina Press, 1959), available at: http://press-pubs.uchicago.edu/founders/documents/v1ch15s61.html

9. This is a central theme of R. R. Palmer's *The Age of Democratic Revolution*. For a more recent argument about the declining respect for monarchy, rooted in cultural history, see Robert Darnton, *The Literary Underground of the Old Regime* (Cambridge, Mass.: Harvard University Press, 1982). For one influential example of eighteenth-century European investigations of "oriental despotism," see Montesquieu, *Persian Letters*, trans. C. J. Betts (New York: Penguin, 1973, originally published in French in 1721).

10. On late eighteenth-century American criticisms of both legislative assemblies and popular opinion, see Wood, *The Radicalism of the American Revolution*, 11–92.

11. James Madison notes on "Term of the Executive," 17 July 1787, in *The Papers of James Madison Digital Edition*, J. C. A. Stagg, ed. (Charlottesville: University of Virginia Press, 2010), available at: http://rotunda.upress.virginia.edu.ezproxy.lib.utexas.edu/founders/JSMN-01-10-02-0061.

12. On Locke and his influence on Thomas Jefferson and the US Declaration of Independence, see the superb historical annotations in Jack N. Rakove, ed., *The Annotated US Constitution and Declaration of Independence* (Cambridge, Mass.: Belknap Press of Harvard University Press, 2009), 75–99. Rakove's historical annotations for the US Constitution emphasize the former colonists' fears of "legislative encroachment" as well as royal prerogative. See ibid., 103–215. On early American criticisms of legislative tyranny, see J. G. A. Pocock, *The Machiavellian Moment: Florentine Political Thought and the Atlantic Republican Tradition* (Princeton: Princeton University Press, 1975), esp. 506–51; Erik Nelson, *The Royalist Revolution: Monarchy and the American Founding* (Cambridge, Mass.: Belknap Press of Harvard University Press, 2014), esp. 184–228. On early American criticisms of monarchy, there is a much larger literature. For example, see Bernard Bailyn, *The Ideological Origins of the American Revolution* (Cambridge, Mass.: Belknap Press of Harvard University Press, 1967); Wood, *The Radicalism of the American Revolution*, esp. 11–92.

13. See David C. Hendrickson, *Peace Pact: The Lost World of the American Founding* (Lawrence: University Press of Kansas, 2003).

14. See the 1 November 1783 report from the Continental Congress on this issue, available at: http://memory.loc.gov/ammem/collections/continental/defects.html.

15. John Locke, *Two Treatises of Government* (December 1689), Book 2, paragraph 156.

16. Ibid., Book 2, paragraph 155. For a further analysis of Locke's thinking about executive power, and its influence on the American founders, see Mansfield, *Taming the Prince*, 181–211

17. David Hume, "On the Independency of Parliament," in *Essays: Moral and Political* (1742), Book 1, Essay 6. See also, Hume, "Idea of a Perfect Commonwealth," in Ibid., Book 2, Essay 16.

18. Edmund Burke, *Reflections on the Revolution in France* (1790). Quotation available from Edmund Burke, *The Works of the Right Honourable Edmund Burke*, Volume 3 (Project Gutenberg e-book, 2005), 497–498, available at: http://www.gutenberg.org/files/15679/15679-h/15679-h.htm#Page_231.

19. Harvey Mansfield points to Machiavelli as the first modern thinker about executive power. Machiavelli's *Prince* and his *Discourses on Livy* were indeed deeply influential for later thinkers. Machiavelli was, however, writing about a prince who ruled a small republic without a legislature or other counterbalancing political institutions. For that reason, Machiavelli was less influential in the eighteenth and nineteenth centuries than Locke, Hume, Burke, and others. The American founders were familiar with Machiavelli,

but they looked most closely to the later writers. See Mansfield, *Taming the Prince*, 121–49. See also Pocock, *The Machiavellian Moment*, esp. 156–217.

20. See the excellent etymology for the word "executive" in the *Oxford English Dictionary*, 2015 online edition.

21. Text of the Virginia Plan, presented to the Constitutional Convention, 29 May 1787. There are three variant texts of the Virginia Plan, one of which includes the language that the National Executive should "consist of a single person, with powers to carry into execution the National Laws, and to appoint to Offices, in cases not otherwise provided for, to be chosen by the National Legislature, for the term of seven years." See the three variant texts of the Virginia Plan at: http://avalon.law.yale.edu/18th_century/vatexta.asp

22. Randolph added a fifth point: the federal government "was not even paramount to the state constitutions, ratified, as it was in many of the states." See James Madison's Notes of Debates in the Federal Convention of 1787, Tuesday, 29 May 1787, available at: http://teachingamericanhistory.org/convention/debates/0529-2/#9. Madison's notes on the Constitutional Convention are one of the principal records used by historians for following debates among the delegates.

23. US Constitution, Article II, Section 2.

24. On 30 May 1787 the Convention's Committee of the Whole passed a resolution stating that a "national government ought to be established consisting of a supreme Legislative, Executive, and Judiciary." The resolution passed with yes votes from the representatives of six states (Massachusetts, Pennsylvania, Delaware, Virginia, North Carolina, South Carolina.) Connecticut voted no, and the New York delegation was divided. After this vote on the fifth day of the Convention, it was agreed that the new national government would have an empowered executive. This was a major departure from the Articles of Confederation. See Madison's Notes of Debates in the Federal Convention of 1787, Wednesday, 30 May 1787, available at: http://teachingamerican history.org/convention/debates/0530-2/#10.

25. Akhil Reed Amar, *America's Constitution: A Biography* (New York: Random House, 2005), 132.

26. One scholar observes that in the entire text of the US Constitution, the only use of the personal pronouns "I" and "my" appears in the specifically delineated oath of office for the president of the United States. He writes that this is "America's most personal office." See Amar, *America's Constitution*, 177. Article II, Section 1 of the US Constitution closes with the exact words for the US presidential "Oath or Affirmation": "I do solemnly swear (or affirm) that I will faithfully execute the Office of President of the United States, and will to the best of my Ability, preserve, protect and defend the Constitution of the United States." Gouverneur Morris quotation in Jack N. Rakove, *Original Meanings: Politics and Ideas in the Making of the Constitution* (New York: Alfred Knopf, 1996), 266. Second quotation from Amar, *America's Constitution*, 195.

27. See Rakove, *Original Meanings*, 244–87.

28. Quotation from Rakove, *Original Meanings*, 268. On the role of virtue in the framers' considerations of executive power, see Mansfield, *Taming the Prince*, 247–78.

29. Quotation from Amar, *America's Constitution*, 162.

30. James Madison, "The Union as a Safeguard Against Domestic Faction and Insurrection," Federalist No. 10, 23 November 1787, available at: http://thomas.loc.gov/home/histdox/fed_10.html.

31. Quoted in Wood, *Radicalism of the American Revolution*, 220.

32. Wood quotes Jeremiah Atwater, *A Sermon Preached Before His Excellency Isaac Tichenor, Esq...on the Day of the Anniversary Election, October 14, 1802*, in Wood, *Radi-*

calism of the American Revolution, 220. For a fuller discussion of early American assumptions about virtue, benevolence, enlightenment, and republicanism, see Wood, *Radicalism of the American Revolution*, 95–225.

CHAPTER 2

1. George Washington, First Annual Message to Congress on the State of the Union, 8 January 1790, available at: http://www.presidency.ucsb.edu/ws/?pid=29431.

2. Ibid.

3. Ibid.

4. Ibid.

5. See Bernard Bailyn, *To Begin the World Anew: The Genius and Ambiguities of the American Founders* (New York: Alfred Knopf, 2003).

6. Edmund S. Morgan, *The Genius of George Washington* (New York: Norton, 1980), 21.

7. See the many revealing entries from Washington's diary: Donald Jackson and Dorothy Twohig, eds., *The Diaries of George Washington*, Volume VI: January 1790–December 1799 (Charlottesville: University Press of Virginia, 1979). Available at: http://memory.loc .gov/cgi-bin/ampage?collId=mgwd&fileName=mgwd/gwpagewd06.db&recNum=2 3&itemLink=r?ammem/mgw:@field(DOCID+@lit(wd069))%23wd060022&linkText=1

8. Alexis de Tocqueville famously argued that the crucial cause of the French Revolution was the growth of the monarchy into a ubiquitous power across the country, and the resistance that encouraged, as well as the rigidity in monarchical policies that resulted. See Alexis de Tocqueville, *The Old Regime and the French Revolution*, trans., Stuart Gilbert (New York: Random House, 1955, originally published in French in 1856).

9. Quoted in Don Higginbotham, *George Washington and the American Military Tradition* (Athens: University of Georgia Press, 1985), 17.

10. Higginbotham, *George Washington and the American Military Tradition*, 77.

11. This assessment of Washington's decision-making style draws heavily on Morgan, *The Genius of George Washington* and Higginbotham, *George Washington and the American Military Tradition*.

12. George Washington to William Fitzhugh, 25 March 1781, quoted in Morgan, *The Genius of George Washington*, 89 fn 22.

13. Morgan, *The Genius of George Washington*, 19.

14. George Washington, First Annual Message to Congress on the State of the Union, 8 January 1790, available at: http://www.presidency.ucsb.edu/ws/?pid=29431.

15. Alexander Hamilton, Report on Public Credit, 9 January 1790, available at: http:// press-pubs.uchicago.edu/founders/documents/a1_8_2s5.html.

16. See Ron Chernow, *Alexander Hamilton* (New York: Penguin, 2004), esp. 295–308; idem., *Washington: A Life* (New York: Penguin, 2010), 619–22; Joseph J. Ellis, *His Excellency: George Washington* (New York: Random House, 2004), 203–06.

17. In 1780 Washington displayed remarkable insight about the long-term strength of British national finance and the fragility of French national finance. He wrote: "Though the [British] government is deeply in debt and of course poor, the nation is rich and their riches afford a fund which will not be easily exhausted. Besides, their system of public credit is such that it is capable of greater exertions than that of any other nation…France is in a different position. The abilities of her present Financier [French Minister of Finance Jacques Necker] have done wonders. By a wise administration of the revenues aided by advantageous loans he has avoided the necessity of additional taxes. But I am well informed, if the war continues another campaign he will be obliged to have recourse to the

taxes usual in time of war which are very heavy, and which the people of France are not in a condition to endure for any duration." Quoted in Morgan, *The Genius of George Washington*, 17–18. On the "northern financial revolution," see Chernow, *Washington*, 622. On the British "financial revolution" and the rise of the "fiscal-military state," see P. G. M. Dickson, *The Financial Revolution in England: A Study in the Development of Public Credit, 1688–1756* (London: St. Martin's Press, 1967); John Brewer, *The Sinews of Power: War, Money, and the English State, 1688–1783* (Cambridge, Mass. Harvard University Press, 1990).

18. George Washington to Henry Laurens, 14 November 1778, reprinted in Morgan, *The Genius of George Washington*, 63. The text of this letter is also available at: http://www.loc.gov/teachers/classroommaterials/presentationsandactivities/presentations/timeline/amrev/turning/laurens.html.

19. George Washington to James Madison, 5 November 1786, available at: http://founders.archives.gov/documents/Washington/04-04-02-0299.

20. See David C. Hendrickson, *Peace Pact: The Lost World of the American Founding* (Lawrence: University Press of Kansas, 2003).

21. George Washington to Alexander Hamilton, 4 April 1783, available at: http://rotunda.upress.virginia.edu/founders/default.xqy?keys=FOEA-chron-1780-1783-04-04-6. On Washington's efforts to balance the military need for a professional army with democratic concerns about protecting civil liberties, see Higginbotham, *George Washington and the American Military Tradition*, 69–105.

22. Alexander Hamilton conveyed Washington's instructions to Virginia Governor Henry Lee III in a letter dated 20 October 1794, available at: http://founders.archives.gov/documents/Hamilton/01-17-02-0317.

23. *National Gazette* quotation in Chernow, *Washington*, 693. See also Chernow, *Washington*, 684–99; Ellis, *His Excellency*, 221–24.

24. George Washington to Thomas Jefferson, 12 April 1793, available at: http://founders.archives.gov/documents/Washington/05-12-02-0353.

25. See Chernow, *George Washington*, 690–91.

26. The Proclamation of Neutrality from 1793, available at: http://avalon.law.yale.edu/18th_century/neutra93.asp.

27. Madison's "Helvidius" letters from 24 August 1793 and 14 September 1793, reprinted in Morton J. Frisch, ed., *The Pacificus-Helvidius Debates of 1793–1794* (Indianapolis: Liberty Fund, 2007), 59, 89. Emphasis in original.

28. Hamilton's "Pacificus" letter from 29 June 1793, ibid., 8–17.

29. Hamilton's "Pacificus" letter from 10 July 1793, ibid., 33.

30. Hamilton's "Pacificus" letter from 17 July 1793, ibid., 46–47. Emphasis in original.

31. See Ellis, *His Excellency*, 206–40; James MacGregor Burns and Susan Dunn, *George Washington* (New York: Henry Holt, 2004), 77–117.

32. On the rise of the American party system, but the continued commitment to a strong president, see Jeffrey L. Pasley, *The First Presidential Contest: 1796 and the Founding of American Democracy* (Lawrence: University Press of Kansas, 2013).

33. This is a point made very well by Walter McDougall in his book, *Promised Land, Crusader State: The American Encounter with the World Since 1776* (New York: Houghton Mifflin, 1997), chapters 1–4.

34. The best book on the Jay Treaty, and the domestic debate surrounding it, remains Samuel Flagg Bemis, *Jay's Treaty: A Study in Commerce and Diplomacy* (New Haven: Yale University Press, 1962). See also Pasley, *The First Presidential Contest*, 102–08.

35. See Washington's Farewell Address, 19 September 1796, available at: http://avalon.law.yale.edu/18th_century/washing.asp.

36. Ibid. The best analysis of Washington's Farewell Address, its origins, and its enduring legacies remains Felix Gilbert, *To The Farewell Address: Ideas of Early American Foreign Policy* (Princeton: Princeton University Press, 1961).

37. See Washington's diary entry for 16 March 1790, in Jackson and Twohig, eds., *The Diaries of George Washington*, Volume VI, 47.

CHAPTER 3

1. Quotation from Harry L. Watson, *Liberty and Power: The Politics of Jacksonian America* (New York: Farrar, Straus, and Giroux, 1990), 78. See also H. W. Brands, *Andrew Jackson: His Life and Times* (New York: Random House, 2005), 3–95.

2. Quoted in Sean Wilentz, *The Rise of American Democracy: Jefferson to Lincoln* (New York: W.W. Norton, 2005), 251.

3. President Andrew Jackson's Farewell Address, 4 March 1837, available at: http://www.presidency.ucsb.edu/ws/?pid=67087.

4. Ibid.

5. Ibid.

6. On Jackson's supporters, see Watson, *Liberty and Power*, 73–95; Wilentz, *Rise of American Democracy*, 301–58.

7. Quotations from Jackson's Farewell Address.

8. Quotation from Robert Remini, *Jacksonian Revolution* (the World and I Online, available through Amazon.com Kindle, 2014). Also cited by the same author in *Andrew Jackson: The Course of American Democracy, 1833–1845* (New York: Harper and Row, 1984), 127.

9. Most notorious, see Arthur M. Schlesinger, Jr.'s Pulitzer Prize winning book: *The Age of Jackson* (Boston: Little Brown, 1945).

10. John Quincy Adams, Daniel Webster, Henry Clay, and John C. Calhoun were four of Jackson's most formidable critics in his time. For a sampling of historical criticisms, often invoking Adams, Webster, Clay, and Calhoun, see Anthony F. C. Wallace, *The Long, Bitter Trail: Andrew Jackson and the Indians* (New York: Hill and Wang, 1993); Daniel Walker Howe, *What Hath God Wrought: The Transformation of America, 1815–1848* (New York: Oxford University Press, 2007), esp. 328–524; Merrill Peterson, *The Great Triumvirate: Webster, Clay, and Calhoun* (New York: Oxford University Press, 1987).

11. This is the central argument of Robert Remini, *Andrew Jackson and the Course of American Freedom, 1822–32* (New York: Harper and Row, 1981). This is volume two of Remini's magisterial three-volume biography of Jackson.

12. Jackson's Farewell Address.

13. For a thoughtful analysis of Jackson's views and behavior toward American Indians, see Robert Remini, *Andrew Jackson and His Indian Wars* (New York: Viking, 2001). See also Wallace, *The Long, Bitter Trail*. Contrast Wallace's account of Jackson's Indian hatred with his assessment of Jefferson's assimilationist impulses: Anthony F. C. Wallace, *Jefferson and the Indians: The Tragic Fate of the First Americans* (Cambridge, Mass.: Harvard University Press, 1999).

14. The best account of the War of 1812, with attention to the roles of Indians and Loyalists as supporters of the British, is Alan Taylor, *The Civil War of 1812: American Citizens, British Subjects, Irish Rebels, and Indian Allies* (New York: Random House, 2010).

15. Quoted in James Parton, *Life of Andrew Jackson* (Boston: Houghton Mifflin, 1885), Volume 1: 426. This very old three-volume biography of Jackson is still a valuable source for its use of original materials and its deep analysis of Jackson's career and

personality. I thank Daniel Feller for drawing me to this and other often-neglected sources on Jackson.

16. For a careful and detailed account of Jackson's role in the First Seminole War, see Howe, *What Hath God Wrought*, 96–107.

17. For a thoughtful but very controversial psychological investigation of Jackson's Indian hatred, and its popularity among his followers, see Michael Paul Rogin, *Fathers and Children: Andrew Jackson and the Subjugation of the American Indian* (New York: Alfred Knopf, 1975).

18. For an assessment of the role slavery played in Andrew Jackson's career, see Mark Cheathem, "Andrew Jackson, Slavery, and Historians," *History Compass* 9 (2011), 326–38.

19. Andrew Jackson's First Inaugural Address, 4 March 1829, available at: http://www.loc.gov/exhibits/treasures/trr075a.html.

20. Andrew Jackson's First Annual Message to Congress, 8 December 1829, available at: http://www.presidency.ucsb.edu/ws/?pid=29471.

21. Ibid.

22. Ibid.

23. Quoted in Watson, *Liberty and Power*, 103.

24. On the nature of Jackson's appointments, and a comparison with his predecessors' appointments, see Ibid., 103–04; Sidney Aronson, *Status and Kinship in the Higher Civil Service: Standards of Selection in the Administrations of John Adams, Thomas Jefferson, and Andrew Jackson* (Cambridge, Mass.: Harvard University Press, 1964). See also Jon Meacham, *American Lion: Andrew Jackson in the White House* (New York: Random House, 2008), 81–83.

25. For an excellent short history of the Second Bank of the United States, see "The Second Bank of the United States: A Chapter in the History of Central Banking," published by the Federal Reserve Bank of Philadelphia (December 2010), available at: https://www.philadelphiafed.org. On Nicholas Biddle, see "The Rise and Fall of Nicholas Biddle," Federal Reserve Bank of Minneapolis (September 2008), available at: https://www.minneapolisfed.org/publications/the-region/the-rise-and-fall-of-nicholas-biddle; Thomas P. Govan, *Nicholas Biddle: Nationalist and Public Banker* (Chicago: University of Chicago Press, 1959).

26. Andrew Jackson, Veto Message Regarding the Bank of the United States, 10 July 1832, available at: http://avalon.law.yale.edu/19th_century/ajveto01.asp.

27. Ibid.

28. See Meacham, *American Lion*, 137–41, 278–79. On Washington, see chapter 2.

29. Jackson, Veto Message Regarding the Bank of the United States.

30. Ibid.

31. Quotations from Andrew Jackson's First Annual Message to Congress, 8 December 1829.

32. Ibid.

33. *Worcester v. Georgia* 31 US 515 (1832); Tim A. Garrison, "*Worcester v. Georgia* (1832)." *New Georgia Encyclopedia* (April 2015), available at: http://www.georgiaencyclopedia.org/articles/government-politics/worcester-v-georgia-1832. See also Jill Norgren, *The Cherokee Cases: The Confrontation of Law and Politics* (New York: McGraw Hill, 1996).

34. Among the many thoughtful books on this topic, see Wallace, *The Long, Bitter, Trail*; Steve Inskeep, *Jacksonland: President Andrew Jackson, Cherokee Chief John Ross, and a Great American Land Grab* (New York: Penguin, 2015); Daniel Feller, *The Jacksonian Promise: America 1815–1840* (Baltimore: Johns Hopkins University Press, 1995), 179–83.

35. Quoted in Meacham, *American Lion*, 134.

36. See Feller, *The Jacksonian Promise*, 171.

37. See Charles Louis de Secondat, Baron de Montesquieu, *The Spirit of the Laws*, trans. and eds., Anne M. Cohler, Basia Carolyn Miller, and Harold Samuel Stone (New York: Cambridge University Press, 1989, originally published in French in 1748). For Montesquieu's influence on the writers of the US Constitution, see Jack N. Rakove, *Original Meanings: Politics and Ideas in the Making of the Constitution* (New York: Alfred Knopf, 1996), 245–56.

CHAPTER 4

1. John Murray Forbes to Charles Sumner, 27 December 1862, quoted in Eric Foner, *The Fiery Trial: Abraham Lincoln and American Slavery* (New York: W.W. Norton, 2010), 243.

2. See Eric Foner's account of Abraham Lincoln's 20 June 1862 audience with Quaker visitors, *The Fiery Trial*, 210. On George Washington's 16 March 1790 audience with the Quaker representatives, see chapter 2. For an insightful account of Warner Mifflin's life, especially his abolitionism, see Michael R. McDowell, "Warner Mifflin: A Founding Father of Abolitionism," *Quaker Hill Quill* 3 (Summer 2013), available at: http://www.halebyrnes.org/newsflash01.pdf.

3. Abraham Lincoln to Horace Greeley, 22 August 1862, *New York Times* (24 August 1862), available at: http://www.nytimes.com/1862/08/24/news/letter-president-lincoln-reply-horace-greeley-slavery-union-restoration-union.html.

4. Abraham Lincoln, Special Message to Congress, 4 July 1861, available at: http://www.presidency.ucsb.edu/ws/?pid=69802 .

5. Ibid.

6. See Jon Meacham, *American Lion: Andrew Jackson in the White House* (New York: Random House, 2008), 355–57; Foner, *The Fiery Trial*, 159.

7. Lincoln's long-time law partner, William Herndon, observed Lincoln's driving ambition throughout his pre-presidential career: "The man who thinks Lincoln calmly sat down and gathered his robes about him, waiting for the people to call him, has a very erroneous knowledge of Lincoln. He was always calculating and always planning ahead. His ambition was a little engine that knew no rest." William H. Herndon and Jesse W. Weik, *Herndon's Lincoln*, eds., Douglas L. Wilson and Rodney O. Davis (Urbana: University of Illinois Press, 2006), 231.

8. Abraham Lincoln, Special Message to Congress, 4 July 1861.

9. Ibid.

10. Abraham Lincoln to Albert G. Hodges, 4 April 1864, available at: http://www.abrahamlincolnonline.org/lincoln/speeches/hodges.htm.

11. Lincoln, Special Message to Congress, 4 July 1861.

12. On this point, see James M. McPherson, *Abraham Lincoln and the Second American Revolution* (New York: Oxford University Press, 1991), 93–112.

13. Lincoln quoted in Francis B. Carpenter, *Six Months at the White House with Abraham Lincoln* (New York: Hurd and Houghton, 1866) 312–13. Carpenter was a painter who, in 1864, spent six months in close proximity to Lincoln and his cabinet, painting *First Reading of the Emancipation Proclamation of President Lincoln*, which now hangs in the US Capitol.

14. Abraham Lincoln, First Inaugural Address, 4 March 1861.

15. McPherson, *Abraham Lincoln and the Second American Revolution*, 93–96.

16. Abraham Lincoln, First Inaugural Address, 4 March 1861.

17. Lincoln, Special Message to Congress, 4 July 1861. Emphasis in original.

18. Ibid.

19. On this point, see Lincoln's famous letter to Kentucky journalist Albert Hodges, 4 April 1864, available at: http://www.loc.gov/exhibits/treasures/trt027.html.

20. Historian William Hesseltine observed: "Bull Run's sobering lesson that war meant bloodshed and death had been rapidly learned." See Hesseltine, *Lincoln and the War Governors* (New York: Alfred Knopf, 1948), 182.

21. Lincoln, Special Message to Congress, 4 July 1861. See also Phillip Shaw Paludan, *"A People's Contest": The Union and Civil War, 1861–1865* (New York: Harper and Row, 1988), esp. 375–93.

22. "Remarks to Deputation of Western Gentlemen," 4 August 1862, reprinted in Roy P. Basler, ed., *The Collected Works of Abraham Lincoln* [hereafter *CW*] (New Brunswick, NJ: Rutgers University Press, 1953), Volume 5, 356–57.

23. Quotations from James McPherson, *Battle Cry Freedom: The Civil War Era* (New York: Oxford University Press, 1988), 502.

24. See McPherson, *Battle Cry Freedom*, 500; Foner, *The Fiery Trial*, 228–30.

25. See Eugene C. Murdock, *One Million Men: The Civil War Draft in the North* (Madison: State Historical Society of Wisconsin, 1971).

26. On nineteenth-century nation-building policies, led by powerful state leaders and military organizations, see C. A. Bayly, *The Birth of the Modern World, 1780–1914* (Oxford: Blackwell, 2004), esp. 125–243.

27. Abraham Lincoln, speech at the close of the Illinois Republican State Convention that nominated Lincoln as a candidate for the US Senate, Springfield, Illinois, 16 June 1858, available at: http://www.abrahamlincolnonline.org/lincoln/speeches/house.htm.

28. Abraham Lincoln, Address at the Cooper Institute, New York City, 27 February 1860, available at: http://www.abrahamlincolnonline.org/lincoln/speeches/cooper.htm.

29. On presidential uses of war power at home see: William G. Howell, Saul P. Jackman, and Jon C. Rogowski, *The Wartime President: Executive Influence and the Nationalizing Politics of Threat* (Chicago: University of Chicago Press, 2013); Arthur M. Schlesinger, Jr., *War and the American Presidency* (New York: W.W. Norton, 2004).

30. Lincoln, Special Message to Congress, 4 July 1861. On the connection between idealistic claims and American war-fighting, see Jeremi Suri, *Liberty's Surest Guardian: American Nation-Building from the Founders to Obama* (New York: Free Press, 2011); Robert A. Divine, *Perpetual War for Perpetual Peace* (College Station: Texas A&M University Press, 2000); Russell F. Weigley, *The American Way of War: A History of United States Military Strategy and Policy* (New York: McMillan, 1973).

31. On the "culture of death" in the Civil War era, see Drew Gilpin Faust, *This Republic of Suffering: Death and the American Civil War* (New York: Alfred Knopf, 2008).

32. Abraham Lincoln, Gettysburg Address, 19 November 1863, available at: http://avalon.law.yale.edu/19th_century/gettyb.asp. This is the final text of the Gettysburg Address, known as the "Bliss Copy," for its long possession in the family of Alexander Bliss. It was typeset and corrected after Lincoln's oral presentation at the battlefield. For Lincoln's earlier drafts and slight re-writes of the Gettysburg Address, see *CW*, Volume 7, 17–23.

33. Quotations from Garry Wills, *Lincoln at Gettysburg: The Words that Remade America* (New York: Simon and Schuster, 1992), 20, 174. This book offers a stunning analysis of Lincoln's rhetorical strategies and the intellectual impact of the Gettysburg Address.

34. For Lincoln's emphasis on "nation" instead of "union" at Gettysburg and thereafter, see McPherson, *Battle Cry Freedom*, 859.

35. See Edward Everett's letter to Lincoln, 20 November 1863, and Lincoln's response of the same date, in *CW*, Volume 7, 24–25.

36. This is the central argument of Wills, *Lincoln at Gettysburg*.

37. Emancipation Proclamation, 1 January 1863, available at: https://www.ourdocuments.gov/doc.php?flash=true&doc=34&page=transcript

38. See Steven Hahn, *A Nation Under Our Feet: Black Political Struggles in the Rural South from Slavery to the Great Migration* (Cambridge, Mass.: Belknap Press of Harvard University Press, 2003), 62–115.

39. Quotations from the Emancipation Proclamation.

40. On Lincoln's management of his cabinet, particularly around the Emancipation Proclamation, see Doris Kearns Goodwin, *Team of Rivals: The Political Genius of Abraham Lincoln* (New York: Simon and Schuster, 2005), esp. 459–500.

41. Quotation from Gideon Welles, *Diary of Gideon Welles* (Boston: Houghton Mifflin, 1911), Volume 1, 70.

42. See Foner, *The Fiery Trial*, 248–89.

43. See McPherson, *Battle Cry of Freedom*, 490–567.

44. Quotation from Lincoln's Special Message to Congress, 4 July 1861.

45. Lincoln's Annual Message to Congress, 1 December 1862, available at: http://www.presidency.ucsb.edu/ws/?pid=29503.

46. Lincoln to James C. Conkling, 26 August 1863, available at: http://www.abraham lincolnonline.org/lincoln/speeches/conkling.htm. For confirmation of Lincoln's judgment about the positive effect of emancipation on the Union war effort, see Louis P. Masur, *Lincoln's Hundred Days: The Emancipation Proclamation and the War for the Union* (Cambridge, Mass.: Belknap Press of Harvard University Press, 2012); Joseph E. Stevens, *1863: The Rebirth of a Nation* (New York: Bantam Books, 1999).

47. Lincoln to James C. Conkling, 26 August 1863.

48. See Louis P. Masur, "Read It Very Slowly," *New York Times Opinionator* (21 August 2013), available at: http://opinionator.blogs.nytimes.com/2013/08/21/read-it-very-slowly/.

49. Abraham Lincoln to Albert G. Hodges, 4 April 1864, available at: http://www.abrahamlincolnonline.org/lincoln/speeches/hodges.htm.

50. For this crucial period, including Robert E. Lee's surrender and the transition from Civil War to early postwar Reconstruction, see McPherson, *Battle Cry of Freedom*, 831–62.

51. For a very thoughtful analysis of the sources, rhetoric, and meaning in Lincoln's Second Inaugural Address, see Ronald C. White, Jr., *Lincoln's Greatest Speech: The Second Inaugural* (New York: Simon and Schuster, 2002).

52. Abraham Lincoln's Second Inaugural Address, 4 March 1865, available at: http://avalon.law.yale.edu/19th_century/lincoln2.asp.

53. Ibid.

54. See White, *Lincoln's Greatest Speech*, 121–63.

55. "The war came" is from Lincoln's Second Inaugural Address, 4 March 1865. "Better angels of our nature" is the closing phrase from Lincoln's First Inaugural Address, precisely four years earlier.

56. For the text of Lincoln's last speech, 11 April 1865, see http://www.abraham lincolnonline.org/lincoln/speeches/last.htm. See also Louis P. Masur, *Lincoln's Last Speech: Wartime Reconstruction and the Crisis of Reunion* (New York: Oxford University Press, 2015).

57. Lincoln to Thurlow Weed, 15 March 1865, in *CW*, Volume 8, 356.

CHAPTER 5

1. Theodore Roosevelt, "The Strenuous Life," speech delivered to the Hamilton Club, Chicago, Illinois, 10 April 1899, available at: http://www.theodore-roosevelt.com/images/research/speeches/trstrenlife.pdf.

2. Ibid.

3. Theodore Roosevelt, speech in Buffalo, New York, 26 January 1883, available at: http://www.theodore-roosevelt.com/images/research/speeches/trdoac.pdf.

4. The "bully pulpit" quotation comes from an account of Roosevelt's words in *The Outlook* (27 February 1909). Doris Kearns Goodwin emphasizes the rise of presidential oratory and other forms of mass communication in the early twentieth century in *The Bully Pulpit: Theodore Roosevelt, William Howard Taft, and the Golden Age of Journalism* (New York: Simon and Schuster, 2013).

5. Roosevelt to Cecil Spring-Rice, 3 July 1901 reprinted in *Theodore Roosevelt: Letters and Speeches* [hereafter TRLS], Louis Auchincloss, eds. (New York: Library of America, 2004) 232.

6. Ibid; Roosevelt to Henry Cabot Lodge, 29 April 1896, in TRLS, 86. Racial prejudices obviously underpinned Roosevelt's racialism.

7. For an interpretation of Theodore Roosevelt's career that concurs with this assessment, focused on the overwhelming importance of New York City for Roosevelt's development, see Edward P. Kohn, *Heir to the Empire City: New York and the Making of Theodore Roosevelt* (New York: Basic Books, 2014).

8. See Edmund Morris, *The Rise of Theodore Roosevelt* (New York: Random House, 1979), xi–xxxiv.

9. Richard Washburn Child quotation from Morris, *The Rise of Theodore Roosevelt*, xxxi. Richard Washburn Child became a campaign advisor for Warren G. Harding, US ambassador to Italy, and then ghost-writer for Benito Mussolini's book, *My Autobiography*, published in 1928. One can question Richard Washburn Child's ethics, but he surely had close proximity to some of the leading political personalities of the early twentieth century.

10. Roosevelt to George Bird Grinnell, 24 August 1897, in TRLS, 116.

11. Roosevelt to George Otto Trevelyan, 24 November 1904, in TRLS, 369–72.

12. Theodore Roosevelt speech at the Sorbonne, Paris, France, 23 April 1910, available at: http://www.theodore-roosevelt.com/images/research/speeches/maninthearena.pdf. For the "Strenuous Life" speech, 10 April 1899, see: http://www.theodore-roosevelt.com/images/research/speeches/trstrenlife.pdf.

13. Mark Twain, Autobiographical dictations 18 October 1907 and 2 December 1907, in *Autobiography of Mark Twain, Vol. 3* (Berkeley: University of California Press, 2015).

14. Roosevelt speech in Chicago, 17 June 1912, available at: http://www.theodore-roosevelt.com/images/research/speeches/trreactionairies.pdf.

15. Ibid.

16. Ibid. On these core progressive beliefs, and the larger progressive movement that influenced Theodore Roosevelt so deeply, see, among many others, Michael McGerr, *A Fierce Discontent: The Rise and Fall of the Progressive Movement in America* (New York: Oxford University Press, 2003); Alan Dawley, *Struggles for Justice: Social Responsibility and the Liberal State* (Cambridge, Mass.: Harvard University Press, 1993); Eldon J. Eisenach, *The Lost Promise of Progressivism* (Lawrence: University of Kansas Press, 1994).

17. See chapter 3. Lincoln quoted in Richard D. White, Jr., *Roosevelt the Reformer: Theodore Roosevelt as Civil Service Commissioner, 1889–1895* (Tuscaloosa: University of Alabama Press, 2003), 17.

18. White, *Roosevelt the Reformer*, 18.

19. Ibid., 18–22. The full text of the Pendleton Act is available at: http://www.our documents.gov/doc.php?flash=true&doc=48&page=transcript.

20. White, *Roosevelt the Reformer*, esp. 54–140.

21. Roosevelt to William Warland Clapp, 7 August 1889, in TRLS, 34.

22. White, *Roosevelt the Reformer*, 119–40.

23. The literature on the War of 1898 is huge. For some of the most important recent works see: Louis A. Pérez, *The War of 1898: The United States and Cuba in History and Historiography* (Chapel Hill: University of North Carolina Press, 1998); Alfred W. McCoy and Francisco A. Scarano, eds., *Colonial Crucible: Empire in the Making of the Modern American State* (Madison: University of Wisconsin Press, 2009); David Brody, *Visualizing American Empire: Orientalism and Imperialism in the Philippines* (Chicago: University of Chicago Press, 2010); Paul A. Kramer, *The Blood of Government: Race, Empire, the United States, and the Philippines* (Chapel Hill: University of North Carolina Press, 2006).

24. Theodore Roosevelt's Naval War College Address, Newport, Rhode Island, 2 June 1897, available at: http://www.theodore-roosevelt.com/images/research/speeches/tr1898 .pdf.

25. See, among others, Kristin L. Hoganson, *Fighting for American Manhood: How Gender Politics Provoked the Spanish-American and Philippine-American Wars* (New Haven: Yale University Press, 1998); Evan Thomas, *War Lovers: Roosevelt, Lodge, Hearst, and the Rush to Empire, 1898* (New York: Little, Brown, 2010).

26. Roosevelt quoted in H. W. Brands, *T. R.: The Last Romantic* (New York: Basic Books, 1997), 357.

27. Roosevelt to Leonard Wood, 27 March 1901 and 17 April 1901, in TRLS, 224–27.

28. Roosevelt to Henry Cabot Lodge, 23 September 1901, in TRLS, 243.

29. Roosevelt, State of the Union Message, 3 December 1901, available at: http://www.theodore-roosevelt.com/images/research/speeches/sotu1.pdf.

30. Ibid.

31. For a superb account of the simultaneous praise and criticism for Roosevelt's approach to the presidency, see John Milton Cooper, Jr., *The Warrior and the Priest: Woodrow Wilson and Theodore Roosevelt* (Cambridge, Mass.: Belknap Press of Harvard University Press, 1983), esp. 69–88.

32. See Roosevelt to George Otto Trevelyan, 24 November 1904, in TRLS, 367–72. On the progressive preference for knowledge and expertise over populist democracy, see the classic account: Robert H. Wiebe, *The Search for Order, 1877–1920* (New York: Farrar, Straus, and Giroux, 1967).

33. Quotations from Brands, *T. R.*, 438–39. On William Jennings Bryan, see Michael Kazin, *A Godly Hero: The Life of William Jennings Bryan* (New York: Random House, 2006).

34. On the power of railroad monopolies over American industry and parts of government in the late nineteenth century, see Richard White, *Railroaded: The Transcontinentals and the Making of Modern America* (New York: W.W. Norton, 2011).

35. Northern Securities Co. v. United States 193 US 197, available at: https://www .law.cornell.edu/supremecourt/text/193/197#writing-USSC_CR_0193_0197_ZO.

36. See John Morton Blum, *The Republican Roosevelt* (Cambridge, Mass.: Harvard University Press, 1977), 73–105.

37. Roosevelt speech delivered in Dallas, Texas, 5 April 1905, available at: http://www.theodore-roosevelt.com/images/research/speeches/trsquaredealspeech.pdf.

38. Ibid.

39. See Douglas Brinkley, *The Wilderness Warrior: Theodore Roosevelt and the Crusade for America* (New York: Harper Collins, 2010); Char Miller, *Gifford Pinchot and the Making of Modern Environmentalism* (Washington, D.C.: Island Press, 2001).

40. Roosevelt, Address to the Deep Waterway Convention in Memphis, Tennessee, 4 October 1907, available at: http://babel.hathitrust.org/cgi/pt?id=chi.086563523.

41. Ibid.

42. Railroad regulation and the ICC have received extensive scholarly attention. See, among many others, Stephen Skowronek, *Building a New American State: The Expansion of National Administrative Capacities, 1877–1920* (New York: Cambridge University Press, 1982), esp. 248–84; Richard D. Stone, *The Interstate Commerce Commission and the Railroad Industry: A History of Regulatory Policy* (New York: Praeger, 1991); Ari Arthur Hoogenboom and Olive Hoogenboom, *A History of the ICC: From Panacea to Palliative* (New York: W.W. Norton, 1976). The classic critical study of the ICC and railroad regulations in general is Gabriel Kolko, *Railroads and Regulation, 1877–1916* (Princeton: Princeton University Press, 1965).

43. On the enduring influence of the new administrative capacities for the federal government, particularly the independent expert commission, see Skowronek, *Building a New American State*, 248–92.

44. Quotation in Howard K. Beale, *Theodore Roosevelt and the Rise of America to World Power* (Baltimore: Johns Hopkins University Press, 1956), 382. See John Quincy Adams, Independence Day Speech to the US House of Representatives, 4 July 1821, available at: http://teachingamericanhistory.org/library/document/speech-on-independence-day.

45. Beale, *Theodore Roosevelt and the Rise of America to World Power*, esp. 224–382.

46. Theodore Roosevelt, Naval War College Address, 2 June 1897, available at: http://www.theodore-roosevelt.com/images/research/speeches/tr1898.pdf. Before his presidency, Roosevelt wrote, among other books, an acclaimed naval history of the War of 1812. See Theodore Roosevelt, *The Naval War of 1812* (New York: G.P. Putnam's Sons, 1882).

47. Alfred Thayer Mahan, *The Influence of Sea Power Upon History* (Boston: Little Brown, 1890). See Walter LaFeber's classic account: *The New Empire: An Interpretation of American Expansion, 1860–1898* (Ithaca: Cornell University Press, 1963), 80–95. See also Peter Karsten, *The Naval Aristocracy: The Golden Age of Annapolis and the Emergence of Modern American Navalism* (New York: Free Press, 1972).

48. Quotation from Henry J. Hendrix, *Theodore Roosevelt's Naval Diplomacy: The US Navy and the Birth of the American Century* (Annapolis: Naval Institute Press, 2009 Kindle Edition), Location 3787.

49. See, among others, Frank Ninkovich, *The Global Republic: America's Inadvertent Rise to World Power* (Chicago: University of Chicago Press, 2014), 81–86; Emily S. Rosenberg, *Spreading the American Dream: American Economic and Cultural Expansion, 1890–1945* (New York: Hill and Wang), 38–62.

50. See Odd Arne Westad, *Restless Empire: China and the World Since 1750* (New York: Basic Books, 2012), chapters 2–3; Warren I. Cohen, *East Asia at the Center: Four Thousand Years of Engagement with the World* (New York: Columbia University Press, 2000), chapters 9–10; Akira Iriye, *After Imperialism: The Search for a New Order in the Far East, 1921–1931* (Cambridge, Mass.: Harvard University Press, 1965).

51. See the classic account in Eugene P. Trani, *The Treaty of Portsmouth: An Adventure in American Diplomacy* (Lexington: University of Kentucky Press, 1969).

52. See Cumings, *Korea's Place in the Sun*, chapter 3; Louise Young, *Japan's Total Empire: Manchuria and the Culture of Wartime Imperialism* (Berkeley: University of California Press, 1998); Trani, *The Treaty of Portsmouth*.

53. Quotation from Roosevelt to Cecil Spring-Rice, 16 June 1905, in TRLS, 392.

54. Theodore Roosevelt, Nobel Lecture, Oslo, Norway, 5 May 1910, available at: https://www.nobelprize.org/nobel_prizes/peace/laureates/1906/roosevelt-lecture.html.

55. Ibid.

56. See the classic work: F. H. Hinsley, *Power and the Pursuit of Peace: Theory and Practice in the History of Relations between States* (New York: Cambridge University Press, 1967). See also Mark Mazower, *Governing the World: The History of an Idea, 1815 to the Present* (New York: Penguin, 2012).

57. Theodore Roosevelt, Nobel Lecture, Oslo, Norway, 5 May 1910.

58. On this point, see among many others, Rosenberg, *Spreading the American Dream*, 38–62; Cooper, *The Warrior and the Priest*, 346–61.

59. On the connections between internationalism and paternalism in the early twentieth century, see Susan Pedersen, *The Guardians: The League of Nations and the Crisis of Empire* (New York: Oxford University Press, 2015), esp. 1–105.

60. Frank Ninkovich has analyzed Theodore Roosevelt's concept of "civilization" in great depth. My analysis draws on Ninkovich, although my interpretation differs in a few areas. See Frank Ninkovich, "Theodore Roosevelt: Civilization as Ideology," *Diplomatic History* 10 (July 1986), 221–45; Ninkovich, *Modernity and Power: The Domino Theory in the Twentieth Century* (Chicago: University of Chicago Press, 1994), 1–20.

61. The literature on Theodore Roosevelt's Latin American imperialism is enormous. See, among others, Lester D. Langley, *The Banana Wars: United States Intervention in the Caribbean, 1898–1934* (Lexington. University Press of Kentucky, 1983), chapters 1–5; Alan McPherson, *A Short History of US Interventions in Latin America and the Caribbean* (Malden, Mass: John Wiley and Sons, 2016), chapters 2–3; Walter LaFeber, *Inevitable Revolutions: The United States in Central America* (New York: W.W. Norton, 1983), chapter 1.

62. Theodore Roosevelt, Fourth Annual Message, 6 December 1904, available at: http://www.presidency.ucsb.edu/ws/index.php?pid=29545.

63. See Beale, *Theodore Roosevelt and the Rise of America to World Power*, 101–09; John Taliaferro, *All the Great Prizes: The Life of John Hay from Lincoln to Roosevelt* (New York: Simon and Schuster, 2013), 493–503.

64. See Beale, *Theodore Roosevelt and the Rise of America to World Power*, 31–63; Ninkovich, *The Global Republic*, 65–95.

65. See John Milton Cooper, Jr., *Woodrow Wilson: A Biography* (New York: Alfred Knopf, 2009), esp. 198–534; Joan Hoff Wilson, *Herbert Hoover: Forgotten Progressive* (Boston: Little, Brown, 1975); David M. Kennedy, *Freedom From Fear: The American People in Depression and War, 1929–1945* (New York: Oxford University Press, 1999), 70–103.

CHAPTER 6

1. Saul Bellow, "In the Days of Mr. Roosevelt," reprinted in Bellow, *There is Simply Too Much to Think About: Collected Nonfiction*, ed. Benjamin Taylor (New York: Viking, 2015), 328–29.

2. Ibid., 320.

3. Quotations from ibid., 321.

4. Quotations from ibid., 319–20, 395.

5. See John Maynard Keynes, "Economic Possibilities for our Grandchildren," originally published in 1930, written in 1929, reprinted in Keynes, *Essays in Persuasion* (New York: W.W. Norton, 1963).

6. See George N. Nash, *The Life of Herbert Hoover: Master of Emergencies, 1917–1918* (New York: W.W. Norton, 1996); Bertrand Patenaude, *The Big Show in Bololand: The American Relief Expedition to Soviet Russia in the Famine of 1921* (Stanford: Stanford University Press, 2002).

7. See Joan Hoff Wilson, *Herbert Hoover: Forgotten Progressive* (Boston: Little, Brown, 1975); David M. Kennedy, *Freedom from Fear: The American People in Depression and War, 1929–1945* (New York: Oxford University Press, 1999), 70–103.

8. Robert E. Sherwood, *Roosevelt and Hopkins: An Intimate History* (New York: Harper and Brothers, 1948), 9.

9. Josephus Daniels, *The Wilson Era: Years of Peace, 1910–1917* (Chapel Hill: University of North Carolina Press, 1944), 127.

10. Daniels, *The Wilson Era*, 125–26.

11. Roosevelt's long-time speech writer, Samuel Rosenman, was puzzled by his boss's combination of aristocracy and populism. Rosenman confessed that after many efforts to find a clear explanation, including countless conversations with Roosevelt himself, he "never found a satisfactory and complete answer." Rosenman concluded that Roosevelt's populism was indeed part of his elite background—his security in his own status and his pride in helping others: "It was in the heart and soul of the man, in his love of people, his own sense of social justice, his hatred of greed and exploitation of the weak, his contempt for the bully—whether it was a Hitler or Mussolini or an owner of a sweatshop or an exploiter of child labor." Samuel I. Rosenman, *Working with Roosevelt* (New York: Harper and Brothers, 1952), 14.

12. Governor Franklin Roosevelt, Inaugural Speech, 1 January 1929, in *Public Papers of the Presidents of the United States: Franklin D. Roosevelt*, Volume 9 (Washington, D.C.: US Government Printing office, 1941), 76.

13. Franklin Roosevelt, Inaugural Address, 4 March 1933, available at: http://www.presidency.ucsb.edu/ws/?pid=14473.

14. Ibid.

15. On Bellow's work for the Writers' Project in the Works Progress Administration, and the work of many contemporary writers there, see James Atlas, *Bellow: A Biography* (New York: Random House, 2000), chapter 4. On the WPA see, among many others, Anthony Badger, *The New Deal* (New York: Hill and Wang, 1989), chapter 5; David M. Kennedy, *Freedom from Fear*, esp. 252–57.

16. Franklin Roosevelt, Inaugural Address, 4 March 1933. See chapter 4 and Lincoln's statement of April 1864: "I felt that measures, otherwise unconstitutional, might become lawful, by becoming indispensable to the preservation of the constitution, through the preservation of the nation."

17. Franklin Roosevelt, Address Accepting the Presidential Nomination at the Democratic National Convention in Chicago, 2 July 1932, available at: http://www.presidency.ucsb.edu/ws/?pid=75174.

18. Ibid.

19. Franklin Roosevelt, Fireside Chat 1, On the Banking Crisis, 12 March 1933, available at: http://millercenter.org/president/fdroosevelt/speeches/speech-3298.

20. On the limits of executive administrative capabilities before Franklin Roosevelt's presidency, see Peri E. Arnold, *Making the Managerial Presidency: Comprehensive Reorga-*

nization Planning, 1905–1980 (Princeton: Princeton University Press, 1986), 3–80; John P. Burke, *The Institutional Presidency* (Baltimore: The Johns Hopkins University Press, 1992), 1–6.

21. Roosevelt quoted from his Inaugural Address, 4 March 1933.

22. See Max Weber, *Economy and Society*, 2 volumes, trans., Guenther Roth (Berkeley: University of California Press, 2013); Reinhard Bendix, *Max Weber: An Intellectual Portrait* (Berkeley: University of California Press, 1978).

23. This analysis of Franklin Roosevelt and presidential power in general draws on Richard E. Neustadt, *Presidential Power: The Politics of Leadership from Roosevelt to Reagan* (New York: John Wiley & Sons, 1960, expanded and revised edition 1990); Matthew J. Dickinson, *Bitter Harvest: FDR, Presidential Power, and the Growth of the Presidential Branch* (New York: Cambridge University Press, 1996); William G. Howell, *Thinking about the Presidency: The Primacy of Power* (Princeton: Princeton University Press, 2013), esp. chapters 1, 6–7.

24. See, among many others, Joanna L. Grisinger, *The Unwieldy American State: Administrative Politics since the New Deal* (New York: Cambridge University Press, 2012); Brian Balogh, *A Government out of Sight: The Mystery of National Authority in Nineteenth-Century America* (New York: Cambridge University Press, 2009); Stephen Skowronek, *Building a New American State: The Expansion of National Administrative Capabilities, 1877–1920* (New York: Cambridge University Press, 1982); Burke, *The Institutional Presidency*; Michael Nelson, "A Short Ironic History of American National Bureaucracy," *Journal of Politics* 44 (1982), 747–78.

25. Quotation from Eric Rauchway, *The Money Makers: How Roosevelt and Keynes Ended the Depression, Defeated Fascism, and Secured a Prosperous Peace* (New York: Basic Books, 2015), 53.

26. Quotation from Rauchway, *Money Makers*, 65. On the positive public reactions to Roosevelt's decision to leave the gold standard and take monetary affairs into his own hands, see ibid., 85–89.

27. See Rauchway, *Money Makers*, 65–67.

28. From John Steinbeck, *The Harvest of Gypsies*, quoted in Eric Foner, ed., *Voices of Freedom: A Documentary History*, Volume 2, Third Edition (New York: W.W. Norton, 2011), 168.

29. See Jess Gilbert, *Planning Democracy: Agrarian Intellectuals and the Intended New Deal* (New Haven: Yale University Press, 2015); Edwin G. Nourse, Joseph S. Davis, and John D. Black, *Three Years of the Agricultural Adjustment Administration* (Washington, D.C.: Brookings Institution Press, 1937).

30. See Gilbert, *Planning Democracy*; Raj Patel, *Stuffed and Starved: The Hidden Battle for the World Food System* (Brooklyn, NY: Melville House Publishing, 2012).

31. Franklin Roosevelt, Fireside Chat 3: "On the National Recovery Administration," 24 July 1933, available at: http://www.presidency.ucsb.edu/ws/index.php?pid=14488.

32. Lizabeth Cohen, *Making a New Deal: Industrial Workers in Chicago, 1919–1939* (New York: Cambridge University Press, 1990), 268.

33. Historian Lizabeth Cohen explains: "When workers needed welfare, security for their savings and homes, and better jobs during the 1930s, they increasingly looked to the government they had put in office, not to their old community institutions or bosses." Ibid., 282. "Dole" and "saved" quotations on 268 and 273.

34. See Lawrence W. Levine and Cornelia R. Levine, *The Fireside Conversations: America Responds to FDR during the Great Depression* (Berkeley: University of California Press, 2010); Kennedy, *Freedom From Fear*, esp. 363–80.

35. This is the core argument of Lizabeth Cohen's ground-breaking book, *Making a New Deal*, 283. On the social connections across class and ethnicity during the New Deal, and their importance for the transformation of midcentury American society, see Jefferson Cowie, *The Great Exception: The New Deal and the Limits of American Politics* (Princeton: Princeton University Press, 2016).

36. Hopkins quoted in Sherwood, *Roosevelt and Hopkins*, 52.

37. On Roosevelt's disastrous effort at "court-packing" and the declining momentum of the New Deal in 1937, see Roger Daniels, *Franklin D. Roosevelt: Road to the New Deal, 1882–1939* (Urbana: University of Illinois Press, 2015), 317–333; Kennedy, *Freedom From Fear*, 331–62. See also Alan Brinkley, *The End of Reform: New Deal Liberalism in Recession and War* (New York: Alfred Knopf, 1995). On the limits of New Deal liberalism, and the endurance of racial segregation, particularly because of Southern conservative power in Congress, see Ira Katznelson, *Fear Itself: The New Deal and the Origins of Our Time* (New York: W.W. Norton, 2013).

38. See Elizabeth Borgwardt, *A New Deal for the World: America's Vision for Human Rights* (Cambridge, Mass.: Belknap Press of Harvard University Press, 2005), esp. chapter 2.

39. See Stanley G. Payne, *A History of Fascism, 1914–1945* (Madison: University of Wisconsin Press, 1995).

40. Franklin Roosevelt, Quarantine Speech, Chicago, Illinois, 5 October 1937, available at: http://millercenter.org/president/speeches/speech-3310. On the links between Roosevelt's thinking and American Cold War containment policies, see John Lewis Gaddis, *Strategies of Containment: A Critical Appraisal of American National Security Policy during the Cold War* (New York: Oxford University Press, 2005 edition), 3–23.

41. Quotations from Dorothy Borg, "Notes on Roosevelt's 'Quarantine' Speech," *Political Science Quarterly* 72 (September 1957), 430–31; Alonzo Hamby, *Man of Destiny: FDR and the Making of the American Century* (New York: Basic Books, 2015), 291.

42. On this crucial period and Roosevelt's leadership, see David Kaiser, *No End Save Victory: How FDR Led the Nation into War* (New York: Basic Books, 2011), 19–56; Hamby, *Man of Destiny*, 283–300.

43. Franklin Roosevelt, Address to Congress, 21 September 1939, available at: http://teachingamericanhistory.org/library/document/address-delivered-by-president-roosevelt-to-the-congress.

44. Franklin Roosevelt, Fireside Chat 16, 29 December 1940, available at: http://www.presidency.ucsb.edu/ws/?pid=15917. One of the best accounts of Lend-Lease and Roosevelt's leadership during this period is Warren F. Kimball, *The Most Unsordid Act: Lend-Lease, 1939–1941* (Baltimore: Johns Hopkins University Press, 1969).

45. Transcript of Franklin Roosevelt's press conference, 17 December 1940, available at: http://docs.fdrlibrary.marist.edu/odllpc2.html.

46. Hamby, *Man of Destiny*, 320-38.

47. Let me be absolutely clear: there is no evidence that Roosevelt knew in advance of a planned Japanese attack on Pearl Harbor. He expected a Japanese attack, but in the Philippines, not Hawaii. The historical literature, cited throughout this chapter, agrees firmly on this point.

48. Franklin Roosevelt, Address to Congress Requesting a Declaration of War with Japan, 8 December 1941, available at: http://www.presidency.ucsb.edu/ws/?pid=16053.

49. Franklin Roosevelt, Fireside Chat, 9 December 1941, available at: http://www.presidency.ucsb.edu/ws/?pid=16056.

50. See, among others, Greg Robinson, *By Order of the President: FDR and the Internment of Japanese Americans* (Cambridge, Mass.: Harvard University Press, 2001); Roger

Daniels, *Prisoners without Trial: Japanese Americans in World War II* (New York: Hill and Wang, 1993).

51. On this point, see Melvyn P. Leffler, *A Preponderance of Power: National Security, the Truman Administration, and the Cold War* (Stanford: Stanford University Press, 1992), 25–140.

52. See Richard Rhodes, *The Making of the Atomic Bomb* (New York: Simon and Schuster, 1986); Kai Bird and Martin Sherwin, *American Prometheus: The Triumph and Tragedy of J. Robert Oppenheimer* (New York: Vintage Books, 2005).

53. See Bernard Brodie, "The Absolute Weapon," in Bernard Brodie et al., ed., *The Absolute Weapon: Atomic Power and World Order* (New York: Harcourt, Brace, 1946).

54. Franklin Roosevelt, Annual Message to Congress on the State of the Union, 6 January 1941, available at: http://www.presidency.ucsb.edu/ws/?pid=16092.

55. See Jeffrey A. Engel, ed., *The Four Freedoms: Franklin D. Roosevelt and the Evolution of an American Idea* (New York: Oxford University Press, 2016).

56. See Borgwardt, *A New Deal for the World*; Robert A. Divine, *Second Chance: The Triumph of Internationalism in America During World War II* (New York: Atheneum, 1967).

57. See, among many others, Vladislav Zubok and Constantine Pleshakov, *Inside the Kremlin's Cold War: From Stalin to Khrushchev* (Cambridge, Mass.: Harvard University Press, 1996); Vojtech Mastny, *The Cold War and Soviet Insecurity: The Stalin Years* (New York: Oxford University Press, 1996).

58. See, among others, Melvyn P. Leffler, *For the Soul of Mankind: The United States, the Soviet Union, and the Cold War* (New York: Hill and Wang, 2007), 11–83; Vladislav Zubok, *A Failed Empire: The Soviet Union in the Cold War from Stalin to Gorbachev* (Chapel Hill: University of North Carolina Press, 2007), 29–61; Campbell Craig and Fredrik Logevall, *America's Cold War: The Politics of Insecurity* (Cambridge, Mass.: Harvard University Press, 2009), chapters 1–2; Odd Arne Westad, *The Cold War: A World History* (New York: Basic Books, 2017), especially chapters 3–5.

59. See Jeremi Suri, *Liberty's Surest Guardian: American Nation-Building from the Founders to Obama* (New York: Free Press, 2011), chapter 4; Leffler, *A Preponderance of Power*, esp. chapter 1; Gaddis, *Strategies of Containment*, esp. chapters 2–3.

60. Bellow, "In the Days of Mr. Roosevelt." For Beard's criticism of Roosevelt, see, for example, Charles Beard, *President Roosevelt and the Coming of War, 1941* (New York: Transaction Publishers, 1948). Former President Herbert Hoover continued his crusade against Franklin Roosevelt's alleged abuses of power, long after Roosevelt died. See Herbert Hoover, *Freedom Betrayed: Herbert Hoover's Secret History of the Second World War and its Aftermath*, ed., George N. Nash (Stanford: Hoover Institution Press, 2011).

61. Franklin Roosevelt quoted in Sherwood, *Roosevelt and Hopkins*, 3.

CHAPTER 7

1. President John F. Kennedy, Inaugural Address, 20 January 1961, available at: http://www.jfklibrary.org/Research/Research-Aids/Ready-Reference/JFK-Quotations/Inaugural-Address.aspx.

2 Arthur Schlesinger, Jr., "The Shape of National Politics to Come," 12 May 1959, Folder 280, Box 216, Chester Bowles Papers, Yale University Library—Manuscripts and Archives [hereafter Bowles papers]; Arthur Schlesinger, Jr. to Chester Bowles 18 August 1959, Folder 280, Box 216, Bowles papers. Schlesinger's "Shape of National Politics" essay reached other prominent Democrats, including Adlai Stevenson. See Folder 1, Box 74, Adlai Stevenson Papers, Seeley Mudd Manuscript Library, Princeton, NJ. Arguments similar to Schlesinger's were common among various political groups—American and non-American, Left and

Right—during the late 1950s and early 1960s. See Jeremi Suri, *Power and Protest: Global Revolution and the Rise of Détente* (Cambridge, Mass.: Harvard University Press, 2003), chapter 3.

3. Roger Hilsman Oral History, 14 August 1970, 28, John F. Kennedy Presidential Library, Boston, Mass. Hilsman served in the Kennedy administration as director of the State Department's Bureau of Intelligence and Research, and later assistant secretary of state for far eastern affairs.

4. Representatives from newly independent postcolonial states and advocates for civil rights called upon the American president, especially in the late 1950s and 1960s, to increase US commitments to reform at home and abroad. See Mary Dudziak, *Cold War Civil Rights: Race and the Image of American Democracy* (Princeton: Princeton University Press, 2000); Thomas Borstelmann, *The Cold War and the Color Line: American Race Relations in the Global Arena* (Cambridge, Mass.: Harvard University Press, 2001); Brenda Gayle Plummer, ed., *Window on Freedom: Race, Civil Rights, and Foreign Affairs, 1945–1988* (Chapel Hill: University of North Carolina Press, 2003).

5. John F. Kennedy, speech to the Democratic National Convention in Los Angeles, 15 July 1960, available at: http://www.jfklibrary.org/Asset-Viewer/AS08q5oYz0SFUZg9uOi4iw.aspx.

6. On the significance of Kennedy's Irish Catholic heritage, and his "outsider" status from traditional American national political leadership, see Robert Dallek, *An Unfinished Life: John F. Kennedy, 1917–1963* (New York: Little, Brown, 2003), 229–96.

7. This was the central argument of John Kenneth Galbraith's best-selling book, which deeply influenced Kennedy and many close to him: *The Affluent Society* (Boston: Houghton Mifflin, 1958).

8. On the urge to affirm masculine strength and the "strenuous life" among Kennedy and his supporters, see Robert Dean, *Imperial Brotherhood: Gender and the Making of Cold War Foreign Policy* (Amherst: University of Massachusetts Press, 2003).

9. See Richard Neustadt to Senator John F. Kennedy, 15 September 1960, reprinted in Charles O. Jones, ed., *Preparing to Be President: The Memos of Richard E. Neustadt* (Washington, D.C.: The AEI Press, 2000), 21–37.

10. John F. Kennedy, "Forward," June 1963, in Theodore Sorenson, *Decision-Making in the White House* (New York: Columbia University Press, 1963), xi.

11. Ibid., xii-xiii.

12. Quotation from Sorenson, *Decision-Making in the White House*, lectures delivered at Columbia University, April-May 1963 (New York: Columbia University Press, 1963), 37.

13. Quotations from Dallek, *An Unfinished Life*, 372.

14. See, among many others, Howard Jones, *Bay of Pigs* (New York: Oxford University Press, 2008); Peter Kornbluh, ed., *Bay of Pigs Declassified: The Secret CIA Report on the Invasion of Cuba* (New York: New Press, 1998); Lawrence Freedman, *Kennedy's Wars: Berlin, Cuba, Laos, and Vietnam* (New York: Oxford University Press, 2002); Andrew Preston, *The War Council: McGeorge Bundy, the NSC, and Vietnam* (Cambridge, Mass.: Harvard University Press, 2006).

15. The domestic and international pressures encouraging presidential interventions in the Cold War, despite damage to American interests, have received attention from numerous scholars. See Campbell Craig and Fredrik Logevall, *America's Cold War: The Politics of Insecurity* (Cambridge, Mass.: Harvard University Press, 2009); Odd Arne Westad, *The Global Cold War: Third World Interventions and the Making of Our Times* (Cambridge: Cambridge University Press, 2005), esp. chapters 1–2; Suri, *Power and Protest*, esp. chapter 4. For a systematic analysis of this dynamic in the history of great powers, see Paul Kennedy's classic: *The Rise and Fall of the Great Powers* (New York:

Random House, 1987). On the Munich analogy, see Ernest May, *"Lessons" of the Past: The Use and Misuse of History in American Foreign Policy* (New York: Oxford University Press, 1973); Hal Brands and Jeremi Suri, eds., *The Power of the Past: History and Statecraft* (Washington, D.C.: Brookings Institution Press, 2015), esp. 1–129.

16. See chapter 6.

17. Among many others, see Westad, *Global Cold War*, chapters 4–5; Piero Gleijeses, *Conflicting Missions: Havana, Washington, and Africa, 1959–1976* (Chapel Hill: University of North Carolina Press, 2002); Matthew Connelly, *A Diplomatic Revolution: Algeria's Fight for Independence and the Origins of the Post-Cold War Era* (New York: Oxford University Press, 2002); Stephen G. Rabe, *The Most Dangerous Area in the World: John F. Kennedy Confronts Communist Revolution in Latin America* (Chapel Hill: University of North Carolina Press, 1999).

18. David Halberstam, *The Best and the Brightest* (New York: Random House, 1972), 128.

19. On the pervasive crisis atmosphere in the Kennedy White House, see Lloyd Gardner, *Pay Any Price: Lyndon Johnson and the Wars for Vietnam* (Chicago: Ivan Dee, 1997), chapter 1.

20. Arthur M. Schlesinger, Jr., *A Thousand Days: John F. Kennedy in the White House* (New York: Random House, 1965), 626.

21. The history of the Gross Domestic Product as a measure and policy input has received extensive critical treatment, including: Ehsan Masood, *The Great Invention: the Study of GDP and the Making and Unmaking of the Modern World* (New York: Pegasus Books, 2016); Dirk Philipsen, *The Little Big Number: How GDP Came to Rule the World and What to Do about It* (Princeton: Princeton University Press, 2015); Philipp Lepenies, *The Power of a Single Number: A Political History of GDP* (New York: Columbia University Press, 2016). On the history of the Consumer Price Index, see "The First Hundred Years of the Consumer Price Index: A Methodological and Political History," *Monthly Labor Review* (April 2014), available at: http://www.bls.gov/opub/mlr/2014/article/the-first -hundred-years-of-the-consumer price-index.htm. On the nuclear balance, see, among many others, Robert Jervis, *The Meaning of the Nuclear Revolution: Statecraft and the Prospect of Armageddon* (Ithaca: Cornell University Press, 1989); Richard Rhodes, *Arsenals of Folly: The Making of the Nuclear Arms Race* (New York, Random House, 2007); Francis J. Gavin, *Nuclear Statecraft: History and Strategy in America's Atomic Age* (Ithaca: Cornell University Press, 2012).

22. See chapter 6; Max Weber, *Economy and Society*, 2 volumes, trans., Guenther Roth (Berkeley: University of California Press, 2013).

23. Arthur Krock, *Memoirs: Sixty Years on the Firing Line* (New York: Popular Library, 1968), 376–77.

24. As many scholars have shown, the public "consensus" in 1950s America was much thinner than often remembered. See, among others, Kevin M. Kruse, *One Nation under God: How Corporate America Invented Christian America* (New York: Basic Books, 2015); Lizabeth Cohen, *A Consumer's Republic: The Politics of Mass Consumption in Postwar America* (New York: Alfred Knopf, 2003).

25. See W. W. Rostow, *The Diffusion of Power, 1957–1972* (New York: Macmillan, 1972); Roger Hilsman, *The Politics of Policy-Making in Defense and Foreign Affairs* (New York: Harper and Row, 1971); Krock, *Memoirs*; Jonathan Swift, *Gulliver's Travels* (New York: Penguin, 2000, originally published in 1726).

26. Samuel I. Rosenman, *Working with Roosevelt* (New York: Harper and Brothers, 1952), 38. Also, all of President's Roosevelt's daily calendars are available, along with a

helpful timeline, at: http://www.fdrlibrary.marist.edu/daybyday. The calendars on pages 193 and 194 are available at: http://www.fdrlibrary.marist.edu/daybyday/daylog/december -8th-1941.

27. Robert Dallek's ground-breaking biography of Kennedy recounts in detail how sick Kennedy was for much of his life, including the presidency, and how often he required extensive medical treatment. Health was a serious and continual struggle for Kennedy, mostly hidden from the public. See Dallek, *An Unfinished Life*, esp. 73–81.

28. See Memorandum from Richard Neustadt to Senator John F. Kennedy, 30 October 1960, in Jones, ed., *Preparing to Be President*, 40–41.

29. On the rising importance of the newly independent states and their increasing presence on Kennedy's schedule, see Dudziak, *Cold War Civil Rights;* Borstelmann, *The Cold War and the Color Line*; Plummer, ed., *Window on Freedom*.

30. Kennedy secretly recorded the meetings of his Executive Committee ("Excomm") during the Cuban Missile Crisis. These and other quotations are based on the transcripts of those audio recordings edited by Ernest May and Philip Zelikow: *The Kennedy Tapes: Inside the White House during the Cuban Missile Crisis* (Cambridge, Mass.: Belknap Press of Harvard University Press, 1997), 71. Italics in transcript. An alternative set of transcripts, from the same recordings, are available in Sheldon Stern, *Averting "The Final Failure": John F. Kennedy and the Secret Cuban Missile Crisis Meetings* (Stanford: Stanford University Press, 2003). Also, President Kennedy's Daily Schedules are available at the John F. Kennedy Presidential Library, Boston, Mass. An online digital version is available at: http://www.jfklibrary.org/Exhibits/Interactives.aspx.

31. May and Zelikow, eds., *The Kennedy Tapes*, 60. On premature cognitive closure, see Robert Jervis, *Perception and Misperception in International Relations* (Princeton: Princeton University Press, 1976), 187–95.

32. On American nuclear "overkill," see David Alan Rosenberg, "The Origins of Overkill: Nuclear Weapons and American Strategy, 1945–1960," *International Security* 7 (Spring 1983), 3–71. On the nature of the nuclear balance, the American advantage, and the influence of these issues on American policy-makers during the Cuban Missile Crisis, see Marc Trachtenberg, *History and Strategy* (Princeton: Princeton University Press, 1991), esp. 235–60; John Lewis Gaddis, *We Now Know: Rethinking Cold War History* (New York: Oxford University Press, 1997), 260–80.

33. See Sheldon Stern, *The Cuban Missile Crisis in American Memory: Myth Versus Reality* (Stanford: Stanford University Press, 2012), 155–58. On Soviet decision-making, and the influence of the Bay of Pigs invasion and other covert American activities on Soviet perceptions, see Aleksandr Fursenko and Timothy Naftali, *"One Hell of a Gamble": Khrushchev, Castro, and Kennedy, 1958–1964* (New York: W.W. Norton, 1997); William Taubman, *Khrushchev: The Man and His Era* (New York: W.W. Norton, 2003), 529–77. On the influence of potential nuclear Armageddon on presidential decision-making, see Campbell Craig, *Destroying the Village: Eisenhower and Thermonuclear War* (New York: Columbia University Press, 1998).

34. On the Jupiter missile trade, see Philip Nash, *The Other Missiles of October: Eisenhower, Kennedy, and the Jupiters, 1957–1963* (Chapel Hill: University of North Carolina Press, 1997).

35. On this point, see Stern, *The Cuban Missile Crisis in American Memory*.

36. See Suri, *Power and Protest*, chapters 1–3.

37. This was the main argument of Stanley Hoffmann's devastating and highly influential portrait of American foreign policy at the time. See Stanley Hoffmann, *Gulliver's Troubles: Or, the Setting of American Foreign Policy* (New York: McGraw-Hill, 1968). On

the frustration that Martin Luther King, Jr. and other civil rights leaders experienced with Kennedy's hesitance and indecision, see Julian Zelizer, *The Fierce Urgency of Now: Lyndon Johnson, Congress, and the Battle for the Great Society* (New York: Penguin, 2015), 11–60.

38. Dwight Eisenhower, Farewell Address, 17 January 1961, available at: http://avalon .law.yale.edu/20th_century/eisenhower001.asp.

39. See, among others, Michael J. Hogan, *A Cross of Iron: Harry S. Truman and the Origins of the National Security State, 1945–1954* (New York: Cambridge University Press, 1998), especially chapter 9; Douglas T. Stuart, *Creating the National Security State: A History of the Law that Transformed America* (Princeton: Princeton University Press, 2008), chapter 7.

40. Roswell Gilpatric oral history #2, 27 May 1970, John F. Kennedy Presidential Library, Boston, Mass. See also William Burr, ed., "The Creation of SIOP-62," National Security Archive Electronic Briefing Book 130, available at: http://nsarchive.gwu.edu /NSAEBB/NSAEBB130/index.htm; Scott Sagan, "SIOP-62: The Nuclear War Plan Briefing to President Kennedy," *International Security* 12 (Summer 1987); Peter Feaver, *Guarding the Guardians: Civilian Control of Nuclear Weapons in the United States* (Ithaca: Cornell University Press, 1992), 172–98.

41. Gilpatric oral history #4.

42. On creeping militarization, and its broader political and social implications, see Michael S. Sherry, *In the Shadow of War: The United States since the 1930s* (New Haven: Yale University Press, 1997); Andrew J. Bacevich, *The New American Militarism: How Americans Are Seduced by War* (New York: Oxford University Press, 2005); Jennifer Mittelstadt, *The Rise of the Military Welfare State* (Cambridge, Mass.: Harvard University Press, 2015).

43. Lyndon Johnson, "My Political Philosophy," *Texas Quarterly* 1 (Winter 1958), 18–19.

44. Ibid., 20–21.

45. Lyndon Johnson, Address to a Joint Session of Congress on the Voting Rights Act, 15 March 1965, available at: http://www.presidency.ucsb.edu/ws/?pid=26805.

46. The most engrossing book on Johnson's years in the US Senate, and one of the best histories of the Senate, is Robert Caro, *Master of the Senate* (New York: Alfred Knopf, 2002).

47. This interpretation of Lyndon Johnson's populism is central to Randall B. Woods's excellent biography: *LBJ: Architect of American Ambition* (New York: Free Press, 2006),

48. In November 1964 Lyndon Johnson received 61.05 percent of the popular vote, compared to 38.47 percent of the popular vote for his challenger, Arizona Senator Barry Goldwater. In November 1936 Franklin Roosevelt had received 60.79 percent of the popular vote, compared to 36.54 percent of the popular vote for his challenger, Kansas Governor Alfred Landon. Johnson received a higher percentage of the popular vote than Roosevelt, but his margin of victory over his opponent was slightly smaller.

49. Richard L. Strout, reporter for the *Christian Science Monitor*, quoted in Zelizer, *The Fierce Urgency of Now*, 221. See the excellent account of this period in ibid., esp. 131–223. Also, the entire run of President Lyndon Johnson's Daily Diary is available from the Lyndon B. Johnson Presidential Library online at: http://www.lbjlibrary.net /collections/daily-diary.html.

50. See Robert Caro, *The Passage of Power* (New York: Alfred Knopf, 2012), 558–70.

51. For more on George Wallace, and his race-baiting efforts, see Dan T. Carter, *The Politics of Rage: George Wallace, the Origins of the New Conservatism, and the Transformation of American Politics* (New York: Simon and Schuster, 1995).

52. Lyndon Johnson, Remarks on the Signing of the Voting Rights Act, 6 August 1965, available at: http://www.presidency.ucsb.edu/ws/?pid=27140.

53. See Caro, *The Passage of Power*, 598–603.

54. See Zelizer, *The Fierce Urgency of Now*, 225–61.

55. President Johnson's Telephone Conversation with Senator Richard Russell, 27 May 1964, 10:55 A.M., citations 3519–3521, Tape WH6405.10, Recordings of Telephone Conversations, White House Series, Lyndon B. Johnson Presidential Library, Austin, Texas [hereafter LBJL]. My transcription. I have tried to preserve the original speech patterns of the speakers.

56. President Johnson's Telephone Conversation with McGeorge Bundy, 27 May 1964, 11:24 A.M., citation 3522, Tape WH6405.10, Recordings of Telephone Conversations, White House Series, LBJL. My transcription.

57. Lyndon Johnson's decision-making during the Vietnam War has inspired its own cottage industry. Among many others, see Fredrik Logevall, *Choosing War: The Lost Chance for Peace and the Escalation of War in Vietnam* (Berkeley: University of California Press, 1999); Woods, *LBJ*, esp. 483–864; Gardner, *Pay Any Price*.

58. On Johnson's use of "law and order" rhetoric, see Michael W. Flamm, *Law and Order: Street Crime, Civil Unrest, and the Crisis of Liberalism in the 1960s* (New York: Columbia University Press, 2005).

59. Harry McPherson, Oral History, Interview 5, Tape 2: 14, LBJL.

CHAPTER 8

1. Ronald Reagan handwritten diary entries, 10 October 1983 and 18 November 1983, reprinted in Douglas Brinkley, ed., *The Reagan Diaries* (New York: Harper Collins, 2007), 185–86, 198–99.

2. Ronald Reagan, Remarks at the Franklin D. Roosevelt Presidential Library 50th Anniversary Luncheon, 10 January 1989, available at: https://www.reaganlibrary.archives .gov/archives/speeches/1989/011089c.htm.

3. Quotations from ibid.; Reagan diary, 14 February 1981, in Brinkley, ed., *The Reagan Diaries*, 4.

4. Ronald Reagan, "A Time for Choosing" speech, 27 October 1964, available at: http://www.americanrhetoric.com/speeches/ronaldreaganatimeforchoosing.htm.

5. Ibid.

6. On McCarthyism and its influence on the Republican Party in the late 1940s and 1950s, see David M. Oshinsky, *A Conspiracy So Immense: The World of Joe McCarthy* (New York: Oxford University Press, 2005); Sam Tanenhaus, *Whittaker Chambers: A Biography* (New York: Random House, 1997).

7. Ronald Reagan, Commencement Address at Eureka College, 7 June 1957, available at: http://www.freerepublic.com/focus/f-news/913473/posts.

8. On the migration of Midwesterners to California, and their influence on the emerging New Right, see Lisa McGirr, *Suburban Warriors: The Origins of the New American Right* (Princeton: Princeton University Press, 2001).

9. See Lou Cannon, *Governor Reagan: His Rise to Power* (New York: Public Affairs, 2003).

10. Ronald Reagan handwritten radio speech, 8 January 1975, reprinted in Kiron K. Skinner, Annelise Anderson, and Martin Anderson, eds., *Reagan in His Own Hand* (New York: Simon and Schuster, 2001), 255–56.

11. Ronald Reagan, Inaugural Address, 20 January 1981, available at: https://www .reaganlibrary.archives.gov/archives/speeches/1981/12081a.htm.

12. See the very insightful book on conservative politics, race, and Reagan in Mississippi by Joseph Crespino, *In Search of Another Country: Mississippi and the Conservative Counterrevolution* (Princeton: Princeton University Press, 2007).

13. Transcript of Ronald Reagan's 1980 Neshoba County Fair Speech, Mississippi, 3 August 1980, available at: http://neshobademocrat.com/Content/NEWS/News/Article/Transcript-of-Ronald-Reagan-s-1980-Neshoba-County-Fair-speech/2/297/15599.

14. See Crespino, *In Search of Another Country*, esp. 267–78. There is an extensive literature on the merger of New Deal aspirations for social uplift and conservative commitments to racial and religious separation in the 1970s and 1980s. Reagan was a product of this "New Right" phenomenon, and he contributed to its furtherance and normalization in late twentieth-century America. See, among many others, Kevin M. Kruse, *White Flight: Atlanta and the Making of Modern Conservatism* (Princeton: Princeton University Press, 2005); Matthew Lassiter, *The Silent Majority: Suburban Politics in the Sunbelt South* (Princeton: Princeton University Press, 2006); Darren Dochuk, *From Bible Belt to Sunbelt: Plain-Folk Religion, Grassroots Politics, and the Rise of Evangelical Conservatism* (New York: W.W. Norton, 2011); Michelle M. Nickerson, *Mothers of Conservatism: Women and the Postwar Right* (Princeton: Princeton University Press, 2012).

15. See Doug Rossinow, *The Reagan Era: A History of the 1980s* (New York: Columbia University Press, 2015), chapter 2; W. Elliot Brownlee, "'Reaganomics': The Fiscal and Monetary Policies," and Michael R. Adamson, "Reagan and the Economy: Business and Labor, Deregulation and Regulation," both in Andrew Johns, ed., *A Companion to Ronald Reagan* (Malden, Mass.: Wiley, 2015), 131–66.

16. White House Report on the Program for Economic Recovery, 18 February 1981, available at: https://www.reaganlibrary.archives.gov/archives/speeches/1981/21881c.htm.

17. In 1980 national defense spending was 4.8 percent of GDP. In 1983 national defense spending reached 5.9 percent of GDP. See Ronald Reagan, Address Before a Joint Session of the Congress on the Program for Economic Recovery, 18 February 1981, available at: https://www.reaganlibrary.archives.gov/archives/speeches/1981/21881a.htm; White House Historical Tables, "Table 6.1: Composition of Outlays, 1940–2021," available at: https://obamawhitehouse.archives.gov/omb/budget/Historicals. These historical budget tables were produced by non-partisan staff in the Office of Management and Budget, and they have been verified by economists of diverse backgrounds. The tables were originally on the whitehouse.gov website for easy public access, but the Trump administration quickly removed them, without notice, in early 2017. Fortunately, the historical budget tables are still available to everyone through the online archives of the Obama administration.

18. Ronald Reagan, Address to Members of the British Parliament, 8 June 1982, available at: https://www.reaganlibrary.archives.gov/archives/speeches/1982/60882a.htm.

19. National Security Decision Directive (NSDD) 75, "US Relations with Russia," 17 January 1983, available at: https://reaganlibrary.archives.gov/archives/reference/Scanned%20NSDDs/NSDD75.pdf. See also NSDD 32, "US National Security Strategy," 20 May 1982, available at: https://reaganlibrary.archives.gov/archives/reference/Scanned%20NSDDs/NSDD32.pdf.

20. NSDD 75.

21. Ibid.

22. See Martin Anderson, *Revolution: The Reagan Legacy* (Stanford: Hoover Institution Press, 1990), 83. For the earlier origins of Reagan's anti-nuclear thinking, see Paul

Lettow, *Ronald Reagan and His Quest to Abolish Nuclear Weapons* (New York: Random House, 2005), chapter 1.

23. See chapter 7; Aleksandr Fursenko and Timothy Naftali, *"One Hell of a Gamble": Khrushchev, Castro, and Kennedy, 1958–1964* (New York: W.W. Norton, 1997).

24. Quotation from Lettow, *Ronald Reagan and His Quest to Abolish Nuclear Weapons*, 40.

25. See Robert Scheer, *With Enough Shovels: Reagan, Bush, and Nuclear War* (New York: Random House, 1982), esp. 3–17, 120–24.

26. Ibid. On Soviet fears of Reagan's nuclear naïveté and belligerence, see Christopher Andrew and Oleg Gordievsky, *KGB: The Inside Story of its Foreign Operations from Lenin to Gorbachev* (New York: Harper Collins, 1990), chapter 13.

27. Ronald Reagan, Remarks at the Annual Convention of the National Association of Evangelicals in Orlando, Florida, 8 March 1983, available at: https://www.reagan library.archives.gov/archives/speeches/1983/30883b.htm.

28. See Frances Fitzgerald, *Way out There in the Blue: Reagan, Star Wars, and the End of the Cold War* (New York: Touchstone, 2000); Garry Wills, *Reagan's America* (New York: Doubleday, 1986).

29. Ronald Reagan, Address to the Nation on Defense and National Security, 23 March 1983, available at: https://www.reaganlibrary.archives.gov/archives/speeches /1983/32383d.htm.

30. See Sanford Lakoff and Herbert York, *A Shield in Space? Technology, Politics, and the Strategic Defense Initiative* (Berkeley: University of California Press, 1989).

31. See David E. Hoffman, *The Dead Hand: The Untold Story of the Cold War Arms Race and its Dangerous Legacy* (New York: Random House, 2009), esp. 143–54.

32. See the iconic 1984 Reagan presidential reelection campaign television advertisement, "Morning in America:" http://www.livingroomcandidate.org/commercials/1984.

33. Newspaper reporter Lou Cannon covered Reagan's career during his years as governor and president. Cannon argues that Reagan always viewed himself as a public performer, but he was performing his deepest beliefs in politics. Cannon argues that Reagan's effectiveness came from the combination of his authenticity and communication skills. See Lou Cannon, *President Reagan: The Role of a Lifetime* (New York: Touchstone, 2000).

34. For two alternative views, see Beth A. Fischer, *The Reagan Reversal: Foreign Policy and the End of the Cold War* (Columbia: University of Missouri Press, 2000); Paul Kengor, *The Crusader: Ronald Reagan and the Fall of Communism* (New York: Harper Collins, 2006).

35. Data from White House Historical Tables, "Table 6.1: Composition of Outlays, 1940–2021," "Table 7.1: Federal Debt at the End of the Year, 1940–2021," and "Table 14.6: Total Government Surpluses or Deficits (-) in Absolute Amounts and as Percentages of GDP, 1948–2015," all available at: https://obamawhitehouse.archives.gov/omb /budget/Historicals.

36. See David Stockman's searing and still powerful memoir of his service in the Reagan administration: *The Triumph of Politics: Why the Reagan Revolution Failed* (New York: Harper and Row, 1986), 398–99. See also David Stockman, *The Great Deformation: The Corruption of Capitalism in America* (New York: Public Affairs, 2013); William Greider, "The Education of David Stockman," *Atlantic* (December 1981).

37. Reagan diary entry, 30 September 1983, in Brinkley, ed., *The Reagan Diaries*, 183–84.

38. Reagan diary entries, 17–18 September 1983 and 2 December 1983, in Brinkley, ed., *The Reagan Diaries*, 180, 202.

39. Reagan diary entry, 21 October 1983, in Brinkley, ed., *Reagan Diaries*, 189.

40. See "Operation Urgent Fury: The Invasion of Grenada, October 1983" US Center for Military History Publication 70–114–1, available at: http://www.history.army.mil /html/books/grenada/urgent_fury.pdf.

41. Reagan diary entry, 22–23 October 1983, in *Reagan Diaries*, 189–90.

42. Among others, see Jack Snyder, *The Ideology of the Offensive: Military Decision Making and the Disasters of 1914* (Ithaca: Cornell University Press, 1984); David G. Herrmann, *The Arming of Europe and the Making of the First World War* (Princeton: Princeton University Press, 1996).

43. Soviet pilot Col. Gennadi Osipovitch quoted in Thom Patterson, "The Downing of Flight 007: 30 Years Later, A Cold War Tragedy Still Seems Surreal," CNN.com (31 August 2013): http://www.cnn.com/2013/08/31/us/kal-fight-007-anniversary.

44. Ronald Reagan, "Address to the Nation on the Soviet Attack on a Korean Civilian Airliner," 5 September 1983, available at: https://www.reaganlibrary.archives.gov/archives /speeches/1983/90583a.htm. Reagan quoted Abraham Lincoln's famous Address at the Cooper Institute, New York City, 27 February 1860, available at: http://www.abraham lincolnonline.org/lincoln/speeches/cooper.htm. See chapter 4. For Soviet perceptions that Reagan was threatening war after the Korean airline shoot-down, see the memoirs of the Soviet ambassador to the United States, Anatoly Dobrynin, and the Soviet foreign minister, Andrei Gromyko: Anatoly Dobrynin, *In Confidence: Moscow's Ambassador to Six Cold War Presidents, 1962–1986* (New York: Random House, 1995), 537; Andrei Gromyko, *Memories: From Stalin to Gorbachev*, trans., Harold Shukman (London: Arrow Books, 1989), 381–86.

45. Many of the details of the "Able Archer 83" exercise remain classified, but some chilling materials are available. See Benjamin B. Fischer, "A Cold War Conundrum: The 1983 Soviet War Scare," Center for the Study of Intelligence, Central Intelligence Agency, available at: https://www.cia.gov/library/center-for-the-study-of-intelligence/csi -publications/books-and-monographs/a-cold-war-conundrum/source.htm#HEAD- ING1-13; "The Soviet 'War Scare,'" President's Foreign Intelligence Advisory Board, 15 February 1990, available at: http://nsarchive.gwu.edu/nukevault/ebb533-The-Able-Archer -War-Scare-Declassified-PFIAB-Report-Released/2012-0238-MR.pdf; Nate Jones, ed., "The 1983 War Scare: 'The Last Paroxysm' of the Cold War, Part II," National Security Archive Electronic Briefing Book 427, available at: http://nsarchive.gwu.edu/NSAEBB /NSAEBB427; Douglas Birch, "The USSR and US Came Closer to Nuclear War than We Thought," *Atlantic* (28 May 2013), http://www.theatlantic.com/international/archive /2013/05/the-ussr-and-us-came-closer-to-nuclear-war-than-we-thought/276290/; Jamie Doward, "How a NATO War Game Took the World to the Brink of Nuclear Disaster," *Guardian* (2 November 2013), https://www.theguardian.com/uk-news/2013/nov /02/nato-war-game-nuclear-disaster.

46. See "The Soviet 'War Scare,'" President's Foreign Intelligence Advisory Board, 15 February 1990. For a different interpretation that downplays Soviet war fears during the Able Archer 83 exercise, see Simon Miles, "Engaging the 'Evil Empire': East-West Relations in the Second Cold War," Ph.D. dissertation, University of Texas at Austin, April 2017.

47. William Casey, June 1984 memorandum to President Reagan, quoted and described in "The Soviet 'War Scare,'" President's Foreign Intelligence Advisory Board, 15 February 1990.

48. Quotations from ibid.; Don Oberdorfer, *The Turn: From the Cold War to a New Era* (New York: Simon and Schuster, 1991), 66–67.

49. Reagan handwritten diary entry, 18 November 1983, in *The Reagan Diaries*, 198–99.

50. Ronald Reagan, *An American Life* (New York: Simon and Schuster, 1990), 588–89.

51. Reagan diary entry, 16 January 1984, in *Reagan Diaries*, 212; Reagan, Address to the Nation and Other Countries on United States-Soviet Relations, 16 January 1984, available at: https://www.reaganlibrary.archives.gov/archives/speeches/1984/11684a.htm.

52. Reagan, Address to the Nation and Other Countries on United States-Soviet Relations, 16 January 1984.

53. Ibid.

54. Ibid. On the shift in Reagan's rhetoric and thinking about the Soviet Union, see Melvyn P. Leffler, *For the Soul of Mankind: The United States, the Soviet Union, and the Cold War* (New York: Hill and Wang, 2007), 338–450; H. W. Brands, *Reagan: The Life* (New York: Anchor Books, 2015), 431–701.

55. The emergence of the "new thinkers" in the Soviet Union is very well documented. Among many others, see Anatoly S. Chernyaev, *Moya zhizn' i moye vremya* (Moscow: Mezhdunarodnye Otnosheniya, 1995); Robert English, *Russia and the Idea of the West: Gorbachev, Intellectuals, and the End of the Cold War* (New York: Columbia University Press, 2000); Jeffrey T. Checkel, *Ideas and International Political Change: Soviet/Russian Behavior and the End of the Cold War* (New Haven: Yale University Press, 1997); Georgi Arbatov, *The System: An Insider's Life in Soviet Politics* (New York: Random House, 1992); Robert G. Herman, "Identity, Norms, and National Security: The Soviet Foreign Policy Revolution and the End of the Cold War," in Peter J. Katzenstein, ed., *The Culture of National Security: Norms and Identity in World Politics* (New York: Columbia University Press, 1996), 271–316.

56. See Mikhail Gorbachev, *Perestroika: New Thinking for Our Country and the World* (New York: Harper and Row, 1988).

57. See James Wilson, *The Triumph of Improvisation: Gorbachev's Adaptability, Reagan's Engagement, and the End of the Cold War* (Ithaca: Cornell University Press, 2014); Raymond L. Garthoff, *The Great Transition: American-Soviet Relations and the End of the Cold War* (Washington, D.C.: Brookings Institution Press, 1994).

58. Reagan quoted in Stanley Meisler, "Reagan Recants 'Evil Empire' Description," *Los Angeles Times* (1 June 1988).

59. Data from White House Historical Tables, "Table 6.1: Composition of Outlays, 1940–2021," "Table 7.1: Federal Debt at the End of the Year, 1940–2021," and "Table 14.6: Total Government Surpluses or Deficits (-) in Absolute Amounts and as Percentages of GDP, 1948–2015," all available at: https://obamawhitehouse.archives.gov/omb/budget/Historicals.

60. Thomas Piketty, *Capital in the Twenty-First Century*, trans. Arthur Goldhammer (Cambridge, Mass.: Harvard University Press, 2014), 294–98.

61. Reagan was 69 when he assumed office, and 77 when he departed; Trump was 70 when he was elected president. Dwight Eisenhower was 70 when he left the presidency.

62. See the historical data in the US Census Bureau report, "Income, Poverty, and Health Insurance Coverage in the United States: 2012," issued September 2013, available at: http://www.census.gov/prod/2013pubs/p60-245.pdf. See also the World Bank data on economic growth: http://data.worldbank.org/indicator/NY.GDP.MKTP.KD.ZG?end=2015&locations=US&start=1961&view=chart.

63. See the historical data in the US Census Bureau report, "Income, Poverty, and Health Insurance Coverage in the United States: 2012," issued September 2013, available at: http://www.census.gov/prod/2013pubs/p60-245.pdf..

64. On the limits of economic innovation in the 1980s, see Robert J. Gordon, *The Rise and Fall of American Growth: The US Standard of Living since the Civil War* (Princeton: Princeton University Press, 2016), esp. chapter 15. On the enormous gains for the privileged elite, see Piketty, *Capital*, 298–300. See also W. Elliot Brownlee, "'Reaganomics': The Fiscal and Monetary Policies," and Michael R. Adamson, "Reagan and the Economy: Business and Labor, Deregulation and Regulation," both in Johns, *A Companion to Ronald Reagan*, 131–66.

65. See Robert O. Self, *All in the Family: The Realignment of American Democracy since the 1960s* (New York: Hill and Wang, 2012), 383–95; Rossinow, *The Reagan Era*, 129–34.

66. Reagan quoted in Michael S. Sherry, *In the Shadow of War: The United States since the 1930s* (New Haven: Yale University Press, 1995), 457.

67. Ibid., 454–60; Randy Shilts, *And the Band Played On: Politics, People, and the AIDS Epidemic* (New York: Macmillan, 1988).

68. On the Boland Amendment of 1982 and other congressional legislation explicitly prohibiting American military aid to the Contras, see Malcolm Byrne, *Iran-Contra: Reagan's Scandal and the Unchecked Abuse of Presidential Power* (Lawrence: University Press of Kansas, 2014), 42–44.

69. Byrne, *Iran-Contra*, 3, 40.

70. See chapter 6.

71. See chapter 7.

72. Reagan, Address to the Nation on the Iran Arms and Contra Aid Controversy and Administration Goals, 12 August 1987, available at: https://www.reaganlibrary.archives.gov/archives/speeches/1987/081287d.htm.

73. On declining trust in political leadership since Reagan's presidency, and increasing partisan polarization, see Marc Hetherington and Thomas J. Rudolph, *Why Washington Won't Work: Polarization, Political Trust, and the Governing Crisis* (Chicago: University of Chicago Press, 2015).

CHAPTER 9

1. Bill Clinton, *My Life: The Early Years* (New York: Alfred Knopf, 2004), 5.

2. Barack Obama, *Dreams from My Father: A Story of Race and Inheritance* (New York: Random House, 1995), 5; "Dinner with Barack: Two Teachers, an Army Veteran, a Small Business Owner, and the President," Obama presidential campaign video (21 November 2011): https://www.youtube.com/watch?v=Tb5D71aQAoo&t=5m30s.

3. My analysis of Clinton and Obama's early lives draws on a number of excellent biographies, and their memoirs. The best two biographies of the presidents' rise to power were written by David Maraniss: *First in His Class: The Biography of Bill Clinton* (New York: Simon and Schuster, 1995) and *Barack Obama: The Story* (New York: Simon and Schuster, 2012). Both books reflect the author's prodigious digging in the archival record and his dogged pursuit of interviews with people who knew Clinton and Obama throughout their lives. Much of what I write in the first sections of this chapter is deeply influenced by Maraniss's foundational research. I was also deeply influenced by Michael Tomasky's thoughtful and even-handed biography of Clinton: *Bill Clinton* (New York: Henry Holt, 2017). See also the recent detailed biography of Obama: David Garrow, *Rising Star: The Making of Barack Obama* (New York: William Morrow, 2017).

4. The decline in American social and economic mobility, and the entrenchment of stratified classes of citizens in late twentieth-century America, is well chronicled in a diverse range of studies. Some of the best books in this important and growing genre include: Claudia Goldin and Lawrence F. Katz, *The Race Between Education and Technology*

(Cambridge, Mass.: Belknap Press of Harvard University Press, 2008); George Packer, *The Unwinding: An Inner History of the New America* (New York: Farrar, Straus, and Giroux, 2013); Robert D. Putnam, *Our Kids: The American Dream in Crisis* (New York: Simon and Schuster, 2015).

5. Clinton, *My Life*, dedication page; Barack Obama, *The Audacity of Hope: Thoughts on Reclaiming the American Dream* (New York: Broadway Books, 2006), dedication page.

6. This paragraph, in particular, draws deeply on Maraniss's two books: *First in His Class* and *Barack Obama*.

7. This is the central point of David Remnick's thoughtful and frequently moving biography of Barack Obama, *The Bridge: The Life and Rise of Barack Obama* (New York: Alfred Knopf, 2010).

8. German sociologist Max Weber popularized the term "charisma" in the early twentieth century, and it has attracted an enormous literature ever since. For a good start, see the very helpful entry on charisma in Richard Swedberg and Ola Agevall, eds., *The Max Weber Dictionary*, second edition (Stanford: Stanford University Press, 2016), 34–36.

9. Toni Morrison letter to Senator Barack Obama, quoted in Tom McGeveran, "Toni Morrison's Letter to Barack Obama," *Observer* (28 January 2008), available at: http://observer.com/2008/01/toni-morrisons-letter-to-barack-obama. On Clinton, see Morrison, "Comment," *New Yorker* (5 October 1998), available at: http://www.newyorker.com/magazine/1998/10/05/comment-6543.

10. See John Stauffer, *Giants: The Parallel Lives of Frederick Douglass and Abraham Lincoln* (New York: Hachette, 2008); David W. Blight, *Frederick Douglass' Civil War: Keeping Faith in Jubilee* (Baton Rouge: Louisiana State University Press, 1991); Randy Roberts and Johnny Smith, *Blood Brothers: The Fatal Friendship between Muhammad Ali and Malcolm X* (New York: Basic Books, 2016); David Remnick, *King of the World: Muhammad Ali and the Rise of an American Hero* (New York: Vintage, 1998).

11. Remarks by President Obama at the Lyndon B. Johnson Presidential Library Civil Rights Summit, 10 April 2014, available at: https://obamawhitehouse.archives.gov/the-press-office/2014/04/10/remarks-president-lbj-presidential-library-civil-rights-summit.

12. See Michael Kelly, "The 1992 Campaign," *New York Times* (31 October 1992): http://www.nytimes.com/1992/10/31/us/1992-campaign-democrats-clinton-bush-compete-be-champion-change-democrat-fights.html; "Yes We Can," video produced by will.i.am (2008): https://www.youtube.com/watch?v=jjXyqcx-mYY.

13. See Katherine J. Cramer, *The Politics of Resentment: Rural Consciousness in Wisconsin and the Rise of Scott Walker* (Chicago: University of Chicago Press, 2016).

14. See Goldin and Katz, *The Race Between Education and Technology*.

15. President Barack Obama quoted in David Remnick, "Obama Reckons with a Trump Presidency," *New Yorker* (28 November 2016): http://www.newyorker.com/magazine/2016/11/28/obama-reckons-with-a-trump-presidency.

16. President Clinton's calendars are available at: President Clinton's Daily Schedule, http://clinton.presidentiallibraries.us/collections/show/39.

17. President Barack Obama quoted in David Remnick, "Obama Reckons with a Trump Presidency," *New Yorker* (28 November 2016): http://www.newyorker.com/magazine/2016/11/28/obama-reckons-with-a-trump-presidency. On Republican partisan efforts to oppose Clinton and Obama at all costs, see Geoffrey Kabaservice, *Rule and Ruin: The Downfall of Moderation and the Destruction of the Republican Party, From Eisenhower to the Tea Party* (New York: Oxford University Press, 2012), esp. 363–88.

18. See Kabaservice, *Rule and Ruin*, esp. 363–88.

19. On this point, see Jill Lepore's disturbing book: *The Whites of Their Eyes: The Tea Party's Revolution and the Battle over American History* (Princeton: Princeton University Press, 2010).

20. On the decline of public trust ("social capital") in the United States and other advanced societies, see Robert D. Putnam, *Bowling Alone: The Collapse and Revival of American Community* (New York: Simon and Schuster, 2000); Francis Fukuyama, *Political Order and Political Decay: From the Industrial Revolution to the Globalization of Democracy* (New York: Farrar, Straus, and Giroux, 2014), esp. 455–548.

21. For a powerful defense of gradualism and selectivity in policy intervention, see Richard H. Thaler and Cass R. Sunstein, *Nudge: Improving Decisions About Health, Wealth, and Happiness* (New York: Penguin, 2008); Cass R. Sunstein, *Simpler: The Future of Government* (New York: Simon and Schuster, 2013).

22. On the continuing growth of inequality during Clinton's presidency, see Thomas Piketty, *Capital*, trans. Arthur Goldhammer (Cambridge, Mass.: Belknap Press of Harvard University Press, 2014), 294–303.

23. See Office of Management and Budget, US Government, Table 1.1—Summary of receipts, outlays, and surpluses or deficits, 1789–2021, available at: https://obamawhitehouse.archives.gov/omb/budget/Historicals.

24. See, among others, Derek Chollet and James Goldgeier, *America between the Wars: From 11/9 to 9/11* (New York: Public Affairs, 2008); Hal Brands, *From Berlin to Baghdad: America's Search for Purpose in the Post-Cold War World* (Lexington: University Press of Kentucky, 2008).

25. On Yugoslavia, see Norman M. Naimark, *Fires of Hatred: Ethnic Cleansing in Twentieth-Century Europe* (Cambridge, Mass.: Harvard University Press, 2001), 139–183. On Somalia, see Mark Bowden, *Black Hawk Down: A Story of Modern War* (New York: Grove Press, 1999).

26. Samantha Power, *"A Problem From Hell": America and the Age of Genocide* (New York: Harper Collins, 2002), 508.

27. Transcript of President Barack Obama's Nobel Peace Prize Address, Oslo, Norway, 10 December 2009: https://www.nobelprize.org/nobel_prizes/peace/laureates/2009/obama_lecture_en.html.

28. This analysis of the president's liberal internationalism matches James Kloppenberg's analysis of Obama's intellectual roots in pragmatic political philosophy: *Reading Obama: Dreams, Hopes, and the American Political Tradition* (Princeton: Princeton University Press, 2011). See also David Milne's insightful analysis of Obama's emphasis on "pragmatic renewal": *Worldmaking: The Art and Science of American Diplomacy* (New York: Farrar, Straus, and Giroux, 2015), chapter 9.

29. Barack Obama, *The Audacity of Hope: Thoughts on Reclaiming the American Dream* (New York: Broadway Books, 2006), 281. Obama drew on John Quincy Adams and other early American thinkers in writing these words, and he criticized the excessive interventionism of Cold War and post-Cold War American policy-makers.

30. Transcript of Remarks by President Barack Obama at Cairo University, 4 June 2009, available at: https://obamawhitehouse.archives.gov/the-press-office/remarks-president-cairo-university-6-04-09.

31. See, among others, Mark Mazzetti, *The Way of the Knife: The C.I.A., a Secret Army, and a War at the Ends of the Earth* (New York: Penguin Books, 2013); Jack Goldsmith, *Power and Constraint: The Accountable Presidency after 9/11* (New York: W.W. Norton, 2012).

32. For a thoughtful and even-handed analysis of the Iran nuclear deal (officially, the "Joint Comprehensive Plan of Action,") see Kenneth M. Pollack, testimony before the

US Senate Foreign Relations Committee, 5 August 2015, available at: https://www
.brookings.edu/wp-content/uploads/2016/06/Kenneth-Pollack-Testimony-before-the
-Senate-Foreign-Relations-Committee-1.pdf. See also Jeremi Suri, "The Iran Deal Offers Time and Openness," *Austin American-Statesman* (26 July 2015), available at: http://
www.mystatesman.com/news/opinion/iran-deal-offers-time-and-openness/XfsmeeXp
WNgzMu0hGiZ5uL/.

33. See Robert Legvold, *Return to Cold War* (Malden, Mass.: Polity Press, 2016);
Derek Chollet, *The Long Game: How Obama Defied Washington and Redefined America's
Role in the World* (New York: Public Affairs, 2016), 159–79. The evidence of Russian
meddling in the 2016 US presidential election is still unfolding.

34. See Daniel Byman, *Al Qaeda, the Islamic State, and the Global Jihadist Movement*
(New York: Oxford University Press, 2015), 163–86; Joby Warrick, *Black Flags: The Rise
of ISIS* (New York: Doubleday, 2015); Andrew Thompson and Jeremi Suri, "How America Helped ISIS," *New York Times* (1 October 2014).

35. Jeffrey Goldberg, "The Obama Doctrine," *The Atlantic* (April 2016), 85.

EPILOGUE

1. On the need to reform fundamental elements of the American constitutional system for modern purposes and values, see Sanford Levinson, *Our Undemocratic Constitution: Where the Constitution Goes Wrong (And How We the People Can Correct It)* (New
York: Oxford University Press, 2006), esp. chapter 3.

2. On the rise of privately funded idea advocates, see Daniel Drezner, *The Ideas Industry: How Pessimists, Partisans, and Plutocrats are Transforming the Marketplace of Ideas*
(New York: Oxford University Press, 2017).

2. Abraham Lincoln, Second Annual Message to Congress, 1 December 1862, available at: http://www.presidency.ucsb.edu/ws/?pid=29503.

INDEX